Austin
to ATX

To Liz

who loves books

and Texas music

like I do.

Image Wrangling

forever!

[signature]

Austin
TO
ATX

THE HIPPIES, PICKERS, SLACKERS & GEEKS WHO TRANSFORMED THE CAPITAL OF TEXAS

JOE NICK PATOSKI

Texas A&M University Press   •   College Station

Photograph editing by William Howze
Indexing by Rosemary Wetherold

Cover art from mural, *Paradise of the Violet Crown*, by Kerry Awn. Used by permission from HEB/Central Market. The mural is located at Westgate Central Market in south Austin.

Jacket art scanned by Digital Service Center, Texas A&M University Libraries

LIBRARY OF CONGRESS CATALOGING-IN-PUBLICATION DATA

Names: Patoski, Joe Nick, 1951– author.
Title: Austin to ATX: the hippies, pickers, slackers, and geeks who
transformed the capital of Texas / Joe Nick Patoski.
Description: First edition. | College Station: Texas A&M University Press,
[2019] | Includes bibliographical references and index. |
Identifiers: LCCN 2018027856 (print) | LCCN 2018031712 (ebook) | ISBN
9781623497040 (ebook) | ISBN 9781623497033 | ISBN 9781623497033 (cloth:
alk. paper)
Subjects: LCSH: Austin (Tex.)—Biography. | Austin (Tex.)—Social life and
customs. | Austin (Tex.)—Intellectual life. | Austin
(Tex.)—Civilization—20th century. | Subculture—Texas—Austin.
Classification: LCC F394.A953 (ebook) | LCC F394.A953 P38 2019 (print) | DDC
976.4/31—dc23
LC record available at https://lccn.loc.gov/2018027856

Contents

Austin
to ATX

Introduction

(ALMOST) LOVE AT FIRST SIGHT

You always remember the first time.

Mine came after an extended flirtation: childhood glimpses of the Colorado River and the lights of the baseball park on the south bank as the family motored south on vacation; stops for a schooner of cold beer at Scholz Garten on the way to Padre Island; high school football games; fraternity rush parties where you drank until you blacked out.

None of that counted.

The heavy petting started on a visit during my early college years when my friends Don Crowell and Dave Thompson took me to the Split Rail on a Sunday night to see and hear Freda and the Firedogs, a band of hippies who played retro country music.

But true love didn't happen until several weeks after my girlfriend Kris and I moved into a backyard rent house on Avenue H in the middle of August 1973.

I had been running the record department of the Electric Fetus in Minneapolis, Minnesota, the granddaddy of what were known as head shops in the Upper Midwest—places that sold incense, cigarette papers, accessory items for illicit drug use, and a whole lot of records. Being paid well to immerse myself in music was a dream job. I could listen to any record I wanted, and order any record I didn't have. The record distributor representatives who dropped by always had a couple extra tickets to any show I wanted to see, and I saw a lot.

But Minneapolis wasn't home, and I was homesick. Snow in May will do that to a lost Texas soul.

Chet Flippo had been writing articles in *Rolling Stone* and *Creem* magazines about Austin and the cool little music scene that was unfolding there. One story Flippo wrote really stuck with me. It was about a musician named Doug Sahm, an extremely talented Texas hippie rock and roller good at writing songs for homesick Texans. Whenever I listened to his song "At the Crossroads," especially the line "You can't live in Texas if you don't have a lot of soul," I couldn't help but feel a tug.

While in Minneapolis, I'd started to write about music, thinking it might be a career path. I reviewed an album by my favorite blues club and house band back in my hometown of Fort Worth, *Robert Ealey and His Five Careless Lovers Live at the New Blue Bird Nite Club*, for the first issue of a giveaway music magazine published in Dallas called *Buddy*. I made a big deal about how this lowdown form of music was the important stuff that everyone should listen to, not contemporary mainstream commercial rock, which was pretty much what *Buddy* magazine was all about. The recording was primitive, as if documented by folklorists fifty years earlier. In fact, the producers were two very sophisticated cats: Stephen Bruton, brother of Careless Lover Sumter Bruton, who also happened to be singer-songwriter Kris Kristofferson's guitarist; and Bruton's friend T Bone Burnett, who had been making records in Fort Worth since he was a teenager buying records at Record Town, the record shop owned by the Brutons' parents.

Buddy magazine let me know they received a hate letter saying that I didn't know what I was talking about. The sentiment did not seem to be well-articulated, but if I moved someone to write a letter, regardless of how they reacted, I knew I was on to something.

I sent an unsolicited record review to *Creem*, the irreverent, smart-ass competitor to *Rolling Stone*, the bible of music journals. Mercury Records had just issued *Rough Edges*, an album of outtakes by Doug Sahm's old band the Sir Douglas Quintet, issued to capitalize on the new Atlantic album being released by Sahm with an all-star cast of supporting musicians, including Bob Dylan and Dr. John. I'd received promotional copies of both albums at the Fetus, and liked the outtake throwaway album better. So I wrote a short review.

A few weeks later, I received a check for thirty dollars folded inside a letter from Lester Bangs at the magazine, urging me to write more. Lester had been something of a role model as the wildest, most unpredictable, hardest to pin down, and most entertaining of all the music writers I was reading. He was so passionately off-the-wall, it didn't matter what he was writing about, or whether I knew the material. It was the way Lester called 'em as he saw 'em that made me want to read his work.

Lester Bangs's letter motivated me to go back to Texas and write about music. Fort Worth had been a fine place to grow up. After high school, I ran a small record shop there called Natural Records and worked at KFAD-FM, a free-form radio station in suburban Arlington where I was paid $1.60 an hour minimum wage to play anything I wanted from a record library that filled three walls. It was a pretty good job until the station changed its programming format to Top 40, a pretty good reason to wander off to Minneapolis.

After the Electric Fetus, Fort Worth wouldn't do.

The Texas I missed so dang much was somewhere where I'd never lived, but a place I already knew I enjoyed: Austin, where the datelines of those *Rolling Stone* and *Creem* articles were coming from.

Kris and I arrived in mid-August, that time of the summer when the sun baked the green grass white. Our friend Don Crowell sublet his two-room back house behind a fifties-vintage bungalow in the avenues of Hyde Park, north of campus. Since he'd arrived in Austin a year earlier, Don had foresworn killing all living things, including insects, as some sort of spiritual deal. Our first night was spent in the company of cockroaches crawling on the floors, walls, and ceiling. They were three times the size of the roaches we'd become accustomed to in Minneapolis. At one point, I tried to swat one particularly noisy roach scurrying across the ceiling, and it flew straight at my face. A roach had never attacked me before. On the morning after our first night, I wasn't so sure about Austin.

By day, Austin was a comfortable place to hang out, play in, and explore, a pleasing-to-the-eye marriage of oaks, hills, creeks, a river running through the middle of the city, and Barton Springs, the biggest spring-fed community swimming hole I'd ever seen, within a mile of downtown.

Music, the subject I'd moved to town to write about, was everywhere. On any given night there were five times as many bands playing around Austin as in the much larger Minneapolis. Original and roots sounds were the attraction. Cover bands had little standing. Listening and dancing to music and drinking beer appeared to be some kind of refined pastime.

Austin was loose, easy, and cheap. It was fun.

Over the course of those first eight weeks, we went out almost every evening. We hit the Armadillo, Split Rail, One Knite, Soap Creek, and a dozen other clubs. We heard Greezy Wheels, Freda and the Firedogs, Kenneth Threadgill, Doug Sahm, Willie Nelson, Jerry Jeff Walker, W. C. Clark, Mance Lipscomb, Lightnin' Hopkins, Angela Strehli and Southern Feeling, the Storm, Paul Ray and the Cobras, Bill Neely, Clifton Chenier, and loads of other musicians and bands. We were meeting people and dancing and grooving the nights away.

The giant roaches of Avenue H were worth tolerating. I'd found my place. My girlfriend liked it too.

1

Seat of Future Empire, Home of the Armadillo

◉ ◉ ◉

It was a fine day for a hunt. The fall of 1838 had brought sweet relief from the brutal summer heat to the several hundred residents of the village of Waterloo. Folks were in a celebratory mood, having welcomed Waterloo's most esteemed visitor ever, Mirabeau Buonaparte Lamar, vice president and soon-to-be president of the Republic of Texas. Word had spread early one morning throughout the frontier settlement that the prairie was thick with buffalo that had come from the hills to graze on the grassy plains.

The herd was unlike any the men in the small hunting party had seen before, so massive it would have been difficult to fire a shot and not hit anything. The handsome man leading the party, Mirabeau Lamar, Waterloo's visiting dignitary, took his time pursuing his prey on horseback. Somewhere near the present-day intersection of Congress Avenue and Eighth Street, he fixed his eyes on the biggest bull in the herd, no more than twenty-five yards away, slowly unsheathed his pistol from his holster, raised his arm, aimed, and squeezed the trigger.

The big buff bull snorted loudly, shuddered, lurched backward briefly, and then crumpled to the ground.

Afterward the hunters gathered on a hill with an expansive view of the Colorado River, Waller Creek and the prairies and woodlands to the east, and Shoal Creek and the oak- and juniper-canopied hills to the west.

Lamar, a poet and a war hero from Georgia who led General Sam Houston's cavalry in the decisive Battle of San Jacinto for Texan independence, saw beauty in every direction. The setting moved him. This was God's country. Still pumped up by the thrill of the hunt, Lamar declared in a full-throated voice to the rest of his party, "This should be the seat of future empire!"

⊙ ⊙ ⊙

On an early summer night in 1970, a mile south and across the river from that hill where the buffalo hunters celebrated, another man of exceptional physical presence and nobility (Marine reserves, former beer lobbyist) stood outside the Cactus Club bar flanked by two musicians from West Texas, Jimmie Dale Gilmore and John X. Reed, relieving himself. The weather was hot, humid, and soul-sapping, like Austin could be this time of the year. Low evening clouds from the Gulf covered the city like a gray blanket, reflecting what little glow of urban life the small city offered at ten in the evening, when most of the town had already retired.

The plumbing in the men's room at the club had sprung a leak. Rather than wade through sewage to get at the long trough with ice at the bottom, the men at the club had the option of going outside. The women at the club were pretty much SOL (shit outta luck).

Gazing off in the distance, Eddie Wilson, the big man in the middle, spied a building he'd never noticed before, and squinted hard to make out the details. Zipping up, he jumped in his Dodge Charger and drove around the corner to investigate. The headlights revealed a structure that had at one time been a cavernous armory, but had been vacant for months if not years. The big man had been at the club on behalf of the musical group he was managing, Shiva's Headband, trying to figure out where they could score a regular weekly gig now that their old reliable, the Vulcan Gas Company, had shut down. This place would be perfect, he thought, with a little . . . OK, with a lot of work. Since he was alone, Eddie Wilson had no one to shout to, even though he was barely able to contain his excitement: "This should be a hippie music hall!"

⊙ ⊙ ⊙

These two events, separated by 132 years, were Austin's big bangs. The first declaration by Mirabeau Lamar created the town and sited the capital that grew into a city. The second declaration by Eddie Wilson led to the opening of the Armadillo World Headquarters, the first modern institution of a whole other Austin. This Austin was a creative capital of global importance with a seductively attractive lifestyle and an abundance of jobs and opportunity—a model city for the twenty-first century.

Land, cattle, oil, and gas built Texas.

The creative mind and a strong sense of place made Austin Austin.

It was always an outsider's city, contrarian and tolerant by nature, a refuge apart from the state surrounding it.

Physical location had everything to do with it. Austin was about as pleasant as Texas could be in its rugged, semiarid, sun-scorched splendor. A river ran through the heart of the city, several lakes spread out upstream, and the urban grid was laced with still-abundant creeks and springs winding through forested hills pocked with hidden valleys and canyons. Stunning overlooks tantalized the eyes. The natural beauty was obvious.

The landscape in and around Austin could be described as pretty, an adjective not often used to describe the natural surroundings of Dallas, Houston, Fort Worth, Midland, Lubbock, Port Arthur, or other Texas cities—even San Antonio.

Austin looked like nowhere else in this particular corner of the world because it was where five distinct eco-regions converged—the Edwards Plateau, South Texas Brush Country, Western Gulf Coastal Plain, Texas Blackland Prairie, and East Texas Woodlands. The Balcones Fault uplift, where the landmass rose abruptly out of the coastal plain, began less than a mile west of the capitol. Oaks flourished in the thin layer of soil that covered the limestone and granite subsurface of the region. The Hill Country's Swiss-cheese-like karst topography harbored an abundance of caves and underground pools that emerged at the surface in the forms of artesian springs that fed the region's extensive system of creeks and rivers. Whenever heavy rains fell on the rocky undulating hills west of Austin, the steep terrain transformed in a matter of minutes into Flash-Flood Alley, one of the most dangerous flood-prone areas of the United States.

The Blackland soil that stretched from east of the capitol all the way to the coast was some of the richest, most productive farmland found outside of river bottoms in the southern and southwestern United States.

Depending on the hour, day, month, season, or year, the local weather could be tropical, fed by the current of warm moist air scudding in with the low clouds from the Gulf Coast, 120 miles away; arid and hot enough to bleach the sky white, as if the Chihuahuan Desert had expanded 200 miles east; windy and stormy, not untypical for that part of the southern Great Plains known as Tornado Alley; dank and damp, like a lost piece of the Big Thicket, the densest, most biologically diverse part of the great eastern hardwood forest; or simultaneously bone-dry and suffocatingly humid, typical conditions for the brush country and the Texas-Mexico borderlands where the Tamaulipan thorn forest dominated.

Overall, the climate was tolerable enough—and the hills, woodlands, creeks, rivers, and lakes of Austin were inviting enough—that locals responded to the environment in a manner that seemingly escaped folks living elsewhere in Texas. People in Dallas and Houston worked harder,

Austinites liked to reason, because those places were so butt-ugly; there was nothing worth looking at, much less playing in, so a person might just as well keep their nose to the grindstone. Compared to those places, Austin sometimes felt so downright idyllic that work could be distracting. Why slave and toil in the blazing July heat when you could be immersed in the clear, cool sixty-eight degree artesian waters of Barton Springs, the soul of Austin and its wellspring of cool?

Before the first Spanish friars arrived in 1730 to establish three missions near Barton Creek (La Purísima Concepción, San Francisco de los Neches, and San José de los Nazonis), then leaving for more hospitable climes near San Antonio a year later, human settlements were largely in close proximity to springs such as Barton Springs. The springs at San Marcos and Comal, thirty and fifty miles to the south, respectively, provided sustenance to local inhabitants for at least eleven thousand years. Small migratory bands of nomadic hunters and gatherers passed through and around Austin, fishing its rivers and creeks, and pursuing buffalo that wintered in the hills, along with other wildlife. Tonkawa, Comanche, and Lipan Apache all paused and camped in the area during different times of the year over the centuries

The city did not come into existence easily. It was another hundred years after the Spanish missionaries moved on before Anglo settlers started show-ing up. In 1835, fourteen years after Mexico won its independence from Spain, Jacob Harrell moved his family from Hornsby's Bend, several miles east, and built a log cabin on a bluff above the Colorado River that would become the center of the settlement of Waterloo, at the northeast cor-ner of the present-day intersection of Congress Avenue and Cesar Chavez Street. It was the farthest Anglo settlement upriver on the Colorado in this northern Mexico territory called Coahuila y Tejas. Threats from a very hos-tile Comanche nation and a Mexican army determined to maintain their hold on Texas were part of everyday life.

The local citizenry was tri-ethnic—white, black, and brown. Anglos controlled politics and business, but Mexico's influence and proximity was the major difference distinguishing Texas from the southern United States.

A year after the Harrells established Waterloo, on April 21, 1836, Anglo Texans defeated Santa Anna's army at San Jacinto, and Texas gained its independence from Mexico. Five different sites served as capital of the new republic (Washington-on-the-Brazos, Harrisburg, Galveston, Velasco, and Columbia), until President Sam Houston decreed his namesake town Houston near the port of Galveston as the seat of government in 1837.

A year later, in 1838, Republic of Texas vice president Mirabeau Buonaparte

Lamar shot his buffalo and declared that Austin should be the republic's capital. If anyone in the buffalo hunting party disagreed with Lamar, they did not say so.

They knew, as did just about everyone in the tender young republic, that Houston was an awfully inhospitable place for a capital. The first president and founding father of Texas, Sam Houston, might have liked it, but few others did. Flat, swampy, and steamy, Houston was something of an acquired taste.

This place Lamar preferred was more agreeable, weather-wise, especially when the river cooled the southerly summer breezes before they swirled onto the north bank where the settlement was. The scenery and the setting made it easy to ignore some hard truths: the Colorado River was not navigable, Austin's town site was far from major trade routes, and hostile Comanche and Mexicans were perilously close.

A site-selection commission appointed by the Texas congress in January 1839 officially chose the western frontier site after viewing it at the instruction of President Lamar, a big booster of westward expansion. The commission opted to buy 7,735 acres along the Colorado River, including the settlement of Waterloo.

The following May, Edwin Waller arrived with a crew to plat the town site, sell lots, and begin construction of the public buildings that would comprise the capitol for the new permanent capital of the Republic of Texas. President Lamar expressed his desire to honor Stephen F. Austin, the first white colonist to settle in this part of what was now becoming known as Texas, by naming the town after him.

Waller became Austin's first mayor. Lamar would later become known for championing public schools, and for his role in removing the Cherokee Nation from the newly created Texas.

Sam Houston hated the idea of having the Republic of Texas capital in what he knew as hostile territory. When Houston was elected President of the Republic of Texas for a second time in 1841, he publicly declared Waterloo/Austin as "the most unfortunate site on earth for a seat of government" and underscored his point by refusing to move into a permanent residence. Instead, he took a room at Mrs. Angelina Eberly's boarding house. When San Antonio, seventy-nine miles southwest of Austin, was twice occupied by Mexican troops in 1842, Houston was able to persuade the Texas congress to move the capital for security reasons from Austin to Washington-on-the-Brazos, about one hundred miles east, where the Texas Declaration of Independence was signed.

The state archives remained in Austin, which had almost dried up and blown away since no government business was being conducted there. Houston sent a party of Texas Rangers to remove three wagonloads of archives. They were met by cannon fire near the present intersection of Sixth Street and Congress Avenue, instigated by Angelina Eberly. The innkeeper's cannon shot missed hitting a Texas Ranger, but did blow a hole in the General Land Office building. Angry locals chased down the rangers, recovered the archives near Brushy Creek, and returned them to their rightful place. Austin would once again be the capital in 1845—of the State of Texas, not the Republic of Texas. President Anson Jones had called a constitutional convention, which approved annexation to the United States of America that summer.

Government, not business, was the reason for Austin's existence, another characteristic that separated the place from the rest of Texas. The town's against-the-grain tendencies were manifested again sixteen years later, in 1861, when its citizens voted against secession from the United States. The majority of voters in the new state elected to secede from the union and join the Confederate states, triggering the American Civil War.

The state university was Austin's second pillar. Establishing an institute of higher education was no easy task. The Constitution of Coahuila y Tejas, written in 1827, stipulated a public university for the arts and sciences, but the Mexican state never acted on it. The Constitution of the Republic of Texas, ratified in 1836, vaguely mandated "a general system of education." The Texas congress of 1839 designated 50 leagues of land, about 288,000 acres, to pay for a publicly funded university. The designation included 40 acres in Austin directly north of the capitol, an area known as College Hill.

The Texas legislature committed one hundred thousand dollars toward constructing a state university in 1845, but those funds were shifted to defending settlers on the western frontier from Indian attacks. The Civil War further depleted funds designated for education. An amendment of the Texas Constitution of 1876 specifically called for establishment of a first-class university; one million acres of state land became the Permanent University Fund, the university's endowment.

The University of Texas opened its doors on September 15, 1883.

The state's designated top college fostered an educated citizenry. Professors from outside of Texas brought outside ideas that did not necessarily mirror those of Texas' political leaders or business establishment. And more new students and new teachers cycled in every year. The constant influx of restless, imaginative migrants cultivated a disproportionately large number of dissidents, outsiders, weirdos, and nonconformists, as well as academic standouts.

If you were academically inclined, philosophically different, or artistically gifted growing up in Texas, the university provided options. You didn't necessarily have to leave Texas to seek whatever it was you were looking for. "Somewhere else" could mean Austin, the one free space in an otherwise harsh, mean culture that tended to look down on education, academics, the arts, outside ideas, blacks, browns, women, and immigrants.

The university and the state also played important roles as employers. With plenty of jobs within their respective bureaucracies, both institutions attracted folks who needed work but still wanted plenty of leisure time for beer-drinking, bullshitting, hell-raising, and thinking. A clear, unfettered head and a relaxed body provided the kind of mental and physical space for a person to work out ideas.

The university and the state were Austin's acknowledged pillars. But there was a third institutional leg of the stool Austin sat upon—the lubricant that encouraged society.

Twenty-eight years after Mirabeau Lamar shot and killed that buffalo, and ten years before the state university welcomed its first students, August Scholz opened the doors of his bar at San Jacinto Boulevard at Sixteenth Street, serving a thirsty clientele of central European immigrants. Scholz added a garten for beer-drinking outside and for hosting *saengerrundes*, German singing clubs from San Antonio, New Braunfels, and Fredericksburg. "Garten" in these parts meant a string of lights woven through the branches of stately oak and pecan trees out back of the building. In 1879, Austin established its own *saengerrunde* at Scholz Garten.

Austin's oldest continuously operating business, and the oldest business in all of Texas, is a beer joint featuring music.

Interesting people showed up. Elizabet Ney, an immigrant from Germany, set up shop in Hyde Park in 1882 after Governor Oran Roberts invited her to the capital city, inspiring her to resume her career as a world-class sculptor.

Will Porter, who would later become better known for his pen name, O. Henry, founded his broadside, *The Rolling Stone*, in Austin, publishing in 1894–95. He gave the big town's natural beauty a boost when he floridly described Austin as "the City of the Violet Crown," the crown being that thin ribbon above the horizon line that is shaded with dark purplish pollen from the Ashe juniper, which blossoms in the winter months when the air is driest and the visibility sharp. In other words, Porter turned one of the area's worst attributes—pollens that left allergy sufferers sniffling and sneezing—into an asset, as locals tended to do.

Maybe there *was* something in the air. Porter wrote fancy prose and short stories with a twist. Another local, Miss Arizona Dranes, sang sanctified music

The pursuit of pleasure in Austin is defined by its oldest business, Scholz Garten, where music, beer-drinking, dancing, and conversation have been a way of life for more than 150 years. (Photo by Tom Davis; courtesy of Scholz Garten.)

with unbridled passion. A young girl from North Texas who enrolled in the Texas Colored School for the Blind in Austin, Dranes would learn to play piano and sing classical music, and eventually make recordings. Her recorded body of work poured the foundation of modern American black gospel music and was the single greatest influence on gospel giant Sister Rosetta Tharpe.

Dranes's spiritual music was the other side of the coin from the music that amused patrons of Guytown, Austin's most storied "sporting" district. Aside from the ladies of the night, the other amusement in Guytown was provided by what were politely called "barrelhouse pianists." A Texas subculture tied together by the railroad and prostitution, the barrelhouse tradition was carried on by two Austin stalwarts in particular: Robert Shaw and Roosevelt T. Williams, better known as the Grey Ghost.

Barrelhouse, blues, and gospel gained importance and significance through the efforts of John A. Lomax, a University of Texas professor who would become known as the father of American music folklore, his wife Bess, and his son Alan, a field collector of American and global folk music. A younger UT academic, Americo Paredes, would follow in the footsteps of the Lomaxes and elevate Mexican-American and border folklore to a field of serious academic study. In Austin, low art was recognized as fine art before anyone else was splitting the difference.

Three other University of Texas academics—Roy Bedichek, J. Frank Dobie, and Walter Prescott Webb—were Texas' first great historians, each eloquently detailing the state's (and the republic's) colorful past. In the process, they created a mythology all their own.

The smart minds and outside thinkers in Austin started veering off course in the 1940s, fifties, and early sixties. They frequently expressed themselves in the pages of the *Texas Ranger*, the campus satire magazine at the University of Texas that started in the 1930s. Often censored by university authorities for exceeding the boundaries of good taste in the name of puerile humor (e.g., "Sex on Sixth Street," "Grab Your Broad and Go Sidewalk Surfin' with Me"), the *Texas Ranger* produced several notable scribes and artists—notably Bill Helmers, who would become a lifer editor/writer at *Playboy* magazine, and cartoonist Frank Stack, who authored the *Adventures of Jesus* under the name Foolbert Sturgeon in 1962, regarded as the very first underground comic strip. Stack's creation was followed two years later by Jack Jackson's full-blown underground comix magazine, *God Nose*, about God and the fools he rules. Jaxon, as he was known, printed one thousand copies after hours on the Texas State capitol's printing press, taking advantage of his day job as a state bureaucrat, before departing for San Francisco.

A writer, cartoonist, and poster artist named Gilbert Shelton began drawing and writing for the *Texas Ranger* on his way to being recognized as one of the best-known underground comix creators of all time, with his characters Wonder Wart-Hog, a twisted variation on Superman who first appeared in a campus humor magazine in 1962, and the Fabulous Furry Freak Brothers, a sitcom based around three characters—Fat Freddy, Phineas, and Freewheelin' Franklin.

Shelton and two *Texas Ranger* cohorts, Joe Brown and Tony Bell, founded the Underground City Hall on the 1600 block of Lavaca. They were hippies, a term not yet in the common language that was being applied to outsiders of a certain bent. Hippies rejected mainstream "straight" society and the materialism that went with it. They embraced their own different kind of culture, which translated into long hair and unconventional dress such as sandals, beads, and tie-dyed fabrics. They preached peace and love, not war—a direct reaction to the United States' failed occupation of Vietnam. They experimented with drugs such as marijuana and mind-altering psychedelics like LSD and psilocybin.

Hippies were descendants of the beatniks and the beat generation, the post–World War II American literary and cultural movement that scorned societal norms, values, and materialism, and embraced spiritual searching through experimentation with Eastern religions and philosophies and with psychotropic drugs. There were just enough lingering beats and newly minted hippies around the university to comprise a community and sort of justify the existence of the Underground City Hall. Shelton, Brown, and Bell used the space to sell hippie clothes and underground comix, many of which Shelton created. In their spare time, of which they had plenty, they launched a satirical campaign for governor of Texas.

Their candidate was Oat Willie, a large-nosed cartoon character drawn by Gilbert Shelton who wore an airman's hat and red polka dot boxer shorts—the winning candidate Preston Smith favored polka dot ties. Based on a real person named Wally Stopher, Oat Willie carried a torch, riding in a two-wheeled oak bucket chariot while declaring "One vote, One oat." When artist Jim Franklin heard Stopher utter the phrase "onward through the fog," he erased Shelton's saying and replaced it with Stopher's. Oat Willie was not elected governor of Texas in 1968. But Austin hippies had a new icon, catchphrase, and guiding light.

Shelton, Brown, and Bell sold the Underground City Hall to Doug Brown and George Majewski for seventy-five dollars following the 1968 election. Inventory consisted of a pile of *Los Angeles Free Press* underground newspapers and a pile of free clothes. Brown and Majewski renamed the place Oat

Dueling Billboards on the Drag: Preston Smith runs for governor while Shiva's Headband releases their first album, 1968. (Photo by Burton Wilson.)

Willie's Campaign Headquarters and operated it as a hippie head shop with cigarette papers, incense, black light posters, candles, and other accessories to complement their extensive selection of underground comix.

Enough like-minded outsiders lived, studied, worked, and played together to comprise a scene, even though it may have only consisted of four houses on Thirty-Third Street, "the Ghetto" student apartment complex on Rio Grande, the Chuck Wagon restaurant inside the Texas Union student center, the Vulcan Gas Company music club downtown, and the Underground City Hall.

A favored hangout was a gas station on North Lamar that sold beer and encouraged live music, operated by a pot-bellied gentleman with mutton-chop sideburns named Kenneth Threadgill, who liked to step from behind the counter and yodel like his favorite singer Jimmie Rodgers. Mr. Threadgill organized weekly folk music hootenannies that attracted college students, including a jug band known as the Waller Street Boys that included a female "boy" named Janis Joplin. Joplin, a UT student from Port Arthur who was part of the Ghetto crowd, possessed an assertive, powerful voice and was delving into old blues records for inspiration like everybody else.

The best and brightest of Austin's counterculture in the 1960s instinctively hightailed it to Northern California, a considerably more tolerant place. Longhairs were on some kind of cutting edge in San Francisco. Longhairs in Texas got beat up. Janis Joplin's friend Travis Rivers talked her into going with him to San Francisco in 1966 to audition for a band that another hippie Texan named Chet Helms was managing called Big Brother and the Holding Company. She aced the audition to lead the most popular of all the San Francisco psychedelic bands.

What really separated Austin hippies from hippies everywhere else was peyote, which people were eating to induce visions long before Timothy Leary first experimented with LSD. A spineless cactus that resembles an overinflated pincushion growing close to the ground in the limestone scrub soil of South Texas' brush country and the Chihuahuan Desert in Western Texas and Northern Mexico, peyote contains psychoactive alkaloids that when ingested induce visions, hallucinations, and a sense of well-being in an out-of-body experience.

Indigenous peoples in Mexico had been using peyote as a sacrament in ceremonial rituals for centuries. The practice was embraced in the nineteenth century by the Kiowa and Comanche tribes living in and around present-day Texas.

When those tribes were forcefully moved to reservations in Oklahoma by the US government, the peyote cults survived and were legitimized as the

Native American Church, which counted 13,000 members in 1922, and grew close to a quarter-million members by midcentury. Young Texans interested in the life of Quanah Parker, the last chief of the Comanche, whose mother had been a white captured by the Indians, learned about his embrace of peyote.

One of those young Texans, an inquisitive kid in North Austin named Don Hyde, went the extra step. Hyde had also read *The Peyote Cult* by Westen La Barre and Aldous Huxley's *Doors of Perception*, the latter about tripping on mescaline in 1953. It was all the inspiration he and his friend Tom Tischler needed to embark on their own vision quests with peyote, which was readily available at Hudson's Cactus Garden, where Hyde worked, and other gardening stores in and around Austin, where it was sold as a decorative plant.

On his first trip, Hyde thought he was dead until he saw the sun rise. "I couldn't believe the colors as the sun seeped into the woods," he recalled in a 2018 interview. "So many shades of green, even the blackest of blacks was dark green. The clouds in the sky were purple! Everything was incredibly gorgeous, and I'd never felt so good."

Hyde was hardly the only one to make this discovery. Tasker Hudson was shipping "dope cactus," as he called it, collected in South Texas, to New York, Los Angeles, Paris, Rome, Germany, and Japan by mail order. At the time, peyote was completely legal, in contrast to possessing marijuana, which could get someone ten years in prison in Texas. Some of the Texas Union music folkies and the Ghetto hippies who lived near campus bought direct from Hudson.

Hyde had started hanging around with the Texas Union/Ghetto crowd at about the same time he became interested in peyote while attending Lanier High School. He was attracted to the music being made by folkies such as John Clay and the Waller Creek Boys, and to the scene that music people circulated in. He was well-read and grew up watching movies, particularly the B movie fare preferred by Mexican Americans at the Capitol Theatre just west of Woolworth's at Sixth Street and Congress Avenue. His poetry was published in the *Texas Observer*. His interest in peyote was shared by several older friends, among them Gary Maxwell-Scanlon, Jim Franklin, and Roger Baker.

Chewing the bitter buttons to get high could be unpleasant, since some of the alkaloids in the plant induced vomiting. In search of a more palatable way of taking peyote, the group tried teas, tar concentrate, and downing the cactus with Dr Pepper. They settled on boiling the buttons into a liquid extract, which they cooked in rural rent houses near Luling and Dripping Springs. A sheriff's deputy who had been alerted by neighbors about suspicious activities by hippies paid a visit to the Luling house, where Jim Franklin calmly informed him, "We're UT artists and we are extracting plant dye for a special color we need for an art project we're doing." Satisfied with the explanation, the deputy said, "You boys be careful," and drove off.

Baker's knowledge of chemistry led to a process involving butane to create mescaline sulfate, peyote's psychedelic component, in crystal form from the extract. That led to work-vacations to San Francisco for Don Hyde. Mescaline found immediate popularity in Northern California as a pleasant psychedelic alternative to LSD with few side effects.

Hyde traded mescaline for the last of the high-quality batch of White Lightning LSD that had been made for the Human Be-In in 1967, one of several events where crowds converged to hear live music and trip on hallucinatory acid. He decided to try to replicate what he saw going on in San Francisco by opening the Vulcan Gas Company in a former dry goods store at 316 Congress Avenue, the low-rent part of the grand avenue, in the fall of 1967. The Vulcan featured live music and psychedelic light shows with the unspoken understanding that the music and the lights were a whole lot more fun under the influence of LSD, which Hyde had plenty of—particularly the Clearlight, or Windowpane, variety. Joining Hyde in running the Vulcan were Houston White, Gary Maxwell-Scanlon, and Sandy Lockett. Doug Brown and George Majewski helped set up concessions.

The Vulcan became home to a wide array of bands, including the Thirteenth Floor Elevators, the first psychedelic band anywhere, led by a Travis High School dropout named Roky Erickson and Tommy Hall, a UT philosophy major who played electric jug. Their slash-and-burn single "You're Gonna Miss Me" actually snuck onto the Top 40 pop music chart, and they sold out the club three nights in a row before the band fell apart. Other high-profile local psychedelic/blues outfits such as the Conqueroo; Shiva's Headband, led by violinist Spencer Perskin; and the Wig, which featured Bennie Rowe and Rusty Wier, regularly appeared at the Vulcan.

Touring bands such as Steve Miller and the Velvet Underground, and bands that rarely toured, like the Fugs, an obscenity-slinging New York street band led by poet Ed Sanders (who were barely known outside Greenwich Village), played the Vulcan in front of full houses. Hyde brought in blues players Muddy Waters, Jimmy Reed, Big Joe Williams, and John Lee Hooker—who requested Mexican food when Hyde picked him up at the bus station. The Texas blues institutions Lightnin' Hopkins and Mance Lipscomb appeared so frequently they were regarded as family.

Gilbert Shelton started making bright, multicolored posters at the Vulcan in the tradition of San Francisco posters that advertised shows at the Fillmore and Avalon ballrooms. When Shelton left to pursue a career in making posters and drawing underground comix in San Francisco, where expat Texans Fred Todd, David Moriaty, and Jack Jaxon had started the underground comix publisher Rip Off Press, he was succeeded by Jim Franklin.

Johnny Winter, an albino guitarist from Beaumont, got the attention of the blues and rock worlds when he opened for Muddy Waters at the Vulcan and recorded his breakthrough album *Progressive Blues Experiment* there in 1968 for the local Sonobeat label. Winter left for New York with the Vulcan's Houston White and Sandy Lockett in tow, and scored one of the first six-figure advances in the history of the record business.

The Vulcan functioned as more than a music venue to the regulars who frequented the place. It was a touchstone of all the things they heard were going on in California and in a few other hip pockets of the country, a cool place to hang among like-minded people, maybe score some drugs, and have a good time. Authorities in Austin viewed the Vulcan as some kind of den of iniquity crawling with dirty hippies zonked out on dope. They were half right.

The business model was sketchy. Revenue was the cover charge collected at the door, which usually meant about two dollars per person. Even on those rare occasions when the club reached its eight hundred persons capacity, there was never enough money. But Hyde and company weren't in it for the money.

For two years, the Vulcan managed to get by. The daily newspaper would not accept its advertisements because of what the club represented. Police maintained their suspicion that something illicit was going on there. In the fall of 1969, Jerry Spain, a neighbor of Don Hyde's growing up and a member of the Austin Police Department's vice squad, informed Hyde the police were watching him and did not like what they saw going on at the Vulcan. If he wanted to avoid being arrested on some charge they'd make stick, it would be best that he leave town within twenty-four hours.

On January 2, 1970, Don Hyde left Austin for good. The last hippie to get run out of town did not look back. He would land in Marin County as the roommate of Sam Cutler, the business manager of the Grateful Dead, work with the band Quicksilver Messenger Service, and later run a movie theater and music venue in Healdsburg, California, produce an award-winning documentary on real-life hobos riding the rails, become archivist for the film director Sam Peckinpah, and pass some years in Florence, Italy. But Austin never left Hyde.

The outward migration had become pretty much static by 1971, when

Willie Nelson planted roots in Austin after his house outside of Nashville had burned down. People were still leaving for various reasons, but just as many were filtering in. Only these weren't the traditional instate malcontents for whom Austin was the only place in Texas tolerable enough to live in, but increasingly, interesting people from outside of Texas.

The rest of Texas would derisively refer to the People's Republic of Austin, a label that locals wore as proudly as the Keep Austin Weird bumper sticker they later embraced. Those same detractors streamed into Austin to party whenever the occasion called for it, because even rednecks, peckerwoods, bulletheads, and reactionaries recognized that Austin people knew how to have a good time.

They were all cut from the same cloth: Jacob Harrell, Mirabeau Lamar, Angelina Eberly, Elizabet Ney, O. Henry, the Lomaxes; the academics and philosophers Dobie, Bedichek, and Webb; the yodeler Threadgill; Hattie Valdes, whorehouse madam and friend of state legislators; Chano Cadena, Cowboy Donley, Lonnie Guerrero, and Johnny Degollado, the fathers of Austin *mexicano* music; Hemann Sweatt, the first black man to attend the university; professional football's first black defensive star Dick "Night Train" Lane; Congresswoman Barbara Jordan, the Houston orator and legislator who chose to spend her postpolitics life in an Austin bungalow; the Negro Baseball League Hall of Famer Willie Wells; the blacklisted storyteller and humorist John Henry Faulk; the cartoonist Roy Crane; the jazz trumpeter Kenny Dorham; bootmaker Charlie Dunn and saddlemaker Buck Steiner; the photographer Russell Lee; the sculptor Charles Umlauf; and B. L. Joyce, the L. C. Anderson High School marching band director and future arranger and writer for Motown Records. They were outsiders, even if they grew up in Austin, so set in their own peculiar ways that this was the only place where they could work out their ideas and put them into action. They were all part of the prequel of what was to come.

Austin was a big small city in 1970, with 253,000 residents. The skyline was dominated by the pink-granite-domed, 302-feet-tall Texas state capitol building, completed in 1888, and the 307-feet-high University of Texas main building, better known as the UT Tower—symbols of the city's two primary institutions. Between those two iconic structures was the newly constructed semibrutalist glass-and-concrete Dobie Towers, a twenty-eight-story student housing high-rise that looked like it was trying to elbow its way into the picture.

But just as Scholz Garten was the underappreciated third institution that provided the foundation for Austin culture, a few dozen tall structures scattered throughout the core of the city separated Austin's skyline from every-where else. They were called moon towers. These metallic interstice girders, each about 165 feet in height, topped by a small cluster of large lights, with a 15-foot base at the bottom, were part oil derrick, part mini–Eiffel Tower. Their functionality informed their beauty.

When they were first installed in 1894–95, moon towers were intended to mimic moonlight and provide artificial illumination throughout the city at night. Austin had purchased thirty-one towers from the city of Detroit, which had decommissioned their use, to take advantage of the electricity generated by the recently constructed Austin Dam on the Colorado River.

By the early twentieth century, as street lighting became more pervasive, New Orleans, Louisiana; San Jose, California; Aurora, Illinois; Hannibal, Missouri; and Wabash, Indiana, followed Detroit and decommissioned their moonlight towers.

Austin was the only city in the world that held on to its moon towers, a matter of local identity and quirk, rather than practical function. Beginning in 1967, the moon tower in Zilker Park was festooned with three thousand lights every November and transformed into the Zilker Holiday Tree, which attracted thousands of celebrants to twirl around the base of the tower.

A moon tower would provide the locale for a beer bust party in the Richard Linklater coming-of-age film *Dazed and Confused*. A local band adopted the name. And in 1993, the city would rehab the seventeen extant towers and throw a festival in their honor.

In 2011, the Moontower Saloon, a dog-friendly outdoor music venue built on eleven acres would rise just off Manchaca Road in deep South Austin. Set around a fifties-era ranch house, the Moontower featured picnic tables under large oak trees with light bulbs strung through them, a volleyball court, food trucks, and the establishment's own small-scale metal tower.

Austin was still small and sleepy enough in 1970, and the university so dominating, that many local businesses closed up during spring break every March because students had either gone to the beach or went home. Austin got so quiet during the summer that the Chamber of Commerce organized a two-week-long bash in August called Aqua Fest, featuring music and drag boat races, as an excuse to get citizens out.

Music was considered a hobby. Musicians had day jobs. A cover charge higher than two dollars was considered excessive. Writing was a pursuit for the well educated, highly refined, and sufficiently bankrolled. The mid-century-modern thousand-seat Americana Theater with a seventy-milli-meter screen was the coolest thing going in film. H-E-B supermarkets did not sell beer or wine, and closed on Sundays. The Made-in-Austin IBM self-correcting Selectric typewriter was the latest technological innovation.

The wave of change that swept through San Francisco in the late sixties didn't reach Austin full on until the early seventies. In the tradition of the African American celebration of Juneteenth, when news of President Lincoln's Emancipation Proclamation freeing slaves reached Texas two-and-a-half years after the fact, at the end of the Civil War, change often came a little bit slower in Texas. But once that wave finally did crash ashore, it did so with dramatic flourish, spawning new, not-necessarily-obvious institutions, starting with the Armadillo World Headquarters that eventually reimagined Austin into the all-purpose Alternative City.

The peace and love experiment that started in Haight-Ashbury in San Francisco in 1966 didn't turn out all that well, considering the violence that broke out at the Rolling Stones concert at Altamont and insipid, indulgent rock bands such as Journey and Huey Lewis that came along after the Summer of Love. What began with the Cosmic Cowboy in Austin in 1970 was still playing out well into the twenty-first century in the forms of Americana and roots music, with an eternal constant named Willie Nelson. In Austin, everyone was either in a band or knew someone in one.

Music, not politics, defined Austin's counterculture. After the hippies and pickers came the slackers, overeducated deadbeats who approached film and life in general with the same enthusiasm that music clubbers had for rock shows at 2:00 a.m. The geeks who arrived next overwhelmed and outnumbered them all, shapeshifting the culture, the economy, and the city. All these outsiders built their own alternative communities and institutions.

Their cumulative vision of Austin represented the Other Texas that was progressive, forward-thinking, innovative, and environmentally aware, with an abundant population of smart, creative minds, built upon a tradition of tolerance and openness to new ideas and new people, and a strong attachment to place.

The people and institutions here made an impact in spite of Texas, and in spite of the business and political establishment. Artists, creators, and entrepreneurs were by nature outsiders. The hippies, pickers, slackers, and geeks who made Austin Austin fit right in because they didn't fit in anywhere else. Politicians, dealmakers, insiders, and bigwigs were beside the point; those were folks who largely resisted creative change, rather than fostered it. But they served a purpose by giving the creators something to rebel against, providing motivation and permission to paint outside the lines.

The university, Austin's greatest, most valuable institution, historically, enabled this unleashing of creative force, even though more and more out-siders were making up their own curriculum and establishing their own values and rules to get where they needed to go, outside the confines of the classroom. They got what they were chasing after in spite of traditional means and institutions, not because of them. They made their own way.

Music mecca, film industry hangout, source point of the retail organic food movement, high-tech hub and game development hotbed, noncorpo-rate tourist destination, and, for at least a fortnight every March, the Coolest Place in the World.

These origin stories, each with its own chronology, tell how it happened. Woven together, they explain Austin's ascendance from state capital to cap-ital of all things alternative.

2

City of the Violet Crown, the Gay Place

◉ ◉ ◉

A man can do a lot of thinking mowing lawns. There is something calming about the full-throated, muffler-less sputter and pop of the combustible engine, the high-pitched whine and whirr of the blade, the smell of fresh-cut grass mixed with gasoline exhaust, the order and symmetry each pass of the mower deck brings to wild nature.

Steve Harrigan credited his brief career mowing lawns for making him the writer he became. The pay was good. The mowing season was long enough to stay busy March through October. As long as he worked fast, there was always time to think and ponder and plan and plot. When he was done mowing, before the midafternoon heat made the job insufferable, he would go home, sit at his desk, and write.

Writing was pretty much all Harrigan knew he wanted to do when he came to Austin in the fall of 1966, enrolling at St. Edward's University, a small Catholic men's school that was admitting females for the first time. He'd liked what he saw when he'd visited the previous spring—but it wasn't the sweeping vista from the South Austin hilltop campus of the entire Colorado River basin draining into Town Lake with downtown, the capitol dome, and the University of Texas tower looming in the distance. It was skateboards. "My one college visit was to St. Edward's," the soft-spoken Harrigan said over lunch at the Frisco Shop. "There were these people on skateboards. I'd never seen skateboards before. These kids were riding skateboards on campus. I said, 'That's it for me. I'm going here.'"

Simple enough. Austin wasn't Corpus Christi, where he had lived since he was ten. It was time to go to college. "You were supposed to go to college, so I went," he said. His older brother was already enrolled at St. Edward's. "I came to St. Edward's because we were a good Catholic family and it was a good Catholic college."

Although he wanted to be a writer, "I didn't know what it meant," he said. "I didn't know what it entailed. I'd never met a writer. So I thought I'd study English and go to college to become a writer. That was the vague notion."

The prematurely balding Harrigan looked the part. His measured, soft-spoken but intense manner fit the stereotype. All he had to do to complete the profile was write.

By the time Harrigan made it through his freshman year at St. Edward's, he was ready to cross Town Lake and enroll at the University of Texas. He'd gone with some friends to see the film A Farewell to Arms, which was screened in the Texas Student Union. "I couldn't believe a movie like that could be shown on a college campus," he said. "It wasn't the politics of the film. It was my naïve discovery that a film could be shown outside of a conventional movie theater." Universities and colleges around Corpus Christi did not show classic films. "I'd never experienced that, so I decided 'I gotta go to UT.' I transferred the next year."

"People moved to Austin because it was the only place where things were happening," he said. "It looked like Paris in the twenties if you came from Corpus Christi or Abilene or some place like that. Everything felt so alive, so happening, particularly in the late sixties when everything was going berserk. There'd be riots, tear gas, there'd be a big march. The cops would come into the student union and start beating people over their heads with clubs. It was exciting."

His sophomore year he met someone with similar ambitions. "I think his name was Rick, and he claimed to be a writer," Harrigan recalled. "I later learned he was from Amarillo, but he had a British accent. He was said to be working on a novel. I was so impressed. He was self-assured, urbane. I thought the idea that somebody would be working on a novel and would say they were working on a novel was daring and exciting. I never knew what became of him."

He made indirect contact with a real writer. Harrigan had read Thirteen Days to Glory by Lon Tinkle, a book about the Alamo, when he was a kid. Tinkle taught at Southern Methodist University in Dallas and a friend of Harrigan's was taking a class from him. He asked his friend if he'd get his book signed. "And he did," Harrigan said. "I had a real author sign my book." He attended lectures by authors Truman Capote and Jorge Luis Borges when they spoke at the university. "But I'd never talked to one [a writer]."

Harrigan knew lots of poets. Thomas Whitbread, one of his instructors, was a published poet. Writing poetry seemed like a noble thing to do, like writing a novel. "But I didn't know what I was doing, honestly," he said. "I didn't know anything about poetry. I didn't read a lot of it. I just wrote some of it. I was obviously trying to bluff my way through as a poet."

As a junior he took poetry and short story workshops. If a creative writing program existed, he did not know about it. By declaring himself an English major, "I was shunted into this English major world where it was all about analysis and explication of text, stuff like that, which I had zero interest in. I just wanted to write."

Harrigan graduated in 1971, and attended graduate school for a year and a half, where he was doing even deeper textual analysis. "I couldn't handle it; it was so repellent to me," he said. "I knew I didn't want to teach. I knew I didn't want an academic career. I stopped doing that and worked at the University Co-op in the textbook department and in the advertising department."

Mowing changed his life.

"A friend of mine named David Woodland had a lawn-mowing business, and I went to work for him," Harrigan said. "He taught me the trade, which was basically *work fast*. I could do a lawn in fifteen minutes."

Mowing allowed him time for his primary obsession: writing. "I felt it was more of an obligation than a recreation," he said. "I was writing all the time. I was writing poetry; it was short. The poetry I wrote was so cryptic, it was ridiculous. I started a poetry magazine called *Lucille*, with David Moorman, Gunnar Hansen (who played the crazed character Leatherface in the film *Texas Chainsaw Massacre*), and Alice Gordon. We did ten issues while I was mowing yards."

He also wrote two hundred pages of what he hoped would be his first novel. It didn't happen. But it didn't matter. "It was a really good time for me."

He had money in his pocket, and he was chasing his muse. "For the first and only time of my life, I was kind of flush," he said. "My place was ninety-five dollars a month. I had a Toyota Corolla. I think my payment was two twenty a month. I owned my lawn mower and edger outright. Everything I made beyond four, five hundred dollars was money I could keep."

The financial reward allowed Harrigan to appreciate the Zen of it all. "The work was contemplative," he said, cracking a slight grin at the memory. "Actually, mowing for a living was pretty great. You're aware of the contour of the landscape. You watch the grass cuttings in your wake. You're always doing something productive. There is something about mowing that can flush the mind. For one thing, you're thinking all the time. There are endorphins being released. You're free-associating. You're wondering what you can write next. You're wondering how to solve a problem that you've got writing. It was mindless labor in the best sense."

Harrigan was admiring the long piles of grass clippings trailing behind the mower early one afternoon, thinking there must be something better out there, when an idea came to him: "Maybe I could write a magazine article." He'd seen the film *The Last Picture Show*, based on a Larry McMurtry novel. "And in *The Last Picture Show* there was a cameo by Grover Lewis. He played Sonny's father. I wrote to Grover Lewis, because I knew he was at *Rolling Stone* magazine, and asked if he'd be interested in an article about Jim Franklin and the Armadillo culture of Austin."

Rolling Stone was the rock-music-focused biweekly from San Francisco that was becoming the literary voice of American counterculture. What was happening in Austin with Franklin and the Armadillo World Headquarters might be right up their alley. "I got a letter back saying, 'Yeah, send it to us. If we like it, we'll run it and we'll pay you.'"

Harrigan had figured out how to use words to be persuasive and sell his idea. Now he had to do the hard work. He'd never interviewed anyone. He'd never profiled a person for a magazine. He didn't know Jim Franklin. So he called him up and went to see him at the Armadillo World Headquarters, where he lived upstairs. "I interviewed him about armadillos and wrote this article," Harrigan said. He sent in the story, and Grover Lewis wrote back. "'We like it. We are going to pay you $150.' That was my big break."

"I thought I was on my way to literary stardom because I had a piece in *Rolling Stone*," Harrigan said. "But I didn't have any idea how to write a magazine article for real, or what a magazine article was supposed to be. I wrote them a couple more times with ideas but never heard back."

The Jim Franklin armadillo story in *Rolling Stone* gave Harrigan street cred. Kaye Northcott at the *Texas Observer* thought he was cool enough to let him write articles about caves and killer whales, two very un-*Texas Observer* subjects. She ran the piece about the killer whales in an aquatic theme park in Galveston as a cover story.

He was on a roll.

◎ ◎ ◎

Writers were Austin's first creators. They were here from the start, a good twenty years before Scholz Garten, the beer joint and music club known as Austin's oldest business. Mirabeau Lamar, the second president of the Republic of Texas, the man who declared Austin to be a fine location for a capital while on a successful buffalo hunt, was a recognized poet.

A champion of public education, Lamar's words decorated the exteriors of many schools across the state: "The cultivated mind is the guardian genius of Democracy, and while guided and controlled by virtue, the noblest attribute of man. It is the only dictator that freemen acknowledge, and the only security which freemen desire."

At the end of December 1839 when the settlement of Waterloo formally incorporated as the City of Austin with a population of 856, two printing presses were operating.

Austin's first nationally known writer moved to town forty-five years later. William Sydney Porter had drifted west from North Carolina, first to a ranch in La Salle County, and then to Austin. He was seeking a place where he could get some relief from a chronic cough.

Porter settled in, got enough relief from his ailment to join a men's singing quartet that serenaded the women of Austin, worked a series of jobs including pharmacist and accountant, married and raised a family, and wrote. Porter described Austin as the "city of the violet crown" in the short story "Tictocq the Great French Detective, in Austin," which appeared in the October 27, 1894, edition of *The Rolling Stone*, the humorous weekly publication Porter wrote, edited, and published.

The description set the scene for a local high society function, O. Henry—Porter's pen name—wryly teased: "Austin society is acknowledged to be the wittiest, the most select, and the highest bred to be found southwest of Kansas City."

O. Henry was both a satirist and smart-ass, qualities many subsequent writers from Austin seemed to possess. O. Henry short stories in *The Rolling Stone* were widely read in spite of a circulation that never exceeded fifteen hundred. Porter supported his family and himself while publishing the paper by working as a teller at the First National Bank.

The bank gig interrupted his writing career—and then boosted it, in a twisted kind of way. Porter was charged with embezzling, which may or may not have been true. He responded to the charges by fleeing to Honduras, but turned himself in when he learned his wife was dying in Austin. Convicted, he spent three years in prison in Ohio, working as the prison pharmacist and enjoying privileges that included his own private bedroom separate from the captive population. He continued writing and getting published.

Upon his release, Porter hightailed it to New York, where the big publishers were. Many of the stories he wrote in prison were published in a 1904 collection, *Cabbages and Kings*. O. Henry enjoyed recognition and a career as a short story writer known for works such as "The Gift of the Magi" and "The Caballero's Way," which introduced readers to a character named the

Cisco Kid. J. Frank Dobie called O. Henry's "The Last of the Troubadours" "the best range story in American fiction." But he died an alcoholic, destitute at the age of forty-seven.

Three larger-than-life personalities dominated the literary scene in Austin during the first half of the twentieth century, such as it was. J. Frank Dobie, Walter Prescott Webb, and Roy Bedichek were held in high regard as wise men, and their regular conversations at Barton Springs on warm afternoons composed what came to be known as the Salon of the West.

Bedichek was a writer and naturalist who liked to cook outdoors, sleep outdoors, and relieve himself outdoors. Dobie was a folklorist, Webb a historian. Dobie and Webb taught at the University of Texas. Bedichek was director of the University Interscholastic League, the University of Texas–affiliated organization that oversaw public high school academic and sports competition in the state. Webb wrote the epic tale *The Great Plains* that looked at the heartland of the United States as a whole, citing the gun, barbed wire, and the windmill as the forces that civilized the region. He presided over the Texas State Historical Association.

Dobie collected and wrote folk tales about the vanishing South Texas ranch life he grew up in, most notably the book *The Longhorns*. An academic and an unabashed liberal, he was unsparing in his take on Texas politicians and politics, writing, "When I get ready to explain homemade fascism in America, I can take my example from the state capital of Texas." Attracting the ire of Governor Coke Stevenson, Dobie was dismissed from the faculty of the university for his political views in 1944. Twenty years later, one-time Stevenson rival and then-president of the United States Lyndon B. Johnson awarded Dobie the Medal of Freedom.

Dobie and Webb were instrumental in goading Bedichek to finish his first book, *Adventures with a Texas Naturalist*, at the age of sixty-eight. Fluent in several tongues, including ancient Greek, Bedichek had written volumes of letters before then that could have just as well been books.

Well-read, hard-working intellectuals who happened to be friends, the three shared a respect (and fascination) for the natural world. They loved Austin, especially Barton Springs, where they would hang out at Conversation Rock, nicknamed Bedi's Rock, just above Parthenia, the main spring of Barton Springs, and talk about whatever was on their minds.

Their apostles included humorist and writer John Henry Faulk, a Dobie understudy who hosted his own nationally broadcast radio program from 1951 until 1957, when he was blacklisted as part of a communist witch hunt; William Owens, a Bedichek disciple who was an author, folklorist, and professor; and Ronnie Dugger, a bright student who founded the *Texas Observer* in 1954 at the age of twenty-four. Dobie, Bedichek, and Webb all wrote for the *Texas Observer* in its early years. In gratitude, Dugger assembled a collection of tributes into the book *Three Men in Texas* (1967).

The *Texas Observer* was political in nature, championing progressive ideas in a state known for its staunch conservatism. But by the sheer nature of its existence, *Texas Observer* was a literary publication, too. The feisty fortnightly gained considerable literary clout in 1960 when Dugger hired the crusading editor of the student-run *Daily Texan*, Willie Morris. Morris's *Daily Texan* editorials railing against segregation, censorship, and the cozy relationship between the university and oil and gas money had already royally pissed off the Board of Regents, the governor, and state legislators. He invested three years as the editor of the *Texas Observer* before going to New York, where at the age of twenty-seven, he became the youngest editor ever at *Harper's* magazine. It was from New York that Morris wrote his autobiography, *North toward Home*, which covered growing up in Yazoo City, Mississippi, coming to Texas, and moving to New York, with his unequivocal take on Texas politics, especially regarding race.

Shelby Hearon, a 1953 graduate of the University of Texas who started her first novel *Armadillo in the Grass* in 1962 (it was published in 1968), wrote novels and short stories from Austin while nurturing other writers, including onetime companion Jan Reid.

In other words, there were writers in Austin when Steve Harrigan arrived, although no one was making much of a living from the craft.

You could sort of scratch out a subsistence living by editing and writing at the *Texas Observer*, as Molly Ivins, Kaye Northcott, and Jim Hightower were doing. Ivins launched a long run as an acerbic, acid-tongued politics columnist at the *Texas Observer*. Hightower took a detour and served a four-year term as Texas Agricultural Commissioner, embracing the nickname "Whole Hog," and became a syndicated national columnist and radio commentator.

The daily newspaper was competent and paid a salary, but it did not present much opportunity to write. *The Rag*, a beacon of underground journalism, operated like a cooperative rather than a business, meaning just about anything could be published, but at no or low pay. The *Texas Ranger* provided exposure for several talented young writers before ceasing publication in 1972. But neither the *Daily Texan* nor the *Texas Ranger* paid a living wage.

The University of Texas and the Texas Institute of Letters attempted to address the issue indirectly in 1967, establishing the Dobie Paisano Fellowship. The six-month grant provided a writer with a place to live for six months, J. Frank Dobie's Paisano Ranch on Barton Creek in the hills west of Austin, along with a monthly stipend. The Dobie Paisano provided critical breathing room and a much-needed revenue stream for a range of aspiring writers, including Billy Porterfield, A. C. Greene, Sarah Bird, Cecilia Balli, Jan Reid, Gary Cartwright, Laura Furman, Sandra Cisneros, and our friend Steve Harrigan.

Writing wasn't considered much of a career track. What there was in Austin, as Harrigan astutely perceived, was the opportunity to write.

There was one high-profile writer making a living with words: Edwin "Bud" Shrake. He had come to Austin the same year Harrigan enrolled at St. Edward's. Austin was cheap and Austin was cool, which was good enough for the Fort Worth–raised staff writer for *Sports Illustrated*, who moved from New York in 1966. Shrake was on the road so much that his editor OK'd the relocation. He could live wherever he wanted, as long as he met deadlines and filed the kind of stories that kept everyone happy. He had been spending more and more downtime in Mexico, as well as back in his home state. In Austin, he could work on novels and screenplays. Shrake's longtime Fort Worth friend and colleague Gary Cartwright joined him in Austin from Philadelphia, where he'd been writing for *Sport* magazine and, briefly, the *Inquirer* newspaper.

The two met at the *Fort Worth Press* tabloid in the mid-1950s, where both were mentored by the sports editor Blackie Sherrod. Sherrod taught his minions (who also included the writer Dan Jenkins) to make a story interesting, since the outcome, the score—the only vital information in a sports story—was usually already known. "We quoted Shakespeare, even if we didn't know what we were talking about," Cartwright said. They invented teams, made up schools and players, and conjured coaches when real sports were too boring. Sherrod, Cartwright, and Shrake moved to Dallas newspapers to cover the fledging Dallas Cowboys when that National Football League franchise was established in 1960, along with their cross-town rivals, the Dallas Texans of the new American Football League.

While covering the Cowboys for the *Dallas Morning News* in the early sixties, the imposing 6'6" Shrake lived with a similarly statuesque stripper named Jada (who worked for Jack Ruby), partied with the owner of the Cowboys Clint Murchison and women who were not Murchison's wife, briefly opened a nightclub, and wrote well enough to be called to the big leagues, joining his Paschal High School / *Fort Worth Press* buddy Dan Jenkins at *Sports Illustrated*, the best sports magazine in America.

Shrake lived the writer's life in New York. He was given wide latitude about what he wrote, and he took advantage of it. He ran with a fast crowd, supported by a generous expense account that made for many long nights into days at P. J. Clarke's, Elaine's, "21," and other Manhattan bars and drinking establishments.

In Austin, Bud Shrake and Gary Cartwright were writing stars.

Billy Lee Brammer was an even bigger one. Brammer's novel The Gay Place had been published in 1961, when Brammer was thirty-one. The book was recognized as the definitive political novel, and the definitive Austin novel, capturing the place and people and their tendencies for quirk and peculiarity.

The opening passage offered a distinctive whiff of place: "It is a pleasant city, clean and quiet, with wide rambling walks and elaborate public gardens and elegant old homes faintly ruined in the shadow of arching poplars. Occasionally through the trees, and always from a point of higher ground, one can see the college tower and the Capitol building. On brilliant mornings the white sandstone of the tower and the Capitol's granite dome are joined for an instant, all pink and cream, catching the first light."

Brammer got to Austin as a reporter for the Austin American-Statesman, armed with a journalism degree from North Texas State Teachers College in Denton. Whipsmart, animated, and fast-talking, the wiry Brammer was an engaging conversationalist who could run a con when he needed to. He enjoyed drinking beer and talking politics at Scholz Garten with Texas Observer publisher Ronnie Dugger and future Observer editor Willie Morris, the Mississippi kid who at the time was editor of the Daily Texan.

Brammer wrote about the filming of Giant in Marfa, one of several articles he wrote for the Texas Observer, but a writer or editor could not subsist on the wages paid by the feisty progressive voice. Brammer was more than happy to go to work for Senator Lyndon B. Johnson to write policy speeches, letters to his daughters, and serve as the token liberal on his staff as LBJ prepared to seek the office of President of the United States in 1960.

Brammer became a Johnson confidante, traveling with him and hanging out at Johnson's ranch with the family. The experience gave him plenty of material to work into the novel he was writing. It was about a fictional Texas governor named Arthur Fenstemaker, who bore close resemblance to former US senator, present vice-president, and future president Lyndon Johnson. "Arthur Goddam Fenstemaker, hah yew?" was later described as the greatest politician in American literature.

The Gay Place got Brammer banished from LBJ's circle. Johnson dissed him directly, telling him, "I tried reading your novel, Billy, but I couldn't get past the first ten pages because of all the dirty words." Brammer's subsequent writing was hit-or-miss as his fondness for stimulants and inebriants grew. He never finished another book. But by getting that one novel published, he became a role model to a generation of Texas writers.

Brammer lived Austin's split personality. After running with pols, he ran with hippies, not the least of which was Ken Kesey, while the latter was driving around the United States in a psychedelic school bus with a ragtag bunch of friends. They dropped LSD, and brought weirdness into the hinterlands, including Texas, where the merry pranksters stopped in Houston to visit future literary giant Larry McMurtry, who was teaching at Rice University, a story told in Tom Wolfe's *The Electric Kool-Aid Acid Test*, published in 1968.

Brammer and his wife, Dorothy Browne, fell in with Texas hippies in exile in San Francisco—namely the founders of Rip Off Press, the publishers of underground comix, and Chet Helms, the big dog of the Family Dog music collective. Through Helms and the Family Dog, Brammer briefly ran a music club in Denver called the Family Dog. He dropped a lot of LSD along the way. The experiences provided plenty of material for the rock and roll novel that Brammer had started. He lived rock and roll, settling back in Austin in the early seventies when the music scene was blowing up. Brammer found fellow travelers in Bud Shrake, Gary Cartwright, future governor Ann Richards, and other Mad Dogs, as a group of outlaw writers, actors, musicians, sculptors, and associated creatives and cohorts imagined by Shrake were called. They drank, smoked, and ingested copious amounts of weed, coke, acid, and other dope. In Brammer's case, drugging also meant mainlining methamphetamine.

Shrake took a snapshot of that time as Willie Nelson's ghostwriter for his 1988 book *Willie: An Autobiography*, when Willie rented an apartment on Riverside Drive in 1971:

> If you stand downtown and look west across the river to the limestone cliffs that rise up abruptly on the other shore, you are looking at the place where the West literally begins.
>
> The cliffs are a tall wall of rock that runs in an arc from Waco south to Del Rio. The old cotton economy of the South ended where it struck those limestone cliffs. Farther west beyond the cliffs is the Hill Country, which used to be Comanche territory.
>
> Built on seven hills in a river valley where pure artesian water flowed from the rocks and with a mild climate and deer and other wild animals roaming through the oaks and cedars, Austin was like Palm Springs for the Comanche nation long before the Anglo real estate developers turned

it into a town in 1840. Houston had been the capital until then. The brazen act of building a new capital right in the middle of the Comanche's favorite resort started the bloodiest Indian war in Texas history.

You know the Indians lost, but it was hard to tell in Austin in the early seventies. A hell of a lot of young people wore feathers and beads and necklaces and bells and doeskin pants and skirts with fringes and moccasins and long hair and headbands.

It was cheap living. Low taxes, no traffic to speak of. Billy Lee Brammer, who wrote *The Gay Place*, a novel about Austin, was legally blind without his glasses, but Billy Lee was forever taking a bunch of acid and losing his glasses and driving safely all over town in the middle of the night. Austin was a stable place that depended on the state government offices and five universities for much of its economy.

There was no way to get rich in Austin. Only half a dozen houses in town would be allowed in Beverly Hills. People who did have money didn't show it off. Car dealers and beer distributors were big socialites.

You couldn't legally walk around Austin smoking weed or eating acid or mescaline or peyote—dope was very much against the law in Texas—but it seemed like you couldn't walk around Austin for very long without at least being offered a joint.

Every few blocks in Austin you saw some new, unexpected vista—a Victorian house framed against the water and the purple hills, a pair of hawks circling above Mount Larson, a Mexican family eating dinner on the front porch of a house painted pastel yellow with statues of Jesus and the Virgin in the front yard behind a little iron fence.

Barton Springs was the greatest outdoor swimming hole in the country. You could fish and swim in the river right beside your house. You could go out on Lake Travis in a houseboat and putter around hundreds of miles of shoreline for days before somebody found you.

For a population of about 250,000, Austin was a real piece of paradise, an oasis, the best-kept secret in America.

Shrake, Cartwright, Brammer, and this wild bunch wrote about Texans and their Texasness, and enjoyed making fun of, as well as wallowing in, all the stereotypes.

"Billy Lee Brammer was the first writer I ever spoke with," Steve Harrigan said. A friend told him that Billy Lee, which is what everyone called him, really liked what Harrigan had written for the *Texas Observer*. "I had the chutzpah to call him," Harrigan said. "He told me there was this new magazine starting called *Texas Monthly*. Through him, I met Greg Curtis and Bill Broyles, and I got a couple assignments from them."

Texas Monthly magazine was the brainchild of Mike Levy, the kinetic twenty-three-year-old son of a Dallas plumber. Levy had developed an interest in the new city magazine sector of print journalism while attending Wharton School at the University of Pennsylvania. He drove cabs, worked as a jailer, and for United Press International while going to school. After graduating, he sold advertising for *Philadelphia* magazine, one of the hottest city magazine titles going. Levy brought back to Texas a business model for *Texas City*, a magazine focusing on urban Texas—specifically Texas's two biggest cities, Dallas and Houston, along with Fort Worth, San Antonio, and Austin.

Rather than risk resentment by the other city if the magazine was based in Dallas or Houston, Levy wisely chose Austin, the smallest of the state's five largest cities and the state capital, near the geographic center of the state, as a suitably neutral home base.

Levy hired William Broyles, the public affairs spokesman for the Baytown school district, near Houston, as editor. Broyles, an upbeat, curly-haired natural leader, brought in fellow Rice University graduates Paul Burka, Griffin Smith Jr., and Gregory Curtis to help build a small staff working for next to nothing—the alternative Austin business model at work. Levy found an office on the second floor of an insurance company two blocks from the capitol. He hit the streets selling his idea, and then sold ads for the magazine, starting with the debut February 1973 issue. Along the way, the scope broadened. The magazine wasn't just about cities. This was about Texas. As in *Texas Monthly*.

Richard West, a newspaperman and legislative aide, would set out in his VW van to report stories from the hinterlands, while most of the staff focused on the urban areas, determined to put out a publication as good as anything coming out of New York. If things worked out, *Texas Monthly* aimed to pay semi–New York rates too, in the three figures, at least (compared to the two-figure checks the *Texas Observer* offered) holding out the faint premise a writer might actually be able to make a living without having to take a newspaper job, wait tables, or heaven forbid, mow lawns.

Billy Lee Brammer wrote articles for *Texas Monthly*, contributed ideas at meetings, and briefly served as unofficial elder. He willingly shared his experiences of climbing the literary mountain, at least when he wasn't getting tore down or trying to outhustle Larry L. King for the extra bed in the back of Richard West and Susan Streit's Shoal Creek house between marriages.

Brammer directly encouraged and influenced West, Bill Broyles, Greg Curtis, Gary Cartwright, Jan Reid, Al Reinert, and Steve Harrigan.

Harrigan made his debut in the October 1973 issue of *Texas Monthly* with two articles. "One was about the Children of God [religious cult]. I spent three days in Dallas proselytizing with the Children of God," he said. "The other was about the Aurora Spaceman. I kept doing stuff for *Texas Monthly*, teaching myself how to write. *Texas Monthly* was the gateway for me. Nobody knew what they were doing. It was wide open. You could just start writing for them. I wrote for the *Austin Sun*. I wrote a piece for *Esquire*, for *The Atlantic*, but *Texas Monthly* was the crucial thing.

"I had no contacts. I had no money to fly to New York. I had no one to meet. Moving to New York was off the table. When *Texas Monthly* happened, it created this cluster of possibilities for writers in Texas. Also, we were doing world-class work. There were people like Gary Cartwright who were already big deals. I was really intrigued by people like John McPhee or Tom McGuane—stuff that was kind of natural history–based that was kind of apropos of nothing. That was the kind of stuff I wanted to write. That put me a little bit at odds with the thrust at *Texas Monthly*, which was all about power and politics and business.

"I remember sitting in the office and there would be a big story by Richard West or Harry Hurt that would come in at one hundred pages and everybody in the whole office would go berserk because they had to get this thing in the magazine, and it had to be cut down. I remember feeling like, 'I'm doing something wrong. Because my story is only twenty pages and nobody seems to care.' But it would slip into the magazine. The stuff I wrote didn't excite the readership, but it steadily got some awareness over the years."

Eventually, Harrigan stopped mowing lawns.

"I started making enough money writing magazine articles that I could quit," he said. "One of the people whose lawn I was mowing was [*Texas Monthly* editor] Bill Broyles. He claimed he discovered me when I was his yardman. That's not quite true. I was writing for *Texas Monthly* and still mowing. I wasn't getting paid enough from *Texas Monthly* to make a living. I was married to Sue Ellen and making two thousand a year from freelancing— that was enough to live on. By the time we started having kids, I was making enough to get by."

Sue Ellen Harrigan liked the idea that her husband was a writer. "I don't think she liked the idea that I was not a huge, best-selling writer," he laughed.

A *Texas Monthly* article about capturing dolphins turned into a new idea for a novel; this one became real. *Aransas*, the first novel by Steve Harrigan, was published in 1980. It told the story of a dolphin trainer on the Texas coast near where Harrigan had grown up. His second novel, *Jacob's Well*, about a dangerous diving cave in the Texas Hill Country, reflecting his interest in scuba diving, was published in 1984.

Harrigan was a real novelist, one of the "literary sodbusters on the literate frontier," as fellow *Texas Monthly* staffer Al Reinert described this generation of Texas writers. But he had already figured out that being a novelist wasn't really all that big a deal.

As much as Harrigan fancied being a novelist, he'd also been smitten with the idea of writing a movie ever since he'd seen *Lawrence of Arabia* at the Tower Theater in Corpus Christi when he was fourteen. "I was always a movie person and had always imagined myself writing or making movies," he said. "But I had no awareness of how to do it." He'd tried to write a screenplay on Cabeza De Vaca, the first European to explore Texas, twenty years after Columbus sailed into the New World. But the script went nowhere. Then he met Bill Wittliff.

"Lo and behold, he was writing movies," Harrigan said. "For real."

Bill Wittliff was an all-around Renaissance man. He had grown up in the Hill Country town of Blanco and ran a small publishing company, Encino Press, in Austin. He enjoyed photography as much as writing. Along the way, he worked as a writer on the films *Honeysuckle Rose* and *Barbarosa* for music man Willie Nelson, who had a hankering for acting, and wrote the screenplay of the film *Red-Headed Stranger*, based on the Willie Nelson song-cycle album of the same name, in 1979. After playing tug-of-war with Hollywood producers, who wanted Robert Redford to play the lead role that Willie envisioned himself in, Nelson and Wittliff bought back the rights to the film and Wittliff directed *Red-Headed Stranger* in 1986.

Three years later, Wittliff's screenplays were the basis for the four-part television western mini-series *Lonesome Dove*, based on the book by Larry McMurtry. The saga focused on two retired Texas Rangers, Gus McCrae and Woodrow F. Call, on a cattle drive from Texas to Montana. The series snagged several Emmy awards and earned consensus recognition as the best western broadcast on television.

Wittliff wasn't the only screenwriter in town. The first screenplay Bud Shrake ever attempted was made into the 1973 film *Kid Blue*, starring Dennis Hopper, the Hollywood actor who was an honorary Mad Dog. Shrake wrote twenty-nine more scripts through the eighties into the nineties, including several made-for-TV collaborations with Gary Cartwright. Screenplays that actually made it to the silver screen included *J. W. Coop* (1972), starring Cliff

Robertson; *Tom Horn* (1980), starring Steve McQueen; and *Songwriter* (1984), with Willie Nelson and Kris Kristofferson.

Warren Skaaren, a sculpture major who graduated from Rice University two years prior, had been appointed the founding director of the Texas Film Commission in 1971. His assignment? Get film companies to shoot their movies in Texas. Forty films were made in the state during his three year tenure. Skaaren hung around enough movie people, helping support and promote the groundbreaking *Texas Chainsaw Massacre*, among other things, that he decided to take a chance and dive into writing screenplays. By the end of the eighties, Skaaren had burnished a reputation as Hollywood's go-to script doctor (even though he remained in Austin), known for rewriting—and saving—several screenplays on which a considerable amount of money was riding. Four rewrites, *Batman*, *Top Gun*, *Beverly Hills Cop II*, and *Beetlejuice*, cumulatively grossed more than $1 billion.

Harrigan and his best friend, another writer named Lawrence Wright, who'd grown up in Dallas, decided if Bill Wittliff could write screenplays, then they could too.

"We took two weeks of vacation and sat in Larry's office," he said. "Bill had loaned us a script, so we could see where the margins were. We'd come up with this idea about an astronaut who'd been to the moon and didn't know what to do with the rest of his life." Working on manual typewriters, Harrigan and Wright took turns writing scenes, one after the other. "We banged out this script for two weeks, and we sold it to Sydney Pollack."

Harrigan and Wright were extremely lucky.

"There was an agent named Tina Nides who represented *Texas Monthly*. CBS Films bought it for Sydney Pollack. We flew out to LA and hung out with Sydney. He'd ask, 'Where does the first act end?' 'Where does the second act end?' We had no idea what he was talking about. Ours was only the second script we'd ever seen."

Moonwalker, later retitled *Ocean of Storms*, was never made. The script was revised, reworked, and rewritten by many other writers. "Warren Beatty owns that script, last I heard," Harrigan said. Seeing the project completed was almost beside the point. "We made real money off it."

Harrigan and Wright tried to write a comedy for Jane Fonda next. "It became clear at that time we didn't know how to write a movie script, but we both separately kept at it," Harrigan said. "We wrote three scripts together that didn't go anywhere after that, then we went on our separate ways."

Harrigan's first novel, *Aransas*, was optioned for a made-for-television movie by the NBC network. "The producer of that, Robert Lovenheim, contacted me and asked if I'd be interested in writing the Ishi movie." Ishi was the last surviving member of the much-persecuted Yahi people of Northern California, who spent his last years as a public exhibit at the San Francisco Museum of Anthropology. The film, titled *The Last of His Tribe*, aired on the HBO channel in 1992. Getting the film to production "got me in that world," Harrigan said. "I was in the long-form television world, churning out script after script."

One oddly prophetic Lawrence Wright screenplay became *The Siege*, the 1998 film starring Denzel Washington about a terrorist attack in New York.

Harrigan and Wright were instrumental in hatching the idea for Texas Writers Month that eventually was absorbed into the Texas Book Festival. "Larry and I were in a book store, and they didn't have any of our books, or any books by anyone we knew," Harrigan said. "We thought, 'That's not right. This is Austin. There ought to be Austin writers in this book store.'

"If there was a community when I was starting out, it was all at the university, and it was all professors. We had a meeting with bookstore owners and said we'd like to have this thing called Texas Writers Month. Book Stop [bookstore] said yes, and helped organize an evening that welcomed Austin writers, considerably expanding the playing field beyond the university. This brought everybody out of the shadows."

Aware of his role in Texas Writers Month, Mary Margaret Farabee recruited Harrigan to attend organizing meetings for a Texas book festival that Laura Bush, the first lady of Texas, was advocating for. Bush, a former librarian, wanted a literary event that would benefit public libraries. The first Texas Book Festival launched in and around the capitol over a November weekend in 1996.

"The first year, it was just Texas writers," Harrigan said. "It was almost a competitor to Texas Writers Month. I felt strongly that it ought not to be about just Texas writers. It ought to be national or international. Texas was starting to open up in a literary sense. Until that time, it had been a provincial place. You either had to get out of it, or entrench yourself in it. It was like we were trying too hard to be Texas. Texas writing needed to be open to the world and vice versa."

Under the direction of Cyndi Hughes, a former copy editor at *Texas Monthly*, the Texas Book Festival stepped up from being a regional, provincial event into the biggest book festival hosted by any state in the United States.

By 2015 the festival had stretched out into tents along Congress Avenue for several blocks and along Eleventh Street, and into the Paramount Theater, as well as the book festival's core, the Texas capitol and the underground capitol extension. Because it was Austin, two tents on Congress featured music, not books, with a singer-songwriter lineup designed to appeal to a literate adult audience, and a children's music lineup appealing to kids. The crowd count grew to more than fifty thousand.

The early years of the Texas Book Festival coincided with the height of Steve Harrigan's so-called Hollywood career. Throughout the 1990s, he was being paid very handsomely—bigger money than most novelists were getting—to write screenplays and adaptions for original movies on television. "The kind of stuff I specialized in was, for the most part, Movies of the Week, known in the business as MOW's," Harrigan wrote in an article for *Slate* magazine. "They were called movies of the week because, in the days before reality television swept away the old scripted paradigm of TV entertainment, every broadcast network had at least one night a week devoted to the airing of an original movie or miniseries. As a writer of what I call colon movies (such as *Beyond the Prairie: The True Story of Laura Ingalls Wilder*, or *Take Me Home: The John Denver Story*), the '90s were my golden decade. I was an A-list writer of B-list productions."

He peaked (or bottomed out, depending on perspective) with *The O. J. Simpson Story*, a screenplay he was hired to write within weeks of the murder of Simpson's wife and her boyfriend. "I thought the idea was insane," Harrigan admitted. But he took the money, met the challenge, and withstood the criticism. The *New York Times* called the Simpson MOW "another of television's scavenger productions, eager to pounce on the bare bones of any sensational story that might turn up a few gold fillings for the network bottom line."

Harrigan felt like he was always trying to aim high even though his primary task was to crank out competent content. "I never thought of myself as a TV-movie hack. I wrote with the anguish and conviction of an uncompromising indie auteur."

A writer for the popular midnineties television dramatic series *Knots Landing* let Harrigan be the indie auteur he wanted to be, at least to some of the brightest young writing minds anywhere. Jim Magnuson had been hired by the University of Texas to oversee the James A. Michener Center for Writers, a master of fine arts writing program that admitted twelve students a year on three-year residency fellowships to study fiction, poetry, playwriting, and screenwriting. Located in J. Frank Dobie's old house on Park Row, now Dean Keeton Boulevard, the Michener was quickly recognized as one of the top ten writing programs in the United States by *The Atlantic* magazine.

Author James Michener made his name for long, meticulously researched, multigenerational novels he wrote about specific geographic regions, including *Hawaii*, *Tales of the South Pacific*, *Chesapeake*, *Caribbean*, and *Alaska*. His books sold more than seventy-five million copies, giving him the wherewithal to endow the writing center with twenty million dollars. *Texas*, published in 1985, was one of Michener's most popular epic novels (despite Steve Harrigan's less-than-favorable review in *Texas Monthly*), and the writing experience led his third wife, Mari, and him to put down roots in Austin, where he passed away in 1997 at the age of ninety.

Harrigan loved his gig instructing the Michener fellows. "It's astonishing to me that I teach these people," he said. "They're much more plugged-in than I ever was, so much more aware. The possibilities are so much more wide-open. The editor of the *New York Times Book Review* or an agent will come to talk to the students. They know what the Michener Center is. People are aware if somebody graduated from there. Nobody's career is ever made, but you have more of an open door. In the seventies, there was no door. It was another dimension that you couldn't find your way into.

"Here, there's a pipeline. It's up to the individual, to fate, to chance. But there's a strong possibility a person coming out of the Michener would make an impact."

Three Michener graduates, Philipp Meyer, author of the novel *The Son* (2013), and writers Lee Shipman and Brian McGreevy, went beyond writing to create El Jefe Productions to give authors greater control over adaptions of their work. Their first rollout was the AMC cable channel's Western series *The Son*, based on Meyer's novel about a Texas ranching family whose patriarch, captured by Comanche as a child, has a mean, vengeful streak.

One of Harrigan's students, Jake Silverstein, had been an overqualified newspaper reporter in Marfa, Texas. After the Michener, he became editor of *Texas Monthly* magazine before editing the *New York Times* Sunday magazine. "Jake wasn't the standard applicant," Harrigan said. "He was more of a nonfiction guy. It's satisfying to say, this guy was my student. You do feel this wonderful sense of continuity."

Harrigan had come full circle. "I was the bewildered student. Now I'm the bewildered teacher."

Michener director Jim Magnuson wrote his own novel in 2014 based around the center, *Famous Writers I Have Known*, which followed a con enrolled in a writing program.

Of all the institutions Harrigan had been attached to, he was proudest of the nonprofit Capital Area Statues, Inc. (CAST). "That was Larry's idea. He called me one day back in the early nineties and said, 'There aren't enough statues.'" Wright envisioned a statue of Walter Prescott Webb, Roy Bedichek, and J. Frank Dobie at Barton Springs, sitting around on a rock in their bathing suits, just as the three homespun intellectuals once did.

They convened a committee that included writer Bill Wittliff, musician Marcia Ball, publicist Vincent Salas, and attorney Amon Burton. Sculptor Glenna Goodacre agreed to do a maquette. A total of $250,000 was raised to make the full bronze statue, Philosopher's Rock, at the entrance of Barton Springs.

The CAST committee followed with a bronze of Angelina Eberly on Congress Avenue created by Patrick Oliphant and sited at the exact spot where Eberly fired a cannon at the General Land Office to prevent the removal of the Republic of Texas archives from Austin to Houston in 1842. In 2013, CAST dedicated their third statue, a bronze of a braided Willie Nelson sitting at the entrance of the Austin City Limits music venue.

"It's harder to do now," Steve Harrigan said. "It's hard to find a location. It's harder to get the buy-in with the city. It's harder to find the right subject matter that is not subject to pressure from one group or another."

Capital Area Statues cast around the Willie statue: writer Lawrence Wright (left), writer Stephen Harrigan, writer-photographer Bill Wittliff, musician Marcia Ball, film producer Elizabeth Avellan, attorney-professor Amon Burton, and publicist Vincent Salas. (Photo by Kenny Braun.)

But it was more than worth it.

"There's nothing more satisfying than seeing something you've thought of, in bronze," Harrigan said. "I see my grandchildren playing on Philosopher's Rock. That's pretty cool." He smiled a smile of satisfaction while his eyes wandered off for a nanosecond, and then composed himself to add, ". . . even though they're not supposed to; we strongly discourage that." He did not sound very convincing.

Harrigan had managed to keep his sense of humor. He self-deprecatingly described his body of work that had spanned more than ten books, scores of magazine articles, and dozens of films as "somewhere between emeritus and irrelevant."

Readers would determine that. Harrigan had a hometown edge. Austin had the highest per capita book sales in the United States, according to the American Booksellers Association.

Booksellers had been a presence in Austin ever since there was a university. In 1970, three retailers—University Co-op, Garner and Smith, and Congress Avenue Booksellers—dominated the local trade. But an outsider book business was also thriving. Oat Willie's Campaign Headquarters head shop in an old wood frame house at Sixteenth and San Antonio Streets, south of campus, stocked books normally not-for-sale in conventional bookstores, such as the *Whole Earth Catalog*, how to grow marijuana guidebooks, and underground comix, the vast majority of which were drawn and produced by former Austinites in San Francisco.

Right around the corner from Oat Willie's on the bottom floor of an old two-story duplex at 503B West Seventeenth Street, another specialty bookstore opened in 1970. Grok Books, owned by two couples, stocked books of a metaphysical, Eastern religion, and philosophical nature. The name for the store came from the phrase coined by science fiction novelist Robert Heinlein in his 1961 book *Stranger in a Strange Land*.

Philip Sansone, a bright-eyed, idealistic former customer bought Grok Books in 1978. He was freshly returned from seven years in Honduras and Paraguay as a Peace Corps volunteer, teaching sustainable agriculture. Sansone worked to make the store a place to hang out as much as buy a book, hosting talks and readings by Timothy Leary, Buckminster Fuller, Ram Dass, John Lilly, and Ray Bradbury. Change did not come without resistance. A manager quit when Sansone added air conditioning.

The name and the scope of the store expanded with a move to Brodie Oaks shopping center on the southwestern edge of Austin in 1984. BookPeople, the new name, referenced the small passionate band of word-lovers in Ray Bradbury's 1953 science-fiction classic *Fahrenheit 451*.

In 1995, Whole Foods Market at Brodie Oaks, BookPeople's neighbor and quasi-partner, closed. The second store opened by the hometown natural grocery chain had outgrown the location in ten years. A bigger store would open on the western edge of downtown at the intersection of West Sixth Street and Lamar Boulevard, an area occupied by new car dealerships and used car lots. Whole Foods CEO John Mackey was paying a lot for the move and new space. Sensing an opportunity of convergence, he talked Philip Sansone into moving BookPeople into the building along with Whole Foods. Mackey made Sansone's decision easier because Mackey was the biggest of twenty investors underwriting the bookstore. With their financial backing and encouragement, BookPeople took on a forty thousand square foot space, filling three floors with three hundred thousand titles, along with accessories and knickknacks. BookPeople instantly qualified as the largest independent bookstore in Texas.

As tricked out as the store appeared with its custom wood shelves and stuffed chairs, investors were not happy. Sales lagged. The wrong accessories were being hawked. BookPeople claimed the biggest selection of crystals in Austin, but Austin folks weren't buying many crystals at the bookstore.

Sansone stepped aside in 1999 to become president and executive director of the nonprofit Whole Planet Foundation, which offered microcredit in communities in sixty-eight countries that supplied Whole Foods Market stores. He remained on the board of BookPeople, whose continued viability, he believed, was a result of the conscious capitalism philosophy he had embraced.

New CEO Steve Bercu, an attorney and one of the twenty BookPeople investors, recalibrated, seeking to maximize the space and improve odds of profitability. The Internet was triggering all kinds of chaos in media and business, sweeping away most independent bookstores and all but one major bookseller chain in the process.

Bercu faced the same challenges as his counterpart across Lamar Boulevard, John T. Kunz, the owner of Waterloo Records—the leading independent record store in Austin. Record stores had pretty much vanished as a chain concept by 2000, and indies were shutting down too, suggesting there was no money to be made in CDs or vinyl, since music could be downloaded for free on the Internet. Kunz and other indie record store owners responded by banding together nationally and sharing marketing strategies such as National Record Store Day and ancillary product ideas, keeping the emphasis on highly educated staffs and full customer service. Bercu and Kunz joined forces as principals in the Austin Independent Business Alliance, championing local businesses and passing out more than three hundred thousand Keep Austin Weird stickers.

Bercu, like Kunz, built the business on the simple premise of having a staff that knew their stuff. His people loved books as much Waterloo's employees were schooled in the breadth of recorded music.

Waterloo had bands and beer. BookPeople had readings and signings and book clubs and beer. And coffee. And massage. And literary camps for kids and teenagers.

The reading culture it fostered through hand-written book reviews, comfy chairs that invited customers to sit and linger, and events tailored to all age groups almost every day of the week separated BookPeople from other book retailers.

BookPeople worked because it operated like a mom-and-pop indie bookshop, but on a big volume basis.

Twenty years after BookPeople opened at Sixth and Lamar, the retail book landscape had dramatically changed. Online retailer Amazon dominated the book trade nationally. More than one thousand independent bookstores closed between 2000 and 2007.

But BookPeople kept choogling on.

In the tradition of *Texas Monthly*, a twenty-first century homegrown startup publication made an impact that resonated far beyond Austin. Its focus was hyperlocal, as in the state politics of Texas played out at the capitol. The idea was to report extensively and thoroughly on the sausage-making processes of legislating and governing in a state storied for its dysfunction in both aspects. Evan Smith had witnessed the disruption of print publishing along with most all of old media firsthand when he became editor of *Texas Monthly* in 2000. Advertising revenue stagnated, circulation stalled, and the parent company, a Midwestern radio chain, watched that medium's value plummet, further squeezing the bottom line. The same squeeze impacted every daily newspaper in Texas. The papers responded with cutbacks. All but two eliminated their capitol bureaus. Smith, venture capitalist John Thornton, and Ross Ramsey, editor of the *Texas Weekly* newsletter, joined together to fill the void.

The *Texas Tribune* started publishing in 2009 as a nonprofit, online newspaper with a full team of journalists—many of them former newspaper reporters—covering Texas politics in a neutral manner, unlike the opinionated *Texas Observer*. The staff quickly grew to more than fifty, the largest statehouse bureau in the nation. The unconventional method of funding compromised the traditional wall between editorial and advertising, with underwriting sometimes coming from the same corporations, institutions, and people that *Texas Tribune* covered, which frequently necessitated disclaimers accompanying articles. But their bet was on the mark: many of the same Texas daily newspapers that once maintained capitol bureaus in Austin now ran stories from the *Texas Tribune*.

Texas Monthly persevered as the best writers' magazine in the Southwest. At the end of the seventies, the publication claimed a circulation of three hundred thousand, each issue fat with advertising, sandwiched between content that earned the National Magazine Award for editorial excellence. Maintaining that level of readership for the next forty years, *Texas Monthly* was regarded as the most successful of all city/regional magazines.

In its first seven years of existence, *Texas Monthly* grew from an idea into a big business and the modern publishing institution of Texas, the established linchpin of a bubbling literary community that few cities between the coasts could claim.

The original *Texas Monthly* crowd moved out and up. Mike Levy bought a second magazine *New West* from media mogul Rupert Murdoch and brought in *Texas Monthly* editor William Broyles to edit the magazine, retitled *California*. But Broyles and Levy quickly learned California was nothing like Texas. Broyles was hired away to edit *Newsweek*, where *Texas Monthly* writer Richard West also landed briefly.

Broyles wrote the screenplay for the film *Apollo 13* with Al Reinert, and scripted other films including *Cast Away* and the television series *China Beach*. Joe Nocera joined the *New York Times* as a business columnist. Nicholas Lemann wrote for the *New Yorker* and was dean of the Columbia University School of Journalism. Dominique Browning and Barbara Paulsen edited national magazines. Dick J. Reavis wrote books about the Branch Davidians in Waco and the Oklahoma City domestic terrorist Timothy McVeigh. Helen Thorpe wrote theatrical plays and books about immigrant women and females in the military. Mimi Swartz was a staff writer at the *New Yorker* before returning to *Texas Monthly*. Robert Draper blossomed into a national political writer. Pam Colloff joined the *New York Times Sunday Magazine* as a staff writer.

Sarah Bird wrote nine novels, numerous screenplays, and scripts. Her breakthrough was *Alamo House* (1986), a comic novel about her college years at the University of Texas. S. C. Gwynne, a *Texas Monthly* editor, took on the tale of the Comanche, which he described as the most powerful tribe in American history, for his third book, *Empire of the Summer Moon* (2010), one of the best-selling books written in Austin.

After his groundbreaking 1974 book about the Austin music scene, *The Improbable Rise of Redneck Rock*, Jan Reid wrote about the land where he grew up (*Deerinwater* in 1985), his own near-death experience (*The Bullet Meant for Me* in 2002), political sleazeballs (*Boy Genius: Karl Rove* in 2003, and *The Hammer Comes Down* in 2006, both with Lou Dubose), peyote-eating Indians (*Comanche Sundown: A Novel* in 2010), a cosmic cowboy (*Texas Tornado: The Times and Music of Doug Sahm* in 2010), and a governor (*Let the People In: The Life and Times of Ann Richards* in 2012).

Gary Cartwright carved out a career at *Texas Monthly* writing about strippers, drug smugglers, dogfighting, the Great Galveston Storm of 1900, devil worshippers, Viagra, and football, earning the title as "best damn magazine writer who ever lived."

Don Graham took on war hero and movie cowboy Audie Murphy (*No Name on the Bullet*, 1989), the King Ranch (*Kings of Texas*, 2002), the film *Giant* (*Giant: Elizabeth Taylor, Rock Hudson, James Dean, Edna Ferber, and the Making of a Legendary American Film*), and other mythic Texas icons in his books

Angela Shelf Medearis, another *Texas Monthly* ex who spent her brief time at the magazine as a secretary, wrote *Picking Peas for a Penny*, a counting rhyme picture book published in 1990, her first of more than one hundred children's books and seven cookbooks, with more than 1.5 million copies of her books in print.

Texas Monthly was hardly the only finishing school for writers.

H. W. Brands bicycled to his math and history teaching gigs at Austin Community College and Kirby Hall prep school while chasing his doctorate at the University of Texas before cranking out twenty-five plus titles, including *TR* (1998), *The First American* (2002), *The Age of Gold* (2003), *Andrew Jackson* (2006), *Traitor to His Class* (2009), *The Man Who Saved the Union* (2013), and *The General vs. the President* and *Reagan* (both published in 2017). A frequently cited authority on television's History Channel, Brands also wrote a history of the United States in haiku form, publishing the haikus over four years of tweets on the Twitter social media platform.

Historical novelist Elizabeth Crook wrote about the Texas war for independence from Mexico in *Promised Lands: A Novel of the Texas Rebellion* (1994); the leader of the Texas war for independence and his eleven-week marriage in *Raven's Bride: A Novel of Eliza Allen and Sam Houston* (1991); and the first mass murderer of the modern era, Charles Whitman, in *Monday, Monday* (2014), before turning her sights on a girl growing up in a Hill Country community of German freethinkers during the Civil War in the 2018 novel *The Which Way Tree*.

Mary Helen Specht, an Abilene native and Dobie Paisano fellow who taught creative writing at St. Edward's, snagged numerous awards for her 2015 debut novel *Migratory Animals*, a tale of an American climate-change scientist working in Nigeria who returns home to Austin. The *New York Times* praised Specht for capturing the "minute details of contemporary life in a certain social niche of culture-rich, cash-poor pseudo-bohemians"—the Austin cool kids, the once-upon-a-time slackers who were evolving into another version of conspicuous consumers.

Bud Shrake's best-selling work was *Harvey Penick's Little Red Book* (1992), a humble volume of philosophy and insight imparted by the Austin Country Club golf instructor who taught touring pros Ben Crenshaw and Tom Kite, as well as nonprofessionals including Shrake. He also wrote a historical novel about early Austin and early Texas, *The Borderland: A Novel of Texas* (2001), more than a dozen other novels, and was escort and companion for Governor of Texas Ann Richards.

Bill Wittliff remained a man of multiple interests, maintaining his office in the eighteenth century Victorian where O. Henry lived and worked, writing, photographing, illustrating, and archiving. Frustrated when items purchased by his wife Sally and him at an auction of J. Frank Dobie's estate did not interest the University of Texas, they established the Wittliff Collections at Texas State University in San Marcos, beginning with the Southwestern Writers Collection, where there were repositories for the papers of Harrigan, Shrake, Reid, Cartwright, John Graves, Elizabeth Crook, Cormac McCarthy, Sandra Cisneros, and other prominent Texan and southwestern writers. A photography element, a music element, and a book series were added later. The most-visited part of the collections was the exhibit for *Lonesome Dove*, for which Wittliff wrote the screenplay and photographed the filming.

Twenty years after the Mollie Ivins/Kaye Northcott era at the *Texas Observer*, another talented duo emerged from the feisty publication. Nate Blakeslee was a budding investigative reporter, having published an exposé about black folks in the small Panhandle town of Tulia who were being set up in drug busts by local law enforcement and wrongfully convicted on trumped-up charges. Blakeslee's reporting led to Governor Rick Perry, a staunch right-wing conservative, pardoning thirty-five black Tulia residents in 2003 who had been wrongfully imprisoned.

Karen Olsson wrote the novel *Waterloo* (2005), about a struggling alt-weekly reporter writing about politics, set in a place that looked a whole lot like Austin. Her book was touted as the first significant novel about Austin since *The Gay Place*, portraying a love affair with the city that had slightly soured. Olsson and Blakeslee moved to writing gigs at *Texas Monthly*.

One of the unlikeliest and most-read authors tied to Austin was a Plan II graduate of the University of Texas who'd grown up in Houston and introduced the Frisbee to natives in Borneo while in the Peace Corps. Richard "Kinky" Friedman first made his mark as the satirical front man of a band called the Texas Jewboys who were marginally associated with the Cosmic Cowboy phenomenon. Serving up titles such as "They Ain't Making Jews Like Jesus Anymore" and "Get Your Biscuits in the Oven, and Your Buns in the Bed," Friedman was what he liked to call "an equal opportunity offender."

Kinky Friedman toured with Bob Dylan and the Rolling Thunder Revue before moving to New York in the late seventies, where he was a regular at the Lone Star Café, the city's premier Texas music outpost. He started writing mystery books that were chockfull of one-liners, beginning with *Greenwich Killing Time*, published in 1986. Flimsy plot lines faded as Friedman amped up the focus on humor in subsequent books such as *Elvis, Jesus, and Coca-Cola* (1993).

Friedman became a national figure by playing on his Jewishness, his Texas roots, and his quick-witted ability to insult and simultaneously make people laugh (usually): "Well, I just said that Jesus and I were both Jewish and that neither of us ever had a job, we never had a home, we never married and we traveled around the countryside irritating people."

Friedman moved back to Texas in the nineties and began writing a humor column at *Texas Monthly*. He was one of the few people welcomed to the White House by both President Bill Clinton and President George W. Bush. Friedman ran for governor of Texas as an independent in 2006, campaigning on the premise that "musicians can run this state better than politicians. We won't get a lot done in the morning, but we'll work late and be honest." He garnered 12.6 percent of the vote to place fourth in a six-candidate race (Rick Perry won with 39 percent of the vote). Friedman was defeated in the Democratic primary for Texas Agricultural Commissioner in 2010, and again in 2014, losing the primary runoff to a Cleburne cattle rancher who did not campaign.

Friedman preferred spending time at the Utopia Animal Rescue Ranch outside of Medina in the Hill Country, once his family's ranch. That's where Friedman revealed himself as the softy he was, surrounding himself with dogs and cats. "Money can buy you a fine dog," he liked to say. "But only love can make him wag his tail."

Steve Harrigan's best friend Larry Wright won a Pulitzer Prize for his book *The Looming Tower: Al-Qaeda and the Road to 9/11*, published in 2006, which explained the roots of Middle Eastern terrorism and the United States' involvement in that part of the world. Wright followed *Looming Tower* with another bestseller, *Gone Clear* (2013), about the cult religion of Scientology, and a comprehensive look at contemporary Texas, *God Save Texas* (2018).

Steve Harrigan did alright his own self. His string of books included his epic *Gates of the Alamo* (2000), the novel *A Friend of Mr. Lincoln* (2016), and a one thousand page history of Texas. He paid someone else to mow his lawn. Once he had started to earn enough money to focus on writing instead of mowing, his wife had stepped in. "Sue Ellen used to love to mow and took over the grass-cutting for decades," Harrigan said. "But she finally hung up her mower."

Austin had grown into a legitimate literary community. Journals such as *A Strange Object, American Short Fiction, Bat City Review, The Austin Review, Lone Star Literary Life,* and *Write Bloody Publishing* and the Writers' League of Texas provided outlets for aspiring writers. The Austin Book Arts Center in the East Austin building that housed Flatbed Press took love of books one step beyond, celebrating the Art of the Book. Anyone could take a workshop in letterpress printing, bookbinding, papermaking, typography, book history, and design. The delivery system was as worthy as the content.

The relocation of *Kirkus Reviews* furthered the perception. *Kirkus*, founded in 1933, was the bible of unbiased, prepublication book reviews. Its most recent owners, the Nielsen Company, shut down the publication in 2009, only to have two rabid booklovers, Herb Simon and Marc Winkelman, resuscitate *Kirkus* and engage in an aggressive expansion. Operations moved to Austin, where Winkelman resided and where Clay Smith, the editor in chief, lived.

For every fellow admitted to the Michener Center there were one hundred others figuring out other ways to write, get published, get read, and maybe even get paid. For all the literary institutions that had been built in Austin over the past half century, there was a whole other generation bubbling under who had nothing to do with those institutions, but were managing to produce quality literature.

It was always like that, really. In 1973, the same year Mike Levy started *Texas Monthly* magazine, the new television columnist for the *Austin American-Statesman*, Lisa Tuttle, cofounded the Turkey City Writer's Workshop with fellow outside writers Bruce Sterling, Stephen Utley, and Howard Waldrop. The four loved reading science fiction and futuristic literature, and learning to write it. Each developed the chops to enjoy distinguished careers in those realms.

Tuttle quit her day job at the newspaper in 1978 and moved to England, where she wrote dozens of science fiction books and a novella with George R. R. Martin that became the novel *Windhaven*, published in 1981. Bruce Sterling, whose work resonated globally, eventually relocated to Belgrade, Serbia, then Turin, Italy, carving out his own niche as the cyberpunk of cyberpunks, an intense, riveting teller of stories from the dystopian future.

Sterling was the major influence in Austin being recognized as a cyberpunk hotbed, and the Turkey City group was instrumental in starting ArmadilloCon in 1979, an annual Austin meetup for cyberpunk writers.

Austinite Ernest Cline saw his debut novel *Ready Player One* (2011), a dystopian teen adventure about virtual reality, be translated into twenty languages and turned into a major motion picture of the same name produced by Steven Spielberg in 2018. The movie rights were sold within forty-eight hours of selling the book to a publisher.

A handful of scribes had been able to support themselves, more or less, writing about music, following in the footsteps of Margaret Moser of the *Austin Chronicle*, who started covering the scene in the seventies and writing for punk fanzines such as *Sluggo* and for the *Austin Sun*. Moser went on to mentor younger writers while upping her own game to write Austin's music history. Another *Austin Chronicle* music writer, Michael Corcoran, turned his love of contemporary music and gossip into deep dives into African American gospel and blues music in Texas, uncovering new information on little-known musical giants such as the blind gospel singer Arizona Dranes and Washington Phillips, who played a one-of-a-kind zither-like instrument he called the "manzarene," and writing and revising his book *All Over the Map: True Heroes of Texas Music* (2005).

Austin American-Statesman music columnist Ed Ward became a music history contributor to the National Public Radio program *Fresh Air*. Riffing off his historical radio work, he wrote *The History of Rock and Roll, Volume One*, published in 2016, a biography of the guitarist Michael Bloomfield, and another rock history book.

Spike Gillespie, Jersey-raised, turned her extremely first-person *Austin Chronicle* column into a life as a writer-of-all-trades, with side businesses as a wedding official and writing workshop teacher.

By the early twenty-first century, Austin was a place ambitious writers moved to, not *from*. The British-born Owen Egerton and his spouse Jodi Egerton were the power couple of the latest wave of outsider writers. Egerton described himself as a screenwriter first, novelist second, and a performer too—a nice way of saying being a writer was no longer enough. He was one of the Master Pancake Theater and Sinus Show cast at the Alamo Drafthouse Theater, based on his ability to talk back to movies and make people laugh. His first feature film *Follow*, a psychological horror film, debuted at Fantastic Fest in 2015. Jodi Egerton was the one-woman operation behind Write Good Consulting. A University of Texas PhD in English who'd done a turn in academia as the assistant director of the Division of Rhetoric and Writing and a training specialist at the Undergraduate Writing Center at UT, she was also part of the Typewriter Rodeo collective, who composed poetry on vintage typewriters on demand, working parties, events, and performances. Both Egertons had author credit on *This Word Now* (2016), one of several Egerton how-to-write books. Once a month, Owen Egerton hosted the One Page Salon, during which selected writers read one page of a work in progress.

Neal Pollack was a One Page Salon regular. A quick-witted satirist, he'd written ten "semi best-selling books of fiction and nonfiction," including the *Neal Pollack Anthology of American Literature* (2000) for the prestigious *McSweeney's*. He promoted himself as "the greatest living American writer" for the book and continued using the superlative in the column he wrote for the online magazine *Salon*. ("Breaking: The Greatest Living American Writer: 'Hug the kids under the tree this year. It's all over. There will never be another Christmas.'") A multitasker who wrote a motorsports column, taught yoga, and was a three-time champion on the television game show *Jeopardy!*, Pollack captured the Austin twenty-first century zeitgeist in his official biography, which stated he was an Austin resident "seemingly against his will."

The One Page Salon was one of dozens of regular meetups around Austin devoted to words and writing. One particular gathering of four older men sat at a table at Sweetish Hill Bakery every Monday morning to discuss the world situation over coffee, eggs, muffins, and croissants. To most of the bakery's customers, they were the four old guys who always sat in the corner, like old guys tend to do. The customers who did recognize Steve Harrigan, Larry Wright, Bill Brands, and Greg Curtis knew better. These were real writers, each exceptionally accomplished in his respective field. In fact, this was the smartest breakfast table in Texas. And they were having themselves a genuine literary salon, the kind Steve Harrigan used to read about.

3
Willie Nelson in Groover's Paradise

⊙ ⊙ ⊙

Writers may have come first, but Austin didn't have an identity or a soul until the musicians arrived, especially one in particular.

They were a stripped-down trio, a little scruffy around the edges. The man in the middle, a shaggy-haired, clean-shaven fellow who smiled with an instinctive ear-to-ear grin scanned the audience as he walked onto the stage, nodding when he recognized a familiar face, nodding even when he didn't, as he stepped toward the microphone. The bassist was a rail-thin hippie Indian in buckskin with a headband. The drummer wore a black hat and black cape. His prominent jet-black sideburns and distinctive goatee projected a menacing countenance. He looked like the Devil.

The people who had gathered to bear witness were an odd lot. At least half of the crowd of three hundred were authentic, puredee, unreconstructed Texas hippies—meaning long hair, T-shirts and jeans, cutoffs, granny dresses, beads, stash bags, tie-dye, sandals, and patchouli oil. They either sat on the concrete floor of the Armadillo World Headquarters or stood up, sometimes dancing in place, as was the protocol when bands like Greezy Wheels, the popular local country-rock ensemble opening this particular show, were performing.

The hippies were a fairly sophisticated bunch, musically speaking, having already been exposed to bluegrass titan Bill Monroe, the neo-bluegrass group Country Gazette, and country rock acts such as the Flying Burrito Brothers and Delbert and Glen. The response Bill Monroe had received transformed the crabby old performer from suspicious hard-ass wondering what the hell his booking agent had done into an enthusiastic convert. These young people knew how to show their appreciation.

The not-quite-other-half of the Armadillo house was composed of straights, as the hippies described the conventional folks in their slacks,

Poster for Willie Nelson's first appearance at the Armadillo World Headquarters, August 12, 1972, as drawn by Micael Priest. (Courtesy of the South Austin Museum of Popular Culture.)

pantsuits, dresses, and beehives. These were country music fans willing to put up with the funky environs so they could hear the main attraction—the small man crooning into the microphone named Willie Nelson.

No matter how nicely the country music folks may have dressed, the temperature inside the massive building, lacking air conditioning on this hot August night, was making everyone sweat before Nelson sang a note. When he finally did, his reedy, twanged-up voice instinctively prompted some couples in the crowd to find room on the side to dance the Texas two-step. Most just watched, many in thrall, as Nelson serenaded them with songs that he wrote and with a few that he didn't.

Gazing at the crowd in front of him while uttering, "Well, hello there," the opening line to "Funny (How Time Slips Away)," Willie didn't quite know what to think. This crowd definitely transcended the country label slapped on him after living and working in Nashville for more than ten years. Maybe his daughter Lana was right. After attending the Atlanta International Pop Festival two years earlier, she had told him he should be playing rock festivals, not honky-tonks. That was where his audience was.

A house fire and blind luck landed Nelson and his musicians at a bankrupt dude ranch outside of the Hill Country resort town of Bandera in 1971. Willie, his wife Connie, and their daughter Paula, with another baby girl, Amy, on the way, had planned to move to Houston, where Connie was from.

Then they saw Austin.

"[Willie's sister] Bobbie had been living in Austin and she kept saying, 'You need to come and see,'" Connie Nelson said. "We drove over from Bandera just to look around, to consider Austin." They were crossing the South First Street Bridge over Town Lake when Willie turned to Connie and said, "This is pretty cool, all this here in the middle of Texas." Houston didn't have an urban lake or a hike-and-bike trail; Barton Springs, where women could bathe topless; Hippie Hollow at Lake Travis, where one could bathe in the nude; or anything like that.

"This is where we should be," he said to her.

A Woodstock-inspired country music festival that featured Ernest Tubb, Tex Ritter, Hank Snow, Dottie West, and other country traditionalists over a long weekend in March 1972 sealed the deal. The Dripping Springs Reunion, held on a ranch twenty-five miles west of Austin, was a financial bust, with less than twenty thousand fans turning out for the three-day event. But the appearance of Willie along with his friends Kris Kristofferson, Waylon Jennings, and Merle Haggard on the last day, Sunday, and their jam at Coach Darrell K Royal's afterward, sparked a buzz around Austin.

Connie was sold. People were genuinely friendly. After Connie had given birth to Paula while they were still living in Ridgetop north of Nashville, she remembered getting the cold shoulder at the grocery store. "I never got 'What a cute little baby,'" she said. "Women would look away. I didn't realize Willie was well-known and to these people, I was yet another Other Woman. In my head, it was more like, 'These people aren't very friendly.' When we moved to Austin, everybody was sincerely friendly."

Willie and Connie found an apartment on the south shore of Town Lake. He sat in with Freda and the Firedogs, young hippies playing old country at the Split Rail. He played an antiwar benefit in Wooldridge Park, along with the Conqueroo, a popular Austin psychedelic rock band recently returned from San Francisco; Greezy Wheels; the bar band Lee Ann and the Bizarros; and a white blues band called the Storm, featuring a hotshot guitarist from Dallas named Jimmie Vaughan. Willie, wearing a black flat-brimmed cowboy hat, and his band, bassist Bee Spears and drummer Paul English, were joined onstage by Sweet Mary Egan, the fiddler from Greezy Wheels, whose rendition of "Orange Blossom Special" could bring any crowd to its feet.

That led Willie and his business manager, best friend, and literal back, Paul English (the drummer who looked like the Devil), to the Armadillo World Headquarters, which in turn led to Willie standing on the stage, reveling in the beer-addled, weed-scented hooting and hollering adulation. The hippies seemed to like the music even more than the old fans did. Raised on literate singer-songwriters such as James Taylor, Leonard Cohen, and Bob Dylan, they hung onto every word that Nelson sang. The lyrics to "I Never Cared for You" were as deep and meaningful as anything those other composers had written. Plus, Willie was one of them—a shaggy-haired Texan who liked to smoke dope as much as he liked to drink beer, an iconoclast and contrarian moving to his own rhythm.

Willie and Connie broke the lease for the apartment on Riverside Drive. It was upstairs, Connie was pregnant with Amy, and Willie wasn't going to carry groceries up and down the stairs or do heavy lifting. They found a duplex west of the city on Cuernavaca Road near Lake Austin. Connie, Paula, and Willie lived on one side; Billy and Susie Nelson, Willie's adult children from his first marriage, lived in the other duplex. Across the way, Paula Carlene and Paul English and their son Darrell Wayne lived in another duplex.

At the time, Austin had the lowest cost of living of the hundred largest cities in the United States. Marijuana sold for ten dollars an ounce. Cheap beer was less than two dollars a six-pack. The Armadillo World Headquarters was the kind of place where you argued whether or not to pay the two dollar cover to see Delbert McClinton and Glen Clark perform inside the concert hall, or to just stay in the beer garden and keep buying dollar fifty pitchers of Lone Star, Pearl, and Shiner with your friends while another band played for free.

The Armadillo developed a reputation built upon the local and touring music presented there, for its hippie staff who dug music and musicians, for its cheap beer and nachos, and for its hippie poster artists.

Acts that would have otherwise bypassed Texas, such as roots rockers Commander Cody and His Lost Planet Airmen, the guitar virtuoso Ry Cooder, and the avant-garde Captain Beefheart and His Magic Band played Austin because of the Armadillo. The Armadillo also served as home for the Austin Ballet Theatre, original theatrical performances, art openings, a kitchen and bakery, a beer garden, and a recording studio. Its beer garden was a regular afternoon and evening social hang, just as Scholz Garten had been to previous generations of Austin beer drinkers and music lovers. Like so much of alternative Austin that would follow, the Armadillo worked for all the wrong reasons. The financial bottom line was almost beside the point. The Armadillo was all about music, not money.

Eddie Wilson, the beer-lobbyist-turned-psychedelic-band-manager, who first spied the future home of the Armadillo World Headquarters in June of 1970, secured the lease to what had once been a National Guard Armory and practically willed the 1,500-capacity music hall into existence. Spencer Perskin contributed a few thousand dollars from the advance he received

A concert crowd at the Armadillo World Headquarters during its first year, 1970. (Photo by Burton Wilson.)

from a Capitol Records recording contract for his band Shiva's Headband, whom Wilson managed. *Sports Illustrated* magazine staff writer Bud Shrake, who left New York for Austin by choice, threw in another thousand. A couple dozen dedicated friends and music lovers sweated and hammered and imagined and hauled. Two months later, the Armadillo World Headquarters opened, effectively elevating eclectic music into a fine art while planting the seed of creativity that would come to be identified as the Austin groove.

Nobody got paid, and nobody minded, because everyone agreed a concert hall run by hippies was a great idea. Austin needed a place like this. It was chaotic spontaneity from the get-go, a shoestring operation with no formal infrastructure, no air conditioning, and no budget; just a common desire to make a cool place where people could hear good music, smoke dope, and drink beer.

Bud Shrake headquartered Mad Dog Inc., the imaginary enterprise he dreamed up with writer Gary Cartwright ("Doing Indefinable Services to Mankind") in an empty space upstairs at the Armadillo, where they often brought visiting dignitaries including actor and fellow Mad Dog Dennis Hopper and Dallas Cowboys football star Don Meredith.

The poster artists distinguished the Armadillo from all other venues. Inspired by San Francisco poster artists of the sixties, this loose collection of creative minds made each event at the Armadillo special with their vivid imagery, which would then be plastered all over town, a service performed for maybe one hundred dollars, some weed, or other considerations.

Armadillo poster artist Jim Franklin at work, while humans dressed as armadillos kneel behind him. (Photo by Watt Casey.)

Jim Franklin was the Vulcan Gas Company's last poster artist and the Armadillo's first, mainly because JFKLN started the whole obsession with the nine-banded placental mammal with the leather-like armored shell by painting armadillos in all sorts of strange situations, including emerging from a crack in the earth and humping the capitol dome. Pretty soon, the armadillo was the recognized symbol of Texas hippies—hard-shelled on the outside for survival purposes, but soft and sweet on the inside, with peaceful, nonthreatening habits and intentions.

Franklin, a native of La Marque near the Texas coast, had trained as a fine artist in San Francisco but went off the track thanks to LSD and the electroshock therapy he'd received after a dustup with authorities. Dave Hickey, owner of the short-lived, cutting edge A Clean, Well-Lighted Place art gallery in Austin, exhibited Franklin's work, in addition to hiring him to paint the walls between shows. One thing separated Franklin from mainstream fine artists, according to Hickey: "He wasn't mansion-trained."

Franklin would be joined by Micael Priest, the burly colorblind poster artist who left a commercial design career to draw and emcee shows. Franklin got distracted, first by rock star Leon Russell, who hired him to paint his swimming pool in Oklahoma; then by Texas blues guitarist Freddie King, who took him on the road; and later by Bill Livingood, the T-shirt entrepre-

Micael Priest's rendering of the Armadillo poster artists. (Courtesy of the South Austin Museum of Popular Culture.)

neur with whom Franklin operated the Ritz, a sagging B movie house on Sixth Street downtown reinvented as a music hall.

Other poster artists moved in. Sam Yeates, who grew up on a farm outside Stephenville in near West Texas and had a bachelor of fine arts degree, left a teaching gig in Dallas to dive into the Armadillo, drawing richly detailed images that were as much painting as advertising poster. De White gave up his formal art training to join a commune in his hometown of San Angelo that led him to the Armadillo, where he became Guy Juke, the distinctive cubist bebop stylist. Bill Narum was an established poster artist and designer from Houston who created the logos and staging for the rock group ZZ Top and did a deep dive into video. Danny Garrett sought out Narum in Houston when he returned from Vietnam, and hit the Armadillo within days of its opening, turning out several posters before moving on to Castle Creek, the Texas Opry House, and Antone's. Ken Featherston, recognized for his trippy phantasmagorical style, and Henry Gonzales, the one Chicano of the bunch, came from Corpus Christi. (Featherston was tragically shot dead in 1975 in the parking lot by a disgruntled customer who'd been kicked out of the Armadillo.) Kerry Awn from Houston did most of his cartoony renditions for Soap Creek Saloon's monthly calendar, even though he ran with the Armadillo bunch.

◎ ◎ ◎

Presenting Willie Nelson was in keeping with the wide variety of music the Armadillo had been booking since the start. Rock music was the AWHQ's meat and potatoes, but folk, blues, bluegrass, and jazz were also in the mix. Why not country?

Willie Nelson may have been offbeat and something of an iconoclast, but the hits he wrote for others, including "Crazy" for Patsy Cline; "Night Life," made famous by Ray Price; Faron Young's "Hello Walls"; and "Funny," a rhythm and blues hit for Joe Hinton, were about as country as it got.

Country was indigenous to Texas and arguably the most popular form of music among its citizens. But many of those citizens were hostile, reactionary rednecks—the kinds of folks who liked to verbally and physically harass hippies. Finding common ground in Willie Nelson's country music, beer-drinking, and pot-smoking bridged a great divide.

◎ ◎ ◎

Willie Nelson had such a good time playing the Armadillo that he called his friend Waylon Jennings in Nashville to tell him "something is going on down here." Jennings, Tom T. Hall, and other country music mavericks seeking to broaden their audiences booked into the Armadillo.

A month after his Armadillo debut, Nelson returned to co-headline with Michael Murphey, the blond-haired folk-country singer-songwriter riding high with the popular anthem "I Just Want to Be a Cosmic Cowboy." Together the two would hit the road and play cities around Texas as the Armadillo Country Music Review. The idea was to show off this exciting new country and rock hybrid sound that was being cooked up in Austin. Evidently, not too many people cared. Turnout at shows in San Antonio, Dallas, Midland, Amarillo, and Corpus Christi was light to nonexistent. The tour was a bust, although a subsequent television taping of Nelson and Murphy at the Armadillo the following year helped spark interest in Austin music and the two artists in particular.

In the spring of 1973, Willie and the Armadillo crew joined forces as co-promoters of a weekend festival like the Dripping Springs Reunion the previous year, only with Willie's music friends filling the bill, along with some rock and roll. The first Willie Nelson Fourth of July Picnic was a one-day affair staged on the same ranch west of Austin as the Dripping Springs Reunion the year before. Jim Franklin designed a poster depicting the American flag unfurled across a two-lane road with a tiny armadillo bearing a Texas flag crawling out from under it.

Fifty thousand music fans trekked to an open field to hear music and be part of a festival. Chaos reigned as fences were knocked down; ticket receipts grabbed; and the drunk, drug-addled masses went crazy from the

Willie Nelson, band mates, and crew compete in the Willie Nelson Run for Your Life 5K. (Photo by Watt Casey.)

heat. The show itself was an unqualified success, with a lineup that featured the biggest act in rock, Leon Russell, who was becoming Willie's new running buddy; Willie's country music friends Waylon Jennings, Tom T. Hall, Kris Kristofferson, Sammi Smith, Charlie Rich, Billy Joe Shaver, John Prine, Hank Cochran, Johnny Bush, Ray Price, and Ernest Tubb; recent Austin immigrants Doug Sahm, Jerry Jeff Walker, Asleep at the Wheel, and the Nightcrawlers, Marc Benno's band that featured a very young Stevie Ray Vaughan; and the yodeling granddaddy of Austin music, Kenneth Threadgill.

Austin American-Statesman columnist Billy Porterfield summarized the event: "It was miserable and it was great, one of the glorious heathen stomps between the Americas of J. Edgar Hoover, Joe McCarthy and Ronald Reagan."

"Willie was tough as shit," Eddie Wilson said, admiring his tenacity in pulling off the picnic. Willie had spent the previous fifteen years or so knocking around beer joints, hanging around promoters of broken dreams making promises. If the Armadillo people helped moved the ball forward, he was OK with any bullshit that went with it.

But when it came time to book another Willie show at the Armadillo, following the Armadillo Country Music Review concert that was videotaped, Bobby Hedderman, the Armadillo's booker, voiced a complaint. He definitely wanted another Willie date, but he did not appreciate Willie's people toting guns backstage and told him to his face. Willie needed to control his friends and keep them from pushing around Armadillo staff. Hedderman's comment touched a nerve. Guns had been an effective form of persuasion on the hardscrabble club circuit that Willie had been working. Without someone toting a pistol during the settlement after a show, Willie would be even more broke than he was.

"They don't all carry guns," an irritated Nelson informed Hedderman, telling him to call his manager in New York to confirm the next Armadillo booking. When Hedderman followed up, his manager relayed a message from Willie: "Fuck you. If his friends aren't good enough for you, then neither is he."

By the time the second Willie Nelson Fourth of July Picnic rolled around, staged over three days at an automobile raceway outside of Bryan ninety miles east of Austin, Willie Nelson and his Family Band had grown to include two drummers and two bassists, as well as Willie's sister Bobbie and a nice Jewish kid from Dallas who played harmonica named Mickey Raphael. They warmed up for the picnic in a new venue less than a mile from the Armadillo called the Texas Opera House, a spacious room that was once a hotel conference center that had air conditioning and sold mixed drinks, two amenities the Armadillo World Headquarters lacked.

Willie Nelson was the second act signed to Jerry Wexler's new Atlantic Nashville record label, the first being Willie's fellow new Austinite Doug Sahm. Sahm had enjoyed pop hit records in the midsixties with his band, the Sir Douglas Quintet ("She's About A Mover," "Mendocino") and lived and recorded in Northern California in the late sixties in the midst of San Francisco's Summer of Love hippie explosion. He returned to his hometown of San Antonio in 1971 but discovered locals were intolerant of longhairs in cowboy boots, so he moved to Austin, residing about a hundred yards from a roadhouse tucked back in the cedar breaks of West Lake Hills called Soap Creek Saloon.

Jerry Wexler had good ears. He was responsible for discovering and producing Ray Charles, Wilson Pickett, Aretha Franklin, Led Zeppelin, and numerous other rhythm and blues and rock giants. Now he wanted to dive into country. He brought Willie Nelson and band to the Atlantic Studios in New York to record the album Shotgun Willie in February 1973. Willie had learned how to record so efficiently during his ten years as a Nashville recording artist that he set a speed record at Atlantic, recording two albums (the second was a gospel album, The Troublemaker, issued a few years later) in less than one week.

Shotgun Willie did not set the woods on fire with sales, but a positive response to the record's loose, rocked-up sound showed Willie the possibilities of recording outside the Nashville assembly line system, and set the table for his second Atlantic release, a thematic song cycle about marriage and divorce called Phases and Stages. "Bloody Mary Morning" came out as a single, followed by "I Still Can't Believe You're Gone," and then by a separate track, "After the Fire Is Gone," a spirited duet with the husky-voiced soul singer Tracy Nelson. The duet was moving up the country charts when the plug was pulled on Wexler and Atlantic Nashville in September 1974. Before the label shut down, engineers recorded Willie and family's two-night stand at the Texas Opera House just before the second Fourth of July Picnic. Both shows extended beyond three hours and were powered by extended jamming in the style of the Grateful Dead and the Allman Brothers Band, with assistance from some illicit white powder.

By the third Fourth of July Picnic in 1975 near Liberty Hill, about thirty-five miles northwest of downtown Austin, Willie Nelson was a very big deal. The picnic drew close to seventy-five thousand fans. The promoters, meaning Willie and the outlaw country music hustlers who'd been booking Willie for years, turned a profit. His new album, Red-Headed Stranger, a spare, thematic song cycle about a preacher who kills his lover and goes on the lam, his first for Columbia Records, was taking off. The single "Blue Eyes Crying

Willie Nelson's Fourth of July Picnics made broiling in the hot Texas sun along with tens of thousands of other drunk and stoned music lovers a Texas tradition. (Photo by Marlon Taylor.)

in the Rain," a old country music ballad, reached number one on the country charts, a first for Willie.

Nelson purchased the old Texas Opera House, which closed a year after it opened for not paying taxes, along with surrounding apartments and land at a bargain price, giving many local musicians a place to live as well as play. The music room was renamed the Austin Opry House. Then he bought a bankrupt country club and condos and land in Spicewood, twenty-five miles west of Austin, where producer Chips Moman designed and built a tricked-out recording facility called Pedernales Studios, adjacent to the country club's nine-hole golf course. Willie's world even had a western town left over from a movie shoot that he dubbed Luck, Texas ("You're either in Luck, or you're out of Luck").

⊚ ⊚ ⊚

There had never been much of a music business in Austin, like there was in Nashville, Los Angeles, and New York. Traditional music businesses such as record companies, song publishers, jukebox operators, recording studios, and independent distributors maintained offices in Houston and Dallas, Texas's largest cities. Yet Austin was filthy with folks who liked to pick, sing, write, and perform, and folks who liked to listen and dance to them. The vast majority of the music being made in and around Austin was for the sheer pleasure of making music, not for aspirations of commercial success. In other words, for all the wrong reasons. But in a good way.

Music in Austin meant live performances in clubs. During the sixties, the IL, the Victory Grill, and Charlie's Playhouse on the east side catered to black folks. The Green Spot and La Plaza on East Sixth Street and the Rockin' M on the Lockhart Highway attracted a Mexican American audience. The Old New Orleans Club, the Eleventh Door, and the Jade Room on Red River Street presented rock and roll. The San Francisco–inspired Vulcan Gas Company was the place for psychedelic rock and blues.

As the scene shifted in the early seventies, one old club gained considerable cachet, mainly for the musicians playing its tiny stage. The Split Rail on South Lamar, a half block south of what was then known as Town Lake, was an Austin classic, featuring live bands seven nights a week with no cover charge. The former drive-in restaurant's big night was Sunday, when Freda and the Firedogs packed the joint to overflowing. Marcia Ball was Freda, a Cajun hippie chick who was on her way to San Francisco with her boyfriend when she got sidetracked after stopping in Austin. Staying at a house full of Louisiana expats, she followed one of them, a songwriter named Bobby Charles, to the Split Rail to hear Kenneth Threadgill.

By the time Marcia Ball's band started playing the Split Rail a year later, the hippie/redneck line had been breached, in no small part due to Threadgill, who had started letting his white hair grow longer, just as Lyndon Johnson had done after he stepped down as President of the United States and set up residence in Austin. Threadgill was a traditionalist dedicated to singing and yodeling the songs of Jimmie Rodgers, a yodeler from the 1920s who was known as the Singing Brakeman. Threadgill's regular fiddler Cotton Collins was a storied music veteran who had songwriting credits for the dance standard "Westphalia Waltz." But Threadgill had hippies in his band too, which was renamed the Velvet Cowpasture, a play on the New York underground rock band the Velvet Underground.

Kenneth Threadgill, the yodeling godfather of Austin music. (Photo by Marlon Taylor. Courtesy Austin History Center, Austin Public Library.)

Freda and the Firedogs, Marcia Ball's band, played hardcore country standards straight and serious. West Coast rock bands that had embraced country music such as the Flying Burrito Brothers and the New Riders of the Purple Sage usually did so with their tongues firmly in cheek. The three front players of the Firedogs—pianist Marcia Ball a.k.a. Freda, guitarist John X. Reed, and bassist Bobby Earl Smith—were all business, faithfully quoting from the songbooks of Buck Owens, Patsy Montana, Flatt and Scruggs, George Jones and Tammy Wynette, Loretta Lynn, and Buddy Holly, along with a handful of originals written and sung by Smith.

Freda and the Firedogs helped bridge the hippie-redneck gap when they played a benefit for state legislature candidate Lloyd Doggett at the Broken Spoke on July 9, 1973. The Spoke on South Lamar Boulevard was one of several country honky-tonks scattered around Austin with a reputation for not welcoming hippies. But owners James White and Joe Baland saw the crowd that Freda and the Firedogs pulled and, more importantly, liked the style of country they played, and the invisible barrier dropped. Everybody wanting to dance country would be welcome at the Spoke, no matter how they looked or dressed.

Two listening rooms, the Saxon Pub and Castle Creek, hosted a new generation of singer-songwriters raised on folk music who were embracing the country rock hybrid, including Willis Alan Ramsey, Jerry Jeff Walker, Michael

Murphey, Townes Van Zandt, B. W. Stevenson, Steve Fromholz, and Rusty Wier.

In 1966, Rod Kennedy, a New Yorker who raced cars and then collected vintage models, opened a car museum at Lavaca and Fifteenth Streets, around the corner from the state capitol—only nobody came. A folk singer named Allen Damron and a banjoist-guitarist Segle Fry talked Kennedy into turning a third of the museum into a music listening room. The Chequered Flag opened in 1967, featuring Damron, whose original songs and twenty album discography guaranteed a draw, with touring folkies including Waco native Carolyn Hester, Kathie Harrison, Big Bill Moss, and the new folk immigrants. The singer-songwriter focus continued after the club became Castle Creek in 1970.

Ray Wylie Hubbard, Michael Murphey, and B. W. Stevenson, the one progressive country folkie to have hit singles, all went to the same high school in Dallas and hung out at a folk club called the Rubiyat, where they met other acoustically inclined song people from the Dallas area like Willis Alan Ramsey and Mickey Raphael, before all of them moved south to Austin. Similarly, folkies including Townes Van Zandt, Guy Clark, and Nanci Griffith, who worked Houston rooms such as Anderson Fair, started drifting west to play for the college kids in Austin.

A friend of Walker's who'd occasionally open up for him at Castle Creek named Jimmy Buffett, a rising singer-songwriter out of Mobile, Alabama, wrote the song of his life, "Margaritaville"—an homage to the tequila-and-lime juice mixed that that was becoming locally popular—while in Austin.

Soap Creek Saloon was more like a secret clubhouse. You had to know about it to even start to look for it. Not everyone was willing to drive seven miles from downtown into the darkened hills west of Austin and find the turnoff at 707 Bee Cave Road. West Lake Hills had a lingering reputation as cedar chopper country, with an encampment or two of the hardscrabble hillbilly types still subsisting on cutting and selling the scraggly Ashe juniper wood abundant in the area. If you got lost, you might run into one of their camps, or the places belonging to those who replaced them—high class folks with money and means to build modern, sometimes unconventional homes, including geodesic domes and a group of Mongolian yurts.

The quarter-mile drive down the bumpy dirt road was its own adventure. At the end of the rocky trail was a larger cleared section of caliche fronting a low-slung, barely-lit-from-the-outside clapboard roadhouse of some faded reddish color, consisting of two large rooms, topped by a tin roof. It could have been someone's ranch house or hunting cabin, or a gambling casino,

Last night at the original Soap Creek Saloon in West Lake Hills, January 18, 1979. (Photo copyright © 1979 Ken Hoge.)

once upon a time. From the outside looking in, the place appeared unassuming and anonymous. Several naked white incandescent light bulbs in the shape of a star identified the entrance. Neon was nowhere in sight.

George Majewski, who owned Soap Creek with his wife, Carlyne, worked the bar. She booked the cool bands that played Soap Creek. Paul Ray and the Cobras and their two hot guitarists, Denny Freeman and Stevie Vaughan, had Tuesday nights. Greezy Wheels, Alvin Crow, Omar and the Howlers, Steamheat, the comedic Uranium Savages, and out-of-town bands like Delbert McClinton's from Fort Worth and Joe Ely's from Lubbock were all part of the weekend lineup.

Doug Sahm played whatever he wanted whenever he wanted. Sahm was the bandleader, the lead guitarist, the main singer, the fiddler, and the steel player. Whenever he got bored, he'd scan the audience and solicit requests, never getting stumped—if he wanted to play it. A confirmed genre-jumper equally fluent in hillbilly, western swing, Tex-Mex, rhythm and blues, and pop, Sahm didn't fit into a single niche, which might have hurt his recording career, but worked perfectly over the course of three forty-five-minute sets. He was a juke joint high priest.

Fans showed up just to see which version would be performing onstage. He could trot out the Sir Douglas Quintet hits from the sixties ("She's About A Mover," "The Rains Came," "Mendocino"); Texas standards such as Ray Sharpe's Fort Worth shuffle "Linda Lu"; the Thirteenth Floor Elevators' psychedelic classic "You're Gonna Miss Me"; and "Talk to Me," made famous by

Sahm's San Antonio compadre Sunny Ozuna and the Sunliners; and western swing tunes by Bob Wills and His Texas Playboys, Charlie Walker, and Lefty Frizzell. He also covered tunes by less-well-known talents such as Link Davis, Freddy Fender, T-Bone Walker, Junior Parker, Bobby Blue Bland, and Guitar Slim. Before or after songs, Sahm would cite each creator by name, giving the crowd little history lessons.

"Is Anybody Going to San Antone," the twin-fiddle-driven single off the album *Doug Sahm and Band*, issued by Atlantic Records in 1973, was instantly recognizable. The album had achieved considerable notoriety before its release due to Sahm's off-key duet partner on the single and on other tracks on the album, Bob Dylan. The Song Poet of His Generation had been keeping a low profile and hadn't recorded in several years when he decided to hang around with Sahm in Atlantic's New York studio.

Imagine that: the guy onstage ten feet away, his long hair rendered into dripping strands by sweat, was Bob Dylan's buddy. As a child prodigy on steel guitar, Sahm had sat on the knee of Hank Williams, country music's first genuine star. As a teenager, he'd learned licks from T-Bone Walker, the first acknowledged master of the electric blues guitar, by hanging out in chitlin' circuit clubs. On Thanksgiving Day 1972, Sahm led an improvised jam at the Armadillo World Headquarters that included the Grateful Dead's Jerry Garcia and Phil Lesh, and the hottest act in rock, Leon Russell. And now here he was entertaining a couple hundred stoned-out Soap Creekers, lording over a scene he would describe in a song called "Groover's Paradise."

⊚ ⊚ ⊚

Two local enterprises pretty much summed up the music business beyond the clubs, such as it was in Austin in the seventies. Inner Sanctum, housed in a two-story building on Twenty-Fourth Street, a block from the Drag fronting the University of Texas, opened three weeks after the Armadillo World Headquarters did. It was Austin's only independent record shop, and stood out from competing chain stores by featuring records by Austin and Texas acts, and as the go-to destination to buy concert tickets. Owner Joe Bryson's staff, headed by a larger-than-life figure known as Cowboy (real name James Cooper), were all music hounds, either playing in bands, trying to manage bands, or at the very least out and about in the clubs almost every night and always ready to offer honest assessments of new music at the store by day.

Texas Monthly magazine tapped Bryson to be the embodiment of the "cosmic cowboy" in that publication's August 1974 photo spread comparing and contrasting real rednecks with pseudo rednecks, in response to the rapidly growing popularity of progressive country music. Bryson understood the lay of the land. "We all knew old country music and the things that went with it, like cowboy boots and hats and 'ritter' shirts (snaps on the front) and blue jeans," Bryson said. "That all merged into the local music scene that was happening. Hard liquor was disdained in favor of beer. We shared everything: food, homes, beds, pot, music. You knew everybody. You probably didn't know their last name (too many people making their money outside the law), but you knew them and saw them all around Austin at the different happening spots."

The other business tied to the nascent music scene was KOKE-FM, a commercial radio station that introduced a progressive country music format in early 1972, reflecting the kind of music being played in Austin clubs. The announcers on KOKE-FM were all local celebrities, as disc jockeys tended to be, but the DJ who took over every morning when format switched from Spanish language to Super Roper Radio stood out. Joe Gracey was a smooth-talking refugee from KNOW-AM, Austin's Top 40 station, and the rock music columnist for the *Austin American-Statesman*. A gadfly and relentless clubber, Gracey brought folks like Willie Nelson and Doug Sahm up to the station and put them on the air. Nelson did one of KOKE-FM's promo spots, to the tune of his sixties-vintage country song "Mr. Record Man"—"I was driving down the highway, with KOKE-FM turned on." Nelson brought along his friend Kris Kristofferson, the tousle-headed Texas native songwriter and

A promo event at Inner Sanctum Records. From left: KOKE-FM's Joe Gracey, Inner Sanctum's James "Cowboy" Cooper, and KOKE-FM's Marty Manning. (Photo by Watt Casey.)

singer who at the time was the hottest act in country music, to perform a spontaneous concert on the radio.

KOKE meant Nelson, Walker, Ramsey, Fromholz, Murphey, Stevenson, the Lost Gonzo Band, Kinky Friedman, Sahm, Guy Clark, Townes Van Zandt, Asleep at the Wheel, Alvin Crow, Billy Joe Shaver, Rusty Wier, Greezy Wheels—any local act with a good record, really—could get airplay alongside Waylon Jennings, Leon Russell, Kris Kristofferson, Johnny Cash, Linda Ronstadt, Emmylou Harris, Ernest Tubb, Bob Wills and His Texas Playboys, the Rolling Stones, Creedence Clearwater Revival, the Byrds, and the Flying Burrito Brothers. Radio raised the scene's profile and helped attract curious listeners to live gigs.

In 1975, the same year Willie Nelson scored big with *Red-Headed Stranger*, Doug Sahm released an album called *Groover's Paradise* on Warner Brothers Records that quickly went nowhere, and produced the comeback of Roky Erickson, the Austin-raised lead singer for the Thirteenth Floor Elevators, Texas' (and maybe the world's) first psychedelic rock band. To avoid prison after being caught with marijuana, Erickson had been incarcerated in the Rusk State Hospital for the criminally insane where he endured electroshock therapy. He was a diminished person when he was released, but Sahm took him under wing and encouraged him to perform again at the Ritz Theater, and produced the forty-five by Roky Erickson and Blieb Alien, his new band,

Cosmic cowboy Jerry Jeff Walker (left) joins psychedelic trailblazer Roky Erickson of the Thirteenth Floor Elevators and rocker Doug Sahm for an onstage jam at Gemini's Club on Guadalupe. (Photo copyright © 1977 Ken Hoge.)

at Odyssey Sound/Pecan Street Studios on Sixth Street, "Starry Eyes" backed with "Two-Headed Dog."

KOKE-FM played "Starry Eyes," other stations around the world picked up on it, and Erickson restarted his career, sharing the Armadillo stage with Doug Sahm and another singer that Sahm had talked into making a comeback, Freddy Fender.

Other local stations would follow KOKE-FM by featuring Austin music, a refreshing exception to homogenized radio playlists nationally. At one time or another, KLBJ-FM, KGSR-FM, KUT-FM, KUTX-FM, KOOP-FM, and a revived KOKE-FM programmed Austin music specifically. Larry Monroe, a KUT-FM disc jockey for several decades before moving to KDRP-FM, and Jody Denberg at KGSR-FM and KUT-FM championed Austin singer-songwriters and Austin music in general.

◉ ◉ ◉

The same month Willie Nelson staged his third Fourth of July Picnic in Liberty Hill in 1975, a new music venue opened in downtown Austin. A nightclub dedicated to blues music would have seemed to be an idea that was forty years too late. Blues was dead people's music. By the midseventies, blues around Austin meant the young white players who congregated at the never-a-cover One Knite at Red River and Eighth Streets, just down the block from the police station. Doyle Bramhall's Nightcrawlers, Angela Strehli and Southern Feeling, the Storm, and the Cobras all had residencies on different nights of the week.

Many of these players, such as Keith Ferguson, John (Toad) Andrews, and Speedy Sparks, came from Houston, where they all frequented the same music places growing up and had a personal story or two to tell about Lightnin' Hopkins. The largest contingent of out-of-towners were the Dallas and Fort Worth delegations of Jimmie and Stevie Vaughan, Denny Freeman, Alex Napier, Paul Ray, Mike Buck, Jackie Newhouse, Lou Ann Barton, and Freddie Pharaoh who shared the common traits of listening to WRR's Kats Karavan and KNOK, North Texas' black station, and getting exposed to hometown guitar great Freddie King in black joints rather than white ones. Young players from all over urban Texas mixed it up in Austin and came away with their own blues style.

A few remnants of Austin's black blues community persisted, such as the Victory Grill on East Eleventh Street—once the main street of Austin's Harlem—and in joints farther east like Marie's Tea Room Number Two on Webberville Road. You could hear the East Side in just about everything W. C. Clark, Blues Boy Hubbard, Hosea Hargrove, T. D. Bell, Erbie Bowser,

Matthew Robinson, and barrelhouse pianists Robert Shaw and the Grey Ghost played.

Austin even had certified big-time jazz cats who came home and mentored: Gene Ramsey, who played bass with Count Basie, Charlie Parker, and Thelonious Monk, among others; and trumpet player Martin Banks, who learned from Kenny Dorham and was a veteran of the bands of Duke Ellington, Dizzy Gillespie, and Ray Charles.

All those sounds had faded from the East Side by the midseventies. Everybody knew blues music was dead.

A college dropout from Port Arthur running the Austin location of his family's business thought otherwise. If you walked into Antone's Imports near the state capitol looking for olives, falafel, or one of those famous Antone's po' boy sandwiches, you'd usually have to go to the back of the store to get service. That's where Clifford Antone, a stocky, dark-haired Lebanese kid would be, strumming away on a stringed instrument while a Muddy Waters or Howlin' Wolf record played.

Clifford wasn't cut out for the imported food trade any more than he was cut out to chase a college degree. He'd come to Austin to attend the University of Texas but got kicked out when he was busted at the border try-

Empresario Clifford Antone standing outside the first Antone's on Sixth Street, the club that triggered a nationwide blues revival. (Photo by Nicolas Russell.)

ing to smuggle a pound of marijuana in a hubcap. An older, much respected white blues guitarist named Bill Campbell told Antone about the "for rent" sign he'd seen in front of an old furniture store downtown. Six hundred dollars later, Antone was in the nightclub business.

Opening night was the kind of steamy, sticky summer evening that normally emptied out Sixth Street after the sun went down. But a large crowd gathered on the sidewalk at the southwest corner of Brazos Street waiting to get into the door. The featured attraction was Clifton Chenier and His Red Hot Louisiana Band. The accordion-powered zydeco group of French-speaking Creoles already had an avid following through regular appearances at Soap Creek Saloon. They would christen this new club with a five-night run that kept the place full of partying drinkers.

Behind the bar and working the tables clustered around the stage were attractive young women in their twenties, mostly in floral prints and tight skirts with well-coiffed hair and makeup even, and clean-cut men of similar ages wearing starched Oxford shirts, tails untucked and hanging out, with slacks, not jeans. They projected a different semidressy kind of hip, per the dictates of Clifford Antone, who declared, "We don't want any hippie shit here. This is a *nice* place."

Antone's brought in headlining blues acts while cultivating the best players from the One Knite to effectively create a blues school. Muddy Waters and his band drove in a station wagon from Chicago and were rewarded with a full house and full pay plus tip. Upon their return to Chicago, word of mouth started spreading about this Antone fellow.

Muddy Waters was followed by a who's who of blues giants—Howlin' Wolf's band, Willie Dixon, John Lee Hooker, Percy Mayfield, Percy Sledge, Big Walter Horton, Sunnyland Slim, Buddy Guy and Junior Wells, Albert King, Albert Collins, Bobby Blue Bland, and Jimmy Reed. Some of the more talented sidemen, such as Luther Tucker and Hubert Sumlin, Howlin' Wolf's guitarist, were paid to hang around for a week or two after a gig and share their knowledge with the young players, including Jimmie Vaughan and Kim Wilson of the Fabulous Thunderbirds and Jimmie's little brother Stevie, who was playing second guitar behind Denny Freeman in Paul Ray and the Cobras. This informal apprentice program armed the young players with the kind of direct insight that allowed them to grow into blues virtuosos in their own right.

Within a year of opening, Antone's was the most famous blues club in the world. *Rolling Stone* magazine ran two photos taken at Antone's. The image of a sassy young white female singer named Lou Ann Barton sitting in the lap of a smiling Muddy Waters projected pure joy. The photo of a prone Boz Scaggs sprawled on Brazos Street was accompanied by a brief mention that the Texas-raised, San Francisco rock and soul singer was cold-cocked by an Antone's lieutenant for trying to push his way backstage to visit blues giant Bobby Blue Bland during a break in Bland's show.

◉ ◉ ◉

Eddie Wilson bailed from the Armadillo World Headquarters in 1976, citing burnout from trying to steer the city's best music hall to the breakeven point. He retreated to a small storefront on Sabine Street, a dead-end one-block street downtown next to the police station. He called it the Raw Deal.

It was a low-concept, intentionally hard-to-find greasy-spoon kind of operation, specializing in grilled steaks and chops, bottle beer, mismatched tables, and a grouchy attitude, as evidenced by a sign that read "Remember, you found the Raw Deal. The Raw Deal didn't come looking for you." Another sign posted by the door promised, "It'll Be Better Next Time."

Like Soap Creek had been to music, Eddie's eatery was a semisecret playhouse frequented by a small circle of politicos, students, teachers, bureaucrats, intellectuals, dropouts, and Mad Dogs, writer Bud Shrake's party gang, which included the writer Gary Cartwright and his wife Phyllis, attorney Dave Richards and his wife Ann, a county commissioner and future governor, and the razor-tongued pundit Molly Ivins.

The intentionally ramshackle joint on Sabine Street was easy to miss, underwhelming upon entering, and wholly captured the spirit of an Austin that didn't particularly care to be noticed as long as the party was still going on. Wilson sold out a little more than a year after the Raw Deal opened. Two regulars, Fletcher Boone and Lopez Smitham, paid $750 for the business in $50 monthly installments. A second location, Another Raw Deal, on far West Sixth Street, persevered into the eighties under Boone, Smitham, and Segle Fry. Despite his brief tenure, what Wilson started as a means to forget all about the Armadillo played an unintended role in the evolution of Austin cuisine, where informality ruled. Dressing up to go out to eat somewhere fancy was for Dallas or Houston.

The Armadillo World Headquarters finally became a moneymaking enterprise under the guidance of Hank Alrich, who'd been a critical underwriter of the enterprise in the early days.

Alrich and booker Dave "Killer" Mabry focused on serving as many of Austin's various music communities as possible, as long as they bought tickets and drank beer. The retooling worked.

For all its association with the Cosmic Cowboy movement, the Armadillo never followed stereotype. In addition to blues guitarist Freddie King, neo-swingsters Commander Cody and the Lost Planet Airmen, and southern rock stalwarts the Charlie Daniels Band, two of the Armadillo's most popular regular touring acts were jazz and blues guitar instrumentalist Roy Buchanan and jazz saxophonist and clarinetist Phil Woods, who recorded a live album at the Armadillo on May 26, 1979.

Similarly, two of the biggest local draws at the Armadillo in addition to organic country rockers Greezy Wheels were Steamheat/Extreme Heat, a salt-and-pepper funk fusion band, and Fools, a hard-rocking power trio fronted by guitarist Van Wilks.

The music and everything the building and the people working in it represented could not stop money. Austin's booming real estate market, which was minting millionaires by the week who were flipping land, outstripped the Armadillo's humble financial achievement. Landlord M. K. Hage sold the property. A ten-story office building rose in its place.

The Armadillo went out with a weeklong celebratory bang, wrapping up on New Year's Eve 1980 with Asleep at the Wheel, Commander Cody and His Lost Planet Airmen, and singer Maria Muldaur crooning "Goodnight, Irene," along with a cameo from Kenneth Threadgill. Armadillo poster artists Jim Franklin and Micael Priest returned to emcee the show. Cody wrote a song about the Armadillo kitchen's shrimp enchiladas. It was a bittersweet sendoff, accompanied by tears and a whole lot of laughter.

The Brothers Vaughan: Stevie Ray trading guitar licks with Jimmie behind the wailing sax of Rocky Morales. (Photo by Martha Grenon.)

Chris Layton (left), Tommy Shannon, and Stevie Ray Vaughan—the band known as Double Trouble—dining at Sam's BBQ. (Photo by Watt Casey.)

In a matter of days, Pee Wee Franks' wrecking ball leveled the institution into rubble. The roof was salvaged and placed above the open-air dance floor of Liberty Lunch.

Several thousand people turned out to mourn the loss of the Armadillo. At least that many were partying just as hard at Club Foot, a spacious music venue that had recently opened in an old warehouse across the alley from the Greyhound Bus Station downtown on Fourth Street. Club Foot was large enough to snag some of the road shows that would have otherwise played the Armadillo, and attract a younger crowd, more geared to punk and new wave music. To those people, this iteration of Austin was as exciting as the previous decade had been to their elders.

What bands like Asleep at the Wheel started when they relocated to Austin in the early seventies (because the locals understood the western swing music they were playing) had turned into a steady influx of newcomers. Lubbock country-flavored rock and roller Joe Ely moved, along with his performing friends Butch Hancock and Jimmie Dale Gilmore, because there was more work around Austin than in the South Plains, meaning much bigger audiences that dug their music. Plus, Austin was cheap enough for Hancock to open his own store downtown showing his photography, Lubbock Lights.

The Dixie Diesels, a retro-country band fronted by a singer-songwriter named Shawn Colvin, who had drifted down from Southern Illinois, were part of the great neo-western swing migration of bands moving to Austin because that's where Asleep at the Wheel was.

Blues bands fostered by Clifford Antone and Antone's Nightclub were instrumental in building the scene at the compact Rome Inn on Twenty-Ninth Street, north of campus, especially on Monday nights when the Fabulous Thunderbirds played. Billy Gibbons, the guitarist in the Houston rock band ZZ Top, famously hired limousines to drive his friends and him to the Rome Inn for the gigs.

The Fabulous Thunderbirds—harmonica man Kim Wilson, guitarist Jimmie Vaughan, bassist Keith Ferguson, and drummer Mike Buck—hit the road and found enthusiastic audiences with their minimalist take on obscure blues, especially in the Northeastern United States and London. T-Birds dressed up, not down, and exuded cool in their sharp suits as much as in their stripped down, authentic sound. Among their biggest fans were British roots rockers Nick Lowe and Dave Edmunds, who both produced albums for the band.

There were always plenty of seats at the Rome Inn on Sunday nights, when Jimmie Vaughan's younger brother, Stevie, took the stage. Jimmie Vaughan was all about saying more by playing less, emphasizing the space between notes as much as the notes themselves. Little Stevie wanted to show you everything he knew, every chance he got to take a lead. He left Paul Ray's band to go on his own, first with the Triple Threat Revue, a collaboration with W. C. Clark, the older East Austin guitarist and soul singer, and singer Lou Ann Barton, along with keyboardist Mike Kindred, drummer Freddie Pharaoh, Jackie Newhouse on bass, and saxophonist Johnny Reno. Triple Threat eventually stripped down to a three piece, with drummer Chris Layton and bassist Tommy Shannon, and renamed Double Trouble.

That did not translate into a sizeable audience at the Rome Inn, but it did get the attention of Frances Carr, a horse-track owner with ties to the Grateful Dead and the Rolling Stones, and her business partner Chesley Millikin, the one-time head of Epic Records in England. Millikin and Carr stirred up interest in Vaughan, having him perform for the Rolling Stones and join the touring and recording bands of British rocker David Bowie, after Bowie heard Vaughan at the Montreux Jazz Festival in Switzerland in 1982.

Stevie Vaughan's lead break on "Let's Dance," Bowie's biggest hit record to date, guaranteed a career. Instead, Vaughan blew off Bowie to tour with his own band, signing a deal with legendary talent scout John Hammond and Epic Records, and recording the album *Texas Flood*, which sold more than a half million copies. SRV was Austin's biggest music act. Except for Willie.

Willie Nelson maintained his home and his holdings in Austin, but his audience had gone global. The simple song cycle album *Red-Headed Stranger* was followed by *Wanted: The Outlaws*, a compilation also featuring Waylon Jennings, Jessi Colter, and Tompall Glaser that became the first platinum country music album, selling more than one million units; and by *Stardust*, a collection of determinedly noncountry standards from the Great American Song Book that would spend ten years on the *Billboard* magazine top-selling country album chart.

"Country rock" no longer sufficed to describe what was popping in Austin that was attracting outsider interest. It was a roots town, where it counted if you knew where the music you were playing came from—the unintended birth of Americana music. Authenticity meant everything. Asleep at the Wheel and Alvin Crow were hardly the only ones playing the roots card. Other music tribes included Latin dance music moving to *ritmos* beyond the traditional regional conjunto and Tejano sounds, Vespa-riding mods in trench coats hooked on British and Jamaican ska, loyalists devoted to African bands and ensembles and nothing but, and devotees of punk and new wave sounds that would morph into tangential extensions of all kinds of alternative rock.

Some Austin acts such as Doug Sahm, the LeRoi Brothers, Omar and

Accordion maestro Flaco Jimenez signs an intimate autograph for music maven Margaret Moser. (Photo by Martha Grenon.)

the Howlers, Joe "King" Carrasco, Roky Erickson, Patricia Vonne, Kimmie Rhodes, and Calvin Russell carved out niches in Sweden, France, Switzerland, the United Kingdom, and other parts of Europe in no small part because they were from Austin, Texas.

Several post-Raul's Austin punk rock bands in particular distinguished themselves as major influences for hardcore bands across the United States and Europe by employing native Texan overkill. Scratch Acid infused their version of hardcore with David Yow's exceptionally caustic, take-no-prisoners sonic yelp, egged on by Rey Washam's power drumming. The Big Boys added horns to make punk funky with an added layer of Busby Berkley-esque showmanship, as conceived by front man Randy Biscuit Turner. The Dicks, led by Gary Floyd, one of the first openly gay punk rockers in Austin, mixed blues into their confrontational version of hardcore punk and issued the classic "The Dicks Hate the Police." The Offenders and Poison 13, which featured Tim Kerr and Chris Gates from the Big Boys, also infused blues and metal into their sounds.

Meanwhile, bands from elsewhere continued relocating to Austin because it was the place to make music. One polyglot band that started in Hawaii, Poi Dog Pondering led by Frank Orrall, recorded and released three albums and built a fiercely loyal following for their sprawling, unpredictable live shows before moving on to Chicago in 1992.

As the variety of music being played increased exponentially, one mideighties sound stood out—a postpunk, post–new wave take on rock and roll with roots showing, minus the pretension and artifice defining popular music scenes in other cities. Punk bandleader and author Jesse Sublett, tongue in cheek, described the sound and the scene as the New Sincerity.

The suggestion that the bands were naïve overlooked their earnestness and honesty, which was genuine. Bands like Zeitgeist, the Wild Seeds, Doctors Mob, and Glass Eye cooked up original music and smart songs, and performed them in front of rabid fans jammed into a small off-campus club called the Beach that was once a convenience store. Together they started a scene.

John Kunz and Louis Karp, ambitious owners of a new indie record shop called Waterloo Records, believed in promoting Austin's music culture as much as retailing records, and bankrolled recording sessions for another New Sincerity band, a three-guitar ensemble called the True Believers, before the finished product was sold to Rounder Records.

Margaret Moser was the reporter who first printed the phrase New Sincerity when she heard Jesse Sublett say it. Her writing was critical in identifying emerging bands and scenes. Moser came to Austin from San

Antonio in 1976 with an ear for music, an appreciation of shock value, and a talent for talking and writing. She contributed to the biweekly *Austin Sun* and to punk zines and other publications, but didn't really find her soapbox until the first issue of the *Austin Chronicle* weekly in 1981. The *Chronicle* covered music more thoroughly than the daily paper, the *Daily Texan* at the University of Texas, or any print publication. Moser's writing brought national attention to the New Sincerity bands and to subsequent groups that emerged from Austin.

Moser also mentored younger music writers, including Michael Corcoran, Raul Hernandez, Chris Gray, and Andy Langer. The Austin Music Awards, the local part of South by Southwest, was Moser's baby from inception until her retirement in 2014. She returned to San Antonio, where she worked at the South Texas Popular Culture Center, teaching locals to appreciate, preserve, and respect San Antonio's musical heritage like folks did in Austin.

The Cosmic Cowboy movement might have been a boy's game, but was relatively diverse, all things considered. Singer/pianist Marcia Ball of Freda and the Firedogs and the Bronco Brothers, fiddler Sweet Mary Egan and Lissa Hattersley of Greezy Wheels, singer/guitarist Chris O'Connell of Asleep at the Wheel, and singer Jerrie Jo Jones of Plum Nelly and Mother of Pearl all managed to stand out among the testosterone, and were good enough to see no need to have to embellish their musicianship with any hoochie-coo.

By the eighties, a female sideperson was practically requisite. The Standing Waves weren't the Standing Waves without Shona Lay. John Croslin may have been the intellectual architect of the Reivers nee Zeitgeist, but Kim Longacre's guitar and Cindy Toth's bass and violin, and their collective vocals, made the band. Kathy McCarthy and Stella Weir of Glass Eye, De Lewellen of D-Day, Kris Cummings of Joe "King" Carrasco and the Crowns were essential elements in their respective bands.

Willie Nelson and His Family Band were out of town during most of the punk and New Sincerity run because they were one of the highest-grossing acts in the concert business, especially whenever paired with Waylon Jennings, with six figure guarantees dotting the touring calendar.

Whenever Willie was off the road, he holed up at his Spicewood ranch/compound with University of Texas football coach Darrell K. Royal, now retired, by his side. They golfed on his nine-hole golf course. Willie got as high as he wanted. He recorded with his band and with anyone he cared to record with, whenever he wanted, as long as he wanted. Among the parade of recording partners coming to Pedernales Sound were Latin heartthrob Julio Iglesias, rhythm and blues giant Ray Charles, mentor Ray Price, and

On the merry-go-round with the Butthole Surfers (left to right: King Coffey, Paul Leary, Gibby Haynes, Terrence Smart, Teresa Taylor). (Photo by Pat Blashill.)

old friends Roger Miller, Waylon Jennings, Merle Haggard, Leon Russell, and Johnny Bush.

By 1990, Willie had dodged a well-publicized thirty-two million dollar tax bill from the Internal Revenue Service and recovered most of his property that had been auctioned off by the government. He was no longer Austin's biggest music star. Album sales and box office receipts had plateaued, leading to tours with the Highwaymen supergroup, with Waylon Jennings, Johnny Cash, and Kris Kristofferson, to maintain the high profile and income bracket he'd become accustomed to.

Stevie Ray Vaughan and Double Trouble had stolen Willie's thunder by spearheading a world blues revival. Vaughan was hailed as the best blues guitarist anywhere, a point underscored during the closing jam at the August 26, 1990, outdoor concert in Alpine Valley, Wisconsin, where Vaughan engaged in a show-closing shootout with his brother Jimmie, Eric Clapton, Robert Cray, and Buddy Guy—the best of the best.

Minutes after the last notes of "Sweet Home Chicago," with the other guitarists deferring to Vaughan, acknowledging his particularly fiery playing that night, he stepped into a helicopter that would carry him back to his hotel in Chicago. After lifting off in dense fog, the helicopter banked sharply and slammed into the side of a ski hill, killing Vaughan and four others. His death hit Austin's music community hard. People like thirty-five-year-old

Vaughan weren't supposed to die playing music, especially after he saved himself from serious drug addiction and then started saving others.

Austin music got even harder to pin down. Singer-songwriter Shawn Colvin left Austin after a brief flirtation in the late seventies for New York, where she joined up with Nashville roots king Buddy Miller, ran with a folk collective, appeared in off-Broadway musicals, sang backup on Suzanne Vega's "Luka," and made two albums of her own, winning a Grammy Award for contemporary folk, before returning in 1993. Marriage and divorce followed, a sour experience that inspired her story song about a woman who burns down her house to wipe out the past, "Sunny Came Home," which won her another Grammy in 1997.

Austin was Fastball, the three-piece alt rock band fronted by the lazily charismatic scene fixture Miles Zuniga. Their hit "The Way" was inspired by a newspaper article about an elderly married couple from Salado, Texas, with cognition issues getting lost and disappearing. The song stayed at number one on the *Billboard* modern rock chart for seven weeks in 1998.

Austin was ground zero for the Butthole Surfers, the wildest band on earth. The four-piece band led by Gibby Haynes, the Dallas-raised son of a children's television show host, consistently pushed boundaries of norm and gleefully went over the edge, ruling the international punk / alternative / Out There universe with anarchic, crazed genius. Haynes was just part of the show. Guitarist and co-conspiracist Paul Leary, bassist Jeff Pinkus, drummers King Coffey and Teresa Taylor all ruled their own creative mini-empires. Haynes and Leary founded the band in San Antonio in the early eighties while both pursued degrees at Trinity University—Haynes in accounting, Leary in finance. Utilizing cockroach confetti, condoms filled with colored dye exploding in Haynes's pants, strobe lights, a bullhorn to distort the vocals, genital mutilation films playing simultaneously on screens behind the band, a writhing naked female dancer, and Haynes's menacing, anarchic stage presence, their reputation as "The Weirdest Band in the World" was well-earned.

Austin was Alejandro Escovedo, who arrived in Austin from California in 1981 with the cow punk band Rank and File before transitioning into the mideighties rock outfit the True Believers and then striking out on his own, building a catalog of albums filled with personal story-songs of love, breakup, beautiful losers, and near-death experiences. He was both a sensitive composer and a rock and roll warrior/survivor with a street punk attitude, and a well-earned international cult following. Three-chord rock was his milieu, but he did not hesitate to augment his various bands with cellos and violins. The son of Mexican immigrants to Texas, the ageless, toothsome Escovedo was recognized in 1998 by the national roots music publication *No Depression* as Artist of the Decade. He continued touring and ran with REM, Los Lobos, and all the cool alternative rock bands, for one stretch sharing Bruce Springsteen's personal manager. But Escovedo was best savored inside Austin, where he was king.

Bob Schneider had a similar Austin-centric reputation. Schneider was the Austin music scene's lady-killer glamour boy, a reputation built upon his dark good looks, smoky bedroom voice, overwhelmingly female audience, and high-profile girlfriend for a couple years, the movie actress Sandra Bullock, who had followed her previous boyfriend, actor Matthew McConaughey, to Austin in 1996. All this overlooked Schneider's skills for assembling intriguing music ensembles, only to tear them down and start another completely different kind of band.

Schneider, a military brat who came to Austin after studying art at the University of Texas at El Paso, was on a constant musical bender. His first groups, the Ugly Americans and Joe Rockhead, led to his show band with dirty lyrics, the Scabs, augmented by the Grooveline Horns. Schneider went solo in 1999 as Lonelyland, which became a band unto itself, and dabbled in a bluegrass ensemble, among other projects. Although Bullock pulled strings to get his music on movie soundtracks and on late-night talk shows (Jay Leno introduced him as "Rob" Schneider), Schneider never found much of an audience beyond Austin. The locals didn't care. Over a ten-year span from 1999 to 2010, Schneider won Band of the Year, Musician of the Year, Song and Album of the Year, Male Vocalist of the Year, and Songwriter of the Year multiple times at the Austin Music Awards.

Austin was *la onda*. During the nineties and early aughts, the city became a staging ground for Nuevo Latino sounds that had nothing to do with the city's Texan-Mexican roots laid down by Chano Cadena's and Johnny Degollado's conjuntos, and Ruben Ramos and Manuel Cowboy Donley's more polished big band sounds. The new kids on the block trafficked in mainstream rock (Los Lonely Boys, Vallejo), alternative (producer and guitarist Adrian Quesada), and big brass. Grupo Fantasma, a nine-piece ensemble that formed in 2000, was recruited by pop star Prince as his backing band for an extended Las Vegas residency that lasted several years. Brownout, a spinoff of Grupo Fantasma, broke beyond the Latino envelope with their big brass renditions of songs by the heavy metal band Black Sabbath.

In the midst of this new burst of expanding musical boundaries, a different kind of money started flying around town. It couldn't buy cool, but it could certainly influence how some people tried to define it. Andy Langer arrived in 1990, during what he described as that brief window where old Austin and new Austin intertwined before high tech, money, and hubris overwhelmed everything.

"There was this three-year lull before the clubs in the Warehouse District started catering to the tech money," said Langer, a native of New York's Long Island, during a break in his KGSR radio program. In fact, there were no clubs in the Warehouse District south of Fourth Street and west of Congress Avenue at the time, except for Liberty Lunch. The blocks between Liberty Lunch on Second Street and Ruta Maya Coffee on Fifth Street were either dark or parking lots.

The fast money that accompanied high tech explained all the bars that had sprung up west of Congress and south of Sixth. Oilcan Harry's, Waterloo Brewing Company, Lavaca Street Bar, and the Bitter End catered to this new high-tech crowd, followed by the openings of Fado, Speakeasy, Ringside at Sullivan's, the B-Side, and Qua, with its translucent dance floor built on top of a shark tank. They were all chasing "the first wave of young people coming to Austin who didn't give a shit about music," Andy Langer said. "These guys were working twenty hours a day and had four hours to party. They didn't like music. Music got in the way. They just wanted to get laid."

Cedar Street Courtyard, tucked in a sunken courtyard/revived alleyway on West Fourth, two blocks west of Congress Avenue, didn't happen until March 1995, but tapped right into the cultural shift as Austin's ultra lounge, sleek with lots of metal and glass, consciously stylish with an adult, not college, bent. The drink menu was tailored for martini drinkers. The open-air patio encouraged cigar smoking. There was music—mostly jazz—for background ambience. But Cedar Street wasn't an Austin music club, at least not in the traditional sense, not at first. Once the new and shiny wore off, Cedar Street devolved into a dependable live music room.

Real estate along Fourth was still cheap enough to turn the street into a magnet for gay bars, beginning with the linchpin Oilcan Harry's, a modern, teched-out multibar and dance space that endured into the twenty-teens as Austin's top gay club.

The developing scene was best savored mingling with the crowd that gathered on the street nightly outside Ruta Maya, Austin's pioneering hip coffee company, at Fourth and Lavaca after the bars closed at 2:00 a.m. This bunch was clearly focused on the party, not on a desk gig in Round Rock.

Andy Langer expanded his reporting platforms from writing for the Austin Chronicle weekly to appearing on a local television news channel, writing columns for Esquire and Texas Monthly magazines, hosting daily shows on

KROX-FM and KGSR-FM, emceeing multiple Austin Music Awards ceremonies, and serving as the go-to announcer for all kinds of music-related events.

Tech and music did mesh in Austin beyond decorating the offices of start-ups with local music posters and booking bands for their parties. Advanced Micro Devices worked with Ray Benson in their development of ADAT digital audio technology at Benson's Bismeaux Studios. The producer of the Beatles, Sir George Martin, came to Bismeaux to road test ADAT.

Spoon, Austin's most popular band of the late nineties and early aughts, came out of the tech world. Lead singer, guitarist, and main composer Britt Daniel had been a sound designer and composer for Richard Garriott's Origin Systems, creating sound effects and music for computer games. Daniel was BOI—Born on Galveston Island—and grew up in Temple, about an hour north of Austin. The son of a neurologist, Daniel came to Austin in 1989 as a freshman at the University of Texas. He worked as a DJ on the student radio station and played in bands. Lean, lanky, and laconic in a studiously detached, indie rock kind of way, Daniel packed an emotive, gritty voice that sometimes slipped into a falsetto that could effortlessly wrap itself around intelligent, kicky lyrics like a comfortable slipper.

Daniel met drummer Jim Eno, his principal collaborator, in a band called the Alien Beats. Eno had worked in microchip design for Compaq in Houston before hiring on with Motorola in Austin. Daniel and Eno started recording together as Spoon in 1992. They built a buzz that extended far beyond Austin with an EP and then with a full album *Teléfono*, released in 1996 on Matador, a beloved New York–London rock indie label whose principal owner, Gerard Cosloy, would relocate to Austin in 2004. Nothing about Spoon adhered to Austin or Texas stereotypes (especially after Daniel moved to Portland, Oregon). No one wore cowboy hats or bothered to invoke Willie. Spoon preferred performing in suits.

Success came in the aughts with a string of indie releases starting with 2001's *Girls Can Tell* and running through 2005's *Gimme Fiction*, and 2007's *Ga Ga Ga Ga Ga* through 2014's *They Want My Soul*. The band made real money placing songs on film soundtracks (*Cloverfield, 17 Again, I Love You, Man, Horrible Bosses, (500) Days of Summer*), television shows (*Veronica Mars, The Simpsons, Bones, Chuck, Numb3rs, House, How I Met Your Mother*), and computer games (*Matt Hoffman's Pro BMX 2, MLB: The Show*).

Rock may have no longer been the dominant form of popular music globally, long ago bypassed by hip-hop and modern rhythm and blues. Austin was a mere satellite as far as those musical forms were concerned, and could not boast of a major black female artist comparable to Dallas's Erykah Badu and Houston's Beyoncé. Rock still mattered in Austin. Several post-Spoon rock ensembles managed to carve out niches working variations of alternative rock, from the eclectic Wild Child and the neo-bluegrass hipster conflagration Whiskey Shivers to the neo-classical Mother Falcon, the bluesy soul shouter Malford Milligan, and the twisted poetic dissonance of Churchwood.

Going back to the roots was a well-trod musical path in Austin. Junior Brown's deep bass voice, his neo-traditional forties-vintage country music stage wear, his one-of-a-kind dual neck guit-steel instrument, and goofy songs like "My Baby Don't Dance to Nothin' but Ernest Tubb" made him the standard bearer of a retro-movement that encompassed Alvin Crow, Bruce Robison and Kelly Willis, Dale Watson, Heybale!, the Derailers, James Hand, Guy Forsyth and the Asylum Street Spankers, Jessie Dayton, High Noon, the Last Real Texas Blues Band, the Texas Mavericks, and the Texas Tornados—the last three ensembles overseen by Doug Sahm until his death in 1999—and by Doug-centric offspring such as the Gourds and Shinyribs, Kevin Russell's twenty teens big band.

◎ ◎ ◎

At its core, Austin was a singer-songwriter storyteller kind of music place, going back to the Lomaxes and the founding of the Texas Folklore Society in 1909.

Castle Creek and the Saxon Pub were the best-known listening rooms to hear songwriters in the early seventies, but hardcore aspirants worked wherever they could get their foot in the door. Over the next three decades, places such as the Alamo Lounge in the basement of the rugged old Alamo Hotel at Guadalupe and Sixth Streets, Spellman's on West Fifth Street, emmajoe's on Guadalupe and Thirty-Second Streets, the Austin Outhouse at 3510 North Lamar, the Hole in the Wall on Guadalupe across from UT, and Chicago House at 607 Trinity championed composers wanting to try out their material in a space where the song was respected and revered, not just a means to sell booze. The most durable, venerable songwriter showcase was the Cactus Café in the Texas Union on the University of Texas campus, which thrived into the aughts and teens thanks to its tireless proprietor Griff Luneburg and the financial wherewithal of the college.

Words counted. The creaky stages of Austin groaned with an embarrassment of hungry, ambitious songsters. Some, such as Nanci Griffith, a sweet-voiced literary-minded Austin native who built her songbook in Houston, a tall rail-thin journalism grad from Texas A&M named Lyle Lovett, and his Aggie buddy Robert Earl Keen drew the kinds of crowds that suggested an artist might actually be able to earn a living wage singing their own songs. Their local popularity presaged their ascents as national recording artists with Nashville bases.

Others came to Austin to polish their material. Townes Van Zandt, Willis Alan Ramsey, Steve Fromholz, Butch Hancock, Guy Clark, Lucinda Williams, Jimmy LaFave, Jimmie Dale Gilmore, and Darden Smith moved for the music, as did younger songsters such as Patty Griffin, David Garza, Kevin Welch, Gurf Morlix, Mandy Mercier, and James McMurtry.

Women increasingly staked out a larger piece of the musical turf. Country singer, DIY singer-songwriter-label czarina Terri Hendrix, host of "Bummer Nights" Sarah Elizabeth Campbell, country and swing vocalist and guitarist Elizabeth McQueen, soul and gospel singer Ruthie Foster, one-time State Musician of Texas Shelly King, singer-violinist Carrie Rodriguez, and blues guitarists and singers Carolyn Wonderland, Kathy Murray, and Jackie Venson shared a common respect for where music came from, while each created individual sounds that were wholly contemporary. Kathy Valentine, an original Austin punk rocker, returned from Los Angeles after her extended stint with the girl group the Go-Go's to record on her own and with the all-female Bluebonnets, and mentor younger women, including the Tiarra Girls.

And there was Blaze Foley, the guy Lucinda Williams called a beautiful loser who moved her to write the song "Drunken Angel," and the same songwriter who inspired the songwriter's songwriter, Townes Van Zandt, to write "Blaze's Blues." A gruff, imposing presence who'd drifted over from Georgia, where he'd been performing under the name of Depty Dawg, Foley (real name Micheal David Fuller) landed in Austin in 1976, started performing with Gurf Morlix, and immediately befriended Townes Van Zandt, who saw a troubled troubadour like himself in Foley and called him "one of the most spiritual cats I've ever met."

Foley fell in with a hard-drinking, hard-writing bunch: Jubal Clark came to Austin with a song he'd written called "Willie" that he wanted Willie Nelson's guitarist, Jody Payne, to record. Rich Minus came up from San Antonio, always trying to pitch the handful of songs he'd written, like the ballad "Laredo Rose." Calvin Russell possessed a squint-eyed, roughed-up face that the French would fall in love with as much they did with his songs. They all drank too much, and seemed to revel in living on the edge, hanging out and swapping bullshit as much as lyrics.

Somehow Foley managed to stand out among his ragtag peers, burnishing a reputation for sleeping in dumpsters whenever he couldn't find a couch to crash on. That BFI insignia on the side of many trash dumpsters? That stood for Blaze Foley Inside. He and his songwriting buddies did not hold day jobs. They were outlaws. All they needed was one song to get covered by someone like Willie.

It happened to Steve Fromholz, one of the original wave of progressive country songsters who had already written and performed a brilliant extended song classic about life in small-town Texas called "Texas Trilogy" as part of the duo Frummox, and played in Steven Stills's Manassas before settling in Austin. Circumstance found Fromholz at Autumn Sound in Garland in 1975, where he could be heard singing along to cue Willie Nelson with the right words to his composition "I'd Have to Be Crazy."

It happened to Townes Van Zandt in 1983, when Nelson and Merle Haggard, at the urging of Willie's eldest daughter, Lana, cut "Pancho and Lefty" in the dead of night at Willie's Pedernales Sound and had a number one country hit with the song.

It happened to Blaze Foley, when Merle Haggard covered Foley's "If I Could Only Fly" in 2000 and called the song "the best country song I've heard in fifteen years." Foley was not on hand to enjoy his success. In February 1989, he was shot and killed senselessly by the son of his homeless friend, Concho January. His larger-than-life persona; his habit of sleeping in cars, dumpsters, and under pool tables; and his penchant for creative presentation, calling himself the Duct-Tape Messiah, often distracted from the fact that Blaze Foley was a pretty great singer-songwriter. Not for nothing did John Prine and Lyle Lovett, two fairly renowned songwriters, respectively interpret Foley's "Clay Pigeons" and "Election Day."

Foley's Austin performing partner, Gurf Morlix, did all right too, joining Lucinda Williams's band as guitarist and producing the 1998 breakthrough album *Car Wheels on a Gravel Road*.

Austin singer-songwriters established lineages. David Rodriguez's daughter Carrie, Jimmie Dale Gilmore's son Colin, Butch Hancock's son Rory, Jon Dee Graham's son William Harries, Kevin Welch's kids Savannah and Dustin, James McMurtry's son Curtis, Champ Hood's son Warren, and Johnny Gimble's granddaughter Emily carried the family tradition well into in the twenty-first century.

There were musician lineages too. Lukas Hubbard grew into the lead guitarist his father Ray Wylie had been wishing for, ever since Terry (Buffalo) Ware went his own way. With a multidecade tenure as the bandleader supporting folk music giant Bob Dylan, Charlie Sexton, who was raised with his brother Will by Speedy Sparks and other members of Austin's music community, matured into Austin's all-purpose instrumentalist, music director, and producer. George Reiff, Michael Ramos, and Adrian Quesada assumed similar roles as behind-the-scenes go-to sources for producing and for putting together ensembles for special performances.

A small core of musicians managed to survive playing clubs, working different gigs four to seven nights a week. This bunch of mostly older players were Austin's musical conscience. Their numbers included the guitarists David Grissom, David Holt, Sarah Brown, Denny Freeman, John X. Reed, Derek O'Brien, Scrappy Jud Newcomb, Redd Volkaert, and Willie Pipkin; the bassists Sarah Brown, Bruce Hughes, Glen Fukunaga, and Speedy Sparks; keyboardists Red Young, Floyd Domino, Emily Gimble, Dr. James Polk, Mike Flanigin, Earl Poole Ball, and Nick Connally; horn players Kaz Kazanoff, Elias Haslanger, and Dr. John Mills; drummers Ernie Durawa, Mike Buck, Lisa Pankratz, Barry (Frosty) Smith, George Rains, and Tom Lewis; and steel guitarist Cindy Cashdollar.

Lloyd Maines ruled as the most prolific producer. A Lubbock native who played progressive steel guitar in the original Joe Ely Band and his family's Maines Brothers Band, the soft-spoken, physically imposing Maines moved to Austin in 1981 because that's where he was in demand to produce albums for roots and country music artists. Maines set the Austin standard for recording. He was affordable, straightforward, and responsible for more than one hundred albums that sounded like Texas. He also happened to be

The Liberty Lunch braintrust: booker and SXSW founding director Louis Jay Meyers, manager Mark Pratz, and owners Sheila and Charlie Tesar. (Photo by Martha Grenon.)

the father of Natalie Maines, the singer who remade the Dixie Chicks into one of the biggest acts in country music.

For all the perception of how deep, meaningful lyrics and smart, seasoned musicianship defined Austin music, the biggest hit record to come out of the city was a very un-Austin-like, easy-listening pop tune. Chris Geppert, a cherubic native of San Antonio, was the sweet-tenor lead of a cover band called Christopher Cross that frequently played Steamboat downtown and was known around town for the radio jingle for Dyer Electronics ("A Dyer deal is a stereo steal, Dyer Ee-lec-tronics"). The single the band put together, "Ride like the Wind," and the album they made, which also included the dreamy pop hit "Sailing" (a future yacht rock anthem for the topsider set), won five Grammy Awards in 1979.

◉ ◉ ◉

Sixth Street, one of the first strips in Austin with clusters of music clubs, gentrified in the wake of pioneering businesses such as the Pecan Street Café, Gordo's Pool Hall, and Antone's nightclub in the early seventies, and then morphed into a regional version of Bourbon Street in New Orleans. By the turn of the century, Dirty Sixth was a great place to get drunk, but not such a great destination for music other than copy bands. The cool music crowds moved around the corner to Red River Street, where rents were cheaper among the secondhand furniture and thrift stores.

The openings of Emo's in 1992 at the corner of Red River and Sixth, with three separate stages among a warren of rooms, and Stubb's, two blocks north, an outdoor concert facility with an inside music room and barbecue restaurant in the former location of the One Knite, fostered a vibrant scene of alternative bands, punk rockers, and a hodgepodge of fringe music, occasionally interspersed with touring acts, which usually played the big stage at Stubb's. Within fifteen years, Stubb's and other clubs would be shadowed by residential high-rises occupied by tenants including a few who did not enjoy hearing loud music at night, much less care about living in the Live Music Capital of the World.

No single event epitomized the squeeze that growth and money put on live music more than the closing of Liberty Lunch at the end of July 1999. This wasn't just another music venue going out of business. Liberty Lunch was sacred, like the Armadillo, only if the Armadillo had been sited in an old lumberyard instead of an old armory. Liberty Lunch was owned by Charlie Tesar, but Tesar preferred to keep his nose out of the business, ceding management to Mark Pratz and J-net Ward and booking to Louis

Jay Meyers. The Lunch was funky, duct-taped, slapped-together, falling-apart, hardly state-of-art anything except for being a genuinely great place to watch locals like the Butthole Surfers, Townes Van Zandt, or the Reivers, or a touring rock, roots, or world music act such as Nirvana or King Sunny Ade, up close and personal. Its demise was a sure sign Austin had sold out and gone to hell.

The city embraced music as part of its civic image and made it a prime selling point by voting for a new official motto for Austin in 1991: The Live Music Capital of the World. Now the same City of Austin was kicking out one of Austin's most popular music venues from city-owned property deemed too expensive for a music club.

Of all the sendoffs anticipating Liberty Lunch's closing, Michael Hall took the cake for most imaginative. The tousle-haired lead singer and composer in the New Sincerity band Wild Seeds ("I'm Sorry, I Can't Rock You All Night Long"), whose day job was senior editor at *Texas Monthly* magazine, had been playing Liberty Lunch since 1982. He appreciated the functional durability of the old lumberyard, and the music Liberty Lunch brought to people like him.

Hall's gift of gratitude was Gloriathon, gathering a bunch of folks together to perform the rock and roll anthem "Gloria" for twenty-four hours straight.

Hall and the band the Brooders hit the first E-D-A chords at 9:00 p.m. on July 23, a warm Friday night. The following day around 3:45 in the afternoon, Van Morrison, the composer of the song and lead singer of the Irish band Them, which had the original hit in 1964, joined the marathon by singing "G-L-O-R-I-A" by telephone live while he was performing at a festival in Chester, England.

Mark Pratz and his partner J-net Ward, who were public school educators by day, had been promised city assistance in the form of a six hundred thousand dollar low-interest loan to find a new location for Liberty Lunch. The largesse came mainly out of guilt, since the Lunch was shuttered due to the construction of the new Austin City Hall across the street and a companion office building on Liberty Lunch's site that the city was leasing to the Computer Science Corporation. Liberty Lunch was supposed to relocate adjacent to Stubb's on Red River, which ironically had been poaching many shows that would have otherwise played Liberty Lunch. But the relo never happened, and the complaints and laments never stopped. "These people aren't just mourning the loss of Liberty Lunch," observed Mark Pratz. "They're mourning the loss of their town."

It was a recurring theme. The campus-area institution Les Amis coffee shop closed in 1997, ending a run that started May 7, 1970, when Michael Beaudette and Ralph McElroy set up some tables on asphalt at the corner of Twenty-Fourth and Nueces so they could watch girls go by. The café became the go-to place to sit and drink and eat and discuss radical politics, or just sit and loaf. Its infamy extended to having three scenes in the film *Slacker* and being the subject of its own documentary film, *Viva Les Amis*, which included flash-forward interviews with employees of the space's ironic replacement tenant, Starbucks Coffee.

Flipnotics, Inner Sanctum, Las Manitas, the Austin Opry House, Club Foot, the first Antone's, the second, third, fourth, and fifth Antone's, One Knite, Quack's on the Drag, OK Records, Cheapo Records, La Zona Rosa, Voltaire's, Electric Lounge, Strange Brew, Maria's Tacos—sooner or later, they would all be just memories.

The marginal economics of operating a club poorly reflected music's impact on the city and its culture. Frequently cited as being one of the best places for jobs in the nation during the early twenty-first century, and as an urban environment with a high quality of life, Austin's unlikely stature circled back to music. The first thing arrivals saw stepping off their flight at Austin-Bergstrom International Airport was a sign identifying that official motto: "The Live Music Capital of the World."

No city in the United States had so much music in its DNA. Local music played on the airport's sound system, and bands played live at Ray Benson's Roadhouse in the terminal. Musicians gigged at the H-E-B Central Markets, Whole Foods Markets, and city council meetings. While hardly anyone was making a full-time living from their craft, on any given day or night, hundreds of people were standing by, ready to break out instruments and play for the fun of it.

Musicians known and unknown gravitated to Austin based on that reputation. Stephen Bruton from Fort Worth set aside twenty years of touring as Kris Kristofferson's guitarist and working in Bonnie Raitt's band to plant roots in Austin in the eighties, recording and producing Alejandro Escovedo, Scrappy Jud Newcomb, and himself while fronting the Resentments, a loose collection of musicians in recovery, including Jon Dee Graham, Bruce Hughes, Newcomb, Mambo Johnny Treanor, and John Chipman. Their regular Sunday evening get-together at the Saxon Pub led to tours of Europe and Japan.

Redd Volkhaert and Earl Poole Ball, who played in the bands of Merle Haggard and Johnny Cash, respectively, moved to Austin and often played together in the band Heybale! while each worked club gigs multiple nights every week—a pleasure that wasn't afforded them in Nashville or Los

Gary Clark Jr. commanding the stage at the Austin City Limits Festival. (Photo by Matt Lankes.)

Angeles. Joining them were Cornell Hurd, a San Francisco expat and western swing convert, and rotund blue yodeler Don Walser from the South Plains town of Lamesa, whose belated singing career took flight after he retired from his job with the State of Texas.

No import won Austin's heart quite like Ian McLagan, the spiky-haired Brit who played keyboards with the Small Faces, a rock group that formed in 1965, which became the Faces in the seventies after Rod Stewart joined the band, and recorded and toured with the Rolling Stones. Elegantly charming and totally hooked on rock, Mac first visited Austin in the eighties to see his old Faces band mate Ronnie Lane, who spent his last years in the city fighting progressive muscular sclerosis. After the 1994 Northridge earthquake near Los Angeles, McLagan and his wife Kim, the widow of Who drummer Keith Moon, packed up to raise horses in Manor, east of Austin, while Mac put together various iterations of his Bump Band, enjoying an extended ten-year residency at the Lucky Lounge downtown. McLagen mentored a slew of younger musicians, among them guitarist Scrappy Jud Newcomb, and wrote a very good book about his adventures on the road, *All the Rage: My High Life with the Small Faces, the Faces, the Rolling Stones and Many More* (1998). With an innate ability to light up any room he walked into, he was a critical cog in Austin's music community until his death in December 2014 at age sixty-nine.

"I don't want to be a has-been," McLagan explained to *Rolling Stone* magazine. "I play every day. It's what I do; it's what I've been doing for fifty years." Mac had Austin attitude.

That ability to play regularly in front of enthusiastic, engaged audiences prompted several movie stars turned rockers to invest hang time in Austin to build their musical street credibility. Johnny Depp, Dennis Quaid, Russell Crowe, and David Keith all fronted bands that performed in Austin clubs for extended runs. Real music people dug Austin too. Robert Plant, the wild-maned vocalist for Led Zeppelin, one of the biggest rock acts ever, passed a

Lubbock BBQ king C. B. Stubblefield, Stubb, followed Joe Ely and his music friends to Austin, where his name built a BBQ brand. (Photo by Will Van Overbeek.)

couple years in town thanks to his intense interest in American roots music and a very attractive female singer named Patty Griffin, a one-time waitress who had drifted down from Boston to become one of Austin's premier singer-songwriters. Esperanza Spalding, the Afro-coiffed jazz bassist, bought a second home in Austin so she could chill whenever she wanted to lay low. Elle magazine, which profiled Spalding, described her new place of residence as the "it small city"—only, at close to a million residents, the "it city" was hardly small.

Festivals became the easy, accessible way to hear lots of music all at once. Regular fest-goers made just as big a deal about the Blues on the Green summer series in Zilker Park, the rootsy Old Settler's Music Festival south of the city in April, the Urban Music Festival and the Reggae Festival at Auditorium Shores, and the Sound on Sound and Euphoria fests east of Austin as they did about ACL Fest and South by Southwest.

The contemporary music landscape grew to encompass management companies, booking agencies, rehearsal spaces, luthiers and guitar factories, nonprofits, and other ancillary ventures. Doug Hanners's twice-a-year Austin Record Convention was the biggest record collectors meetup in the country.

For better or worse, clubs, the venues dependent on beer, wine, and liquor sales and cover charges that had been the backbone of Austin's music community, struggled or faded away, increasingly hemmed in by exorbitant leases and complaining neighbors. So Gary Clark Jr. and Gary Keller each decided to do something about it.

Gary Clark Jr. was raised in Austin and educated by blues guitar elders including Jimmie Vaughan and Bill Campbell and the blues empresario Clifford Antone, who took an interest in Clark and his good friend Eve Monsees while both were students at Austin High School in the nineties. Ninety-five percent of the local guitar players in Austin were white, even though many of them sounded black, including Jimmie Vaughan. Clark was one of the few young African Americans playing blues, even as he continually broadened his scope by incorporating hip-hop, R&B, and rock elements into his sound. His blues chops led to Clark spending his twenties sharing stages around the world trading licks with guitar greats like Eric Clapton, Buddy Guy, B.B. King, Jeff Beck, and Keith Richards. By the time he reached the age of thirty, Clark was good and original enough to be regarded as their peer, and wealthy enough to save Antone's nightclub.

After the club was booted from its original location at Sixth and Brazos to make way for a parking garage in 1979, Antone's moved into a warehouse space near Anderson Lane and MoPac Expressway in north Austin, lasting a year there before relocating to an old Shakey's Pizza Parlor on Guadalupe Street, just north of the University of Texas campus in 1981. The third Antone's became even more storied than the original over its sixteen year run, largely because it was where local blues acts who'd made it big— the Fabulous Thunderbirds and Stevie Ray Vaughan and Double Trouble, in particular—came home to party and play.

Antone's Record Shop opened across Guadalupe Street from the club. In the back of the record shop, Clifford Antone established a record label bearing his name that featured favorite artists Doug Sahm, Marcia Ball, Angela Strehli, Lou Ann Barton, and Sue Foley, quickly gaining traction as a contemporary blues label. Two women, Susan Piver and Connie Kirsch, ran the operation.

The club occasionally found itself short on funds, and benefit fundraisers were held on several occasions to keep the lights burning. Blues wasn't selling like it once was, and there had been serious attrition among elder touring headliners. Antone welcomed a giant-sized black cook from Lubbock named C. B. Stubblefield to open a barbecue operation in the back of the club after Stubb moved to Austin on musician Joe Ely's recommendation. Maybe Stubb's barbecue would bring in more business.

The nightclub's struggles were indirectly tied to Clifford Antone's other enterprise. He was popped in 1982 for dealing fifty pounds of marijuana, which led to a not-quite-three-year stretch in federal prison at Big Spring, Texas. While incarcerated, he raised eighty thousand dollars for Big Spring's flood-ravaged Comanche Trail Park by bringing in musical friends such as Asleep at the Wheel, Stevie Ray Vaughan, the Fabulous Thunderbirds, Kris Kristofferson, and Willie Nelson to play fundraisers.

A 1989 bust sent two growers tied to Antone, guitarist Derek O'Brien and percussionist Mambo John Treanor, to prison.

Antone's record label folded, and in 1997 a new group of investors moved the club back downtown to the corner of Fifth and Lavaca Streets in the Warehouse District. Clifford Antone was sentenced again to four years in federal prison in 2000 for dealing marijuana and served three years in nearby Bastrop. Upon his release, he worked with at-risk kids at American YouthWorks, taught a course at the University of Texas titled "The Blues According to Clifford Antone," was the subject of a film documentary, and became the patron and personal chaperone for Chicago blues piano legend Pinetop Perkins, a nonagenarian who had moved to Austin in 2003 at the urging of Antone and another relocated blues legend, the harmonica player James Cotton.

Clifford Antone's death from natural causes at age fifty-seven in 2006 should have closed the book on the Antone's saga. But the club refused to die, even after a version of Antone's club briefly surfaced under new ownership on East Riverside Drive in 2014 that could have been confused for a generic House of Blues franchise.

Gary Clark Jr. and associates bought the name and opened the sixth Antone's at 305 East Fifth Street in 2015. This version of Antone's reconnected Clark to the lineage that went back to Stevie Ray Vaughan, Jimmie Vaughan, Denny Freeman, Derek O'Brien, Bill Campbell, Lou Ann Barton, Angela Strehli, and Marcia Ball, and extended through several generations of younger players, including Ian Moore, Sue Foley, Jake Andrews, Charlie and Will Sexton, the Keller brothers, the Peterson brothers, and Johnny Moeller.

Drummer Mike Buck, one of the original Fabulous Thunderbirds and charter member of the LeRoi Brothers, and his wife, the guitarist Eve Monsees, took over Antone's Record Shop, which thrived as a collectors' store at its Guadalupe Street location.

The Austin that Gary Clark had grown up in had changed but hadn't vanished. "The things that I love about it: the food, live music, beautiful geography, places to hang out and go swimming and camping," Clark said. "All the things that I loved about growing up here are still alive and kicking. I can't knock it; it's a beautiful place."

The shiny twenty-first century skyline rises across Lady Bird Lake from Doug Sahm Hill. (Photo by Joe Nick Patoski.)

◉ ◉ ◉

Rather than relocate or face eviction from 1320 South Lamar due to escalating rent, the Saxon Pub was saved by Gary Keller, cofounder and CEO of the Austin-based Keller Williams Realty, who bought the property and offered Joe Ables, owner of the Saxon, a more affordable lease. Keller Williams, founded in Austin in 1983, was the world's largest real estate franchise by agent count, and its namesake happened to play a pretty mean acoustic guitar and collect vintage guitars when he wasn't moving properties. Keller saw that the wealth that had been created in Austin was negatively impacting landmarks like the Saxon as well as musicians.

Keller founded a nonprofit called All ATX to work with city leaders and address the affordability issue. "Advocacy is absolutely what's necessary," he said. "When you read the census, you can broadly define it into two categories: One is the issue of affordability, and the other issue is support."

◉ ◉ ◉

In the eyes of young native son Shakey Graves, the music scene had experienced the same paradigm shift as the city at large. But the scene remained contradictory enough to provide material to write and sing about. "Austin is the place where you'll have a shit-kicking cowboy decked out and wearing a bolo tie and a belt buckle and you'll be having a conversation about Wu-Tang Clan while he's passing you a joint," Graves explained to Esquire magazine. "You have people riding their horse to a bar to listen to music. You're allowed to do that here; they never changed the law. There's a guy called the Sixth Street Cowboy that really monopolizes that. He got arrested for drunk driving and took it to court, and won, because you can't drunk drive a horse—the horse isn't drunk."

Shakey Graves was the real deal. Otherwise, Willie Nelson wouldn't have let him sign his weathered Martin guitar, Trigger.

Speaking of the Devil, Ol' Will had matured into an institution unto himself. On April 20, 2012, at 4:20 p.m. at the corner of Willie Nelson Boulevard and Lavaca Street at the footsteps leading to the entrance of the ACL Live at the Moody Theater, a statue of Willie was unveiled. The eight-foot-tall bronze by sculptor Clete Shields depicted Willie in headband and pigtails, sitting on a stool, his left hand resting atop his guitar.

Willie's statue complemented the Stevie Ray Vaughan statue across Lady Bird Lake on Auditorium Shores adjacent to Doug Sahm Hill—two prominent sites visited by locals and out-of-towners seeking touchstones to the city's much vaunted but hard-to-pin-down music scene. Nelson was seventy-eight years old and showed few signs of slowing down. He'd stripped down the sound of his family band in the midnineties, around the time he was recording the albums *Spirit* at Pedernales Studios and the atmospheric *Teatro* produced by Daniel Lanois. Drummer Paul English switched from sticks to brushes, Sister Bobbie's piano went up in the mix, and for the first time in his post–*Red-Headed Stranger* career, you could hear Willie's distinctive picking style on the gut-strings of Trigger.

There were Medal of Arts and Presidential Achievement awards, the first celebrity endorsement of legal marijuana in Colorado and Washington state with his Willie's Reserve brand, weed duets with Merle Haggard, Snoop Dogg, and Kris Kristofferson ("It's All Gone to Pot" and "Roll Me Up and Smoke Me When I Die"), albums of new material and an album of Gershwin standards that won him another Grammy, movie roles, Fourth of July Picnics at the Circuit of the Americas racetrack, Farm Aid benefits, and sharing his adult sons Micah and Lukas with Neil Young, who hired them for his backup band.

Willie's bus, Honeysuckle Rose, was parked in its stall in the back of the W Hotel almost as much as it was on the road or out at Willie's place in Spicewood. The W, with its two performance theaters, satellite radio studios where Willie's Roadhouse channel on Sirius/XM broadcast, the Willie statue, and his annual multinight run leading up to New Year's Eve at ACL Live, was Willie's home away from home.

The statue of Stevie Ray Vaughan and Doug Sahm Hill were tributes to two musicians who left their marks on Austin and on music, and became institutions unto themselves too. Willie, you wanted to believe, would outlive his statue.

4
Austin City Limits

⊙ ⊙ ⊙

The band played like they always did, laying back to accommodate the singer's distinctive voice whenever he needed to carry a ballad, and then charging hard, full-tilt straight ahead whenever a song called for the whole ensemble to weigh in. The crowd sitting on the bleachers behind and flanking the stage could have just as well been at a honky-tonk. Most drank beer, many were smoking cigarettes, as was the custom in bars and beer joints, and a few were smoking marijuana.

It was just one of several hundred performances that year for Willie Nelson and Family. Only this wasn't a honky-tonk, a theater, or an open field improvised into an outdoor festival. This was the windowless television studio on the sixth floor of the rust-colored communications building fronting Guadalupe Street between Twenty-Fifth and Twenty-Sixth Streets.

For all the familiar elements of a gig, the band was standing on shaky ground: big television cameras on the floor and on the stage wheeled around the musicians while men and women wearing headphones scurried around the cameras, around the stage, and in the control booth in the back of the room, nervously but quietly. The activity around the players signaled this was something new and completely different. This was music on television.

Terry Lickona had been hearing about the music scene percolating out of Austin for quite awhile. When his friend Dan Del Santo, who played music and lived down the road in the bucolic Hudson Valley town of Poughkeepsie, seventy-eight miles north of New York City, suggested a road trip to check out what was going on down in Texas, the wiry-haired Lickona didn't need convincing. He was a disc jockey at WPDH-FM, a local radio station with a loose country music format, and had been spinning what seemed to be an inordinate number of new records by Austin musicians, including albums by Willie Nelson, Jerry Jeff Walker, Michael Murphey, Willis Alan Ramsey, Doug Sahm, and Asleep at the Wheel.

Terry Lickona and Dan Del Santo hit the road in late June 1974. Their destination was the Texas World Speedway, an automobile racetrack near Bryan, Texas, where Willie Nelson was staging his second Fourth of July Picnic with a bunch of his musical friends, most of them from Austin.

The idea of hearing music out in the wide-open spaces sounded good, but the reality was harsh. The Texas midsummer heat felt like a blast furnace to the New Yorkers. "The only shade I could find was from a chain link fence," Lickona laughed. Lickona and Del Santo stayed for most of the three-day festival nonetheless. Despite the brain-fry and residual effects of being surrounded by seventy-five thousand hippies and rednecks shit-faced drunk and stoned out of their gourds, they agreed it was a swell Texas music experience.

But they weren't done. They wanted to see the place where most of the music they'd witnessed on the stage of the racetrack was coming from. They escaped Willie's Picnic midday Sunday and drove west for an hour and a half to Austin. Cruising slow down East Sixth Street toward Congress Avenue, they heard the strains of an accordion over a bouncy polka rhythm. The sounds of Tex-Mex conjunto music were emanating from a small bar on the south side of the street. Lickona glanced over to Del Santo. Del Santo looked back at Lickona, eyebrows raised. They broke out into wide grins. They both knew music, but neither had ever heard music like this before. Nothing in Poughkeepsie sounded like that.

Lickona and Del Santo decided then and there they would to move to Austin. Lickona drove into Austin for keeps four months later, three weeks after Willie Nelson videotaped the pilot for a music series on the campus of the University of Texas. Lickona had four hundred dollars in his pocket. "I was going to get a job in radio," he laughed. "I figured I could make the rounds of the radio stations and someone would hire me. But KOKE and KVET weren't hiring. None of the stations were. Apparently there was a pool of RTF grads who didn't want to leave Austin and who would work for minimum wage." He joined the pool by talking his way into a part time gig at KUT-FM, the University of Texas's radio station, doing public affairs, a late night jazz show, and a bluegrass program.

Lickona had bought into the alternative Austin business model, doing something for all the "wrong" reasons (i.e., working on the cheap or for free to get to do what he wanted to do).

Video and music was already a thing in Austin. Austin Community Television, ACTV, the city's community access channel made possible by Capital Cable, the Lyndon Johnson family-owned cable television service to city households, offered video training sessions at the Armadillo World Headquarters in the early seventies. Students learned how to operate Sony

Portapak portable video cameras and recorders, a reel-to-reel setup attached to a handheld camera that one person could operate.

Mike Tolleson, the legal counsel for the Armadillo, had seen his first Portapak at a Rolling Stones concert at Hyde Park in London in 1969. He brought the idea back to Austin, shared it with pioneering video producer Bill Narum and others, and helped organize ACTV.

Once trained, video students made documentaries—many of them music-related. To broadcast their work, students trekked to the hill in West Lake Hills where television and radio broadcast towers were clustered, and plugged in their Portapak into a socket at the base of one of the towers. Cable being a new idea, community access channel viewers numbered in the hundreds, if that. Still, anyone could make a video and show it to viewers at home thanks to ACTV.

Austin Community Television would build a permanent studio on the east side, while the city added a nonprofit music channel to the local cable lineup. By the nineties, ACTV was generating more hours of original content than any single public access television channel outside of New York City, spawning numerous music and talk programs, including a flamboyant character known as Carmen Banana, and a spittle-spewing political conspiracy theorist with a booming voice named Alex Jones, who would use ACTV to launch an alt-right media empire.

The idea of music on television was hardly new. Music shows on national network television such as *Hullabaloo*, *Where the Action Is*, and *American Bandstand* had been programming staples during the sixties. Many local television stations across the United States broadcast shows featuring local teenagers dancing to popular music, including Austin, where Cactus Pryor hosted the *Now Hear This!* dance party on KTBC Channel 7. (Until 1970, Austin was the largest city in the United States with only one television station, a left-handed tribute to the station's president, Claudia Taylor Johnson, a.k.a. Lady Bird Johnson, who until 1968 was the First Lady of the United States. The Johnsons preferred not having competition.)

The advent of video technology that was accessible to anyone who wanted to use it, along with plenty of content to shoot—music, mainly—fostered a small video community. A group of Houston video enthusiasts headed by designer and poster artist Bill Narum set up shop in the small town of Taylor, thirty-four miles northeast of Austin, to run the TaylorVision cable service and provide the small operation with hours of videotaped concert footage from the Armadillo World Headquarters. The number of viewers in the farming community might have been counted on one hand, but the producers were mastering the craft of videotaping music.

Kinky Friedman and Willie Nelson acting like Kinky and Willie. (Photo by Will Van Overbeek.)

Leon Russell, at the time one of the biggest rock acts in the world, sent his newly formed video company ShelterVision to Austin to shoot musicians in clubs and outdoors. ShelterVision's footage was edited into the *Lone Star Cross Country Music Hour*, a music series sponsored by Lone Star Beer that aimed to air on eleven Texas television stations in 1975 while FM stations in each market simulcast the program. Willie Nelson performed and hosted. Acts who were filmed included Asleep at the Wheel, Kinky Friedman, Jerry Jeff Walker, B. W. Stevenson, Kenneth Threadgill, Jimmy Buffett, Willis Alan Ramsey, Ray Wylie Hubbard, Steve Fromholz, Rusty Wier, and Greezy Wheels. But funding for the series fell short, and all the episodes did not air.

The NBC television network filmed portions of Willie Nelson's second Fourth of July Picnic in 1974, airing segments on their *Midnight Special* music program hosted by the radio personality Wolfman Jack.

All this music-video development had not gone unnoticed by producer Bill Arhos at KLRN, the Public Broadcasting System educational television channel for San Antonio and Austin. Mike Tolleson and other Armadillo staff had already talked Arhos into supplying a crew and production gear to videotape a performance of the Armadillo Country Music Review roadshow starring Willie Nelson, Michael Murphey, Billy Joe Shaver, Greezy Wheels, D. K. Little, and Diamond Rio at the Armadillo World Headquarters. The performance aired on KRLN and was simulcast on FM radio stations in San Antonio and Austin.

Other PBS affiliates were broadcasting live music performances, including *Soundstage* from WTTW Chicago and *Boboquivari* from KQED in San Francisco. One music series, *The Session*, filmed at WSIU in Carbondale, Illinois, brought director Bruce Scaife to Austin.

Scaife was hired away from WFFA in Dallas, the biggest commercial television station in Texas, by KLRN in the summer of 1974. KLRN and most other Public Broadcasting System affiliates were airing fourteen episodes of *The Session* that summer, which Scaife had directed in 1971 while at WSIU. "There was a writer's strike going on and PBS was looking for already produced shows done by member stations that were good enough to air and fill their summer schedule," Scaife said. "It was one reason KLRN hired me."

Bill Arhos and Scaife hit it off. Both saw the potential to do music shows in the new studio in the University of Texas communications building. The PBS management had issued a call for more original programming from its affiliates. But Studio 6A, the largest soundstage between either coast, was sitting empty most of the time. *Carrascolendas*, a bilingual children's program, was the soundstage's only tenant. Content was needed to keep the studio busy.

"Bill asked me to think about something we could do that would show off their new capabilities and facilities that might attract national attention," Scaife said. "I was thinking about a music show from the start, but had no idea what it might be about."

Arhos posed the same question to another KLRN employee, Paul Bosner, who had been a cameraman for the CBS television network and an associate producer for a Miss America pageant. He'd been reading a lot about the Austin music scene and noticed it was getting national coverage from newspapers and magazines he subscribed to. When he read Jan Reid's *Improbable Rise of Redneck Rock* (1974), the light bulb above Bosner's head turned on.

"Paul came to me about the possibility we could do something together combining our two different backgrounds and experiences," Scaife said. "We watched a couple of my [*The Session*] shows, visited Soap Creek and the Armadillo, and met at Les Amis to mull over how we might put together an idea to present to Bill Arhos that KLRN could do with Paul producing and me directing."

Arhos didn't bite at first, but Scaife and Bosner kept at it. This redneck rock thing was a cultural happening and wouldn't last forever. And it was unique to Austin. Arhos eventually gave in, wrote a proposal, and carried it to station management. "Bob Schenkkan liked it," Scaife recalled. "Harvey Herbst hated it. It would be a huge undertaking and a too big a risk for KLRN." But Shenkkan and Arhos prevailed, and Bosner and Scaife were green-lighted by management to work on a pilot, committing twenty thousand dollars in funding, whether or not additional outside funding could be secured.

They would film performances in the new studio by Willie Nelson and B. W. Stevenson, a giant, bearded singer-songwriter with a penchant for overalls who had enjoyed two pop hit songs, "My Maria" and "Shambala." The audio of Stevenson's set was so full of glitches that his video performance was shelved. Willie Nelson ended up having the pilot all to himself.

Willie was good enough to use as a fundraiser for PBS stations, further elevating his profile and raising enough money for pledge drives early in 1975 to green-light thirteen episodes with a one hundred thousand dollar budget. Joe Gracey, the disc jockey at KOKE-FM, the Austin progressive country music radio station, was hired as talent coordinator.

Bosner named the show Austin City Limits. Scaife created the picture (i.e., the stage design, shooting plot, and logo). He took a straight-ahead, no-frills approach to capturing the performance, focusing on the players and little else. Arhos protected the production team from management and outside interference. And despite Bosner's embrace of The Improbable Rise of Redneck Rock, Joe Gracey searched beyond the Cosmic Cowboy stereotype for earthier, roots sounds.

The remaining members of the original Texas Playboys, the western swing band led by fiddler Bob Wills in the thirties, forties, and fifties, who were easily the most popular musicians associated with Texas during those decades, got together again for the television cameras. Modern western swing bands Asleep at the Wheel and Alvin Crow; ascendant singer-songwriters Townes Van Zandt, Steve Fromholz, and Bobby Bridger; and popular country-rock acts such as Jerry Jeff Walker and B. W. Stevenson all got face time. So did Clifton Chenier and his Red Hot Louisiana Band, one of the most dynamic live acts playing Austin on a regular basis. Ry Cooder, a Los Angeles guitar virtuoso who had been hanging around South Texas dancehalls learning the bajo sexto twelve-string guitar that accompanied the accordion in the Tex-Mex sound known as conjunto, joined accordion star Flaco Jimenez from San Antonio performing for the show.

At the end of season one, KLRN brass hemmed and hawed and wouldn't commit to a second season, prompting Bosner to accept an offer to take on a Shakespeare project in London. When the station finally relented and green-lighted a second season, Bruce Scaife stepped in for Bosner as the de facto producer (the titled producer, Howard Chalmers, "was of no use at all" according to Scaife) while continuing as director.

Scaife streamlined the show's opening. He came up with Gary P. Nunn's song "London Homesick Blues" to use as the show's theme, as sung by Nunn, one of the Lost Gonzo Band backing Jerry Jeff Walker in his season one ACL appearance.

Scaife departed at the end of season two. "I was trying to save my marriage, which was on the rocks," he said. The Scaifes had made six moves in ten years to get to Austin, and directing *Austin City Limits* had cut into domestic life. "I placed my family above my career," said Scaife, who moved to Colorado. "I sacrificed it all for a marriage that didn't work out anyhow."

Bill Arhos continued doing battle to keep *Austin City Limits* on the air. A new producer-director would be there right alongside him.

Since KUT-FM was located in the basement of the same communications building as Studio 6A, Terry Lickona couldn't ignore what was going on up on the sixth floor. "For the first three seasons, I soaked up this great music and drank beer at *Austin City Limits* tapings, usually with Dan Del Santo." Lickona got to know the people who worked on the program, volunteered to help, and eventually became assistant to the producer.

"Joe Gracey had booked talent for first two years, and was replaced by Craig Hillis for season three," Lickona said. Hillis booked many of the same acts his agency, Moon Hill Management, represented—Michael Murphey, Steve Fromholz, and Rusty Wier—effectively playing to the folkie in cowboy hat Austin music stereotype.

Austin City Limits producer Terry Lickona at work in Studio 6A. (Photo by Scott Newton.)

By the start of season four, most of the original production team had moved on.

"Nobody thought this would last more than a couple years," Lickona said. He talked his way into producing the series for 1978, even though he lacked an RTF degree and any deep broadcasting background. He'd simply been around long enough to understand how the show worked, and was a lot cheaper than importing a producer from Los Angeles and New York.

For his first season as producer, Lickona booked his old friend from Poughkeepsie, Dan Del Santo and his eclectic Professors of Pleasure big band; the Austin barrelhouse blues piano legend Robert Shaw; and Tex-Mex experimental accordionist Steve Jordan. He pushed for George Jones, the hardcore country traditionalist from Southeast Texas who was arguably country's greatest vocalist, but others on the staff pushed back. George Jones was too old school. Higher-ups wanted more Willie Nelsons and young Texas singer-songwriters. Except, there was only one Willie Nelson, and even though singer-songwriters in Austin seemed to be a dime a dozen, the best ones had already been featured.

For a long stretch, Lickona juggled to balance the hour-long show with a mainstream country Nashville act and an Austin act. Arhos found himself defending the show from locals who called his program *Nashville City Limits*. The appearances of Hank Williams Jr., Holly Dunn, Razzy Bailey, Alabama, Larry Gatlin, Chet Atkins, Janie Fricke, the Judds, Gary Morris, Lee Greenwood, Diamond Rio, Wynonna, and Suzy Bogguss made it difficult to refute the point.

The Nashville tie-in eventually faded in favor of a broader range of acts with an emphasis on honest roots music, reflecting the sounds coming out of Austin clubs. The rest of the country started tuning in.

Through the eighties into the nineties, the scope of the music presented on *Austin City Limits* grew in sophistication and star power. Heavyweights were more than happy to get paid the standard television appearance fee in exchange for the nationwide exposure on a show that pretty much left the performance to the performer.

Lickona's hand was evident in the appearances of the song poet Leonard Cohen, Houston blues songster Lightnin' Hopkins, rhythm and blues avatar Ray Charles, blues guitarist B. B. King, the Neville Brothers, Dr. John and Fats Domino from New Orleans, the jam bands Phish and Widespread Panic, the rock band Little Feat, roots giants Los Lobos, folk goddess Joan Baez, dada rockers the Flaming Lips, and the Allman Brothers Band.

Complementing the national acts were Austin-affiliated performers such as Lyle Lovett, Nanci Griffith, Steve Earle, the LeRoi Brothers, Stevie Vaughan, Lucinda Williams, Eric Johnson, Delbert McClinton, Robert Earl Keen, Fastball, Spoon, Junior Brown, and Little Joe y La Familia.

By the early 2000s, global acts such as David Byrne, the Buena Vista Social Club, Ladysmith Black Mambazo, Juanes, Radiohead, Rodrigo y Gabriela, Van Morrison, Manu Chao, and Sufjan Stevens were ACL's bread-and-butter. Artistically, the television program had scaled up and gone wide in its mission to showcase more kinds of different music from around the world. But financially, Austin City Limits was skating on thin ice, as it had been since the very start. Every season's future seemed in doubt at the start of each season. At the last minute, a sponsor would materialize to assure another year of ACL shows.

A stud bicycle racer and new digs would fix that.

The sight of more than one hundred thousand party people jamming Auditorium Shores on the south bank of Town Lake and filling the surrounding streets looked fairly awesome to the cyclist at the center of all the attention. From where he stood, the mass was one big sea of yellow jerseys, with bicycles in every direction. The scene was sort of incongruous since no one in Texas ever got too excited about a cycling competition in faraway France. But the local bicycle racer had just won his third consecutive Tour de France, the world's premier cycling event, and his hometown was responding by going nuts.

The slight, elegantly sculpted young man being feted felt elation, validation, and vindication all at once. Lance Armstrong, cycling champion and cancer survivor, had pulled off the impossible: beating testicular cancer and training up to become the best and most famous cyclist in the world, all while fending off accusations he couldn't have done it without doping.

There was music and dancing in the streets. The crowd cheered "Lance! Lance! Lance!" as Armstrong raised his arms triumphantly, a scene that was broadcast on television around the world. The city had a new one-name superstar to stand next to Willie. Austin never looked so inviting.

You could say Austin was primed for the arrival of the sandy-haired kid from Plano in 1989, as much as the kid was primed for Austin. At the suburban high school he attended north of Dallas, football was everything. A student competing in triathlons and bicycle races was considered, well, exotic, if not a freak. So he didn't mind spending part of his senior year training in Colorado with the US Olympic development cycling team, preparing for the Sprint Triathlon National Championships, which he would win later that fall for his first national title, while planning his exit from Plano. "The day after I graduated, I had a U-Haul loaded up, and headed south," Armstrong said.

Austin was the only place to go. Plano was flat. Austin had hills. Austin offered the best cycling network of nearby rural farm-to-market and ranch roads in the region. "Austin was good, certainly better than Dallas-Fort Worth," he said. "It wasn't Colorado or Northern California where the riding was epic," but he lacked the money to move out of state. Besides, Austin was only three hours away from his mother, Linda, a divorcee who lived alone in Plano.

"We'd done training camps and races in and around Austin but I didn't know a lot," Armstrong admitted. "I didn't know anybody except for one buddy who went to UT. I didn't know where the fuck I'd go riding. I didn't know where to eat. I just did it."

He found a small bungalow on a hidden stretch of Shoal Creek Boulevard between MLK and Enfield Streets for three hundred dollars a month—"a 'bro' deal," he explained. He found a place to eat four blocks down Lamar Boulevard at the corner of Tenth Street: the very first Whole Foods Market.

"I'd walk down there and have lunch at Martin Brothers (the coffee shop/café/ice cream parlor built inside the Whole Foods). Have the same thing every time—once I get onto something, I don't change—soft chicken and black bean taco with a side salad and salad dressing. They made these great mango smoothies. I'd have my lunch, buy my groceries, and walk home up Lamar."

Lance Armstrong had tapped into an enlightened food source that could satisfy his training needs. Right place. Right time.

The eighteen year old found plenty to amuse himself too. He was less than a mile from Liberty Lunch on Second Street and the Black Cat on Sixth Street, which became his two regular music hangs.

The Black Cat, which opened in 1985, operated by different rules than most clubs, in a thoroughly contrarian Austin kind of way. Fashioned out of an alleyway with barely a semblance of a roof, the club was lowdown, just the way owner Paul Sessums and his family intended. The draw was good live bands and cheap beer. The crowd that was cultivated with that policy included a good number of bikers, skinheads, and extreme punks, guaranteeing an edge to any evening. The place didn't have a phone. Beers were no more than three dollars. Hot dogs were free.

Black Cat bands were paid with a very sophisticated tip jar/bucket pulley system that swung above the crowd. If the audience dug the band, the bucket filled fast and frequently. If the crowd didn't approve of the music, it showed in a light bucket. Two Hoots and a Holler, a three-piece high-powered rock-abilly outfit led by Ricky Broussard, packed the place with six hundred fans every week, even though their draw outside the Black Cat was marginal.

The Black Cat turned Lance into a hardcore fan of the band Soulhat, an organic, funky jam band that featured front man Kevin McKinney and the drummer Barry "Frosty" Smith, who'd relocated from California after playing with Lee Michaels and Funkadelic.

Cycling, Lance Armstrong said, "was just a local scene. There were a bunch of riders, and there was this weekly race every Tuesday night, six o'clock, southeast part of town." Fifty-six miles round trip. No rules, no judges, just cycling.

"The first people I met in Austin were people I met on that ride," Armstrong said. "That's where I met Bart Knaggs, who became my business manager. I realized he was a nice guy, smart guy, good rider." But there was no real competition. "Nobody came out of the Tuesday Nighter and went on to any international success," Armstrong said. He was the exception. A year after arriving in Austin, he was recognized as the US national amateur cycling champion, beating numerous professionals to win two major cycling races.

Armstrong competed in multistage races internationally and represented the United States in the 1992 Olympics in Barcelona, Spain, finishing fourteenth in the road race competition. After the Olympics, he turned pro, winning three major US races in 1993, and then winning the 161 mile World Road Race Championship in Norway—the youngest winner ever and only the second American to do it.

The Norway race got the attention of Armstrong's adopted hometown. "The cycling community was like, 'The world's champion lives here, this is amazing!'" Armstrong said. "The Statesman even wrote about it."

Armstrong would win the Tour DuPont in 1995 and 1996 and race for the US Olympic team again in 1996. He was ranked number one cyclist in the world with a $2.5 million annual contract to race, a Porsche to drive, and a million-dollar mansion west of the city on Lake Austin. But a noncycling event was bigger news that year. Armstrong was diagnosed with testicular cancer, which had spread to his abdomen, lungs, lymph nodes, and brain. He was treated aggressively for the disease. Instead of a dead man walking, he beat all odds and was declared cancer-free in February 1997. As Armstrong resumed training, the Livestrong Foundation was created to raise awareness, combat cancer, and beat the disease. The response surprised Armstrong. "That was the first time the city was like, 'One of our guys is sick, one of our guys has a problem, let's rally.'"

At that point, Armstrong and Austin officially became an item. "I was in an outcast sport, where I came from. But me and the city, we kind of grew together."

The romance reached the hot-and-bothered stage when Armstrong won the most prestigious multiple stage competition in the world, the Tour de France, in 1999. Lance was Austin's dude.

He had been blessed with an oversized heart and a lung capacity that separated him from mere mortals, and he'd just beat the cancer that could have just as well killed him. "People were like, 'Huh? The guy who was sick two years ago won the Tour de France?'" Armstrong said. "It was a big deal for this city. We didn't have the Cowboys. We didn't have the Spurs. We've got UT, the football team. Outside of that, there wasn't a sports institution to cheer for. My story became like this team that they adopted and cheered for and invested in."

With his bright eyes, chiseled features, and buff frame, Armstrong was the perfect face for the steroidal boomtown that high tech was supercharging, driving the area population over one million. He spoke the cool kids' lingo, hung out in the clubs digging music, and enjoyed representing the city. He talked the archconservative Texas legislature out of a bill that would have banned cyclists on rural Texas roads. He inspired a global fashion trend with yellow Livestrong wristbands representing his cancer foundation, which surpassed the four million dollar mark in funds raised. He was the highest paid public speaker in the United States, fetching more than a hundred thousand dollars per speech.

Armstrong had been feted with a parade that began at the state capitol after his first Tour de France win in 1999. Afterward, he admitted, "I don't like the idea of just sitting there and [smiling and waving to the crowd]." Being passive was for someone else.

He passed up having another parade after winning the Tour de France again in 2000 because he was training for the Olympics. But following the third consecutive Tour de France victory in 2001, Armstrong let city officials know that he'd prefer something more in tune with Austin's reputation, rather than another parade through downtown. "I love live music, rock and roll," he said. "How 'bout we do a big concert, a big party?"

Six days after Armstrong's third Tour de France win, Auditorium Shores had transformed into the Lance Armstrong rock festival, the streets lined with fans holding "Lance de Triomphe" and "Vive Le Lance" signs. Armstrong flew into Austin on Air Force One, accompanied by the president of the United States after spending the previous day at the White House visiting

George W. Bush, whom Armstrong got to know when Bush was the bicycle-riding governor of Texas.

In a sport dominated by Europeans, three consecutive wins put Lance Armstrong in a zone of his own. No American had done that.

He did not stop at three. It was four Tour de France victories in row in 2002, then five, six, and seven consecutive wins, each an unprecedented achievement.

Every Tour de France victory translated into another bigger, better hometown party, which in turn grew into major civic events. "I much preferred having these concerts," Armstrong said, even though the music was still preceded by a parade. "We did five of them," he said. "As it grew and grew, it got to the point that we closed down Congress Avenue."

The Lance Armstrong victory parties launched careers and saved an Austin institution. Promoter Charlie Jones got his gig producing the Lance celebrations through his MiddleMan Music production company. The College Station native had come to Austin from Howard Payne University in Brownwood in 1990. His dream of being a professional baseball player had ended when he was kicked off the college team for running through a girls' dormitory in his jockstrap. He took a job waiting tables at Pappadeaux's and took a life-changing course at Austin Community College on concert promotion, taught by Austin jazz musician and promoter Mike Mordecai.

Jones hired on with Tim O'Connor, the Willie Nelson protégé who was Austin's biggest independent promoter, starting as an intern answering phones in 1993. O'Connor's Direct Events controlled the 3,000 capacity Austin Music Hall downtown and its smaller neighbor, the 1,400 capacity La Zona Rosa, and the brand new 3,500 capacity Backyard amphitheater near Lake Travis, built on 13 oak-studded acres on the edge of the Hill Country.

After learning the ropes, Jones started MiddleMan Music, getting his baptism by fire stepping in at the last minute to produce Austin's New Year's Eve A2K street celebration on December 31, 1999. The event featured two stages on Congress Avenue with a full slate of Austin favorites, including Lyle Lovett, Miss Lavelle White, Little Joe y La Familia, Kelly Willis, and Robert Earl Keen.

A2K attracted a quarter-million celebrants and was pulled off with a minimum of hitches. That led to Jones scoring the promoter gig for the Lance Armstrong victory concert party at Auditorium Shores in 2001. The Lance celebration ran so smoothly that Charlie Jones was invited to join Bill Stapleton and Bart Knaggs, Lance's business reps. Their business, Capital Sports Ventures, became Capital Sports and Entertainment. It was no longer just Bill and Bart managing Lance. The addition of Jones signaled interest in concert production and music festivals. With shows like the ones Jones produced on Congress Avenue and at Auditorium Shores, how awesome would it be to do an all-day festival in Zilker Park?

Jones and Charles Attal, the promoter who booked Stubb's and other venues, addressed that hypothetical. Both agreed Austin was primed for an annual festival in the fall, similar to the New Orleans Jazz and Heritage Festival every spring. Jones and Attal also agreed that the only thing better than an Austin music festival at Zilker Park would be an Austin music festival with an Austin name—a brand that everyone knew, like the Austin City Limits Festival.

Bart Knaggs and Bill Stapleton at Capital Sports and Entertainment approached the board that oversaw the *Austin City Limits* television show with their festival proposal, signaling they would commit substantial financial resources to make it happen. Some of the more hidebound board members were not so enthusiastic. "You had some old-school board members at *Austin City Limits* who were against it," Lance Armstrong said. "There was always friction. 'How long do we give them the name for?' 'What is it worth?' 'What does that do for our brand?'"

If the Willie/Waylon ACL traditionalists weren't buying in, just about everyone else was. The television series was in danger of going away altogether. Funding and sponsorships were perennially meager. Capital Sports and Entertainment didn't want to just license the *Austin City Limits* name to produce a festival; they were ready to invest a million dollars in new equipment and upgrades to the television show.

That was music to Terry Lickona's ears. "They came to us to use our name," the ACL producer said. "By using our name, they were able to book acts they otherwise wouldn't have gotten. It enabled them to make a deal with the city, secure Zilker Park. But they weren't just licensing the name or the brand to the festival. They wanted to invest in the brand, make the show bigger, more marketable, convert to high definition."

CSE's offer was accepted. *Austin City Limits* would license its name for a musical festival in Zilker Park. In exchange, the Capital Sports and Entertainment partners provided the wherewithal to upgrade the television series and assure some kind of future. "They gave us the resources to do that," Lickona said. "That finally brought us financial stability. Up till then, it was Fly by the Seat of Your Pants. There was a stretch through the nineties when our budget was frozen for ten years."

In the short span of three months during the summer of 2002, Charlie Jones and Charlie Attal sketched out, assembled, and staged the first Austin

City Limits Music Festival over a two-day weekend in September. Sixty-seven bands, including String Cheese Incident, Pat Green, Wilco, Los Lobos, and Emmylou Harris, performed on five stages. The reunited Arc Angels— young rockers Charlie Sexton and Doyle Bramhall Jr. with Chris Layton and Tommy Shannon, the Stevie Ray Vaughan Double Trouble rhythm section (a personal favorite of Lance Armstrong's)—reunited to headline the fest.

Twenty-five thousand ticket buyers were anticipated, but the two Charlies and Knaggs, Stapleton, and Armstrong at Capital Sports and Entertainment started sweating bullets when only seven hundred tickets had been sold a month before the event. They shouldn't have worried.

The actual crowd count for the two-day event exceeded forty-two thousand at twenty-five bucks a ticket. Lance Armstrong introduced most of the acts, including the Arc Angels.

The crowd count increased to sixty thousand for the second ACL Fest in 2003, which was spread over three days instead of two, and featured one hundred bands for the all-inclusive sixty-five dollar price.

An even larger crowd of seventy-five thousand attending the third ACL Fest in 2004 forced a capacity limit after neighbors living near Zilker Park complained. Part of the price for using the city's most popular public park for a month, factoring in setup and teardown, was CSE's investment restoring the park to prefest conditions, and adding improved turf to what would now be known as Zilker Park's Great Lawn.

Charlie Jones continued producing the Lance victory concerts with Charles Attal. The shows were becoming a much-anticipated annual event in Austin following each Tour de France win. The celebration of Armstrong's sixth consecutive victory on August 13, 2004, started with a parade from the state capitol down Congress Avenue, with Lance leading the way on his custom Trek bike flanked by the mayor and the local congressmen on their bikes. That preceded the main event—a free concert on a yellow-colored mega stage facing Congress Avenue.

Texas musician Robert Earl Keen delivered a rousing, raucous set, followed by Lance Armstrong addressing the gathering of seventy-five thousand. "This vibe is a little different than Alpe d' Huez," he said to the crowd, "but this is the greatest town in the whole world." Armstrong and his girlfriend, the pop singer Sheryl Crow, later joined headliner Steve Miller onstage for the song "The Joker." Yellow was the color of the evening. The dome of the Texas state capitol was bathed in bright yellow light, as was the crowd on Congress Avenue.

Armstrong's relationship with Sheryl Crow, a very public high-profile affair that began in 2003, cemented his celebrity. The couple was engaged in 2005 and enjoyed multiple victory smooches under the Arc de Triomphe before breaking up in February 2006 after Crow was diagnosed with breast cancer.

Charlie Jones formalized his partnership with Charles Attal, and with Charlie Walker, who had worked for LiveNation, the biggest concert promoter in the United States, to form C3 Presents in 2007, which would become the Austin City Limits Festival's production company.

The organization quickly expanded to promote and produce a revived version of the Chicago-based Lollapalooza Festival, as well as Lollapaloozas in Brazil, Argentina, and Chile. The Chicago Lollapalooza operated so efficiently, a local candidate for the president of the United States named Barack Obama hired C3 Presents to produce Obama's campaign events and his election night victory celebration in Chicago's Grant Park in 2008. Following his election, President Obama used C3 Presents to produce his inauguration and parade, and major public events.

"We had no idea," Armstrong said. Capital Sports and Entertainment had invested wisely.

ACL Fest further burnished Austin's reputation as a live music hub. The various ways music was being presented and consumed had scaled up from two hundred seat clubs to outdoor spaces accommodating seventy-five thousand. Even with those numbers, most wristband holders could actually see most of the music they wanted to see, albeit from several hundred yards away.

The success of the Austin City Limits Festival provided *Austin City Limits*, the longest-running music series on television, with the resources to move off-campus into new, plush digs in 2011. A studio/theater was built into the W Hotel high-rise at Second and Lavaca Streets downtown. ACL Live at the Moody Theater immediately generated buzz as the place in Austin to hear live music.

"It's as good for a live music experience as it gets," Lickona said. "We sweated bullets for five years while we were designing it. We wanted to keep the experience intimate, and it's the same size footprint as [the original] Studio 6A. So we maintained the vibe, and expanded it vertically."

Studio 6A in the University of Texas communications building had been constructed as a soundstage for television. Accommodating an audience was an afterthought, which made performances feel and look intimate. The Moody featured three tiers of seating, every seat with a direct sightline to the stage. Somehow, despite being the same size as the old studio, the room felt bigger, and the stage more distant.

The Moody was modern, sleek, and minimalist, meaning no more cheap seats. The view from the mezzanine patio outside the theater was Urban-Suburban Anywhere—a cluster of tall, shiny skyscrapers, every building in sight, including the Tex-futuro City Hall across the street, built in the past twenty-five years. The only exception was the two-story mustard brick J. P. Schneider & Bros. building at the southwest corner of Second and Guadalupe that housed Lambert's Downtown Barbecue.

For all its obvious attributes, the Moody Theater, as ACL Live was formally known, was neither funky nor soulful. That was the Austin of the Armadillo World Headquarters and Liberty Lunch. This was a whole other Austin.

The philosophy of presenting as wide a range of acts as possible for ACL Fest mirrored the television series. The Cosmic Cowboy one-trick pony had become lost in the crowd. The "going home to the Armadillo" *Austin City Limits* theme song, "London Homesick Blues" by Gary P. Nunn, was replaced by "Travis County Jail," an upbeat blues-rocker with an earworm-worthy chorus by Gary Clark Jr., the Austin-raised guitarist who'd just turned thirty.

"You can only imagine how long we've heard that phrase 'home with the Armadillo,'" Lickona said, rolling his eyes. "The show is more eclectic. We didn't want to be stereotyped as a regional music show."

Example A was the hip-hop superstar Kendrick Lamar, who bounced around the elevated stage, working both ends of the proscenium and claiming the space in between as his turf, as the floor below moved in an organic swell, ebbing and flowing, heads bobbing to the beats. Capturing the transcendent moment were two giant pedestal cameras on the floor and a handheld camera and two-person crane camera onstage—all trained on different elements of the musical assemblage, but mostly on the singer. Lamar, one of the biggest acts in show business, could have easily played the 14,000-seat Erwin Center arena for two nights, or packed the even larger amphitheater at the Circuit of the Americas racetrack southeast of the city by the airport. Instead, he opted for the Moody Theater downtown that could accommodate 2,750 fans max, many of them bunched up around the stage, experiencing Kendrick Lamar in close to ideal performance conditions. Despite the full house, there were plenty of restrooms and bars to choose from, lines were short, and the air conditioning worked great.

The rap music that Lamar's sound was built on used to be considered the antithesis of what *Austin City Limits* was about. Now it was being enthusiastically embraced. In the spirit of synergy, Lamar would be booked as one of the headliners for the following year's ACL Fest.

"It's not a show anymore," Terry Lickona said about *Austin City Limits* not too long after the television program's fortieth anniversary show from the

Moody Theater aired nationally. "It's a brand, and it's stronger than ever, by any standard. It wasn't our goal to be curator of such a wide strata of music." It just worked out that way.

The technical approach remained no frills and traditional: Cameras on musicians, lingering on front person and solos. Let the musicians play. Don't get in their way. No tricks or funny stuff. "Our direction style hasn't changed," Lickona said. "We've held true to the original template."

As an old-timer still at the top of his game forty years after he started, Terry Lickona made a point of looking forward instead of back. He refused to wax cynical. "I'm not negative about Austin today. I don't dwell on the past. I'm not fixated on the bygone days of the seventies, the eighties, or the nineties. If I was, I wouldn't enjoy what I do today. I continue going out, even if there aren't too many of the old places left, like Antone's. I've never married. I don't have a family. My friends' ages range from their early twenties to their sixties and beyond. When I go out, I'm usually with my younger friends, and we'll go to places I wasn't familiar with."

What Lickona was seeing made him optimistic. "I'm working with a kid through Grammy U, which mentors young people interested in careers in music or the music business, who is a budding Charles Attal. He's putting shows together on a shoestring where he'll combine slam poetry with music and standup comedy. He puts up posters online, and promotes aggressively and is drawing crowds. Tonight he's doing a DJ scratch-off at Red 7. I'm still not completely tuned into that scene. It's not my thing, but I might go to see what he's doing."

Bands remained a cultural force, but trying to make a living playing music was more of an economic struggle than ever, Lickona acknowledged. Music was returning to its previous iteration as a hobby requiring dedication and commitment, rather than a career. "I've got several friends waiting tables at different restaurants to pay the rent and make ends meet who have a band thing on the side, or are recording in someone's studio, or recording at Music Tech where they're taking classes, or in their living room or garage," Lickona said. "Some of the music they're doing is really fascinating. It's out there. There are people out there doing that. Their obsession is to be creative.

"This one kid who's from Mexico City originally, he lets anybody get up on stage and play. He won't even ask if they're musicians; he just lets them get up and do their thing. Sometimes toward the end of a set, he disassembles his drum kit and hands the pieces out to the audience, and lets people join in. If you're there, it's kind of a crazy scene. Now he's got a little following and he's played more shows, and honed the band down to an actual core group of musicians, instead of opening it up to anybody off the street. The music and the people who are creating it seem to have a broader mix of interests."

To folks of a certain age and disposition, Austin continued to offer whatever it was they were looking for. "Some of these younger musicians may have only been here for two or three years," Terry Lickona said. "They were drawn here for their own reasons, like I was, and like you and others were over the years, and they still feel that same sense of community, or that same spirit, that same synergy—OK, I had to use that word—and the ability to collaborate with other people, and get up on a stage and play and not even know if it's any good, or if anybody's going to like it, but just kind of work it out, over time."

The alternative Austin business model still worked. "It's continuing with younger people I know who are committed to staying in Austin and do what they do, be creative artistically," Lickona said. "They're barely getting by. People talk about the cheap rent and cheap pot in Austin in the seventies. People were still scraping by to pay rent. And the ditch weed from Mexico wasn't that good.

"It's not a great business model, as businesses go. But it's sustainable, as long as your expectations aren't great and you don't feel the need for many creature comforts. It's still inspiring for a lot of people. I don't know what it's like in Seattle, Portland, or anywhere else, but I don't think [those cities have] quite the same sense of community or inspiration that motivates people to want to create, to focus on that, instead of 'Fuck it, I can't do this, I gotta get a job or leave.'"

The Austin City Limits Festival grew bigger than the television series that branded it.

In 2015 LiveNation, the biggest concert promoters in the world, paid $125 million dollars to acquire a 51 percent share of C3 Presents, the promoters seeded by Lance Armstrong to create ACL Fest. The three Charlies would never have to work again, if they didn't want to work.

Festivals were the thing now, not clubs, more evidence of Austin's scaling up. ACL Fest expanded to two weekends in 2012. Residents living near the park complained of festival fatigue and demanded the city return the space to its original intended use as a park. But the crowds kept coming. A whole lot of them had seen *Austin City Limits*. Now they wanted to see for themselves.

5
Whole Foods Market

◉ ◉ ◉

This was the grocery of dreams. Everything you ever wanted, plus lots of stuff you never knew you wanted, until now. Walking into the eighty thousand square foot space for the first time was like seeing Disney World the first time as a five year old, only with the informed palate of an adult. The lights, sounds, smells(!), and feel turned the typically mundane chore of shopping for food into a sensuous experience packed with adventure, fun, even romance. Everything looked beautiful: an illuminated rainbow of picture-perfect produce never kissed by the mist of chemicals: the asparagus tips, the celery stalks, the organic Fujis, the dozens of varieties of mushrooms, most of them cultivated locally, everything perfectly arranged. Some items in the seafood display were so fresh, they twitched.

There was a state-of-the-art butchery with grain-fed and grass-fed beef, a state-of-the-art bakery with brick oven, and state-of-the-art chocolate enrobing fountain to dip whatever food item you pleased in a vat of liquid chocolate.

Samples beckoned in all directions. Cheese vault, walk-in beer alley, tea bar, kombucha on tap, coffee bar, juice bar, salad bar, sushi bar, ramen bar, wine bar, made-to-order breakfast taco bar (on spelt tortillas, if you wish), walk-in ice cream freezer, and prepared global fare with the Indian selections almost as extensive as the Mexican. There was something for vegans, the gluten-free, the lactose-intolerant, the peanut-free, and for other specific diets. Carnivores could chow down on authentic Texas barbecued beef brisket that had been slow-smoked for fifteen hours. An open-air patio invited lingering under a shade tree after a meal, at least when the patio wasn't being used as a skating rink or for a music concert.

This was not shopping at your parents' supermarket. This was pleasurable epicurean consumerism at its healthiest and finest. This was eye candy that was good for you. This was entertainment, a destination—Food Mecca.

John Mackey appeared relaxed and vaguely satisfied, as much as a driven type A individual running a company with close to a hundred thousand employees could be satisfied. He knew his job was never done. He was always on a quest.

Wearing a light jacket over a green polo shirt with the company logo and a shiny round employee button attached, he could have easily been mistaken for a team leader maybe, or a vendor. But CEO? Well, if you thought about it long enough, maybe he did look the part, in an Austin casual kind of way. A blunt talker, Mackey carried himself in the direct, straightforward manner of a general or commander. But sometimes he couldn't help himself. He was a hippie at heart. As he measured out a scoop of grain from a bulk barrel bin for the cameras, he gazed around the premises—*his child*—and positively beamed. "With this store, we're pioneering a new lifestyle that synthesizes health and pleasure," he confidently declared to the reporter from *USA Today* on opening day of his grocery's flagship store. "We don't see a contradiction."

Whole Foods Market had come a long way since its inception twenty-five years earlier. The same day that the Armadillo World Headquarters closed, December 31, 1980, John Mackey and his business partners, Craig Weller, Mark Skiles, and Renee Lawson, were sifting through the numbers for the first Christmas season of their business, which had opened that September.

Whole Foods Market had altered how Austin and the nation ate.

When it came to food, Austin had been pretty much like any other medium-size city of a quarter-million not on the East or West Coasts. It was a meat-and-potatoes town, with a few local twists—namely, an abundance of Tex-Mex, or Texas-style Mexican cuisine, food cart vendors around the campus of the University of Texas, a natural food collective/restaurant near campus called Sattva, where students could have an edible vegetarian lunch of brown rice and soy sauce and soup for a dollar, and a scattering of small independent health food stores.

Cheap informed the palate. The Stallion Drive-In, which did not have curb service, featured a not-too-impressive chicken-fried steak plate, a gristly patty of ground beef covered with batter and white-orange colored gravy, accompanied by fries and a sliver of iceberg lettuce with a mini-chunk of a tomato, for one dollar. A Hobo Plate consisting of a taco, beans, and lettuce at Hector's Taco Flats ("Over One Million Returned"), a duct-taped outdoor dive down and across Lamar Boulevard from the Stallion, went for the same price. Hector Alvarado, a native of the Rio Grande Valley, was all about cheap, serving pitchers of Shiner for seventy-nine cents with live bands playing for no cover.

Eggrolls, two for a dollar, from one of the carts on Guadalupe Street across from the University of Texas campus, was about as cheap as it got in Austin.

If Austin dining had an attribute adjective, "earthy" would suffice. The Les Amis Café coffee shop at the corner of Twenty-Fourth and San Antonio, one block from the UT campus, was as authentically bohemian as a coffee shop/hangout was supposed to be, not for the food but for the quirky, quasi-communal staff, notorious for working topless in the kitchen during hot spells in the summer. Dirty's, the shorthand name for Martin's Kum-Bak Place, a white clapboard burgers-and-beer institution on Guadalupe Street dating to 1926, was known for its well-seasoned griddle, which turned out some of the best burgers on earth, and for its staff, beginning with car hop Doc Mallard, who started working at Dirty's in 1947, and eternal familiars Wesley and Marge.

Nothing Strikes Back, an ice cream parlor in a second-story walkup on the Drag (Guadalupe Street) facing campus, was all about atmosphere, with splashed day-glo paint and day-glo posters covering its black interior walls illuminated with black lights and accompanied by psychedelic music. "Please allow 60 seconds for visual decompression," advised a sign posted at the entrance.

Virginia's Café was one-woman home-cookin' operation on South First Street renowned for its proprietor's Southern-style lunches and her stubborn refusal to be helped or assisted by her customers. The Night Hawk earned its rep as the local version of the modern formica-ed coffee shop-restaurant that would have passed for a Bob's or a Kip's in another city if not for its signature grilled Top Chop't chopped sirloin plate, and yeast rolls. The Hoffbrau Steakhouse on West Sixth Street, Austin's oldest steak joint, established in 1934, was the place for inexpensive griddle-fried T-bones and other steak cuts—a concept that inspired imitators in Dallas and Houston. The Tavern at Twelfth and North Lamar, established a year before the Hoffbrau at the end of Prohibition, attracted a beer and burger crowd. Jake's, one block south of the Hoffbrau on West Fifth Street, was the go-to joint for fried oysters in a basket. Hardcore seafood eaters stuck with Quality Seafood fish market on Airport Boulevard.

Before 1980, dining out decisions frequently came down to where to eat Mexican: El Rancho or El Mat downtown, Carmen's La Tapatia, Cisco's, Joe's Bakery, or El Azteca to the east, or El Gallo south of the river. El Patio, President Johnson's family's favorite Mexican restaurant, north of the university, served saltine crackers as well as tortilla chips as complimentary starters, a custom that attracted curiosity seekers. The industrial "truck stop" enchilada plate heavy on the beef chili gravy was the star entrée at the Dart

Bowl. When variety was called for, Vikashmo's Italian-Mexican menu would do just fine. Green Pastures, in a two-story historic home on a South Austin estate, claimed the dress-up fancy crowd for whom fine dining meant roast beef, cotillion rolls, cheese rosettes, and Texas pecan balls, accompanied by milk punch. Regulars patronized the Holiday House burger restaurant for Charley the Alligator, the tropical fish tank, and the totem poles out front as much as for the char-broiled hamburgers.

Exotic cuisine in Austin was the Bob Armstrong Dip at El Rancho, traditional Tex-Mex chile con queso jazzed up with ground beef. Movers and shakers in Austin, such as they were, and meaning mostly UT athletes or coaches and the occasional governor, frequented Janie and Matt Martinez's Tex-Mex fiefdom spread over two buildings on East First Street, a block east of Wilbur Clark's Crest Hotel, where the Four Seasons is now. A meal at El Rancho concluded with a complimentary sherbet or pecan praline candy, and a handshake with Matt Martinez, who often as not stood sentry at the entrance.

The night Leon Russell accompanied Willie Nelson and his family to dinner at El Rancho marked a tectonic shift in the Austin celebrity pecking order, such as it was. Heads turned and the buzzing from tables grew louder among the already loud clientele of the Always Good restaurant. This was even bigger than Coach Royal coming in for his usual Mexican fix.

Barbecue offerings spanned House Park BBQ, a lunch joint six blocks west of the capitol established in 1943, Jerry Jones's Pit BBQ on Barton Springs Road, several locations of The Pit, and Sam's and 3M on the African American east side. Otherwise, you took a road trip to the small towns of Lockhart, Luling, Elgin, Taylor, Coupland, or Llano for real Texas barbecue.

The three recognized basic food groups of Texas—Tex-Mex, chicken-fried steak, and barbecue—were very much the backbone of Austin cuisine. "Cutting edge" was a term reserved for knives.

Several restaurants significantly expanded Austin's culinary girth in the seventies. The Old Pecan Street Café at 314 East Sixth Street was the first modern eatery on that storied entertainment strip, serving steaks, sandwiches, crepes, quiches, and desserts along with drinks in a spacious high-ceilinged room with hardwood floors and exposed limestone walls—a look that would define the interiors of the refurbished Victorian commercial buildings on the street. Old Pecan Street was followed by the short-lived Alana's Bluebonnet, which aimed for a finer dining experience (chicken-fried steak was reinvented as "pan-fried tenderloin of beef") that was simultaneously understated and sophisticated, and by the Paradise Café, the city's first fern bar.

Two Austin dining traditions away from downtown began in 1975. Clarksville, the former slave quarter in Old West Austin that was one of modern Austin's first neighborhoods to gentrify, was the unlikely location for Jeffrey's, a small café owned by Ron and Peggy Weiss and Jeffrey Weinberg that offered the finest dining experience of any Austin restaurant in a determinedly casual, intimate setting of an old storefront.

A few miles further north, a Mexican hacienda appeared in a residential neighborhood on North Loop Boulevard. Fonda San Miguel was an authentically designed Mexican restaurant adorned with Mexican artifacts opened by Tom Gilliland and Miguel Ravago as an expansion and second iteration of San Angel Inn, a high-end Mexican concept they launched in a small rent house on Westheimer Boulevard in Houston's Montrose. Fonda's elevated look complemented a menu refined by Mexico cooking authority Diana Kennedy, emphasizing interior Mexican gourmet fare.

Vegetarian cuisine took awhile to gain traction. Soyawanna Burger turned out an imaginative nonmeat hamburger at its location on Twenty-Third Street for a few years in the seventies. You could go meatless working the quiche, salads, and vegetables on the menus of the Omelettry West, the Magnolia Café, or the Kerbey Lane Café—vaguely related small independent restaurants that would become early adopters of locally sourced ingredients. The first serious all-vegetarian restaurant, Mother's Café, opened its doors in an old frame home on Duval, north of the UT campus, in 1980, and quickly built a loyal clientele.

Texas was still the number-one beef-raising state in the United States, and most of its citizens were largely unabashed carnivores. But a significant number of out-of-towners drove to Austin to eat at Mother's and shop at one of the cluster of small stores selling whole grain, natural, and organic foods within two miles of the UT campus. You could find a health food store in Dallas, Houston, San Antonio, or Fort Worth, if you looked around enough. Austin had critical mass.

The Good Food store on West Fifth and Baylor Streets, which was almost as large as a conventional grocery, was part of a vertically integrated business called Good Food People, a vegetarian-oriented health food retailer, restaurateur, and wholesaler. Good Food made and distributed its own honey, sprouts, whole grain bread, all-natural soap, pastries, and yogurt. It was started by a vegetarian Sikh sect that practiced Surat Shabd yoga and lived simple lives with moral standards. They created the company to supply themselves and greater Austin with more vegetarian options. New owner Stuart "Hoot" Shaw had more of a business head. He saw expansion in Good Food's future.

Natural foods had been the domain of cooperatives and religious groups, a direct result of the Austin Community Project's promotion of the food co-op movement in the early and midseventies. Two smaller food co-ops, Woody Hills and Avenues, joined forces in 1976 to open the Wheatsville consumers' cooperative grocery at Twenty-Ninth and Rio Grande, raising the bar of how large a health food store or co-op could be, and then raising it again in 1981 by moving into a former Kash-Karry grocery store at 3101 Guadalupe, north of the UT campus. The second move was a defensive measure.

Four years after Wheatsville opened, the owners of two competing commercial health food stores got together and created an even larger natural food store. John Mackey and Renee Lawson had been running SaferWay at Eighth and Rio Grande. Craig Weller and Mark Skiles operated Clarksville Natural Grocery on West Lynn Street. Mackey approached Weller and Skiles, suggesting they combine resources and open the largest health food store in Austin, meaning the largest health food store in the Southwest. Mackey also intimated that if Weller and Skiles were not interested, his new store might put them out of business.

John Mackey had grown up a fierce competitor. He butted heads with his suburban Houston high school basketball coach because he wasn't getting enough playing time. Mackey talked his parents into letting him transfer to another high school, where he practiced basketball long and hard enough to make the team and come back and beat his old team, coach, and school.

"That changed my life," Mackey told Nick Paumgarten of the *New Yorker*. "For the first time I realized that if you didn't like the hand you were dealt, you didn't just have to feel sorry for yourself. You could do something about it."

It did not hurt that his father, Bill, was a strong-willed professor of accounting at Rice University who had just become CEO of a health care company whose value would exceed one billion dollars in fifteen years.

Mackey enrolled at Trinity University in San Antonio, eventually dropped basketball, got deep into philosophy, and discovered the pleasures of Austin in due time. He found his calling after moving into a vegetarian co-op in Austin in the midseventies, even though he didn't know it at the time. "I had my food consciousness awakened," he said. "I learned how to cook and eventually I became the food buyer for the entire co-op." He went to work at the Good Food store at Fifth and Baylor, which at the time was the largest and most popular of the natural food stores around Austin and the UT campus, and the flagship of a five-store chain.

One night after working at Good Food, John Mackey told his girlfriend,

Renee Lawson, "You know, we could do this. This isn't that hard. We could open our own store." The two started researching natural foods retail and figuring out how to raise money. Family provided most of the answer.

"Our goal was fifty thousand dollars, but we could only find forty-five, so that's what we started with," Mackey told the *Washington Post*. "It was all equity investments, though my ten thousand dollar portion was a loan from my father. Renee put in a few thousand dollars that she had saved up, and her family, my family and some our friends. It was like a lot of entrepreneurial startups—it started with financing from family and friends."

They leased an early twentieth century Victorian on the western edge of downtown Austin. The neighborhood was largely residential. Rent was cheap. Two cash registers stood sentinel at the entrance on the ground floor in front of shelving for groceries and for vitamins. Bulk food was in one designated area, produce in another. A small dairy cooler and a frozen food freezer provided refrigeration.

The second floor housed a vegetarian café with seating and a porch deck to sit outside. The third floor was their office-residence where the couch turned into Mackey and Lawson's sleeping futon at night. They showered using a hose attached to the Hobart dishwasher. Food was ordered from catalogs; suppliers trucked in orders from out of state. Shelves were stocked, customers purchased the stock, and more orders were made to restock the shelves.

"That was our little retail business." Mackey said. Sales totaled a respectable $400,000 the first year, a loss of $23,000. Sales reached about the same level in 1979, but a more efficiently run store generated a $5,000 profit for Lawson and Mackey.

That was enough for Mackey to approach Craig Weller and Mark Skiles.

The original Whole Foods Market at Tenth and Lamar. (Photo courtesy of Patty Lang Fair.)

The two bought Mackey's pitch. They found and leased a building at Tenth and Lamar, which had been previously occupied by Mother Earth, a rock music club run by the Weinstein brothers that featured generic cover bands and drink specials. On September 20, 1980, Whole Foods Market opened for business. Lawson dropped out within a year, ending her relationship with Mackey and moving to Belize. The remaining three founders, dubbed the Tofu Triplets, grew the business.

Whole Foods Market was an immediate hit. No other retailer could claim such a large selection of organic foods, bulk items, and baked goods. Unlike most health food stores, Whole Foods' version of natural was neither Spartan nor strident, but fresh and better for you than the imported gourmet fare found at specialty stores. You could buy beer and wine at Whole Foods, natural beef raised without hormones or antibiotics in the Rocky Mountains of Colorado, and almond croissants.

"There was some animosity there," recalled Patty Lang Fair, who had worked at the same Good Food store where Mackey was briefly employed, before being put in charge of the Good Food store at Fifty-Second and Airport Boulevard. Some Good Food employees thought Mackey was trying to pick up trade secrets before jumping into SaferWay with Renee Lawson, Lang Fair said. They were probably right.

Patty Lang Fair got to know Whole Foods first as a shopper who happened to work for the competition. "It was incredible," she said. "It was huge. It was six times, eight times anything I'd ever seen before in natural foods."

The blue-eyed, fair-haired Fair moved from Detroit to Austin in 1976, several months after passing through on her way to Mexico. "I was going to this Free School and I went to Mexico for three months to study existentialism as part of their program. We came through here in January. We went by Pease Park and sat in the sun and I thought, 'Why am I living in Detroit?'"

She had intended to enroll grad school at UT but never got around to it. "After the Free School, UT was a little too . . . I couldn't do it." Her first gig in Austin was "serving ice cream to frat boys" at Swenson's. She found her calling when she answered the Help Wanted ad in *Third Coast* magazine for the Good Food store. A vegetarian since age fourteen, she found her tribe at Good Food.

Her tenure at the Good Food stores lasted three years. "Whole Foods put us out of business when they opened," she said. "It took six months. Mark Skiles, who had worked at Good Food, told me to go ahead and take unemployment, but whenever I was ready to come back to work, come to Whole Foods."

Three new takes on Austin's oldest ethnic cuisine, Mexican, followed on the heels of Whole Foods' overnight popularity. Xalapeno Charlie's on Barton Springs Road was Austin's first hippie-Mexican fusion eatery, emphasizing heat (no pepper or salsa too hot) over subtlety, and wild above mild, like the punk and roots bands that played out back. Growly voiced owner Charlie Duggan provided the atmosphere with his Panama hat / Hawaiian shirt / always smelling faintly of weed presence. XC's was one of several enterprises purposefully carrying on the spirit of the Armadillo after the Dillo closed, but on a smaller, more folksy scale, as if the Armadillo kitchen had relocated, but not the entire AWHQ beast.

That same year, 1981, sisters Cynthia and Lidia Perez opened a Mexican restaurant in the old Avenue Café on Congress Avenue between Third and Fourth Streets. They called the place Las Manitas, the little hands, but couldn't afford a new neon sign, so the old Avenue Café remained while a new Las Manitas logo was painted on the streetside window. The home-cooked interior Mexican fare with occasional infusions from Central America established Las Manitas as the go-to downtown spot for breakfast and lunch. Seating expanded from the front counter and a few tables and booths to a slapdash patio out back, accessed by cutting through the kitchen, which was largely staffed by newly arrived immigrants from somewhere south, leaving no doubt as to the cuisine's authenticity. The Perezes played a critical role in elevating the breakfast taco, also known as a taquito, into hip gringo food. At the northern end of the block, at the corner of Third and Congress, the politically active sisters along with Maria Elena Perez founded La Peña, a nonprofit Latino arts group dedicated to artists, poets, and musicians, which grew into a regional umbrella for a number of nonprofit arts groups.

The Perezes sniffed at any inferences their cuisine was Tex-Mex. Las Mañitas was puro mexicano down to the aguas frescas, migas, mole, and enchiladas hongos. Such purity tests would not be applied to another Mexican food venture that began a year later on Barton Springs Road, next to Zilker Park. Chuy's Comida Deluxe was the invention of Mike Young, John Zapp, and Craig Ainsworth, three young Austin restaurateurs behind Mike and Charlie's, one of Austin's first and most popular fern bar restaurants.

Chuy's was conceived as a fun place to go out and eat and drink when it opened as the anchor tenant on Barton Springs Road's informal Restaurant Row. An intentionally kitschy Elvis-on-black-velvet, hubcaps-on-the-ceiling theme accompanied the food, which proudly declared itself Tex-Mex, yellow cheese and all. Chuy's sported one gourmet touch—imported whole green chiles from Hatch, New Mexico, for menu items. The arrival of the new crop of Hatch chiles was celebrated with a green chile festival every August at each Chuy's location. Chuy's expanded to more than a hundred locations in the Southeastern and Eastern United States, each location indirectly selling Austin to the world.

Threadgill's, Eddie Wilson's revival of Kenneth Threadgill's gas station / beer joint, became famous again for its Southern comfort food, especially chicken-fried steak and vegetables. The *Los Angeles Times* aptly described Threadgill's as Austin's first Austin-themed restaurant. A second Threadgill's location opened in the old Marimont Cafeteria in South Austin, about a hundred yards from the remains of the Armadillo World Headquarters.

◉ ◉ ◉

Not quite six months after the Armadillo World Headquarters closed, on Memorial Day 1981, seven inches of rain fell on the city and a flood ripped through Shoal Creek, the primary drainage of West Austin, jumping its banks. The floodwaters floated vehicles off the used car lot of McMorris Ford and into the creek, which had been transformed into a raging torrent. Many of the vehicles caught the current and slammed with an audible crash against the bottom of the bridge where Sixth Street crossed over Shoal Creek.

The flood would prompt the Ford dealership to move to the Motor Mile

Melanie Bounds serves proprietor Eddie Wilson at his home base, Threadgill's Old No. 1 on North Lamar. (Photo by Will Van Overbeek.)

on south Interstate 35. GSD&M, the advertising agency founded in 1971 by some hustling UT grads who didn't want to go to Dallas or New York or Chicago to seek their fortunes as admen and adwomen, moved in to the location, building a one hundred thousand square foot headquarters. GSD&M would snag such valuable accounts as Southwest Airlines and Walmart, as well as the "Don't Mess with Texas" antilitter campaign, as it grew into an agency powerhouse, five hundred employees strong, consistently ranking as one of the coolest companies to work for in Austin.

Four blocks upstream, Whole Foods Market was underwater. The grocery's building was in a notorious low-lying flood plain, but the new business had not purchased flood insurance. The entire inventory, valued at four hundred thousand dollars, was lost. Without prompting, dozens of customers, employees, vendors, creditors, and friends showed up at Tenth and Lamar, sleeves and pants rolled up, ready to clean up, before the floodwaters had completely receded.

The customers wanted to help the grocer because the grocer was providing the goods they wanted.

Several years after the Shoal Creek Flood of '81, John Mackey wrote the Whole Foods Declaration of Interdependence, articulating a stakeholder philosophy that extended beyond the bottom line to factor in employees, suppliers, the community, and the environment, as well as customers—a macro view of retailing food. This wasn't just lip service or advertiser-speak, Mackey insisted. Whole Foods Market would walk the walk, and the Shoal Creek flood had a lot to do with it. It turned out to be a good business strategy.

Love was written into the Higher Purpose Statement of the company's Core Values: "With great courage, integrity and love—we embrace our responsibility to co-create a world where each of us, our communities and our planet can flourish. All the while, celebrating the sheer love and joy of food."

The Whole Foods store was restocked, rebuilt, and reopened less than a month after the flood. Customer response was stronger than ever. Shoppers took Whole Foods' loss personally. One of the neighbors helping her friends clear out the mud and debris in the store was Patty Lang Fair, who would become a team member within the year, enabling her to see the store that she shopped at in a very different light.

"Once I went to work there, I could see there was sixteen feet of Knudsen's apple juice. Everything was double-fronted, double-fronted, double-fronted." Dirty little secret: "We didn't have products to fill the shelves. The only bottled water was Perrier. Dr. Bronner's Peppermint took up a

whole shelf in body care until Rachel Perry natural cosmetics were introduced; Rachel Perry stood out because its scents did not resemble musk or
patchouli."

A significant chunk of the Whole Foods space was leased to Martin
Brothers, a natural foods café with in-house ice cream, coffee, sandwiches,
black bean tacos, and a new frozen liquid concoction that was all the rage—
the smoothie.

Whole Foods Market was a stealth patron of Austin's music scene. "You
could either work at Whole Foods or work in a restaurant," said Patty, who
married the musician Jad Fair. "That was the day job." That policy extended
to openly gay people, and to all sorts of alternative types who didn't fit in
elsewhere.

It helped that Mark Skiles did all the initial hiring. "He didn't care what
you looked like as long as you worked hard," Fair said. "We had a diverse
bunch of people working for us, from Izod and plaid shorts preppies to
hard-core punks and hippies. I was kind of astounded by that.

"It wasn't like going to work," Fair said. "There was no barrier between
the customer and team members. You were a customer one day, then a
team member for six months. Everybody knew each other. Team members' friends and families would show up. We just had fun. If things didn't
work, 'Oh! Too bad!' We'd start something else in terms of what we carried.
At ten o'clock [closing time] we'd crank up that sound system, put on our
own tapes, everybody's dancing, customers boppin' in the aisles. It was so
awesome—go out to clubs afterwards, stay out till two, drink coffee in the
morning, and start over."

Shoppers felt the same way. This wasn't a supermarket, but a cool hang.
Longer lines inevitably formed in front of one Whole Foods checkout register whenever Jimmy Turner was sacking. The charismatic mute dancer wore
roller skates and gave hugs to shoppers at checkout. The habit spread. Pretty
soon, wealthy West Austin matrons outnumbered the unreconstructed hippies cruising the narrow aisles.

Whole Foods was that public place where straight Austin met counterculture Austin, on the latter's terms.

Hair color was as controversial as sugar or meat. "We were always arguing about the dress code: can we have pink hair?" Fair said. The leadership—Mackey, Skiles, and Weller—decided blue hair, green hair, or pink
hair were OK. "But you can't have multicolored hair."

Fair went to talk to leadership on behalf of the team members. "I gave
an impassioned speech. 'That's why Westlake ladies come here. Their kids

couldn't have pink hair, no way. But they loved to be able to say, 'You'll never guess what I saw at Whole Foods! Those crazy people.' They just adored us."

Ladybird Johnson, the former first lady of the United States, helped settle the issue. "In the middle of this colored hair fight, I saw her come in and started bagging for her and asked, 'What do you think about this colored hair?'" Fair said.

Ladybird Johnson smiled sweetly as her eyes grew wide. "Oh, their pink hair just tickles me."

After Fair related what Mrs. Johnson had told her, leadership gave team members their seal of approval to color their hair any way they damn well pleased.

Dress code fights went far beyond hair color to deal with ripped T-shirts, graphic T-shirts, underarm hair, men in skirts, women without bras. The liberals usually won, but compromise was inevitable. Exposed underarm hair was a no-no for women and men both. Some men shaved so they could wear tank tops. "Slightly" ripped T-shirts were fine as long as the shirt was clean. Inappropriate words/images on T-shirts were prohibited; store managers would make the call. Shorts and skirts could be no higher than two inches above the knee for women and men alike.

Battles over food were more heated. Artificial flavors, colors, and ingredients were banned from the outset. The inclusion of coffee, alcohol, and natural meat set off internecine warfare between the purists and the casuals. It was no sugar versus some sugar, no white flour versus who cares? Fair's previous employer, Good Food, had been much stricter in what was and wasn't carried. "We didn't carry eggs; we didn't carry meat. We did carry milk. We didn't carry coffee. It was a strange list of things. That's another reason Whole Foods put us out of business."

Each new product introduced to fill up those increasingly crowded shelves at Whole Foods Market brought its own issues. Coke and Tide were nixed. Seven-Up was on the cusp. Some processed snacks loaded with sugar snuck through.

"We battled about everything," Fair said. "There wasn't anything that showed up we didn't battle about. We were intense. Those original vendors were awesome."

Chico's Tofu, made in a kitchen in Elgin, was one of the first local suppliers to Whole Foods that passed the standards test. Reed Murray's White Mountain Foods Bulgarian yogurt, made with milk and live culture and nothing else, was another. "All these local vendors were getting the picture," Fair said. "They didn't start out thinking they were going to make a lot of money out of this, but then it dawned on them—'Maybe I can make a lot of money doing this.' That was cool. That was a bunch of hippies making good money."

Patty Lang Fair's enthusiasm and love for Whole Foods grew as she moved up from cashier to marketing/merchandising and then store manager. The store opened with nineteen employees; the staff expanded to seventy-five in four years. Almost half were musicians. Fair was especially proud of putting up a suggestion box. "I thought it was the most brilliant idea on the face of the planet," she said with a self-deprecating laugh. "I was excited. I put it up. The next day I opened it up. There were two suggestions. One was, 'Please tell Threadgill's to put baked potato on the menu.' The other was, 'Does Julie [one of the cashiers] have a boyfriend?'" She did.

Fair called Eddie Wilson at Threadgill's to pass along the suggestion. "Tell them to get the broccoli cheese casserole," Wilson replied.

The loose, open community spirit that distinguished Whole Foods from other grocers was put to the test in 1984 when a team member was diagnosed with a disease no one had heard of before. "From day one, if you were gay and open, you worked at Whole Foods. It was never ever a thing," Fair said. "That shaped our culture a lot. Mark had a lot of Houston frat boy in him but he hung out with the punks, gorgeous guy. He worked at the bakery, loved people. He came in one day, took me out to the picnic table [where meetings were held] and said he'd been diagnosed with AIDS.

"The only reason I knew anything about it was because I'd read the *Village Voice* [the New York City alternative weekly]. I told him to go back to work in the bakery, and I called Craig [Weller]. He knew nothing. People thought they were going to die. We had no idea how you caught it. We had the city director of health come and talk to us. He knew nothing. A bunch of team members threatened to quit. 'You need to get him out of the store!' They were afraid they were going to die.

"We were taking little steps, trying to figure things out. We took him out of bakery and had him sack groceries. He came into the office and got a drink of water from the drinking fountain—just a cup. This really nice woman came up and said, 'What the hell are you doing?' There was this huge uproar. John and Craig and Mark got together and said, 'Mark is our family. He's not getting fired. If you don't want to work with him, then quit.' He couldn't use the bathroom. He couldn't drink from the fountain. But he had a job. He eventually got sick enough that he quit, and then . . . But that was the MO from then on, how that was treated. 'We'll take care of you.'"

Spiritual advisors frequently turned up, depending where founder John

Mackey's personal quest took him. For one two-month stretch, Mackey and his wife showed up for work wearing macramé headbands, each with different jewels in them. An advisor suggested they could open their third eye with the jewels he'd made for them. Another spiritual advisor tried to heal a contentious argument by inferring the problems went all the way back to Atlantis.

Mackey, clearly the general of the Tofu Triplets, wasn't around the store that much, Fair said. "He was plotting our future to take over the world with natural foods."

This alternative-to-conventional enterprise had the potential to go long and large.

The second Whole Foods Market store opened in 1984 in the Crossroads shopping center near the intersection of highways 183 and 360 in Northwest Austin, where companies such as IBM and Texas Instruments were driving a population boom. It was a different Austin up north. "Suburbia didn't want a Whole Foods Market," Fair said. "That was a big wake up call. It took a long time for sales to build up there. Half the team members went there. They weren't happy. It took a long time." By 1986, six years after the first store at Tenth and Lamar in Austin opened, there were Whole Foods Markets in Dallas (Bluebonnet Natural Foods was purchased), Houston, New Orleans (the Whole Food Company was purchased), and a third store in Austin in Brodie Oaks shopping center on the southwestern edge of the city.

"The most difficult part was going from one store to two stores," John Mackey said to the Washington Post. "Before that, you could personally be there to look after everything. Once you expand to two stores, you have to start developing systems to organize the company, developing processes and policies, and making sure your culture is being extended. After you get that down, it all comes down to putting the right people in place to help you replicate those systems over and over again."

Driven by his ongoing philosophical quest, Mackey initiated group improvement and empowerment experiments. "We'd try something new every month," said Fair. "For awhile we had these PIQ circles. I'm not even sure what PIQ meant, but every week we'd have these Circles of Quality. We had a Joint Management Team for a while, where there wasn't one store manager, but four. That didn't work."

The team member concept stuck.

Mackey articulated the ideas of teams and members in an essay he wrote and distributed throughout Whole Foods titled "The Self-Responsibility Principle."

"One of the most important keys to individual happiness and success in life is one's willingness to take responsibility for creating it," he wrote. "Unfortunately, many people have disempowered themselves by believing that they are victims of events beyond their control." He concluded the essay, writing, "Since I believe in self-responsibility, my intention has been to foster it throughout the company. Whole Foods is a radically decentralized company with a minimum of internal bureaucracy."

The team was the defining unit of activity throughout the company. Each store was its own profit center with self-managed teams in charge of various parts of the store, each with its own performance goals to meet, and its own leader. Leaders met with other leaders within a store. Store leaders met with other store leaders in their region, and regional team leaders huddled together regularly with other regional leaders. Team members voted on accepting new hires. If someone wasn't doing their part on a team, the others could kick them out.

John Mackey liked to use basketball and baseball as metaphors for the team concept: individuals in those sports had the potential to be game changers, whether it was hitting a home run, making a desperate catch against the outfield wall, or draining a three-pointer when the clock ran out. Improvisation came with the territory. Football, he liked to point out, merely required players to follow orders given by the coach. Execute. Don't stray from the plan or improvise. Do as you were told. Mackey wanted baseball and basketball people on his teams.

Traditional media advertising was initially avoided because Whole Foods couldn't afford it. By the time aggressive expansion was underway, direct consumer outreach and word of mouth worked just as effectively.

Original team member Margaret Wittenberg established quality standards for Whole Foods Market, a key component separating the company from the competition. Industry baselines for sustainable and organic agriculture, seafood sustainability, and the welfare of farm animals were set. Aspartame and high fructose corn syrup were among seventy-eight ingredients banned by Whole Foods. The standards sometimes prompted catcalls about Holy Foods. But the formula worked.

Whole Foods Market would eventually expand coast-to-coast and to Canada and Great Britain, buying out regional grocers along the way, including Wellspring in North Carolina, Bread & Circus in New England, Mrs. Gooch's in Southern California, and Fresh Fields in the mid-Atlantic region to become the largest certified organic grocer in the world. The number of college degrees within a sixteen-minute drive determined the viability of a proposed location, though over time Mackey would observe that "consciousness has gone beyond just being well-educated when it comes to healthy food," as he explained to Fortune magazine. Population density became the main factor in determining locations. And if the numbers didn't work for some urban areas, the Whole Cities Foundation that Whole Foods started could subsidize new stores, as it had done in inner city Detroit, New Orleans, Newark, and South Side Chicago, impoverished areas known as food deserts for their lack of access to fresh food.

◎ ◎ ◎

The real estate boom of the early eighties brought new restaurants to the fore, but also threatened old reliable joints known for cheap and filling Mex cuisine. Four years after Whole Foods Market opened, Moses Vasquez, the owner of the Tamale House Number One, a small taqueria downtown at the corner of Congress Avenue and Cesar Chavez Boulevard (formerly First Street) frequented by bankers, lawyers, politicos, and downtown workers, sold his business and the seven thousand square feet of land it was built on for $1.6 million. It was a record for such a small piece of Austin real estate.

The closing of Tamale House Number One signaled the end of dollar tacos downtown. Old school Tex-Mex and enchilada plates for under five bucks were threatened species. Upscale Mex was ascendant. There was money to spend. During the mideighties, the rest of Texas was mired in an economic slump tied to depressed oil prices. Office occupancy rates in Houston dropped below 70 percent. H-Town's skyline was peppered with ghost high-rises. Austin real estate continued gaining value. When the mild tail end of the recession reached the city in the late eighties, real estate prices flattened for two years before resuming their irrational rise.

The real estate boom had made a lot of speculators a whole lot of money. But the land flipping didn't much impact Austin directly. The small city feel held. The 1982 opening of the 17-story, 484-room Hyatt Regency on the south bank of Town Lake signaled a slight change in that perception, and underscored official Austin's big city aspirations. The Hyatt was Austin's biggest hotel, built with more rooms and more space than any hotel in the city in order to accommodate conventions. The hotel featured an indoor atrium, a requisite amenity of big city Hyatts, only this one featured a recreation of a Hill Country creek running across the lobby floor, a subtle nod to the local surroundings. You weren't spending the night in Generica at this Hyatt.

Perhaps the buzziest amenity offered by the hotel was the specialty of the house at the La Vista restaurant at the top of the Hyatt, with stunning views of downtown Austin across Town Lake and the Hill Country rising to the west.

La Vista's German-born chef George Weidmann had taken notice of the popularity of fajitas in local restaurants. Grilled skirt steak rolled in a tortilla came from the Rio Grande Valley of South Texas, where Mexican vaqueros took what was considered a throwaway cut when cows were butchered on ranches and elevated it to a regional delicacy. Sonny Falcon, the manager of Guajardo's Meat Market in Austin, had Valley connections and introduced fajitas to central Texas in 1969 when he opened a concession stand at a local Diez y Seis celebration. For the next decade, Falcon served his specialty to mexicanos, Anglos, and all colors at parades, festivals, rodeos, fairs, and street celebrations all over Texas. By the time Chef Weidmann decided to add them to La Vista's menu, fajitas were outpacing tacos as a Tex-Mex staple around Austin. Local restaurants such as Manuel's sleek contemporary Mexican on Congress Avenue and the southwestern-infused Z'Tejas Grill on West Sixth Street had already jumped into the game.

Weidmann's sizzling fajitas accompanied by margaritas helped make La Vista the most profitable restaurant in the Hyatt chain. Conventioneers left Austin thinking the food tasted different, with flavors like nowhere else.

◎ ◎ ◎

Most out-of-towners didn't know they could have lunch or dinner at Whole Foods Market, mostly because they hadn't heard of Whole Foods yet.

John Mackey was stretching and then overstretching the company's finances in order to continue expanding. The concept was working. People were responding. The only thing holding back growth was money. Venture capitalists offered cash with strings attached. Mackey likened VCs to "hitch-hikers with credit cards. They get in your car, and as long as you take them where they want to go, they will help pay for the gas. But if you get lost or wander off the road you promised you were going down, they will hijack the car, throw you out, and bring in a new driver."

Whole Foods Market went public in 1992, selling shares of stock in the company. Mackey was thrilled because the company would no longer need to rely on venture capitalists, and because the company could reward "all those people who had shown faith in us and invested back in the early days." The stock offering made many early investors wealthy in one fell swoop.

John Mackey's company aimed to be nothing less than America's natural grocer. While personnel searched for and studied existing regional chains as part of Whole Foods' expansion strategy, its first major competition popped up in Austin.

H-E-B Central Market opened in January 1994 on spacious grounds on North Lamar Boulevard previously occupied by the Austin State Hospital mental institution, some twenty-eight blocks north of the original Whole Foods. Central Market instantly upped the stakes in the natural food/epicure segment of the grocery market nationally. The two business models of that sector were competing head-to-head in Austin.

H-E-B Central Market was a high-end gourmet concept from the dominant grocer in South and Central Texas and the largest privately held business in Texas. The second and third generations of the Howard Butt family under the guidance of Charles Butt had been steadily growing the company since the early seventies, when beer and wine sales began despite the family's devout faith. During the eighties, H-E-B expanded beyond its south Texas base into Houston, and throughout Mexico, while simultaneously warding off Walmart, which was just entering the grocery game but already had a presence that threatened to wipe out all competitors.

H-E-B had witnessed firsthand the impact Whole Foods had in Austin and Houston, where Whole Foods captured a healthy slice of the highly competitive but largely untested sector. Central Market responded by rolling out a kinder, gentler version of Whole Foods—easier to understand, more like a regular store (except for an intentional maze-like layout), less dogmatic, with some organics, lots of cheese and epicurean baked goods, and larger selections of beers, wines, and accessories (the high markup items where stores realize bigger profit margins).

Families moved into the Rosedale neighborhood specifically to be near Central Market.

Over the next ten years, H-E-B Central Markets opened in Dallas, Fort Worth, San Antonio, and Houston, with a second location in Austin—cities where Whole Foods had already planted its flag. Whole Foods viewed H-E-B Central Market as more of a complement than a cutthroat competitor, an entry-level experience for shoppers who might get interested in organics and eventually buy in to the healthy lifestyle that Whole Foods embraced. A Whole Foods regular could easily indulge in Central Market's nondenominational epicurean groove, but it was more specialty food store than natural foods grocer. Anyone all-in on organics eventually stuck with Whole Foods.

Whole Foods responded to Central Market locally a year later in 1995 with a retooling. All three existing Austin locations closed and were consolidated into two new stores: one in Gateway Plaza in Northwest Austin that replaced the nearby Crossroads shopping center store, and a new thirty-eight thousand square foot flagship store at Sixth and Lamar. The south Brodie Oaks store, whose cramped footprint inhibited store traffic since its opening in 1985, was sold and turned into a Sun Harvest grocery. The first Whole Foods at Tenth and Lamar closed for good, with Cheapo Records moving into the space.

Closing the first store was the price of expansion. Despite its limited size, the legacy store was still one of Whole Foods' top twenty grossing locations, even as the chain grew to thirty-five stores in eight states, with eyes on New York and San Francisco. Leadership was clearly ready to remove some of the cult stigma associated with the old store in order to attract more young urban shoppers for whom Whole Foods was neither a lifestyle nor community, but the closest grocery to home. A revised dress code limited the number of rings in pierced noses to one. Eyebrow piercings were banned. Legal and HR decreed team members couldn't hug customers; the customer had to initiate the hug. The spirit of Tenth and Lamar had flown off to some sleek upscale mall in California.

"I know that's true and it's unfortunate that we would lose customers over our move, but we've talked to a number of our customers who felt alienated at our other stores," said Rich Cundiff, who oversaw the Southwest region for Whole Foods at the time. "They felt like they were walking into an exclusive club. We're not a niche market any more. We're a national chain. The market has shifted to the point where we can sell Cheerios now because it doesn't have preservatives. But the fact that we're selling Cheerios doesn't mean we have compromised our quality."

This kind of progress distressed some of Whole Foods' old guard, including Patty Lang Fair. "The turning point came—this was more in California than it was here—when people started figuring out that they could replicate conventional food in a natural, organic form, like Barbara's Bakery, Lundberg, and Arrowhead Mills switching from just providing brown rice and bulk grains to something fast-cooking like a Rice-A-Roni type thing. Then it went crazy. People could relate to that. This isn't rabbit food anymore. 'Oh, I can get animal crackers that are healthy and organic.' But it was also crappier food that was processed, even if it was organic."

Some ideas didn't pan out. Whole Foods leadership saw untapped potential in vitamins and herbal supplements, and bet big, purchasing Amrion, the Colorado-based manufacturer of health supplements and vitamins, in 1997 through a merger. Two years later, the vitamin and supplement division merged with WholeFoods.com into WholePeople.com, an online sales outlet for the products. But the division did not perform as projected. In 2001, Whole Foods sold off its interest in the company, which was renamed NatureSmart.

⊚ ⊚ ⊚

Austin-style food and hospitality, both determinedly provincial, started to resonate nationally and internationally during the last quarter of the twentieth century. Building from the chicken-fried steak, BBQ, and Tex-Mex basics, local cuisine evolved as its customers' worldview expanded, spurred on by funky restaurant concepts that traveled well like Chuy's Tex-Mex, the family-owned H-E-B, the ongoing spread of Whole Foods Market, the cottage industry of salsa and condiment makers that Whole Foods and Central Market inspired and stocked on their shelves, an emerging craft beer and wine industry with a developing Central Texas wine trail, and a hub of craft liquor distilleries.

The one missing ingredient was the most essential—the food that grew out of the soil.

Most raw ingredients, the building blocks of any food-focused community, historically came from either traditional food suppliers such as Ben E. Keith and Sysco, or in the case of organic foods, California. Local growers elevated the food sector into another iteration of an Austin creative-innovative community.

The establishment of Boggy Creek Farm at 3314 Lyons Road three miles east of the capitol marked the start of Austin's urban farm movement. Carol Ann Sayle and Larry Butler had been bit by the "back to the land" bug and in 1992 purchased the derelict five-acre property with a historic nineteenth century home in serious need of rehabilitation. They already farmed several acres of land in Milam County about eighty miles northeast of Austin, which they bought ten years before.

Butler had spent some of his growing up years in Milam County. He was running a big screen video store in Oak Hill on the western outskirts of Austin when he met Sayle, who had opened an art studio a few doors down in the western town strip center. Willie Nelson's business office was nestled between Sayle's studio and Butler's store.

Sayle had grown up middle class in San Antonio and came to Austin in 1964 to enroll at the University of Texas after attending Southwest Texas State Teachers College in San Marcos. "I was afraid [to come to Austin] at first because [UT] was so big," she said. "Then I wasn't afraid anymore." She graduated from UT in 1966, married, had her first child, and taught high school in Kyle for two-and-a-half years until she had her second child. "Back then, if you were pregnant, they'd make you go home," she said.

Her family moved to Oak Hill where Sayle met Butler, a strapping man with an infectious smile. She divorced, married Butler, and the couple moved to South Austin where they bought several rental properties. The couple relocated to Old West Austin, where they restored a historic home on Highland Avenue while Butler worked the Milam County farm whenever possible. Crops started coming in.

Sayle approached Whole Foods Market in 1991 to see if there was interest in their Milam County tomatoes. The bulk of Whole Foods' organic produce was grown in the San Joaquin Valley of California and then shipped to Texas. "I put the tomatoes in sacks and took them to Whole Foods' produce wholesaler at Sixth Street and I-35 and asked if they wanted to buy some certified organic tomatoes. The buyer came out and looked in my trunk, reached in, took a tomato and started eating it. 'Yes,' he said. 'We'll buy every tomato that you can bring us.'"

Sayle didn't have boxes to package the tomatoes. The Whole Foods buyer gave her leftover boxes from California organic produce.

A year later, Sayle and Butler paid forty thousand dollars for the five acres of land fronting Lyons Road in East Austin, including the fallen-down main house that dated back to 1841. That meant the house was as old as the French Legation closer to downtown, the oldest extant frame structure in Austin. "This place was not in that good of shape," Sayle said. "The house was tumbled in, chimney was fallen into the attic, doors stolen, sixteen trailers of junk thrown over the fence by the neighbors. Nobody wanted it."

Boggy Creek Farm was paying its own way six months after it opened. Sayle and Butler rented out their previous residence, now restored, to pay the mortgage on their new homestead. "I told Larry I'd figured out we were making three dollars and twenty three cents an hour, which was well below the minimum wage," Sayle recalled. "He just slumped. 'How are we making it then?' 'We're working seventy hours a week, that's how,' I told him. 'We're not spending any money because we're working all the time. We're eating from the field.' We ate a lot of eggplant."

The first crop to come in at Boggy Creek Farm was head lettuce, harvested in January 1993. This piece of East Austin had gone back to its original intended use. Sayle found a town plat of Austin from 1845. The land east of the capitol was designated farmland to feed the new growing community. Four hundred and fifty-two residents listed their occupation as farmers. Five identified themselves as lawyers.

Eating well mattered more than eating cheap in Austin. Proof could be found on a full-bloom second spring mid-November weekday at Boggy Creek Farm in 2015. The mild autumn weather was close to perfect: clear skies, no wind, air temperature hovering around seventy degrees. The first freeze of autumn was still a few days away. A Halloween deluge had left the soil moist and the landscape greened up, almost making up for the severe drought that had run from mid-June to late October, burning up much of the vegetation.

Workers in the field were pulling up and bringing in lettuce, green beans, broccoli, kale, chard, tomatoes, beets, radishes, carrots, and peppers. Painters from an art group had set up easels around the grounds to work on landscapes for a class. Behind the main house in the center of a gaggle of people scurrying in every direction was the beaming seventy-one-year-old matriarch of East Austin Ag. A spry and spunky Carol Ann Sayle wore the dirt under her fingernails with pride.

Originally a two-person operation—Sayle and her husband, Larry Butler—Boggy Creek had expanded its labor force, but was still running lean. Sayle depended on four full-time workers, one half-time employee ("and during the summer, the two Marias go to half-time too because you know you can die out there"), and two full-time farm associates, as Sayle described her two right-hand women. Five volunteers were helping out, digging in the fields out front and in back of the centerpiece historic home where Sayle and Butler lived. The "work for free because it's fun" alternative Austin business model was definitely in play at Boggy Creek.

Sayle busily directed volunteers carrying fresh-picked produce to the walk-in refrigerator, adjacent washroom, or the Farm Stand screened-in metal building. Boggy Creek Farm had been the first urban farm in Austin to supply wholesale produce to Whole Foods Market, but the practice ended in 2011 when a hard freeze in late spring was followed by record heat and a record drought, which wiped out most of Boggy Creek's crops. "That whole year we got six inches of rain," Sayle said. "There were over ninety days of 100 degree temperature or higher. Everything died except the tomatoes. That was it. We had to try and sell everything retail to recoup some of our losses. It's been slowly coming back since, but we don't wholesale anymore."

"All our food goes here," she said, pointing to the Farm Stand. "Our food's not cheap. We're not subsidized by the government. It's all real, not processed. Our regular customers include several chefs from Austin restaurants. Larry brings in more food on Saturdays from the other farm in Milam County."

The forty-seven acres farmed near the town of Gause was sandy, acidic soil. "We're on the high side of the Brazos, about a mile from the river. They don't spray around there. It's a really clean place to grow. It's the wild hogs, the deer, the possums, raccoons, and gophers, the stinkbugs, the corn worms, the freezes, the heat and all that."

Boggy Creek was a whole 'nother farm, with different worry priorities. "I don't have wild hogs here," she said, surveying the East Austin acreage. "I do have possums and raccoons, but they're mostly interested in the chickens. Squirrels will sometimes eat crops and people will let go of their bunny rabbits when they don't want them anymore and they'll eat whole rows, but that's rare. We have alkaline soil here, but it's bottomland, antique soil, really. It's really wonderful."

Boggy Creek Farm was the heart of Austin's Urban Farm district. "The HausBar Farm is two blocks north of here," Sayle said. "Downstream is Rain Lilly and up near here is Springdale Farm. We're all different." Rain Lilly hosted Shakespeare plays and other events. Susan Hausmann and Dorsey Barger's HausBar included a bed and breakfast "Guest Haus" on-site; Barger had been a founding owner of East Side Café, the first restaurant in East Austin with its own garden. Tecolote Farm opened for business a year after Boggy Creek. Paula and Glenn Foore's five-acre Springdale Farm, which was a landscaping business before the farm was been established in 2008, provided greens to thirty high-end Austin restaurants. Urban Roots, farther north on East Seventeenth Street, was established in 2007 and became a nonprofit in 2011. Its paid intern program focused on getting Austin young people between the ages of fourteen and seventeen to work the crops on the three-and-a-half acre sustainable farm to better understand agriculture. Almost half of the annual twenty-five-thousand-pound harvest at Urban Roots was donated to area soup kitchens and food pantries, while the rest was sold at farmers' markets.

Cumulatively the urban farms made a difference. Chefs shopped the farms. Farm-to-table and locally sourced became restaurant selling points.

Bryce Gilmore's Odd Duck, one of the pioneering food truck concepts in Austin to transition to brick-and-mortar, bragged about their suppliers, listing forty-nine local sources on a weekday winter menu ranging from olive producers and pig butchers to mushroom growers and organic vegetable gardeners.

"People are eating healthier," Carol Ann Sayle said. "Visitors come up all the time to tell me, 'You don't know how much you inspired me to do a garden.' That's one of the greatest outcomes. People see what can be grown here. They may only do it one or two seasons after they see how hard it is, but they understand what's going on. It's created lots of farmers, young farmers. And these other farms around here are here because we're here."

Sayle and Butler didn't mind providing prospective farmers a reality check. Modern farming in America was a prohibitively expensive trade to enter if one didn't inherit the land. "I tell my young ones that they're going to have to be in the country to be able to buy enough land," Sayle said. "You don't want a bunch of mortgages. You've got to be out of debt because farming is precarious. And it's not going to be just about farming. These girls here, they're just farming. They don't come in and do the taxes, the payroll. They don't put in infrastructure. They don't do social media. They're just farmers. But they're not farmers in the sense of a business."

In addition to the usual elements to contend with, East Austin urban farmers got pushback from neighborhood activists who contended the farms were forcing blacks and browns out of historically black and brown East Austin. PODER (People Organized in Defense of Earth and Her Resources), an organization that had successfully closed a fifty-two acre fuel tank facility adjacent to East Austin residences in 1992 and was instrumental in persuading the City of Austin to decommission the Holly Street power plant in East Austin in 2007, lobbied the city to restrict the farms from butchering domestic livestock, as HausBar had been doing, and from hosting events, which all the farms did. A city council vote left zoning of the farms intact while restricting the slaughter of livestock, leaving the farmers who rehabbed the land and buildings they purchased wary and worried.

One clear result of the farms gussying up the surrounding neighborhoods was escalating property values. East Austin was no longer a bargain. East Austin was valued for having the largest stock of yet-to-be-rehabilitated older homes in the city and its proximity to downtown. Boggy Creek Farm and Springdale Farm could each easily net a cool five million selling to a developer. But that wasn't in their plans, Sayle said. "Our lives would be destroyed. We can't put a price on our lives like that."

It weighed on her. "It's a heavy responsibility, this place," Sayle said. "We can't move. It's home. We want to have young people taking this over. We still want to live in this house, because it's our house, and we still want to mentor. Larry would like some time to do woodworking stead of picking beans on his knees at age sixty-eight. I want to paint more. But we still want to be involved.

"We need the sunshine and to be active."

Looking at the dozens of people busily scurrying about Boggy Creek Farm, it was apparent that Sayle and Butler were not the only ones who felt that way.

Food was the new music. Even as the daily newspaper offered veteran reporters early retirement to further reduce staff, coverage of restaurants and the related food movement grew exponentially. Matthew Odam was the new Margaret Moser. He knew all the places and all the standout chefs. If he liked your restaurant, you could expect a good run.

Local sourcing extended from urban farms to the cottage industry of boutique food and drink products trying to tap into the considerable buying power of Whole Foods and Central Market. Everybody knew someone, it seemed, who was working in their kitchen trying to come up with a sauce, salsa, cheese, bread, condiment, or some other specialty food product worthy of being carried by one or both grocers.

The Sass Sisters, twin sisters Lauri and Carol Raymond and their "sister" in sauces Celeste Seay, formed a partnership late in 1987 to produce, market, and distribute the fresh garlic-and-sesame salad dressing/sauce they'd invented. SASS, the acronym for Season All Stuff Sauce, began production in Carol's kitchen and built a fervent following among customers of the several small health food stores in Austin that carried SASS. Increasing demand led them to Woody Hitchcock, owner of another small food company Out to Lunch, who offered to share his kitchen with the sisters and mentor them in the ways of the food business. When the Raymonds took their creation to Whole Foods, their business and their lives changed.

The Raymond Sisters bought out Celeste Seay in 1990, and then Carol Raymond moved to Santa Fe in 1994, leaving Lauri in charge.

Whole Foods was already carrying fresh dressings with high-quality natural ingredients produced by the Martin Brothers, Karl and Jeff, who operated the café–coffee shop–ice creamery inside the original Whole Foods at Tenth and Lamar. The popularity of the café and its salads spurred the brothers to bottle their dressings, starting with mainstream Bleu Cheese and Balsamic Vinaigrette and expanding into exotic dressings such as Calamata Feta and Pecan Smoked Sun-Dried Tomato Ranch.

The Martin Brothers' success hipped Whole Foods to the huge untapped potential of selling prepared foods ready-to-eat in the grocery store. A large number of shoppers preferred buying something they could eat on the spot or that could be heated in a microwave, rather than have to make a meal from scratch. Prepared food offered considerably larger profit margins, too.

Martin Brothers Café was a victim of its own success. When the new flagship Whole Foods opened at Sixth and Lamar in 1995, Martin Brothers was conspicuously absent. Whole Foods leadership had observed Martin Brothers in action long enough to want to keep the action in-house. Martin Brothers moved to a standalone location on Guadalupe Street, just north of the University of Texas campus. The dressings business continued until 2001 when the brothers were acquired by the Sass Sisters, expanding the Sass empire to sixteen sauces and three dips.

New sauce and salsa startups popped up. A radio talk show host who hailed from St. Louis, Patrick J. Timpone, marketed his Mama Rosa's Hot Sauce as a perishable salsa made with all-fresh ingredients, and no additives or preservatives. The product flew out of Whole Foods refrigerated cases. East Side Café, the first organic restaurant on the east side with its own on-site garden, bottled its three most popular salad dressings. Romannee "Foo" Swasdee, owner-chef of the Thai restaurant Satay, bottled spicy peanut sauce, as well as three other Asian-infused sauces. TexaFrance, "Your Secret Sous Chef," founded in 1986 in suburban Round Rock by two chefs, David Griswold and Jean-Pierre Parant, carved out a niche with a variety of sauces, condiments, pestos, chutneys, and jellies. Oka's Miso Dressing was a standalone powerhouse soybean condiment/sauce built from word-of-mouth. Doug Foreman, a thirty-two-year-old burger joint operator who started his Guiltless Gourmet business with two credit cards, was told by his doctor that his cholesterol count was off the charts and that he was way too fat. Foreman responded by experimenting and then introducing fat-free baked tortilla chips as an alternative to the traditional fried variety in 1989. Five years later, Guiltless Gourmet sold to Barq's Root Beer for somewhere between ten and twenty million dollars.

The indie alternative spirit carried over to the alcohol part of the food and drink proposition.

Microbreweries popped up all across the city and county once the Texas legislature legalized drinking on the premises where the beer was made in 1993. The wine trail of wineries extending from Austin to Fredericksburg in the Texas Hill Country evolved into a Texas version of Napa, at least from the tourism standpoint, with fifty-three established wineries. Local beer and wine was hardly unique to Austin.

But no one anywhere was doing a legal microdistillery until Tito Beveridge set up Beveridge's Mockingbird Distillery in deep East Austin, Texas' first licensed distillery and the only one-man distillery in the federal database. Beveridge had been giving friends gifts of cheap vodkas infused with flavors. Perfecting a recipe for a quality homemade, handmade vodka, he produced one thousand cases in 1997, the first year of production. In 2001 Tito's was invited to the San Francisco World Spirits competition and won the double gold medal in the vodka category, beating out Grey Goose, Belvedere, and several dozen other competitors. Ten years after opening for business,

160,000 cases of Tito's Handmade Vodka were being shipped out of Austin annually. Ten floor-to-ceiling stills replaced the original still, which had been duct-taped from two Dr Pepper kegs and a Cajun turkey-fryer. Even as the company had expanded beyond its small batch origins, fending off lawsuits claiming Tito's was too big to call itself "handmade," cool drinkers were buying into the vodka's Austin affiliation. Being from Austin gave Tito's a hipper and younger image than brands coming out of Russia, Poland, and Finland.

Other microdistilleries popped up, including two rival vodkas, Dripping Springs and Deep Eddy, several whiskies, and a rum distillery. Locally sourced booze evolved into a lifestyle as critically specific and disciplined as the food police were once caricatured—telling you what's good for you.

The whole food thing had evolved.

Patty Lang Fair opened twenty Whole Foods Market stores around the country, always returning to Austin. The opening of the Cherry Creek store in Denver led her to quit. "That was our Martha Stewart period," she said of the late-nineties version of Whole Foods. "I thought we were more interested in having beautiful stores than providing healthy, natural foods. It was style over substance. That particular store just seemed the epitome of all that—flashing neon signs, commissioned artwork, marble counters from Italy, handmade tiles in the bathrooms. It was beautiful, but not why I was there."

She gave notice and went to work for Fossil Rim Wildlife Center, a nonprofit endangered species research and conservation center near the North Texas town of Glen Rose. She discovered a very different world outside the Whole Foods bubble. "Something I took for granted at Whole Foods and found wasn't the norm [was] an environment where people can make mistakes. You figure out what went wrong, do your best to fix it, and move on. End of story. It's rare. What I found outside of Whole Foods is a tremendous fear of making mistakes. And if they do make a mistake, they do their best to not admit to it—ignore it, cover it up, lie, blame someone else. It's so toxic. Right? People make mistakes. It's the human condition. At Whole Foods I learned it was OK to make mistakes; we were encouraged to take responsibility for them without fear of punishment, learn from them, and give that same freedom to others. It's pretty radical in the business world."

Residing in a community where biblical creationism was a tourist attraction proved challenging to Lang Fair. The biggest grocery was a Brookshire Brothers, an East Texas chain where organic produce was still considered foreign and exotic. She lasted four years before she returned to Austin and to Whole Foods, just in time for the opening of the flagship store at Sixth and Lamar.

If there was one person in Austin who epitomized good ideas and good ideals gone astray, a sizeable number of grocery consumers would have nominated John Mackey. He took his job personally, referring to the stores and the employees collectively as his "child." His prickly personality and willingness to confront rather than deflect made him an easy mark. He had outlasted a series of partners, collaborators, and spiritual advisers who had his ear to be the last one standing at the top of the Whole Foods pyramid. He was the face of the business.

Whole Foods had grown so ubiquitous in a certain upscale segment of modern America life that it turned into a punch line. Asparagus water—sixteen ounces of water with three stalks of asparagus—selling for $5.99 at one of the New York City Whole Foods made it easy.

Comic Kelly MacLean blogged: "Whole Foods is like Vegas. You go there to feel good but you leave broke, disoriented, and with the newfound knowledge that you have a vaginal disease."

Whole Foods was a meme on Twitter:

"In which aisle can I find the nunchucks?"
"Ma'am, this is a Whole Foods"
"Sorry, in which aisle can I find the gluten free nunchucks?"
—jade (@TheDreamGhoul)

Whole Foods sells $10 gift cards. The perfect gift for a loved one who wants two onions.
—Kevin Farzad (@KevinFarzad)

John Mackey willingly took on labor unions in California and elsewhere. Unions were against everything he believed in, and he liked articulating the point. "The union is like having herpes," he said back in the eighties. "It doesn't kill you, but it's unpleasant and inconvenient, and it stops a lot of people from becoming your lover." He disparaged federal health care, suggesting individuals should eat better to improve their health. His unwillingness to lower prices as competition increased from natural food grocers and from conventional grocers alike made him a big bad boss in many eyes.

The increasing popularity of organic and natural foods that Whole Foods was so vital in fostering came back to bite the company on the ass. Conventional grocers started emulating H-E-B Central Market, stocking organics and selling them for considerably less than what Whole Foods charged, exacerbating the Whole Paycheck perception.

For seven years Mackey posted pseudonymous remarks disparaging Colorado-based natural foods competitor Wild Oats Markets on online financial forums while Whole Foods was trying to buy Wild Oats, which it eventually did. Rather than let the corporate spokesperson speak for the company, Mackey enjoyed writing his own op-ed articles, such as his argument published in the *Wall Street Journal* that President Obama's expansion of federal health care benefits was "fascist." While his commentaries reflected his well-thought-out neo-capitalist beliefs, they often earned him the enmity of many Whole Foods employees and shoppers, and risked lowering shareholder value.

Good intentions and achievements seemed to be forgotten whenever Mackey spoke out. But despite his bad rep, Mackey was recognized as the accounting firm Ernst & Young's Entrepreneur of the Year for 2003, the same year Whole Foods Market became the first organic food grocer certified by the US Department of Agriculture. Company policies based on equanimity continued—for instance, no Whole Foods employee can earn more than nineteen times the average salary of a team member. The concept of team members, in which teamwork was stressed and employees could vote on keeping or rejecting another team member, had been embraced across the corporate world.

When the US Department of Agriculture dragged its heels on labeling genetically modified foods (GMOs), Whole Foods took the lead and required vendors to label all products with GMOs by 2018. Mackey had accumulated so much wealth that he opted to take an annual salary of one dollar. Those good deeds were too often neutered by Mackey's need to express his libertarian hippie views publicly in the interest of exchanging ideas.

Food writer Michael Pollan went after Whole Foods in his book *The Omnivore's Dilemma* (2006), charging that Whole Foods supported the same kind of large-scale industrial agribusiness as conventional groceries. Pollan used organic asparagus from Argentina sold at his Whole Foods in Berkeley, California, rather than local asparagus, as the example: the vegetable that was flown in from South America and priced at six dollars per pound may have been grown organically, he wrote, but it tasted like "damp cardboard."

Those gorgeous displays in the front of Whole Foods stores had to be some kind of Potemkin Village. Nobody could afford to buy all that beautiful produce. What happened to all the unsold produce when it spoiled? As Whole Foods got bigger, its embrace of local and seasonal produce waned,

Pollan wrote, even though the company marketed itself as "Supermarket Pastoral." When Pollan spoke at BookPeople, the indie bookstore across the street from Whole Foods' flagship store in Austin in which John Mackey was the major investor, Mackey showed up, offered Pollan a twenty-five dollar gift certificate to make up for the bad asparagus, and started a conversation that continued across the street and later in public. They engaged in an exchange of public letters and debated in front of two thousand people at the University of California in Berkeley where Pollan taught journalism, and where Mackey had earned considerable enmity for fighting off attempts to unionize workers when Whole Foods opened there.

The debates led to Mackey's pledge to buy more from local growers, underwriting a ten million dollar loan program for small farmers, and to promote the humane treatment of animals.

"He's the real deal," Pollan said of Mackey. "But it's a weird deal: Libertarian capitalist vegan, passion for animal rights, very smart oddball. We came out of our spat in a good place—he made some real changes as a result of the dialog and was very clever in positioning WFM as responsive to its critics."

Increasing competition and an inability to keep up with a torrid growth pace led to a slip in Whole Foods' stock price in 2015. The company responded with a value-focused retail grocery concept, 365, that wasn't quite what it was hyped to be.

CEO Mackey was skating on thin ice, in many respects just as he'd been doing since the very beginning, especially after longtime co-CEO Walter Robb, the realist of the two, was pushed out in 2016 with a ten million dollar parting gift and a 30 percent discount at Whole Foods for life. Mackey, the person, remained curious and hungry for spiritual nourishment on his lifelong path of self-discovery. Gurdjieff, Rand, Jung, Ouspensky, Rajneesh, Casteneda, Buber, Camus, Grof—he'd tried them all. He shared elements of his ongoing spiritual quest in an inspirational CD issued in 2008, *Passion and Purpose: The Power of Conscious Capitalism*. He also wrote his own dietary manifesto, the *Healthy Eating Initiative*.

On Memorial Day 2015, rains fell hard on already saturated soil, and Shoal Creek in downtown Austin jumped its banks again. Lamar Boulevard, the major north-south thoroughfare on the western side of downtown Austin, was submerged from Ninth Street to Fifteenth Street, flooding numerous businesses, including the building at Tenth and Lamar that once housed the first Whole Foods Market. That Whole Foods had been destroyed by the Shoal Creek Memorial Day Flood of 1981 before being rebuilt through the sheer will of its staff and the goodwill of its customers.

John Mackey had not forgotten. Four hundred eighteen stores later, the mega natural grocer purchased a full-page ad in the *Austin American-Statesman*:

> We understand firsthand the power of floods. We also understand the power of love in business.
>
> Our first store was destroyed by a flood in 1981. We survived only because of the outpouring of love and support from local businesses, neighbors, customers and dedicated Team Members.
>
> Now 34 years later, we'd like to return the favor. Whole Foods Market will be issuing up to $1 million in interest-free loans to help our neighborhood businesses get back on track.

John Mackey had grown his idea into the thirtieth largest retailer in the United States. In the process of making healthy profits, Whole Foods Market reformed the American food system. Right or wrong, he still really cared.

Mackey's in-house conscience, Patty Lang Fair, felt like success almost ruined the company, even though that same success brought competition, and competition created pressure for Whole Foods to lower prices. "A lot of the team made too much money and they got scared about losing it," she said. Stock options had created significant wealth for Whole Foods employees, but when the price dropped, shareholders starting pushing for more conventional features in Whole Foods. Fat sells.

"What sells is trust," Fair countered. "People trust us. That trust eroded over the past few years and that just broke my heart. I started hearing from people. 'I'm not really a Whole Foods shopper. I'm not like that.' I thought, 'People used to love being Whole Foods shoppers. What's going on?' Yoga moms wearing yoga pants were saying that."

Patty Lang Fair was still buying in, even though her perception of the company had been challenged. She had become the company's consumer insights coordinator, but more importantly, she was one of the three last team members from Tenth and Lamar still with Whole Foods. "John Mackey, he put his money where his mouth is in terms of sustainable agriculture," she said admiringly. "We do so much in support of that. We have these responsible ratings. I'm in consumer insights. Nobody cares, nobody sees. We're doing it because it's the right thing to do. There's been a huge change in how people grow food, including the big guys [agribusiness]. That's cool.

"Our Animal Welfare Ratings came about from someone just writing us. They were responding to something John had written on his blog and John said, 'Good point. I see your point.' Then wham bam, we have Animal

Welfare Ratings. He's a pain in the butt but he's a visionary kind of guy, let go of the Libertarian thing."

Enough capital had been created to support three foundations: the Whole Kids Foundation designed to feed kids, which helped put together Michelle Obama's White House garden; the Whole Planet Foundation, dedicated to microcredit lending to suppliers; and the Whole Cities Foundation, which helped underwrite stores in underserved, financially risky inner city locations.

"I honestly think we have found our way again," Fair said. "John had the vision and as he got busy with other things such as conscious capitalism and healthy eating, the vision faded. The company leadership was some guys that found themselves millionaires. It was easier for them to believe the hype— Whole Foods didn't have any competitors, everyone loved Whole Foods, Whole Foods ruled the world. They seemed completely blindsided when H-E-B, Safeway, Kroger, and other national conventional grocers picked up on organic and natural foods. People started buying there. The reaction from leadership was fear, which was not the Whole Foods Market I knew. We went into a bit of a frenzy. At a time when I think it was most important to stay our course, we faltered. It seemed like we suddenly wanted/needed everybody's grocery dollars, when in the past we were happy knowing that we would most likely just get 20 percent or so of grocery consumers.

"I'll go with John," she said. 'There's new places to go where we can still be funky and new and different. I hope the next few years proves me right," she said.

"We helped change Austin. Now I want to bring the funk back."

Patty Lang Fair spoke too soon. In 2017, Whole Foods was taken over by Amazon, the electronic commerce company that was the world's third largest retailer. The funk would not return.

6

South by Southwest

◉ ◉ ◉

Louis Black was not an early riser.

When his telephone rang shortly before sunrise on the morning of Saturday, March 14, 1987, he was not a happy camper. The burly, bearded editor of the *Austin Chronicle* liked hitting the clubs at night to hear music like everyone else at the weekly newspaper. Mornings were for other people.

Roland Swenson was on the line.

Future South by Southwest founder and CEO Roland Swenson when he managed the new wave band Standing Waves. (Photo by David Fox.)

"Louis, you know it's today?" Swenson asked, his voice cracking with nervous excitement.

"What's today?" Black mumbled in a gravelly voice.

"The event! South by Southwest! When are you going to come down?" Black squinted toward the alarm clock on his nightstand. It was 6:00 a.m.

"Yeah, I know," he rasped. "Fuck you," he mumbled before hanging up the phone and rolling back to sleep.

Roland Swenson felt very alone. But not for long.

Three hours later, the meeting room at the brand new Marriott Hotel just east of the state capitol had filled to the point of overflowing. All eyes were fixed on the podium where a colorful character with a shiny, sweat-slick forehead jutting in front of a high pompadour of brown hair addressed the gathering in a thick Cajun accent.

"I'll say dis. I knew the radio people and visited them everywhere I could. Disc jockeys didn't make a whole lot of money, so I would help them out whenever I could, leave 'em a hundred dollar bill for running change, throw it in the trash can on my way out the door. You sure better believe it when I tell you there wasn't a janitor at a radio station anywhere who fished a hundred dollar bill out of the trash can."

Huey P. Meaux, the Crazy Cajun, the hustling independent record producer, promoter, and all-around music industry maverick from Houston, was schooling the next generation of music movers and shakers in the traditional methods of record promotion. As an indie working out of Houston, Meaux shared more than a few qualities with the young alternative types who were industry outsiders. Still, despite numerous disadvantages, Meaux managed to score hits with "She's About A Mover" by the Sir Douglas Quintet in 1965 and revive Freddy Fender's career in 1974 with "Before the Next Teardrop Falls," among dozens of top ten records he was affiliated with. Although he was a few generations older than most of the audience, Meaux might have some wisdom to impart to his younger, more idealistic listeners. Plus, he was available.

The first South by Southwest Music and Media Conference almost didn't happen. The registration system set up for the event failed, causing lines to back up. Instead of the anticipated 150 registrants showing up, 700 queued up to pay for credentials admitting them to 15 panel discussions, the clubs where bands were playing, a backyard day party at the residence of punk rocker Jean Caffeine, and the keynote address by Huey P. Meaux.

After Meaux spoke, a young man approached him in the hotel lobby to ask, "Is it true that payola is dead?" Meaux shot him a puzzled look. "Dead?" he said. "I didn't even know it was sick, little bruddah."

That night, the Tailgators, Doctors Mob, LeRoi Brothers, Wagoneers, Dino Lee, Lou Ann Barton, Walter Hyatt, Two Nice Girls, Leroy Parnell, Ray Campi, Butch Hancock, Jimmie Dale Gilmore, Bobby Bridger, Vince Bell, and Angela Strehli, and half of the 177 acts booked for the festival performed in 13 clubs in and around downtown. The audience was a mix of locals familiar with the club scene, joined by music lovers from around the state and around the country, many of whom paid ten dollars for wristbands that would admit them into SXSW-sponsored clubs. Even the odd A&R record company person, has-been record producer, hustling publicist, and wannabe music industry executive could be spotted in the crowds. The music industry had come to Austin.

All in all, the response was positive, considering it was spring break week, when the University of Texas usually emptied out and thousands of students headed to the Texas coast or to the mountains. Student-oriented businesses in Austin typically shuttered during spring break. Antone's, the Continental Club, Liberty Lunch, Texas Tavern, and Steamboat would have otherwise cut back their schedules or closed for the week. Instead, almost every one of the sanctioned clubs was crowded, some at capacity.

Like just about everything else in alternative Austin, it started with music.

◎ ◎ ◎

Louis Black had arrived in Austin on a hot August night twelve years earlier. He and a running buddy had driven from Vermont in a '52 Chevy DeLuxe, looking for an old girlfriend who wasn't at home. They gently broke into her house to leave their bags, picked up a copy of the *Austin Sun* at a convenience store, looked over the club listings, and wound up at Soap Creek Saloon grooving to the musician Doug Sahm—three hours of full-blast Texas music that left him soaking in sweat and convinced he'd found his place. "I knew I was home."

Black decided to stay in Austin to immerse himself in film and film scholarship at the University of Texas, as well as to continue his higher education in music in Austin's clubs. He fell in with a group of similarly inclined graduate film students, including Nick Barbaro, Ed Lowry, Sarah Whistler, Joe Dishner, and Jeff Whittington. He got active in CinemaTexas, the campus film society run by grad students that programmed films that were required viewing for Radio-Television-Film courses being taught during the semester.

CinemaTexas offices were on the top floor of the faculty dining room building at the corner of Twenty-Fifth and Guadalupe Streets across from KLRU, KUT, and the College of Communications building. "CT had two rooms: one, the office for ordering films, editing notes, and meeting; the other, a screening room where the mimeograph machine was housed," Black wrote in a recollection in the *Austin Chronicle*. Equipment included a sixteen-millimeter projector and a two-plate flatbed Steenbeck editing machine for more careful viewing and analysis. "On it, you could watch the film frame by frame, as well as go backward and forward with ease," Black wrote. "Back then, it was an absolute luxury, and UT RTF was one of the few graduate schools where history, theory, and criticism students had access to one."

The grad students running CinemaTexas wrote notes to accompany each screening. "We'd turn in our four to twelve pages of notes, which were edited and typed onto stencils, mimeographed, and distributed at the screening," Black wrote. "Notes consisted of a film's complete credits (which were not as extensive as today's), the feeling being if an assistant sound editor's nephew went to UT, we wanted him to see his uncle's name. They also included an analysis of the film, which often included its history as well as that of the director and actors. The notes were periodically collected together, and a volume of them (usually about ten to fifteen films in a set) would be published and sent to a nationwide mailing list."

The note writing led to a big sky idea: what about an alternative newspaper like the old *Austin Sun*? Austin's counterculture had not stopped growing, and when the *Austin Sun* ceased publication in 1978, it left a void that

Austin Chronicle publisher and SXSW founding director Nick Barbaro at work with Dulcinea in his lap. (Photo by Martha Grenon.)

Founding SXSW director and Austin Chronicle editor Louis Black speaks at South by Southwest. (Photo by Martha Grenon.)

had remained unfilled. Why not? Black, Barbaro, and company were finishing graduate film school, and there weren't any sweet jobs waiting for them in Hollywood.

Although none had journalism backgrounds, they knew how to write and do reviews. Whatever they didn't know, they could learn. With the bulk of the funding coming from Nick Barbaro's mother, a one-time Miss America, the first issue of the Austin Chronicle appeared in news racks on September 3, 1981.

Six years later, Louis Black, the editor of the Austin Chronicle, joined with his old friend Nick Barbaro, the publisher of the Chronicle; Roland Swenson, the blond-haired band manager who was overseeing distribution of the Chronicle; and Louis Jay Meyers, a banjo player and steel guitarist who booked reggae acts into Liberty Lunch, for a series of breakfast meetings. Over coffee and eggs and toast, their idea for a convention of music outsiders came into focus.

Swenson was a descendant of the Swedes who settled in and east of Austin in the mid-nineteenth century. In the late seventies and early eighties, Swenson had managed the Standing Waves, an arty, kinetic ensemble inspired by the Talking Heads and one of the most popular of the punk and new wave groups playing Raul's, the small, former Chicano bar at 2610 Guadalupe Street. Raul's was the incubator for punk bands including the

Skunks, the Huns, the Big Boys, the Dicks, D-Day, Terminal Mind, the Next, the Re-Cords, and the Delinquents.

Most of the Raul's bands were highly derivative of scenes in New York and Los Angeles. What separated the Raul's scene from all other punk scenes was its patron saint, Roky Erickson, who was playing shows fronting the Explosives, a pop power trio with roots going back to Jerry Jeff Walker. Erickson had been lead singer of the Thirteenth Floor Elevators, an Austin band that formed in 1965 and recorded an album in Houston, The Psychedelic Sounds of the 13th Floor Elevators, regarded as the first psychedelic music recording (i.e., music made under the influence of LSD and intended for an audience that listened under the influence).

Powered by Erickson's soulful wail singer and Tommy Hall's electric jug, the Elevators blazed a trail in Austin and Houston before emigrating to San Francisco just in time for the Summer of Love, where they earned semihouse band status at the Avalon Ballroom. But LSD and too much of everything else took its toll, and Erickson wound up receiving electroshock therapy as a result of his incarceration in the State Hospital for the Criminally Insane in Rusk, Texas.

Erickson reemerged on the music scene in the midseventies, egged on by Doug Sahm, and started attracting international label interest through his Raul's appearances. For his part, Erickson connected punks to psychedelic music, tying together two decades of extreme homegrown music-making.

It was out in the Raul's parking lot during a break that Roland Swenson realized how wide the gap was between bands like his own trying to get their foot in the door of the music business and the people in the business who could make or break a music act. Surely there was a more effective way of getting a tastemaker to hear the Standing Waves than exchanging names of important people with another band manager who was as clueless as he was.

Swenson moved to New York with the Standing Waves for a stretch in the early eighties to get closer to the action; dabbled in music promotion representing his friend Patrick Keel, a record producer and performer; and ran his own Classified Records record label, doing business in the same converted two-story house on West Twelfth Street as the Austin Chronicle.

For several years, Swenson attended the New Music Seminar, which started in 1980 in New York as a means of connecting indie bands with the music industry. He was part of an official delegation from Austin attending the New Music Seminar in the summer of 1986 that led to the announcement that a regional version of the NMS would be held in Austin in the spring of 1987. It would be called the New Music Seminar Southwest.

But the New Music Seminar organizers dropped the idea, citing internal organizational challenges, including, according to their critics, way too much partying. Roland Swenson, the *Austin Chronicle*, and the Austin Convention and Visitors Bureau picked up the ball and ran with it. Screw New York. They'd do their own music conference.

The *Chronicle* would sponsor the regional seminar. Publisher Nick Barbaro got on board when Swenson suggested ending the gathering on Sunday afternoon with a barbecue and softball game, two of Barbaro's favorite activities. Black, a hardcore cinephile, came up with the name South by Southwest, a riff on the Alfred Hitchcock film *North by Northwest*. The Austin CVB kicked in funding to make the conference happen.

The focus would be on music and alternate media, meaning publications in other cities that were similar to the *Austin Chronicle*. The *Chronicle* reached out to eleven alt-weeklies across the United States, asking each to sponsor a band from their city. That guaranteed music from outside the Austin area and loads of coverage from the weeklies.

The organizers did not anticipate the response to their idea. "We opened for badge pickup the day before, and we had carefully made and laminated all the badges," Swenson said. "But we didn't expect many people who weren't preregistered to show up. All of a sudden there was a long line of people who wanted to buy a badge or make their case they should be comped. We didn't have a computer and were working from printouts from the one *Chronicle* computer, which primarily handled billing for advertising, and was back at the office. Eventually the line cleared, and SXSW was even bigger than we expected.

"The hotel had given me a sleeping room, so I could be on-site twenty-four hours a day," Swenson said. "I'd had a huge fight with a hotel salesman who was telling me that our people were only allowed to stand around in front of the half of a hotel ballroom we bought, and not in front of the vacant side. I was operating under severe lack of sleep for many weeks. I was in a lot of pain from an injured shoulder I got six months before while delivering the *Chronicle*. I was taking hydrocodone, which gave me weird dreams and kept me from sleeping deeply whenever I had a few spare hours, usually around 4:00 a.m. The night before the keynote, I was having vivid dreams of angry people chasing me around the lobby yelling, 'There he is! He's the one who got us to spend all our money to come to this lame event!'"

Saturday morning came. After Swenson's brief telephone conversation with Louis Black followed by a few more minutes of shut-eye, Swenson got out of bed and went downstairs to see what was going on. "There was a good crowd. Everybody was in a good mood, smiling, and was very nice to me. I went to work and didn't stop until Sunday at the first annual softball tournament and barbecue. We ate Stubb's barbecue with our bare hands. Nobody thought to bring plates or utensils."

By pulling off the first South by Southwest, Swenson, Black, Barbaro, and Meyers jump-started what would grow into Austin's biggest annual event.

The drawing card was music—in the clubs, on the streets, on outdoor stages, at parties, and as the subject of panel discussions. Throw in generally mild and pleasant mid-March weather while the rest of the nation was still locked in a winter chill, and no wonder Austin turned into the spring break destination for the music industry. Getting on a panel and then hanging with your pals, maybe hearing some music, doing some partying was on the calendar of every music biz player with an expense account. This was fun, not work, and definitely not some button-down convention.

Registration the second year increased from 700 to 1,200. The number of bands performing tripled to 415 bands.

Music consumers quickly followed the insiders and those who fancied themselves insiders. For them, doing South by Southwest was like going to a music festival spread out all over a city instead in an open field in the middle of nowhere, plus there were all these parties with bands everywhere

SXSW staffer and serious dancer Peter Turner busts a move with Autumn Deuel outside a sold-out Continental Club while Dianne Scott, Austin's most famous bouncer, watches from the door. (Photo by Martha Grenon.)

all day and all night, with free beer and barbecue. Why bother doing spring break on Padre Island?

The fourth year, SXSW grew up philosophically. The scope of music broadened. Mano Negra from Paris headed an international delegation of music acts, and the first hip-hop showcases were presented. South by Southwest was becoming more than a local or regional event.

By the fifth year, when 2,833 registered for the music conference, South by Southwest hit its first ceiling. The Austin Fire Marshall strictly enforced capacity limits in clubs. Wristband holders, theoretically guaranteed admission to all participating music venues, couldn't get in venues because capacity had been reached, and music conference registrants with their platinum badges were getting priority access.

Some bands got angry about where and when they were booked. One club, Abratto's, charitably described as a "disco meat market" by writer Michael Corcoran and not a live music venue to begin with, withdrew from SXSW after its first night of showcasing bands. Abratto's had been designated as the site for hardcore punk bands from Houston, per SXSW schedulers. The music and venue did not mix well. Acts scheduled to play Abratto's on the following nights, including a hot female country ensemble known as the Dixie Chicks, ended up performing in hotel conference rooms instead. Somebody somewhere got so pissed off by something SXSW did that they set fire to a stack of copies of the *Austin Chronicle* at the entrance of South by Southwest offices on Fortieth Street, causing extensive smoke and water damage.

Backlash had been part and parcel of SXSW from the very beginning, per the SXSWsux and South by So What? epithets bandied about by the whiners.

South by Southwest turned into a pretty big deal. Day parties emerged as a complement to nighttime showcases. Record labels, publications, and corporate sponsors staged invitation-only parties in the afternoon featuring music acts that would later showcase in front of the public. Retail stores and other businesses along Sixth Street, South Congress Avenue, and South First Street got into the act, throwing their own day parties with bands, food, and beer. Partygoers who chose wisely could eat, drink, and hear all the music they wanted for six days and nights, twenty-four hours a day, without spending a nickel.

The same clusters of friends and associates kept coming back, turning SXSW into something of a family reunion as well as spring break for the music industry. Roots rock music journalists who knew each other met for an annual breakfast. Roadies from bands that traveled together planned motorcycle rides around the Hill Country. A&R reps from certain indie labels took road trips to Lockhart, Luling, and Taylor to eat real Texas BBQ.

The Memphis producer and performer Jim Dickinson was one not-so-untypical regular. He made SXSW his family's annual spring vacation, bringing along his wife, Mary Lindsay, and his boys, Luther and Cody. Jim sat on panels and played, and gradually over the course of several SXSWs, introduced his sons, the future founders of the North Mississippi All-Stars, to the musician's life.

As cool as it was having all kinds of music people come to Austin from all over the United States and, increasingly, all over the world, the Austin Music Awards celebrated locals. The music awards started in 1983, four years before South by Southwest, to recognize winners in the *Austin Chronicle*'s annual music poll. *Chronicle* music maven Margaret Moser organized the event, which was held at Club Foot, the Austin Opera House, and Antone's its first three years. The 1984 awards show was highlighted by the surprise appearance of Stevie Ray Vaughan and Double Trouble, previewing their second album, *Couldn't Stand the Weather*. Joining Stevie onstage was his brother Jimmie, whose Fabulous Thunderbirds were one of the award show's headliners.

The Austin Music Awards became South by Southwest's kickoff event. "South by Southwest needed us back then," Moser said. It was the one program on the first South by Southwest schedule that organizers knew would draw a crowd. As SXSW grew in scope and breadth, with more music from elsewhere in the United States and overseas added to the lineup, the Austin Music Awards were dedicated to Austin. Moser, MC Paul Ray, and Moser's army of volunteers dressed up for the occasion, as did many awards recipients, as if this was Austin's Grammys. The backstage crowd visiting and yakking sometimes outnumbered the folks in the audience. Outsiders were welcomed, but the emphasis remained Locals Only, even as the music awards grew along with SXSW.

South by Southwest attempted to spread its brand by organizing similar events in St. Louis, Toronto, and Portland. A South by Southwest panel in 1992 titled "Who Shot JFK?" about the assassination of President John F. Kennedy attracted an overflow audience, which led South by Southwest organizers to produce ASK, the Assassination Symposium on John F. Kennedy in Dallas, the first conspiratorialist convention of its kind. The subject matter interested SXSW staff, but they were just as driven to put to use their knowledge of how to stage an unconventional convention, which they did for three years.

The events kept a year-round staff busy, utilizing their organizing skills.

Meanwhile, the original continued muscling up. In 1993, the SXSW Music and Media Conference moved into the massive new Austin Convention Center downtown with 365,000 square feet covering five exhibit halls, seven ballrooms, and fifty-four meeting rooms. SXSW immediately became the new center's biggest event. Ann Richards, the governor of Texas, delivered the keynote that year.

The three major elements of Austin's rising alternative profile converged for the eighth iteration of South by Southwest in March 1994. Two new components would complement the existing music conference and festival, under a single banner: SFMC—the South by Southwest Film and Multimedia Conference. Louis Black could have his own small-scale version of the Sundance Film Festival. Multimedia dealt in high tech, which was rapidly integrating itself into Austin's cultural fabric while disrupting its financial hierarchy.

The plan was simple: build upon the already hugely popular enterprise of music by adding film and technology to the spring fortnight of serious discussion and serious partying. The three disciplines overlapped. Many people in the different fields already knew one another. The event that made music the cultural totem of Austin would be the event tying together Austin's creative strands.

It was an easy sell. Louis Black may have been editor of the *Austin Chronicle* and a South by Southwest director, but above all, he knew film. Actors like that kid Johnny Depp loved Austin. Depp had started running with Gibby Haynes, the leader of the Dadaist band the Butthole Surfers, and songwriters Bill Carter and Ruth Ellsworth, forming the band P with them while he was filming *What's Eating Gilbert Grape?* in the Austin area. A new resident named Sandra Bullock, who would become the highest paid female actor in movies, found happiness as the girlfriend of singer, bandleader, and all-around heartthrob Bob Schneider, and became a regular at gigs of the Ugly Americans and other bands that Schneider led.

Movie people thought Austin was cool because they didn't get hassled by fans like they did in other cities. They could hang out with musicians, who were like actors, only in a more romantic way. "Who knew that Austin would be America's Paris?" the *New York Daily News* asked.

The mere fact that Johnny Cash was appearing in front of five hundred fans at Emo's Alternative Lounge (a music room that could charitably be described as gnarly and punkish), with Beck as the opener, following Cash's SXSW keynote address, should have been enough to suck the air out of all

other buzzworthy moments at 1994 edition of South by Southwest. But adding film and technology to the mix made Cash's showcase a moment, but
not necessarily *the* moment. The grizzled, mildly bloated sixty-one-year-
old Cash had reemerged as a wizened, talking blues song poet, dressed in
a black tuxedo shirt and a long black waistcoat. His reinvention came under
the guidance of producer Rick Rubin, cofounder of Def Jam Records and
one of the guiding forces of hip-hop music, which Johnny Cash had absolutely nothing to do with.

Cash performed solo with a guitar, and then was joined by the Tennessee
Two, his backup band. He encored with "A Boy Named Sue," tweaking the
familiar tag line at the end to say, "If I ever have another boy, I'm gonna
name him Emo."

The stool Johnny Cash sat upon hung above the bar for the rest of the
club's existence.

Meanwhile, the Friends of Louis Black Film Festival, as the *Austin American-
Statesman* movie critic Michael MacCambridge snarkily described the new
film component of SXSW, generated a whole other buzz in collusion with
some gamers and geeks. Richard Linklater, whose Austin-made indie instant
classic *Slacker* had presented Austin to the film world in a most compelling
manner, headlined the lineup of Louis's friends showing their films and
talking about them.

"We'd talked about [adding film] from early on," Black said. He'd seen
what the Sundance Film Festival in Utah had done to boost independent
film, but also realized that as Sundance grew in prestige, loads of worthy
films weren't getting into that festival. "We thought we'd do a boutique film
festival and a little bit of a conference," he said. If nothing else, the festival
and conference would expose filmgoers to Texas independent filmmakers
that Black had been championing in the *Austin Chronicle*.

Katie Cokinos of the Austin Film Society had been tapped to organize
the film festival, but at the last minute, after walking into SXSW offices and
seeing nothing but chaos, Cokinos introduced Black and Barbaro to twenty-
three-year-old Nancy Schafer, who was hired to program SXSW Film.

The feisty Schafer had come to Austin two years earlier after spending
summers volunteering at the Telluride Film Festival (in other words, working for free for all the "wrong" reasons, but another example of the alternative Austin business model). She'd been the production coordinator for
The Return of the Texas Chainsaw Massacre featuring Matthew McConaughey
and Renee Zellweger, and was working the counter at Waterloo Records to
pay the bills and be around cool people.

"I met Roland, Nick, and Louis at their office," she said. "They sort of asked me for my credentials, but it was so obvious they weren't going to look for anyone else. This was a lark for them. They were going to try it for a year. They didn't know if it would go on. For them the hire wasn't that scary. They were going to do it this one time."

Schafer attended the Sundance Film Festival in Utah in January to meet movie people, talk up South by Southwest, and check out panels. If the people she spoke with had any connection to Texas, they already knew about South by Southwest and were generally receptive. Film people with no connection to Texas gave her blank stares.

The timing of SXSW Film coincided with the rollout of the idea Barbara Morgan and Marsha Milam had been kicking around. They wanted to do an Austin film festival with a specific focus, and had settled on doing it in March. A movie producer from Houston named Fred Miller told Morgan and Milam, "The one area of film that is not being fulfilled in the festival area is the screenwriter." Morgan and Milam had identified a void in need of being filled. "All of these people desperately wanted to share their craft, get together and talk about it," Morgan said.

Several "ugly meetings," as Louis Black cheerfully described them, ensued before Milam and Morgan agreed to move the Heart of Film festival to October. The weather would be just as predictably pleasant, and there would be no conflicts for local or national festgoers.

Black griped about the coverage of the feud by the *Austin American-Statesman*'s movie critic, Michael MacCambridge, a friend of Morgan's and Milam's. But MacCambridge's calling SXSW Film the "Friends of Louis Black Film Festival" didn't feel like a diss to the man it was directed toward. "That was kind of the point," Black said. "We knew everybody in regional independent film, the people in Texas who were making movies. It was an outgrowth of the CinemaTexas mentality. It was all about regional film."

Black pulled out his Rolodex. "We gathered these Texas film luminaries and showed the films they wanted to show," Nancy Schafer said. Bill Wittliff, the Austin screenwriter, director, and author delivered the film keynote address, and showed the film he directed, *Red-Headed Stranger*, starring Willie Nelson, as well as Wittliff's cut of *Barbarosa*, also starring Nelson, which Wittliff wrote. Hector Galan, the Latino independent filmmaker from San Angelo living in Austin who wrote and directed the historical Tejano music film *Songs of the Homeland*, was honored. So were writer and screenwriter Bud Shrake (*Strange Peaches, Kid Blue*), and Texas indie pioneers Eagle Pennell, Ken Harrison, and Andy Anderson, Black's original inspirations for a Texas film festival. Texas-born producer-director Michael Nesmith, a member of the TV band the Monkees who'd embraced music videos, and Rick Linklater, who showed *Slacker* as well as his rarely-seen earlier effort, *It's Impossible to Plow by Reading Books*, had featured screenings, as did Peter Jackson's pre-Hobbit production, *Meet the Feebles*.

Nesmith cancelled at the last minute due to illness, saving him the indignity of watching his films *Tapeheads* and *Repo Man* screen with an audience of maybe seventy people at Hogg Auditorium on the UT campus. Seventy was actually considered a very good turnout by some of the exhibitors, Black learned. "I'd go by the Dobie and there were fifty people in a theater that could hold one hundred fifty for a screening with the filmmaker in attendance. And I'd go up to the filmmaker afterward and apologize, and they would look at me and go, 'Are you kidding? That was the best screening that I ever had!' This happened again and again."

Black credited the film fest audiences, who were not unlike the sometimes overly enthusiastic crowds that showed up to hear music in Austin. "I didn't realize some of these were difficult films," he said. "They weren't getting any more people anywhere else [where these films screened]. Not only were they getting an audience in Austin, but they were getting an engaged and intelligent audience."

About the same time that Louis Black talked Nick Barbaro and Roland Swenson into a film festival, Dewey Winburne, an oversized, gregarious, and very charismatic programmer, was trying to talk Louis and Nick into a tech fest. "Y'all need a New Media component," Winburne kept telling the two. They were missing the boat. South by Southwest needed to embrace technology.

Although they were already taking on a major addition by adding film, Black and Barbaro bought into Winburne's message. They *were* missing the boat and needed to hop onboard.

Black handed Winburne half the program and told him to fill it up. Louis and Nick had other tasks to deal with. More importantly, they both believed Winburne could pull it off. "Dewey knew everybody," Black said. "Even in music, we were still outside and renegade. Dewey knew everyone in the New Media community, locally and nationally."

Hugh Forrest, an Austin High School graduate who'd published the *Austin Challenger* alternative newspaper before joining the *Chronicle* gang, was put in charge of organizing and overseeing the multimedia track that Winburne had cooked up.

OK, so the big high-tech component was actually a two-day open house for "cutting edge visual creatives," as *The Daily Dot* later described the first multimedia confab. CD-ROMs, computer compact disks that held massive amounts of data in the forms of text and graphics, were topic A, since they were on the verge of becoming the Next Big Thing in consumer high tech, due to their unprecedented storage capacity. That's where Winburne put his focus.

So while Johnny Cash might have ruled the SXSW music universe, others were ruling the film and technology universes that SXSW had cooked up.

Three hundred people registered for SXSW Film and another three hundred registered for SXSW Multimedia in 1994. Those numbers were a pittance compared to the almost four thousand registrants who signed up for the music conference. But their presence clearly stretched the definition of what SXSW was all about. Multimedia had a lot of local players, a tribute to Dewey Winburne's networking skills and Hugh Forrest's organizing talents. A good chunk of the Friends of Louis Black film people came from somewhere else.

Richard Garriott, creator of the Ultima online multiplayer game and the force behind Origin Systems, the Austin computer game design company, spoke to the film and technology gathering about how the two worlds were merging in games like the ones Origin Systems was creating. Games were the new form of storytelling, Garriott believed, and the first means of storytelling in which the listener/viewer/player determined the outcome.

Two world premieres and eight panel sessions highlighted the film and multimedia conference, which was based at the Hyatt Hotel. Music and film attracted the crowds and generated the buzz. Real rock stars and movie stars were coming to South by Southwest, and they were no longer necessarily outsiders or indies. Tech people were initially regarded as awkward geeks. As startups and the Internet gained footing, the oversized personalities standing out at SXSW were increasingly tied to tech.

Music, film, and tech were Austin's shiny new industries, and South by Southwest brought them together.

Film and multimedia split into separate tracks for SXSW 1995, with multimedia joining the music conference at the convention center. Registration for multimedia was surprisingly robust compared to film, although neither track came close to the numbers the music conference continued ginning up. Slowly but surely, though, the references to the Next Big Thing at SXSW shifted from hot bands, killer voices, or this year's must-see film to innovations in technology. Whatever the Next Big Thing was in technology could translate into financial windfalls that dwarfed album sales and box office receipts.

But not at the start. Multimedia was on a slippery slope, operating on the premise that what hardware was to the eighties, software would be to the nineties. These were early days. The only people carrying around cellular telephones were record company executives with generous expense accounts. For most users, the Internet meant AOL. South by Southwest multimedia panel discussions were already pondering "Is the Web Dead?" when the World Wide Web had yet to really come alive. South by Southwest's email address was 72662.465@compuserve.com.

SXSW 1995 began minus Louis Jay Meyers. One of SXSW's four founders and the person in charge of booking bands, Meyers decided to sell his stake and bail. "I was tired of being the most hated man in Austin music," he said. He would remain involved peripherally, organizing the SXSW golf tournament, an extremely popular event among record company executives, and continue attending every year. But Meyers had had it being a band picker. Brent Grulke stepped into Meyers's shoes and immediately increased the number of acts invited to the festival from 467 showcasing artists in 1995 to 664 the following year.

SXSW 1995 marked the first year the event was acknowledged as the biggest alternative music gathering going. Its inspiration, the New Music Seminar in New York, folded. Still, for all the hype focused on Austin, its vibrant music scene, and the outsider spirit permeating South by Southwest, no significant acts had been discovered and signed to a big record contract at SXSW, which supposedly was what the conference was all about.

Country pop superstar Billy Ray Cyrus had performed at the second SXSW long before he scored big with "Achy Breaky Heart," and the Hanson brothers from Oklahoma were famously chased by graying Hollywood talent scout and self-promoter Kim Fowley at SXSW before they found their "MMMBop" groove. Even if the promise of being swept up by stardom was rarely realized, few were bitching. It was about the journey. South by Southwest was fun. Bands were willing to travel hundreds and thousands of miles for 250 bucks or some wristbands, which afforded them the privilege of being able to offhandedly say, "Yeah, we played SXSW." Anyone who actually managed to do some business in the midst of ten days of music, film, and tech, well, more power to them.

The appearance of Willie Nelson, Austin's music icon, performing for Microsoft's sponsored closing party spoke volumes of the merging sensibilities. Willie wasn't interested in playing SXSW for $250 or six wristbands. But he was willing to play for Microsoft in exchange for a substantial five-figure fee.

SXSW directors made a conscious decision to allow corporate sponsors and record labels to present music showcases of their own choosing. That brought in bigger, established name acts, but it came at the expense of unknown music acts trying to get their foot in the door and stand out among the noise. SXSW critics pounced, accusing the indie music festival of selling out. Maybe so, but the move helped widen SXSW's appeal. Foreign music delegations, sponsored by their countries, became draws unto themselves. Britain, Germany, the Netherlands, Sweden, Norway, Japan, and Australia all had their own showcase nights, as well as their own day parties.

Sanctioned events were fine. Competition in the forms of nonsanctioned showcases and parties rubbed SXSW directors the wrong way. When Lou Reed was booked to play an outlaw showcase at the same time as the Austin Music Awards, Louis Black accused Reed of "showing disrespect for the Austin music scene." Twelve years later, all would be forgiven—or at least forgotten—when Reed delivered the keynote address kicking off the music conference. After Reed died, SXSW staged a special Lou Reed night at the Paramount Theater.

For SXSW 1997, multimedia officially became South by Southwest Interactive, acknowledging the expanding power and influence of the Internet. Director Hugh Forrest called the name change "an accurate reflection of the industry we service—more and more people are using the Internet more and more often."

Reporters and journalists representing Prodigy, CompuServe, America Online, and other Internet service providers almost outnumbered print media on hand to cover the music portion of the conference.

Thomas Dolby, the digital music pioneer who had a synthesizer-driven hit "She Blinded Me with Science" in the eighties and then went on to develop the software for the polyphonic ringtone in the nineties, delivered the opening keynote. Jaron Lanier filled the closing interactive keynote spot with a speech and performance that combined ancient musical instruments and advanced technology.

SXSW-phile Michael Corcoran noted a turning point at the '97 music conference: a panel chaired by Jon Pareles of the *New York Times* asking "What's Behind the Drastic Slump in Record Sales?" The answer was right in front of everyone, at least those who knew about the Interactive conference that had just wrapped up. The music industry was dying, in no small part due to the rise of digital music, even though more music was being made and performed than ever before.

SXSW responded by further broadening its musical scope, showcasing the ageless crooner Tony Bennett and commissioning Wayne Coyne of the over-the-edge alt band the Flaming Lips from Oklahoma City to stage his Parking Lot Symphony piece in a downtown parking garage. Thirty parked cars, their doors open, had thirty cassette tapes blaring on their players simultaneously. A crowd of more than two thousand witnessed the performance.

By the first Saturday of the fifth iteration of SXSW Film in 1998, Louis Black realized that whatever he'd wanted it to be was actually happening before his very eyes. "I'm looking around and it's like Kevin Smith and Steven Soderbergh and Quentin Tarantino and Guillermo del Toro and Robert Rodriguez and Mike Judge and Rick Linklater . . . and I'm thinking if the roof falls in, American independent film is going to be set back for ten years." Black laughed before turning somber.

"The second thought that came to me was, 'How in the hell are we going to top this lineup?'

"We never had that percentage of important filmmakers. Guillermo, Rick, Robert, Mike Judge were living in Austin. Soderbergh and Tarantino were hanging out with Rick here. It was a coincidence all those people were around at the same time. Austin had become a place to go to, and music was big. There are twenty-five people who really created American independent film—the bookers, lawyers, and managers—and there's six of them walking down the hall; they're going out and having barbecue together."

"I thought we were the center of the universe," SXSW Film director Nancy Schafer said. "People were coming from New York, coming from LA. They knew what we were doing, and they wanted to be there. Industry was starting to call us, 'Can we be on a panel?' The whole thing you want to happen, happened."

It didn't hurt that many of the featured directors were friends who liked to party together. "Quentin, Rick, Robert, Mike Judge—that whole group figured out it was fun to come to Austin and hang out at South By," Schafer said. She would helm SXSW Film for nine years before moving to New York where she was founding director of the Tribeca Film Festival. Matt Dentler, who stepped in as SXSW Film director, put his stamp on the fest by establishing a balance between studio projects and DIY indie films. Janet Pierson, who took over from Dentler in 2009, oversaw the transition to digital while expanding SXSW Film programming to include episodic and television series.

Pierson came to Austin from the Pacific island of Fiji, where she and her husband John and their two children were the subjects of a documentary film *Reel Paradise* (2005). John, a rainmaker producer for indie filmmakers including Rick Linklater, Spike Lee, and Kevin Smith, took over one of the most remote movie houses in the world for a year and exposed the locals to all kinds of cinema, including Three Stooges shorts. The Piersons relocated to Austin when John scored a teaching job at the University of Texas. After spending most of her professional life working with her husband, running SXSW Film was Janet Pierson's deal and hers alone.

South by Southwest Interactive, the stepchild afterthought to music and film when it had been rolled out in 1994, turned into SXSW's driving force. Registration numbers blew past music and film. Like music and film, SXSW Interactive was the alternative to mainstream technology conventions and meetups such as the COMDEX Show in Las Vegas that big tech companies dominated. At SXSWi, an independent developer or a startup had a chance to network, be heard, learn something from a panel discussion, make an impact, and maybe even cut a deal. From an Austin perspective, high tech was the new punk rock: it bothered and sometimes upset people who didn't understand it. Those who did understand dove in full-on without hesitation, like a stage-diving, mosh-pit tumblerocker.

Louis Black pinpointed 2008 as the year South by Southwest reached critical mass. Registration reached 12,651. Among them was Jeff Bezos, founder of online retail giant Amazon, who bought a walkup registration badge and grazed SXSW minus an entourage. Standstill traffic, overflowing sidewalks, and venues filled to capacity were the new normal. The crowd counts were up everywhere, with even more events, more venues, more parties, and more everything, from TV food personality Rachael Ray's day party to Airbnb's launch with two customers—one being Airbnb CEO Brian Chesky.

The previous year, a thing called Twitter was rolled out at SXSW Interactive. By allowing users to communicate by "tweets," short messages that were 140 characters or less, Twitter ushered in the age of social media and text communication on smartphones. Its creator Evan Williams had been an Interactive regular for five years and introduced his previous startup innovation, Blogger, a podcasting company, at SXSW. Twitter was an immediate hit, providing an easy, accessible means of communicating for attendees, but no one left Austin thinking Twitter was going to become the Next Big Thing or a forty billion dollar company. When Twitter did take off over the next three years, its popularity helped establish South by Southwest Interactive as the go-to destination for consumer tech innovation. If there was something new to sell to young people, there wasn't a better place or time to present it to the public than in Austin in March.

Trying to club hop or movie binge between venues with a motorized vehicle during South by Southwest turned into a poor investment of time and money. Seventy-five dollar parking in lots downtown during the peak of SXSW became the going rate—if you could find a space.

◎ ◎ ◎

The Austin that visitors saw during South by Southwest wasn't the Austin that Alejandro Rose-Garcia, the singer-songwriter who called himself Shakey Graves, knew growing up. "As big as Austin has gotten, SXSW, it's not really about Austin bands, or even really about Austin at all," he told *Esquire* magazine. "This doesn't really resemble Austin in any way. When you talk to people and they're like 'I've been to Austin! I've been to SXSW!' it's like, well, you've been to a big, crazy, controlled riot that's happening in the city. It's sort of the same for people who live in New Orleans during Mardi Gras."

Thirty-six years after arriving in Austin, Louis Black, along with Nick Barbaro, Roland Swenson, and Hugh Forrest, was feted as Austinite of the Year at a Chamber of Commerce luncheon at the Austin Hilton. The Hilton opened in 2004, in part to accommodate the unusual convention that the men had started in 1987. Now, in 2012, the chamber was recognizing the South By braintrust for all the good they brought to Austin. Overall, SXSW was the highest revenue-producing event for Austin's economy. The Chamber of Commerce had to recognize them.

The four men remained hippies at heart despite having become very successful businesspeople. But Black, Barbaro, and Swenson put aside their bias, dutifully donned jackets and ties, and joined by Forrest, graciously accepted accolades from the business leaders of the city they helped reinvent.

The fruit of their labors, having the entire creative universe converge on their city, and practically bring everything to a halt with one great big party with a purpose, had altered the city, its self-image, and how Austin appeared to the rest of the world.

The new norm included magic moments such as the one the Austin band Tia Carrera experienced just after finishing their SXSW 2012 showcase set at Headhunters on Red River Street, performing in front of one hundred people in exchange for $250 dollars. One listener in the audience made the band's effort worth it when he showed up to help them load their equipment back into their van after they played. The helper, the comedian and movie actor Bill Murray, asked if he could ride with the band to wherever they were going, but guitarist Jason Morales reluctantly had to inform Murray there was no room in the vehicle. So Murray left the band with huge smiles on their faces. Their friends weren't going to believe them when they told them about their impromptu roadie.

The following March, almost every single band booked at SXSW tried to figure out how to weasel their way into the room where Bruce Springsteen delivered an inspiring keynote address about his life in rock and roll, including his praise of the English band the Animals, whose version of "We've Gotta Get Out of This Place" became "every song I've ever written. I'm not kidding, that's all of 'em," Springsteen said.

One night later, Eric Burdon, founding leader of the Animals and a well-seasoned septuagenarian, joined Springsteen on the stage of the Moody Theater, home of the *Austin City Limits* television program, along with reggae pioneer Jimmy Cliff, Tom Morello of radical rockers Rage Against the Machine, and local heroes Joe Ely and Alejandro Escovedo, to lead the ensemble through the song the Animals made popular.

That show got lost in the dazzle of LL Cool J, Public Enemy, Ice Cube, and Doug E. Fresh performing on Fifth Street in front of a giant sixty-two-foot-tall rendering of a Doritos corn chip vending machine with a four-story LCD screen. Doritos, unsurprisingly, sponsored the show.

Meanwhile, filmmaker Robert Rodriguez stood in front of the W Hotel, swinging an electric guitar. On cue, Rodriguez led his rock band Chingon through an instrumental before unstrapping his axe and stepping up to a microphone. He announced he was starting a new cable television channel, the El Rey network, aimed at young Latinos across the United States who were English speakers first, but nonetheless remained rooted in their Hispanic culture. A week later, Rodriguez was at the White House in Washington, DC, making the same pitch to the president of the United States of America.

Before Rodriguez left for DC, he arranged for Chingon to headline the Doritos stage at midnight on Friday. The band gig was a multimedia extravaganza. Rodriguez knew how to utilize every special effect the interactive stage had to offer. Montages of clips and stills from his films *Roadracers*, *Sin City*, *Kill Bill, Vol. 2*, and *From Dusk till Dawn* flashed on the big screen behind him while his band played.

The Doritos stage was another South By flashpoint. Thousands of kids jamming the street to experience big name acts beneath a giant snack food dispenser was not the SXSW of yore. What had once been alternative and hip out of necessity had evolved into mainstream commercial, as the operating overhead increased with the festival's growth. Despite at least ten indie beer breweries, the hops-and-grain equivalents of the same attitude that started SXSW, within a five-mile radius, Miller Beer was the official SXSW beer sponsor.

It was all about product placement, branding, and what's new. By covering SXSW's expenses, corporate brands got their cool card punched by buying in as a sponsor and being affiliated with something perceived as hipster-approved. These things didn't happen for free, after all. Still, to some weathered eyes, McDonald's and Miller Lite logos on SXSW banners, programs, T-shirts, and official material somehow didn't look right. Taco Bell building its first shipping container store especially for SXSW was no reason to get excited. Austin had grown into a chef's town and a regional brew hub, but it was hard to tell if you read the SXSW program or the back of SXSW T-shirts with all its corporate sponsors clustered at the bottom.

Sponsor money may have been essential to stage South by Southwest, but its impact was minimal compared to the three thousand people who showed up to work for nothing more than the experience of volunteering at South by Southwest.

The SXSW Volunteer Program, as it was formally known, was the stealth infrastructure that kept the whole operation humming. The program's existence generated a steady stream of criticism trashing SXSW for exploiting volunteers and interns. A for-profit company not paying labor was bad business, or at least that's what some labor lawyers and online journalists opined. But from another perspective, it sure looked like the alternative Austin business model at work. People worked for free at South by Southwest because it was fun.

Halfway through SXSW 2014, street traffic had pretty much ground to a halt around the Austin Convention Center stretching north-south along four blocks of Red River and Trinity Streets between Cesar Chavez Boulevard and Fourth Street, and far beyond. Ride shares, rickshaws, bicycles, taxis,

South by Southwest takes over the Austin Convention Center and the rest of the city for a fortnight every March. (Photo by Brittany Ryan, courtesy of SXSW.)

cars, trucks, and all other wheeled vehicles gridlocked. Inside the convention center, several thousand pilgrims swarmed, getting their credentials, attending panels and trade shows, looking at smartphones, ear buds, and other products sponsors were hawking, while scoping each other out.

The intersection at Fourth and Trinity brimmed with representatives from tribes from all around the modern world, most of them under thirty, those older than thirty trying to look younger, everyone decked in some degree of unfashionably hip fashion.

People parading up and down the long escalators on the north side of the building were attired in the requisite array of T-shirts emblazoned with messages and logos, including more than a few advertising the defunct New York punk rock band the Ramones. Some wore flowing scarves wrapped around necks, ubiquitous in Paris in the winter. There was lots of leather. Headgear ranged from the exotic (antique airmen's helmets) to the norm (gimme caps, cowboy hats). An inordinate number wore shorts in spite of late winter temperatures warming no higher than the low sixties. Sunglasses appeared to be the preferred eyewear. Hair of every imaginable length and color, many shades not found in nature, were part of the peacock strut.

Shifting gazes and darting glances suggested everyone was checking each other out but trying to not be too obvious about it, at least when they weren't staring into their smartphones.

This was transition day. Interactive had just wrapped. Some VCs and young entrepreneurs with their business plans lingered to close out deals before heading home. Cutting tech deals on the sidelines was as much a part of SXSW as getting your band signed once was. Film was winding down its five-day rollout of new commercial feature films and edgier independent films. Music—the basic ingredient in what had become a juggernaut that extended to SXSWEdu, SXSWEco, SXSWSports, and V2V, a Vegas spinoff—was about to get underway.

Interactive panels pondered wearables, such as computerized glasses, watches, wristbands, and rings, and social media. The privacy/security tracks garnered the most international media coverage for live video keynotes with Julian Assange, the WikiLeaks whistleblower who was holed up in the Ecuador embassy in Britain; Edward Snowden, the National Security Agency whistleblower who exposed the widespread surveillance and spying on the American public by the National Security Agency, which led to Snowden seeking asylum in Russia; and Glenn Greenwald, the journalist who broke Snowden's story, who was appearing live on video from Brazil.

Snowden spoke from an undisclosed location somewhere in Russia with the US Constitution green-screened behind him. He urged the audience at SXSW to devise programming solutions to prevent unwanted snooping on online users. "The NSA set fire to the Internet," Snowden told the gathering. "You are the firefighters. The people who are in the room at Austin right now, they're the folks who can really fix things, who can enforce our rights for technical standards even when Congress hasn't yet gotten to the point of creating legislation that protects our rights in the same manner. There's a policy response that needs to occur, but there's also a technical response that needs to occur. And it's the makers, the thinkers, the developing community that can really craft those solutions to make sure we're safe."

A few hours later, late night television show host, Jimmy Kimmel, broadcast his ABC television network show from the Long Center in Austin rather than from his usual Los Angeles studio. Kimmel compared notes with actor Seth Rogen about where they had been eating since they arrived in Austin. Both gentlemen plugged Austin as "an enabler" for all kinds of bad habits. "I've been here since Friday and I'm so full of tequila and pork, it's really a problem," Rogen said. Kimmel focused on the most ubiquitous liquid libation. "Here's maybe the best thing about Austin: Everywhere you go, they offer you a beer—for free."

Snowden and Kimmel summed up the yin and yang of SXSW, where somber discussions involving some of the most creative thinkers in the world, such as astronomer Neil deGrasse Tyson and homegrown cyberpunk author Bruce Sterling, occurred simultaneously with some of the most serious party people in the world, including Snoop Dogg, Justin Bieber, Lady Gaga, Neil Young, Jay Z, and Willie Nelson.

To prove their point, the world's highest-paid movie actor, Johnny Depp, flew in on his private jet from France to accompany his girlfriend, Amber Heard, who was receiving a Texas film award. Depp's reward for making the trip was getting to join Willie Nelson and band onstage at the Austin-Travis County Rodeo, several miles and multiple cultures away from SXSW, jamming in front of a cowboy/cowgirl rodeo audience.

Back downtown, outside the Paramount Theater on Congress Avenue, Ian Somerhalder, star of the series The Vampire Diaries, told a newspaper reporter, "Austin during South by Southwest is the most important place to be in the world. The smartest people are all right here, right now, changing the world."

"It feels like a social sculpture here," observed the actress Tilda Swinton on her first trip to the city. "It's as much about the desire to buy a T-shirt saying, 'I was drunk when I bought this T-shirt on Sixth Street' as going to listen to Julian Assange."

Across the street from the tinted glass windows of the Austin Convention Center, a huge crowd massed around two blue-and-white striped tents to illustrate what Swinton was talking about. Underneath one tent, draft beer flowed freely while a snaking queue baby-stepped toward a table where barbecued beef brisket, sausage, chicken, and ribs were being served on paper plates, along with beans, cole slaw, potato salad, slices of onion, white bread, and iced tea, if you weren't drinking beer. This was Texas barbecue, catered, nothing fancy. The majority of the crowd at this gathering hailed from Great Britain, whose music commission was hosting their annual SXSW UK in Austin welcome party, accompanied by a string of new young bands the Brits would be showcasing all week.

The adjacent tent belonged to the Germans, whose government agency promoting German music was sponsoring a similar party with free beer and wine and Texas barbecue.

In the twenty-foot space between the two tents, a thin, well-tattooed German and a hulking Englishman with a shaved head and multiple piercings stood toe to toe. They both clutched cups of beer as they studied a small booklet while talking animatedly. They seemed to be having a good time, heads nodding in unison, a smile now and then, until the German suddenly stood back, shaking his head and waving his hands while muttering "No, no, no," in thickly-accented English. The two weren't arguing about music, their competing meetups and agendas, their countries, or which bands to see that night. They were arguing about the best breakfast tacos in Austin.

Back at the convention center, a passel of geeky kids kept their eyes on their smartphones, trying the new app that let them know where all the free food and booze parties were that afternoon, and which parties had good bands playing. Several raised their heads from staring at the devices in their hand long enough to nod in agreement over another's comment about how a talk she'd just heard was life-changing, before eyes returned to phones and thumbs typed out a shorthand tweet.

Pop-up stores sponsored by Microsoft, Apple, Facebook, ATT, Levi's, and CNN appeared on vacant lots, in empty storefronts, and in leased restaurants. The global brands showcased their newest products to their target audience's tastemakers, who had conveniently appeared from all over the world specifically to sample the latest in music, media, film, technology, and culture.

Two blocks from the convention center, four teenaged girls attired in matching Hello Kitty outfits unloaded amplifiers, microphones, and musical instrumentals out of a rented van to prepare for sound check, just as hundreds of other bands were doing, if they weren't already performing.

Late on the night of March 13, 2014, twenty-one-year-old Rashad Charjuan Owens, a wannabe rapper from Killeen, an Army-base town an hour north of Austin, drove his sports-utility vehicle through a police barricade on the frontage road of Interstate 35, and then tried to elude police cruisers by driving onto Red River Street, which was closed to traffic. Driving recklessly at a high speed, Owens killed three pedestrians and a woman on a moped with his vehicle, and injured twenty-one.

The real story was that something like this hadn't happened before, considering the numbers, the density, and the amount of alcohol involved with the event. South by Southwest had gotten that big—big enough to be the target of considerable pushback from the community. Neighborhood associations near downtown didn't like the crowds and accompanying noise and music, or neighbors who rented out their homes at inflated prices to visitors. Some locals made a point to leave town, like many New Orleanians did during Mardi Gras.

SXSWi 2014 counted 2,800 speakers—more than four times the total number of multimedia registrants twenty years earlier—800 sessions, and more than 30,000 attendees. Interactive effectively captured the dynamic culture of the Internet like no other annual gathering.

"South by Southwest has to stay fluid, always has to change, to be ahead of the curve, instead of emulating what we've done five years ago," Hugh Forrest told *We Are Austin Tech*. "Something launches here, gains traction with this insular cutting edge tech crowd, but won't spread into the mainstream for a couple years. I've had people tell me they register for Interactive to see what will be hot in two years." The mix of ideas and energy SXSW fostered was special. So was the place where all this took place. "What sells a lot of people [on SXSW] is enjoying Austin, the food, the people, the vibe," Hugh Forrest said. "It's such a different city from so many other places. We couldn't pull it off anywhere else."

SXSW Film 2014 showed 133 feature films and 114 curated shorts, selected from 6,494 submissions. For 2015, a record 145 feature films were screened. SXSW Film had grown and matured to the point that it was regarded as one of the most important film festivals in the world, a complement to Sundance and Cannes, and the go-to festival for documentaries and music-focused films.

Louis Black crossed over into the role of producer, backing a Townes Van Zandt music documentary *Be Here to Love Me*, a Doug Sahm music documentary *Sir Doug and the Genuine Texas Cosmic Groove*, a documentary on filmmaker

Richard Linklater, an indie feature film written by the actor Ethan Hawke based on the life of the street musician Blaze Foley, and a documentary on the Church of the Subgenius.

A record 2,200 bands from 62 countries played while the movies screened, the panels pondered, and hundreds of promoters vied for attention at the Interactive trade show. Streets overflowed with parties and improvised music performances starting at noon and going late into the night, most of them having nothing to do with South by Southwest. All that culminated in a twelve-story office building near the Texas capitol, valued at $41 million, constructed in 2017–18 as South by Southwest headquarters.

The event had come a long way. The keynote speaker at the first South by Southwest in 1987 was the independent record producer/hustler Huey P. Meaux, a twice-convicted felon.

The keynote speaker for the thirtieth edition of South by Southwest in 2016 was the President of the United States Barack Obama, who addressed the Interactive conference. The First Lady of the United States Michelle Obama delivered the keynote for the music conference.

"How do you top that?" a friend asked Roland Swenson at the softball tournament that closed out every South by Southwest.

Swenson, who appeared less tired than he did at this juncture in previous years, smiled inscrutably.

"We were working on the Pope."

Later that year, President Obama returned the favor, working with SXSW organizers to stage South by South Lawn at the White House. He'd already taken the Capitol Factory startup incubator tour and had been using C3 Presents to produce his big shows. Obama knew Austin as the place where smart ideas came from.

And everyone knew that for two weeks every March, Austin was the coolest place on earth.

7
Austin Film Society

⊙ ⊙ ⊙

The midnight screening was a calculated risk, and Scott Dinger knew it.
He was the new owner-manager of the Dobie Theater, a two-screen movie
house in a moribund shopping mall at the bottom of a student housing high-
rise across Twenty-First Street from the University of Texas campus. And he
had bought the pitch thrown him by two student-aged movie fanatics. An
effusive, strawberry-haired big guy with horn-rimmed glasses named Lee
Daniel and his mop-topped partner in crime Rick Linklater started a cinema
club and wanted to make a splashy debut. They proposed a once-a-month
Midnight Experimental Film series. Dinger said, "Let's do it." If they could
put butts in the seats and present some cool film, he was all for it.

Cameraman Lee Daniel (left) and director Rick Linklater, founders of the Austin Film Society, at
work with script supervisor Monika Petrillo and actor Patricia Arquette. (Photo by Matt Lankes.)

Daniel and Linklater presented the provocatively titled "Sexuality and Blasphemy in the Avant-Garde" on the first weekend of October in 1985. Five films screened together: Kenneth Anger's *Scorpio Rising*, Luis Bunuel and Salvador Dali's *Un Chien Andalou*, Barbara Hammer's *Multiple Orgasms*, *The Club* by George Griffin, and *Nudes (A Sketch)* by Curt McDowell.

The *Austin Chronicle* provided Linklater and Daniel a free quarter-page ad. The editor, publisher, and most of the *Chronicle* staff had come out of the CinemaTexas/UT graduate film program scene and loved movies as much as Linklater and Daniel did. The ad was augmented by flyers slapped on utility poles around the perimeter of the campus, as if a punk battle of the bands was being promoted instead of five edgy films most students had never heard of.

The Friday night screening sold out. The Saturday night screening sold out. The Sunday matinee was comfortably full, a near sellout. The Austin Film Society was on its way.

Scott Dinger would gain something close to legendary status in Austin cinema as the theater guy who provided screens for ideas like Linklater's and Daniel's and for starting aGLIFF, the Austin Gay and Lesbian International Film Festival two years later.

Rick Linklater and Lee Daniel put Austin film on the map.

"It all grew out of a desire to see films we hadn't seen before," Rick Linklater said. Linklater and Daniel met as Super 8 buffs, two of a gaggle that met at places like Esther's Follies and the Ritz to show their work to one another.

Linklater grew up in Huntsville, a town of thirty thousand in the East Texas Piney Woods, where the Texas prison system was headquartered. He fell in love with Austin over a series of visits in the mid- and late seventies. Grok Books was one of the first windows to this new world. "It was in this old house and it was full of these philosophy and spiritual books you never saw in other bookstores," Linklater said.

He wanted more of that. He'd worked on an offshore oil rig following high school and saved enough money to buy a film camera and move to Austin in 1983 without needing to work. He had two specific goals: watch movies and make movies.

"I was a film freak in a music town," Linklater said. "That first year was glorious. CinemaTexas and the Texas Union Theater were showing five films a day on campus. I was trying to figure out what the scene was here. There wasn't much. It was really loose. There was a group called Heart of Texas Filmmakers, these guys Ray Farmer and Austin Jernigan [who later joined the cast of Esther's Follies]. People made shorts. They had a short film festival every year. I hung out with those guys." One of those guys, Lee Daniel, would be Linklater's collaborator and main cameraman.

"I wasn't in school, but I'd go to student films," Linklater said. "I'd just watch movies and was making my own first movies. I wrote down every movie I saw and at the end of the year, I'd seen six hundred eighty films. Some days I'd see four films."

Linklater's second year of film in Austin was not quite so idyllic. "They're showing the same films, *Wild Strawberries* and *Seventh Seal*," he said. "What about the other forty Bergman films? I started getting frustrated. They were doing them for classes. The same teacher was teaching a new group of students."

He'd seen these movies before.

"I noticed they kept showing the same shit," Linklater said. "I'd sit through a film again, but out of frustration, I got to know Steve Bearden, who was running the Texas Union film program, and the CinemaTexas people. By 1985, their heyday was behind them. Their time was the late seventies and early eighties. All the people who went on to do the *Austin Chronicle*, their energies had shifted to the newspaper. They'd all graduated, Louis [Black], Marge [film critic Baumgarten], Nick [Barbaro], all them. They were doing their own thing. They loved movies more than anything, but slowly but surely, those programs were running out of money. Sixteen-millimeter prints were in worse shape. Professors were starting to show videos and laserdiscs in class instead of showing a movie. That was slowly dying."

Linklater took a couple classes at Austin Community College from Chale Nafus, who became a mentor and would later program films for the Austin Film Society. Linklater got the grades to allow him to transfer to the University of Texas, but it was too late. "I got too far ahead of myself," he said. "I realized I could be teaching that class."

Lee Daniel finished film school and moved in with Linklater. Together they made a charming seven-minute short film about Woodshock, a festival of alternative, New Sincerity, and punk bands, including a very young and innocent Daniel Johnston, the Big Boys, and Glass Eye, staged outside of Austin in the summer of 1985. Using two Super 8 cameras and a Nagra sound recorder, they captured the beer-addled, drug-infused chaos of the crowd and the event. Some scenes employed multiple imagery accompanied by squalling, squealing electric guitar feedback to lend an avant-garde element to the clip, suggesting the two had parachuted into another dimension. The credits at the end read "Film Attempt: Lee Daniel, Rick Linklater."

Conversations between Linklater and Daniel about film turned into talk about a film society. Both wanted to see more experimental film. A film society would allow them to do that. That's when they hatched the idea for the monthly Midnight Experimental Film program at the Dobie Theater.

Film friends showed Linklater how to rent movies. He did the math. Rent a film for one hundred dollars, get fifty people to pay two dollars each to watch it, and—bingo! "We can show anything we want," he said.

Louis Black at the *Austin Chronicle* played matchmaker, introducing Linklater to Chuck Shapiro, a CinemaTexas programmer who offered another money-saving tip to Linklater: "Rent the films, but tell them you're just going to show it once, and actually show it three times. If you pay for all three screenings, you're going to lose money and you'll be out of business."

Linklater learned a lot in a short amount of time—"How to call Canyon Cinema, book the film, pay the shipping, do all the shit work. I didn't have a job because I'd saved my money. So I just devoted myself to that, and writing and shooting film."

The Midnight Experimental Film program was a success. "I was able to rent those films, pay for the rentals, print the flyers at Kinko's," Linklater said. "We were like a band. Lee had no patience to book a film or do any of the bureaucratic shit. Lee liked putting up flyers. At one in the morning, he'd go out flyering."

Linklater and Daniel followed up "Sex and Blasphemy" with four more thematic Midnight Experimental screenings in the spring of 1986. Scott Dinger almost got arrested for showing Pasolini's forbidden *Salo*, part of "The Spirit and the Flesh" series, in conjunction with Austin Community College and that school's director of humanities and all around movie mover-and-shaker Chale Nafus.

That summer, the Linklater-Daniel juggernaut extended to the Laguna Gloria art museum, where German filmmaker Werner Fassbinder's movies were screened in a retrospective that sold enough tickets to pay for itself.

There was an audience for these kinds of films. "We're a music town, a book town, and we're also a film town, but hadn't been much of an outlet for film," Linklater recalled. "Suddenly, there were alternatives. People would come out to Laguna Gloria. One hundred twelve people would fill a classroom to see a film. I'm like, 'Hey man, this is working.' Of course I'm paying a hundred thirty-three dollars a month for a little dive in West Campus, all bills paid. There's no profit, no anything, but we can sustain this thing as long as we want."

With Chale Nafus and *Austin Chronicle* film critic George Morris as advisors, Linklater got ambitious. The edgy programming and the passion stoking it were only the start. "The film programming at the university was kind of the opposition," said Linklater. "We enjoyed our punk status, but I'd go have lunch with Steve Bearden, Chris Anderson, and Mark Alvie when we were getting going. They were real supportive. We would share prints. I'd go over there and just hang out, watch film. But they'd started doing less and less. You could see the budgets were going away. Their funding was getting cut. CinemaTexas went away completely. The very second the student union went into red ink—they lost thirty thousand dollars the same year they built a one hundred million dollar addition to the stadium—film there ended. This was a huge loss for students, not just Austin. If you can't watch great film, what is education?"

Jim Jackson, a film connoisseur who worked at the state capitol and knew powerful people, suggested Linklater apply for a grant.

"Yeah, how do you do that?"

"Oh, you gotta be a nonprofit."

Linklater put on a shirt with a collar and met with a lawyer who set up paperwork for the Austin Film Society. "That's kind of a boring name," he acknowledged. "But it sounds official, not too punky."

He wrote the first Austin Film Society grant application, which effectively persuaded the Texas Commission on the Arts to award the organization six thousand dollars for programming.

Denise Montgomery, another film fanatic who became the film society's blue-sky big dreamer, hatched a plan with Linklater and Daniel to lease an abandoned ice cream shop called Nothing Strikes Back above a popular campus coffee shop and bakery, Captain Quackenbush's Intergalactic Café. Quack's owners, Art and Evelyn Silver, offered the space, which was being used for storage, rent-free. With the help of film friends who volunteered time and labor, they tore up the old space, built a projection booth and a screen and, armed with two sixteen millimeter projectors, created a cinephile's playhouse, Austin Media Arts, the film society's own space, which opened in the spring of 1988. It was the perfect setting for what Montgomery described as a "Beat Happening, eighties style."

Films were screened, workshops held, casting calls staged, and visiting filmmakers spoke. "It was our own cinematheque," Linklater said.

Linklater went overboard with the programming. He booked as many as five films a weekend at AMA. "Then I looked up and saw there were twelve people coming," he said. "Our schedule was ridiculous. I overreached. We lost money. But we were still getting the grants. I realized Austin's good for this, but they don't want to watch eighteen Godard films in a month."

On the other hand, Linklater *would* want to watch eighteen Godard films in a month. And he did.

A film culture emerged at Austin Media Arts. "You met a lot of like-minded people," Linklater said. "Film people are a little shy, a little asocial. A lot of them are quiet. I remember Terry Malick came when we were showing a Bresson film. 'Hey that's Terrence Malick!' Lee Daniel had shot some night sky scenes for him. He talked about *Balthazar*, which he'd come to see. He said it was more sad than he remembered."

Linklater loved hanging around the space. "I'd be up there sweeping the floor, always doing something." He felt a little let down that college film students weren't showing up, even though the AMA was right across the street from campus. So he took note when one awkward UT film student started coming to screenings and discussions. "Students were just too busy with their own shit," Linklater said. "Here we're showing the best films ever. But the ones that did show up were special. This one dorky student was hanging out, always asking questions. I could tell he liked film. He'd ask weird questions." Linklater never caught the student's name. "Over the years, I'd think, 'What happens to guys like that? They don't have the personality or gung-ho to be a director. Do they teach?'"

In 2001, Linklater was showing his animated docufiction drama *Waking Life* at the New York Film Festival, when he was introduced to filmmaker Wes Anderson, the writer and director of the quirky *Bottle Rocket* and *Rushmore*, who was screening his latest film *The Royal Tenenbaums*. "We look at each other and I go . . . 'You're the dorky guy who used to hang at the film society, all grown up!'" Linklater said.

"Yeah, you were the guy projecting those movies!" Anderson replied.

"That had been a big thing for him," Linklater said of Anderson's exposure to Austin Media Arts. And it was a big deal for Austin Media Arts. "He was among the minority of college students taking advantage of what we were showing."

Cinema clubs had been a tradition at the University of Texas. Cinema40 was formed in 1968 by two film buffs, Gregg Barrios and David Berman, as a seat-of-the-pants operation. "We had no budget, but I had a friend running the film program at Rice, so when Jean-Luc Godard went to Houston to do an event at Rice University, we brought him to Austin for nothing, and he screened *Weekend*," Berman said. "He gave some opening remarks, then borrowed my car to drive around because he'd seen the film enough, and then he came back and took questions afterward."

CinemaTexas was dreamed up a couple years later by Ron Lellis and

George Policy to bring in a steady stream of foreign and independent films to screen on campus. Like its predecessor, it too would eventually run its course, as was the case with most college cinema clubs, an indirect result of the availability of film on video, the rise of multiplex cinemas that had enough screens to show beyond-mainstream fare, constant student and staff turnover, and the growing popularity of cable television whose multiple channels filled their schedules with older films.

Austin's film rep had been pretty much tied to an underground horror epic filmed in and around Austin. *The Texas Chainsaw Massacre*, directed by Tobe Hooper, expanded the boundaries of movie gore when it was released in 1974, mainly through the novel use of a chainsaw as an instrument of terror. The film's hero, a cattle truck driver who saves the female lead Sally Hardesty (Marilyn Burns) from the evil Leatherface (Gunnar Hansen) and his chainsaw, was played by Ed Guinn, better known as the leader of the band the Conqueroo. Elder humorist and writer John Henry Faulk made a cameo. Robert A. Burns, the meek and mild-appearing art director, used real animal entrails and body parts in blood-splattered scenes, launching a career as an Austin eccentric and film prop designer (*The Howling*, *The Hills Have Eyes*, *Re-Animator*).

For at least a decade after *Chainsaw*, film in Austin meant either Willie Nelson, who had become a one-man cinematic force unto himself reflecting his One Name Superstar status in music, or some *Chainsaw*-inspired variant. "It was so dispersed," Rick Linklater said. "Once a year, someone would raise a hundred thousand dollars to make a *Chainsaw* wannabe kind of film. But there was no real cultural or unique connection between the people here and the kinds of films being made here. There was no focus."

Austin was ripe with aspiring film people, despite the apparent absence of a scene. Not everyone with talent and cinematic aspirations high-tailed it to Hollywood. Warren Skaaren was the first head of the Texas Film Commission, established by the state in 1971 to attract production companies to film on location in Texas, and went on to rewrite screenplays for *Fire with Fire*, *Beverly Hills Cop II*, *Beetlejuice*, and the first *Batman* film.

Aspiring Austin film directors Eagle Pennell, Kim Henkel, and Doug Holloway deliberately chose the indie path, utilizing local actors including Lou Perryman and Sonny Carl Davis to make low-budget, artsy Texas-fried films, such as Pennell's *Whole Shooting Match*, which was released in 1980, and *Last Night at the Alamo*, released three years later. Rick Linklater called *Whole Shootin' Match* "a big moment in my own film evolution. [Robert] Redford credits that film with waking him up [to the fact] that there is talent all over this country. And he wanted to do a film festival that would nurture that talent out there." In other words, because of Eagle Pennell, directly or indirectly, the Sundance Film Festival happened. Demons got the best of Pennell, and he drank himself to death just before his fiftieth birthday in 2002, never quite attaining the recognition he merited.

Music-themed films starring Willie Nelson put Austin on Hollywood's radar in the late seventies and early eighties. *Honeysuckle Rose* was a major motion picture starring Willie, playing a character based on himself, shot in and around the city during 1978 and 1979. *Honeysuckle Rose*, and subsequent Willie flicks *Songwriter*, *Barbarosa*, and *Red-Headed Stranger* brought real big time actors, directors, producers, and crews to Austin. Willie opened the door for Bill Wittliff, the writer and small press publisher who wrote the screenplays for *Honeysuckle Rose* and *Barbarosa*. The latter was the first script Wittliff had ever written, based on a story he'd heard from his grandfather years before. Writer Edwin "Bud" Shrake saw Wittliff's first script on his desk, picked it up and read it, and got his agent involved. Shrake ended up writing the screenplay for *The Songwriter*.

Roadie was based on a fictional character created by Big Boy Medlin in his column for the alternative *Austin Sun* newspaper. The film featured the singer Meat Loaf in his first lead acting role, playing an equipment lugger for a rock and roll band. Medlin borrowed from his experiences as a roadie for Austin rocker Doug Sahm in 1973 to sketch out the story with collaborator and fellow *Austin Sun* writer Michael Ventura.

Austin was also the scenic backdrop for *Outlaw Blues*, a B movie starring and directed by Peter Fonda, an acolyte of indie drive-in maestro Roger Corman. The film stirred up plenty of local interest when it was released in 1977, despite its schlocky, predictable, chase-scene riddled plot.

Crew people who came to Austin for shoots in and around the city took to the locale, its temperate climate, and laid-back groove as enthusiastically as any touring band ever did. Some, including film editor Sandra Adair, liked Austin so much they put down roots despite the considerable distance from Hollywood.

Texas had plenty to offer as a location for movies. Its physical landscape encompassed coast and desert and a wide range of urban, rural, and suburban settings. The weather was generally pleasant. The absence of unions representing production crews and no state income tax were appealing economic factors. Following her election in 1991, Governor Ann Richards made clear her interest in championing film by hiring a well-connected

Californian, Marlene Saritzky, to oversee the Texas Film Commission and lobby more movie companies to do their filming in Texas.

That was on the surface.

Under the rug, the next wave of filmmakers and creatives was already busily working their way through the process on the fly with a shared street-wise, duct-taped approach to film, accompanied by a missionary determination to do it on their own terms.

⊙ ⊙ ⊙

Rick Linklater plopped down in a metal patio chair at a table at Les Amis Café, the off-campus coffee shop that made an appearance in the film Linklater had just finished. It was winter, early 1991, and Linklater had just returned to Austin from the Sundance Film Festival, where his film Slacker had been nominated for Sundance's Grand Prize award. Linklater's life was about to change, but he either didn't realize it or wasn't letting on. No mirror shades, no shiny leather or turquoise for the twenty-eight-year-old director making his film debut. A blue T-shirt and dark blue jeans would do just fine. He was still very much the deadpan kid from somewhere else in Texas who came to Austin to deep dive into film.

He happened to have an international hit on his hands with the film he scripted and shot at a cost of twenty-three thousand dollars. Its appeal was pegged to Linklater's ability to capture and articulate Austin cool by aiming his camera at the community that lived on the fringe of the University of Texas, the same neighborhood where he lived. The film's characters, he said, "don't know what they're going to do with their lives, but know what they're not going to do."

The plot was minimal, following a thread of characters handing off the story to newer characters, not exactly sure where the story's going, much less where they're going. The conglomeration of permanent grad students, eccentrics, dropouts, and weirdos were the latest iteration of a tradition of offbeat residents in the neighborhood going back to the bohemians and beatniks and running through hippies and punks. The film merely put a name on these smart young adults who embraced aimless drifting during and after college, rather than chasing a career. Slacker.

Everything about the film was quintessentially Austin, at least from a slacker's perspective. And it would not have happened without the film society. "Slacker just sort of plugged into this infrastructure that the Austin Film Society had created," Linklater said. "At our [Austin Media Arts] space, that's where we cast for Slacker. We had our production department there. We segued from film society into filmmaking there. I was struggling just to hang on. It was too overwhelming. I'd done everything—write every grant, do all the programming. It was hard to get someone to do what I did for no money. And when I did it myself, I really couldn't let it step on my program.

"When we screened Slacker at the Dobie in the summer of 1990, we did that all ourselves, putting up flyers and treating it like a punk show. The social aspects of it, and a lot of the people who were in the movie, were just around. They were already part of the Austin vibe."

It helped that the hundred-person cast and crew he assembled for the film all pretty much fit the slacker stereotype. "I couldn't have done it in any other town. Nobody got paid. We all did it for nothing, like a summer art project. Our premise was, 'This film's never going to make money, but if you want to do it, then do it.'" Once again, the alternative Austin business model was in play. Working for free was OK as long as the work was something that you believed in, cared about, or enjoyed doing.

Two years later, Linklater did it again on a considerably bigger stage and with a much larger budget. Dazed and Confused was a coming-of-age

Film director and auteur Robert Rodriguez with his sister, the performer-singer-dancer Patricia Vonne. (Photo by Matt Lankes.)

tale with a comedic twist set in a Texas high school in the seventies—about the same time Linklater was attending high school in Huntsville, and a few years before the film's breakout lead, Matthew McConaughey, would graduate from Longview High. *Dazed* was as iconic as *Slacker* and would inspire its own nostalgia festivals and reunions, and give McConaughey a tag line for an award-winning career, "*Alrightalrightalright.*"

◎ ◎ ◎

About the same time Rick Linklater was applying the final edits to *Slacker*, a gangly, arrestingly charming Mexican American kid from San Antonio was showing his first film around the Austin film community. It was a short called *Bedhead*, a fantasy comedy. His sisters and brothers and a friend served as the actors and crew. He loved movies like Rick Linklater and Lee Daniel did, packed a Super 8, and oozed ambition, tempered by a good street sense. He'd already made a name for himself with his cartoon strip "Los Hooligans" in the *Daily Texan*, following in the *Texan*'s cartooning footsteps of Berke Breathed's "Academia Waltz" and Sam Hurt's "Eyebeam." His business partner was the girlfriend he just married.

Together, director Robert Rodriguez and producer Elizabeth Avellan were determined to take on the world of film.

Avellan and her six siblings grew up privileged in Venezuela, where her grandfather was a pioneering broadcaster. Rodriguez was one of ten siblings raised in a middle class Mexican American family in San Antonio.

They'd met as twenty year olds on the campus of the University of Texas. She was an administrative associate of Provost Gerald Fonken. He worked as a file clerk in the provost's office to subsidize the short films he was making and the cartoon strip he was doing, hoping he could raise his grades to get into film school. On their first date, Robert showed Elizabeth the short films he was making.

She fell in love with his obsession as much as with him. "He was doing all this wonderful work without all the tools normally associated with moviemaking," Avellan said. "He wasn't showbiz at all. His jeans were ripped, and he had holes in his shoes. But he had such a creative mind, I wanted to do whatever I could to help him realize his dream."

After *Bedhead*, Rodriguez started working on *El Mariachi*, a shoot 'em up set in the Mexican border town of Ciudad Acuña. The film, peppered with outlaws and bad hombres going after the good guy with lots of gunfire, blood, and graphic violence, featured an ironic plot twist and subtle comedic turns. The film was shot in two weeks for seven thousand dollars, some of which Rodriguez earned by spending a month in a clinic being a lab rat tested for a cholesterol-lowering drug. Avellan did her provost job and his file clerk job both. Their efforts paid off with El Mariachi winning the Audience Award at the 1993 Sundance Film Festival before going into commercial release.

El Mariachi got the couple to Hollywood, where Robert collaborated with another rising filmmaker named Quentin Tarantino on a film version of the gore comic book classic From Dusk till Dawn while Elizabeth took extension classes on film production at UCLA. Their 1995 stay was brief. Rodriguez was offered the Zorro film project but couldn't come to terms with the studio on a budget. They high-tailed it back to Austin, just in time for the great media disruption of the early twenty-first century. They proceeded to create and build their own vertically integrated film empire, mixing the Spy Kids children's film franchise with gore-noir fare such as the Sin City film series, and doing it themselves.

Linklater and Rodriguez put Austin on the cinema map. Mike Judge validated the perception.

I am the Great Cornholio. I need T.P. for my bunghole-io.
—Beavis

About the same time Rick Linklater was being showered with accolades at Sundance and Robert Rodriguez was firing up his Super 8, a bassist in a Dallas blues band named Mike Judge was applying the finishing touches to Office Space, an animated short cartoon he'd made. Judge's band mates in Anson Funderburgh and the Rockets had observed Judge playing with the Bolex sixteen-millimeter camera he'd purchased and knew he was experimenting with animation. But they were still surprised as much as anyone when Judge told them the Comedy Central cable channel was going to pick up Office Space after he showed it at a Dallas animation festival.

They shouldn't have been. Judge was not just another blues hound. He was a smart, sophisticated, somewhat cynical, very funny blues hound who happened to be born in Ecuador, the son of an archeologist. Raised in Albuquerque, New Mexico, and educated at the University of California at San Diego with a degree in physics, Judge had programmed F-18 jet fighters for Support Systems Associates Incorporated, a military contractor, before moving to Silicon Valley to work as an engineer at Parallax Graphics, which made hardware interface cards for high-resolution screens being developed. He lasted three months. That was long enough to sniff out a tech culture built on incredible piles of cash and bottomless ambition but light on soul or style. The culture was straight out of the *Stepford Wives*, hollow and needy. Judge bailed to play blues. And now he was an animator.

Judge enjoyed drawing, realized he was good with voices when he was in high school, and pondered a career in humor when an essay he wrote in a freshman writing class in college made other students laugh out loud. He had moved to the Dallas suburb of Richardson for his Anson and the Rockets gig when he attended a local animation festival that turned his head around.

"I had always been interested in animation, but I had assumed you needed tons of money and a bunch of people to do it," Judge told Evan Smith. "So I started thinking, 'Wow. I could do this myself.' I went to the library, got out a couple books, and ordered some supplies—at this point I still hadn't met any animators. Then I got a Bolex camera and started playing around with it." His made-up story about an office drone named Milton and The Boss turned into *Office Space*.

"I did it the hard way," Judge said. "I created exposure sheets, timing the lip-sync with a stopwatch to find out where each syllable fell. I had this cassette four-track, and I recorded my own voices. The whole thing was a minute-forty-five. I figured it was a little embarrassing. I mean, you have no reason to think you're going to be successful at something like this. But I knew that when I had played the track for my wife and for somebody else, it made them laugh, so I thought, 'Well, my track's funny even if my animation is bad.'"

Judge developed another short called *The Honky Problem* that aired in 1992 on *Liquid Television*, an animated shorts program on the MTV network, drawing from the peculiar culture he had been living around since moving to Texas. The main character Inbred Jed leads a hillbilly band that plays a concert in front of a hillbilly audience. The clip ends with Jed telling the crowd "inbreeding is everyone's problem."

He sketched out three other Milton-related shorts for the *Night after Night with Allan Havey* show on Comedy Central and for *Liquid Television* that NBC's *Saturday Night Live*, the leading comedy program on television, also picked up. *Liquid Television* premiered Judge's *Frog Baseball*, which featured two crude fifteen-year old juvenile delinquent metal-heads named Beavis and Butt-Head. They were deliberately drawn in a twisted, contemptuous style as if Judge was as deranged as the characters. The appeal was immediate. In two years, the adolescent boys would have their own animated series on MTV, and Mike Judge would be living high in Hollywood while thousands of American teenage boys imitated the snot-nosed laughs and giggles of Butt-Head and Beavis.

Two hundred episodes aired on MTV from 1993 to 1997, with another twenty-two episodes airing in 2011. The Beavis and Butt-Head franchise extended to video games and a major motion picture, *Beavis and Butt-Head Do America*, released in 1996.

Judge didn't fit in well in Los Angeles or New York, the media centers for the kind of work he was doing. He had acclimated to Texas, but not necessarily Fort Worth or Dallas, where he'd been living. The trail Rick Linklater was blazing in Austin looked pretty appealing to the young man with a receding hairline and warped sense of humor. Judge already had a solid feel for Austin from playing gigs with Anson Funderburgh and with Doyle Bramhall, Stevie Ray Vaughan's go-to collaborator. Once the production company in LA for *Beavis and Butt-Head* was up and running smoothly enough, he started spending more time in Austin until he moved for good.

Mike Judge's second cartoon series, a collaboration with Greg Daniels, a writer of the hit animated series *The Simpsons*, drew from Judge's personal experience once again, ginning up even bigger ratings on the Fox television network than *Beavis and Butt-Head* did on MTV. *King of the Hill*, which debuted in 1997, would become television's third-longest running animated series ever.

"I wanted to do something with a conservative, no-nonsense guy up against all these modern, new age hippie, Whole Earth types, but the sympathy would be for the guy," explained Judge. "I also wanted to do something with my neighbors in Dallas, guys sitting around with beers in an alley. I'd done a panel cartoon in 1995 or 1996 of four guys—three saying, 'Yep,' 'Yep,' 'Yep,' and Boomhauer thinking, 'Yep.' It just started from there."

King of the Hill told the story of the middle-class Hill family—Hank, a propane gas salesman; his wife, Peggy, a substitute Spanish teacher with a poor command of the language but mad skills playing Boggle; and their sensitive, pudgy thirteen-year old son, Bobby, who clearly didn't measure up to his father's traditional view of masculinity. Orbiting around the Hills was their saucy, wild-ass niece LuAnne Platter (a riff on the Luby's Cafeteria combo plate), Laotian immigrant neighbor Kahn Souphanousinphone, and Hank's "Yep" buddies—the conspiratoralist Dale Gribble, the pot-bellied Bill Dauterive, and the unintelligible mumbler Boomhauer.

They all lived in Arlen, Texas, a mostly white suburb of tract homes, pickup trucks, and metal sheds out back that resembled the real-life Dallas suburb of Richardson where Mike Judge once lived.

The redneck stereotypes set against a larger canvas of "political correctness" in a rapidly changing world appealed to conservatives and liberals alike. *King of the Hill* aired two 259 episodes over 13 seasons. What had started as a one-man operation learning film animation out of a book had grown into a very big business, with more than a hundred animators in the United States and South Korea. Judge did the voices of Hank Hill and Boomhauer.

Beavis and Butt-Head and King of the Hill opened the door to indie film. Judge directed a full-blown live-action version of Office Space, released in 1999, the bitingly cynical life-imitates-art cult classic Idiocracy in 2006, and the under-rated Extract, inspired by the Adam's Extract Vanilla manufacturer in Austin. He hatched the satiric high-tech HBO series Silicon Valley, which launched in 2013, using his brief experiences in the tech industry to poke fun. The short-lived Goode Family cartoon series, which aired on the ABC network in 2009, told the story of an overeducated, politically liberal, environmentally correct, and rather anal-retentive California family, and featured a boy named Ubuntu and a vegan dog named Che.

Office Space, the film, starring Jennifer Aniston and a repertory cast, flopped when it first hit movie screens. But three years of gradually increasing DVD sales boosted the film to cult classic, celebrating the mundane in cubicle life, down to character Milton's go-to line, "I believe you have my stapler." It wouldn't have happened at all, Judge admitted, "if I hadn't done animated shorts and if I hadn't had two hit TV shows back to back."

Like so many others involved in film in Austin, Judge went the extra mile to support his peers and younger animators coming up. He collaborated with animation savant Don Hertzfeldt in 2003 on The Animation Show, curating a collection of contemporary independent animated shorts and screening the films in two hundred movie theaters across North America. A second The Animation Show launched in 2005 and a third in 2007. Hertzfeldt departed in 2008, leaving Judge to curate a final The Animation Show.

Judge made cameos in the animated series South Park and Space Ghost Coast to Coast. Hank Hill (and Judge's voice) showed up on The Simpsons, Family Guy, and The Cleveland Show. He also appeared as the character Donnagon Giggles in three of the Spy Kids films directed by Robert Rodriguez, and as himself in the film Jackass Number Two, a film inspired by the stupid stunts of Johnny Knoxville and his pals on the MTV program Jackass. For Jackass 3-D, Judge stepped aside and let Beavis and Butt-Head do the cameo.

Through it all, Mike Judge kept improving his bass chops. If he was attending an event with a live band playing that was worth a shit, he was not shy about asking to sit in. The man knew how to hold down the bottom.

◉ ◉ ◉

Terrence Malick was the Austin film outlier. The critically acclaimed New Hollywood director made his mark with two atmospheric films released in the seventies, *Badlands*, about a young Midwestern couple on the run after committing murder, and *Days of Heaven*, a love triangle set in the northern plains at the dawn of the twentieth century. The latter took three years to edit and was considered a commercial flop, although Malick snagged best director honors at the Cannes Film Festival and the film won an Academy Award for cinematography. As time passed, *Days of Heaven* came to be regarded by many critics as one of the finest American films ever made.

The Illinois native quietly settled in Austin in the eighties during an extended break from filmmaking. Malick reemerged in 1998 with *Thin Red Line*, a gritty World War II film that received top honors at the Berlin Film Festival, and *Tree of Life*, which won the prestigious Palme d'Or at the Cannes International Film Festival. Through it all, Malick maintained a low profile around Austin and its nascent film community. But in 2017, he revealed a deep dive into his adopted hometown with *Song for Song*, starring Ryan Gosling and Natalie Portman, a film of two love stories shot in and around the Austin City Limits Festival and the Fun, Fun, Fun music fest. Malick may have been the most reclusive, publicity-adverse filmmaker in Austin, but he clearly had good ears and a good eye, even if his storylines were regarded as overly cryptic, dense, or aimless.

◎ ◎ ◎

Central Texas was no longer merely a fine location to shoot a film. The people behind the camera, making the films, were locals, and many were regarded as champions of independent film. Other young directors started hanging in Austin, including Quentin Tarantino, the celebrated auteur who got his start clerking in a Southern California video store and was as much a fan boy as Linklater and Rodriguez were, and Steven Soderbergh, who in 1989 became the youngest director to win the coveted Palme d'Or at the Cannes Film Festival for *Sex, Lies, and Videotape*. Guillermo del Toro, another movie geek who, like Tarantino and Rodriguez, reveled in horror and dark fantasy films and who was the first major film director to emerge out of Mexico in decades, felt more at home in Austin running with film geeks, as he liked to describe himself, than he did in Los Angeles.

Locals who had roles in *Slacker* became cult celebrities who were recognized on the street. Teresa Taylor, the bassist for the Butthole Surfers, achieved greater fame for her scene in which she holds a glass slide, claiming it was the pop singer Madonna's pap smear, trying to sell it to a pass-erby. A book about the making of Slacker profiled all the cast.

The Alamo Drafthouse Cinema was nothing fancy, just a small fourplex showing second-run features in an old brick warehouse downtown at 409 Colorado Street. But in a matter of weeks after the doors opened in May 1997, the movie house was operating as if it hosting a never-ending film festival. Tim and Karrie League were Rice University grads and film buffs who had tried but failed to open a movie theater that served drinks and dinner in Bakersfield, California. Thwarted by the bureaucracy there, they decided to test the concept in Austin. The appeal of the Alamo Drafthouse Cinema was immediate. People liked to drink beer and eat pizza at the movies.

But eating and drinking at the movies was just the come-on. Other theaters did that. The distinguishing difference was inventive, imaginative programming that cultivated several different hardcore film audiences. Sing-alongs were encouraged at some screenings. Bands provided the soundtracks to silent movies. Theme nights such as Girlie Night dotted the weekly schedule. Directors showed up to present their films and talk about their work. Master Pancake, inspired by Mystery Science Theater 3000, where three hosts with microphones mocked films being shown, became its own institution as host John Erler and a rotating cast of comedians took on movies of questionable taste.

Two months after the Alamo opened, the Leagues heard from Rick Linklater. Any theater showing Thunder Road, half of a Robert Mitchum memorial double feature, was all right by him. How might he be of assistance? Linklater and Detour Productions programmers started huddling with the Leagues, and special conceptual screenings and events emerged, including the Texas Documentary Tour of hot local docs. The Alamo hosted the Quentin Tarantino Film Festival featuring a marathon of films chosen by the director, who was in attendance for the entire run, and Harry Knowles's Butt-Numb-A-Thon.

◎ ◎ ◎

A year before the Alamo's opening, the Austin Film Society established the Texas Filmmakers' Production Fund. Rick Linklater had stayed involved in the Austin Film Society even after he handed the managerial reins to another filmmaker Katie Cokinos in 1990.

"The regional NEA [National Endowment for the Arts] had quit their regional re-grants program," Linklater said. "The Southwest Alternative

Media Project, or SWAMP, in Houston had sucked up most of the re-grant money for this area. The big thing they did was administer this grant. I got a grant. Lee got a grant. A lot of us received a grant for our film, with much thanks. But then it went away. The NEA cut them out. Suddenly there was no more granting agency."

Cokinos and Linklater thought the film society could fill the void. By now Linklater had several films under his belt and knew important people in the business. Benefit premieres and other events could raise funds that would be disbursed in grants to filmmakers in juried competitions. A generation of not-so-old filmmakers could nurture, mentor, and groom an even younger next generation of filmmakers.

"The first year [1996] we raised thirty thousand dollars," Linklater said. "Which was a lot. NEA's grants were fifty thousand. We had panelists come in, did it all official. Ruby Lerner, who ran Creative Capital, the arts organization in New York for years, was a panelist. John Pierson [who helped produce the first films by Linklater] was a panelist. We had a good structure with out of state panelists. It can't be an organization giving grants to their friends. And it was a big deal. Eagle Pennell got a grant for a script that he never finished. That worked so well, we built our way to one hundred thousand a year. That became a real backbone of the organization."

The Texas Filmmakers' Production Fund coincided with the arrival of documentary filmmaker Paul Stekler at the University of Texas. Stekler won Emmy and Peabody awards for his first doc following a North Carolina political neophyte, and had just finished with Luis Alvarez and Andy Kolker *Vote for Me: Politics in America*, a four-hour four-part series on electoral politics in the United States. Stekler's *George Wallace: Settin' the Woods on Fire* was broadcast on PBS in 2000 as part of the American Experience series. His presence drew other documentary filmmakers to campus to teach and guest lecture, including Karen Bernstein, Don Howard, and John Pierson, validating the perception of Austin as a hub of documentary film.

Filmmakers raising money for other filmmakers, filmmakers teaching, and filmmakers doing community outreach all contributed to Austin's rep as the anti-Hollywood, a genuine independent film community, in the tradition of Austin's music reputation as the anti-Nashville and anti-LA.

"Rick staying in Austin after *Slacker* in 1991, that's when Austin film began to change," Louis Black said. "Up until then, it was Tobe Hooper and Eagle Pennell. They made much smaller films. They might have success with regional film, but then they'd go to LA and try to make it in the industry. They would encounter more drugs and alcohol than they would success. Everyone would have to leave and go to LA. Rick stayed, and then Mike Judge moved down from Richardson after he created *Beavis and Butt-Head* and Robert returned to Austin. Guillermo del Toro moved here [from Mexico] because Robert was here."

Katie Cokinos departed the film society to chase her own film career shortly after the filmmaker's production fund grant project got underway. Executive director Elizabeth Peters inventoried the space she and director of programming Jerry Johnson inherited at Detour Productions, Rick Linklater's production company: "A file box of records, a small balance in the bank, four hundred names on our mailing list, a computer, a brand new phone number all our own, and a sun porch at Detour Productions as an office."

Peters and Johnson formalized the Austin Film Society, promoting an increased number of free screenings that attracted capacity houses, establishing a website, publishing a newsletter and a tenth anniversary program, building an email list, and seeking fiscal sponsors for the organization and for filmmakers. Peters was instrumental in launching the Austin Film Society's Texas Documentary Tour at the Alamo Drafthouse Cinema in September 1997. The TX Doc Tour featured established visiting documentarians showing their films while providing high-profile exposure to new documentaries from filmmakers in the region. Jacob Young, director of *Dancing Outlaw*, recalled arriving at a Texas Documentary Tour event that included his film and realizing his work was getting attention like never before. "I pulled up in a taxi, and there was a line around the place. I thought, 'I must be in the wrong place.'"

Elizabeth Peters remained AFS director through 1998 when she accepted the position of executive director of the Association of Independent Video and Filmmakers. Peters's successor, Rebecca Campbell, was fresh blood. The daughter of a foreign service official, she had grown up in Virginia outside of Washington, DC, and lived for extended periods in Ethiopia, South Africa, and Kenya. In 1990, finished with college, she asked herself where she would live if she could live anywhere. She chose Austin for the people and the culture. Most of the original group that started the film society had cycled through and moved on, except for Rick Linklater, who couldn't stay away. Campbell took on the dual tasks of running the film society and spearheading its move to a new home that would bring along most of Austin's working film community.

Robert Mueller Municipal Airport, Austin's commercial airport ten minutes east of downtown, shut down in 1999 when the decommissioned Bergstrom Air Force was refashioned into Austin-Bergstrom International

Airport. Most of the seven hundred acres of Mueller airport land was being transformed into a mixed-use planned urban residential and commercial neighborhood with bike lanes, nature trails, and active rec amenities. Streets in the Mueller development were named Sahm, Antone, and Threadgill. Cool kids with computers known as the Pecan Street Research Group monitored energy usage in 250 Mueller residences to create a smart grid that turned the community into the most energy efficient in the city.

The fate of twenty acres in the northeast corner of the airport land with a cluster of Austin Aero hangers where private aircraft used to park remained up in the air. A projectionist named Sam Ginsel who had been working with Rick Linklater at the Austin Film Center, an editing space and screening room downtown, thought Linklater needed to see the vacant corner of Mueller Airport. Ginsel had dreamed of opening his own studio someday, and in his dream scenario, it would be located there.

Ginsel took Linklater to Fifty-First Street near Manor Road and showed him the array of empty cavernous structures. Linklater liked what he saw and took Ginsel's idea to Louis Black, who gave him a realistic rundown of what would have to be done to pull something like that off.

"We built a coalition," Linklater said. His people went into the surrounding neighborhood to discuss their intentions. "People were warning us there'd a lot of opposition to this," he said. "Never happened." The US Congress did have to sign off on the measure, but more than a few friends helped facilitate that. In a matter of months, Austin Studios came online. "It's a clean deal," Linklater said going in. "The city owns it. The film society will manage it. And the benefit will be Austin." It was so successful from the get-go that Linklater couldn't get space at Austin Studios the first two times he tried because it was booked up.

Enough film was being shot in and around the city to merit the go-to core place for moviemaking. While shooting *The Newton Boys*, Linklater had to drive all over the city to get his business done. "My art department was way up north. Transpo was south, where they can park the trucks. Construction's somewhere else. What the film industry needs is a place to park trucks, a place to build things, some production offices, and a little rehearsal space. If you can build some sets, great. You can build on location. But you really need the hub space."

Mayor Kirk Watson endorsed the project, pointing out film was the kind of industry Austin wanted because it was built on creativity. With enough production crew on hand for four major motion pictures to film simultaneously, Austin Studios was busy from the beginning. "Immediately, it started working," Linklater said. "We could point and say, 'Well there's a couple hundred million in the local economy.'" The numbers looked good.

The film society was a critical part of Austin Studio's viability. "Film studios are losers," explained Linklater. "They should be what this is, municipally owned. Studios are almost like airports because they attract business. Hollywood studios don't even make money, and those things are busy three hundred days a year. It was going to work here only if you kept it small and frugal."

Austin Studios was more than production facilities. The main hanger studio building hosted Women's Roller Derby championships. An open space on the vast tarmac was revamped into the campy retro Blue Starlite Drive-In movie theater, billed as the World's First Mini-Urban Drive-In ("Feel Free to Make Out in Your Car").

An annual gala, the Texas Film Hall of Fame Awards dinner, staged on premises became Austin Studios' glittering glam event with real movie stars (not all of them from Austin) attending.

One nearby hanger already housed a film company when Austin Studios came online. Troublemaker Studios had clustered its production offices, sound stages, and the largest green screen in the state under one roof, all under the watchful eye of the genial Latino fellow in a black cowboy hat who ran the enterprise.

Robert Rodriguez generated more than nine hundred million dollars in box office sales over the course of fifteen films with DVD sales and rentals bringing in tens of millions more. Despite divorcing, Rodriguez and Elizabeth Avellan continued to collaborate as business partners, collectively and individually, with their own studio space, editing facilities, and repertoire of actors. Troublemaker Studios strived to own as much of their creation as possible by the time a finished film reached viewers, rather than be compromised artistically and financially by studios and distributors.

Movie people wanted to come to Austin to make movies, just like tech people wanted to work at a startup in Austin, just like out-of-town musicians lusted to play Austin clubs. A big part of the appeal was a smart, sophisticated audience. It was no big deal when Peter Jackson, the director of Lord of the Rings, flew in from New Zealand to introduce his recently completed movie at the Alamo for its first sneak public screening. It was no big deal when the actor Jack Black sat down beside a stranger at Franklin Barbecue to sample the storied brisket that Bon Appetit magazine declared the finest in all America, and without prompting went on a long jag, telling the stranger what he thought about the 'cue, concluding with the assessment, "It rocked."

Austin audiences provided the template for the Alamo Drafthouse Cinema to expand and hit the road.

◎ ◎ ◎

"Let the sculpting begin!" It was time for the mashed potato sculpting contest, and Tim League was egging on the dozen or so contestants competing to create their own mashed potato Devil's Tower. The real Devil's Tower rose behind the tables where the contestants were shaping their little white mountains of starch, just like the one Roy Neary, played by Richard Dreyfuss, did in the film. It was close to sundown on a late summer afternoon, and 160 movie nuts had trekked to this isolated spot on the plains of northeastern Wyoming to sculpt potatoes and watch movies near the landmark 1,200-foot monolith. Come dusk, a fifty-foot inflatable outdoor screen would command their attention, showing trailers for Steven Spielberg movies including E.T., Raiders of the Lost Ark, and Jaws. Once daylight finally faded, the evening's feature film began, Close Encounters of the Third Kind, the 1977 Spielberg classic about extraterrestrials, featuring several scenes shot on and around the Devil's Tower.

The stop at Devil's Tower, Wyoming, was one of twelve screenings on the Alamo Drafthouse Cinema's 2005 Rolling Roadshow summer road trip, covering six thousand miles over twenty-one days. Once Upon a Time in the West screened at Monument Valley, Utah, where it was filmed. Lake Powell hosted a showing of the original Planet of the Apes, much of which was shot nearby. Canyon City, Colorado, the location for Cat Ballou, hosted that film's screening.

That's how Tim and Karrie League liked to roll. The Alamo Drafthouse Cinema concept expanded locally north to the recently shuttered Village Cinema strip mall fourplex and south to 1120 South Lamar. In 2004, the Leagues sold the Alamo Drafthouse Cinema brand and expansion rights to investors, but kept their Austin properties and the Alamo Rolling Roadshow.

As the chain grew nationally, the local Alamos maintained the original programming focus, screening obscure films and staging special events in addition to presenting mainstream fare. The roadshow with the inflatable screen traveled mostly around Texas, working with cities, towns, and corporate partners. The Goonies screened in Longhorn Caverns, two hundred feet below the surface, with the film's star Corey Feldman in attendance. The Longhorn Speedway hosted the double bill of Russ Meyer's Faster Pussycat! Kill! Kill! and She-Devils on Wheels, with the buxom leading ladies from Faster Pussycat! on hand to answer fans' questions. In 2002, Jaws screened at Lake

Travis in front of fans floating on inner tubes and rafts. Scuba divers were hired to tug at moviegoers' dangling feet in the water during tense scenes in the film to add to the fright factor.

The Alamo Drafthouse national Rolling Roadshow tour for 2005 was lovingly documented in *Ain't It Cool News*, an online film fan website created by superstar fan boy Harry Knowles, who reviewed the on-location screenings. The *Close Encounters* screening at Devil's Tower made quite an impression: "This was a religious experience," Knowles declared in his September 5, 2005, column titled "This Meant Something! Harry and the Rolling Roadshow at Devil's Tower for CLOSE ENCOUNTERS OF THE THIRD KIND!!!"

Knowles wrote: "First, this was the original 1977 35mm Film Print. Which I haven't seen projected since Capital Plaza when I was five—same age as my nephew. I love this version of the film. I love how Teri Garr is shown putting up with an awful lot till it's finally enough. In the Special Edition, her leaving him is kinda bitchy on her part. Here, it's completely understandable."

Austin and film institutions such as the Austin Film Society and the Alamo Drafthouse Cinema informed Knowles's deep movie knowledge and film celebrity. Knowles had been exposed to film by his parents, who traveled the Southwest doing light shows for rock bands before opening Austin's first comic book and movie memorabilia store. When he was six, his folks put on the Austin Fantasy Film Fest, aimed at science fiction fans. The expansive menu of films served up by the Austin Film Society was his textbook.

By the time the Internet became a media force, Knowles, by then a cherubic red-headed, very overweight young adult, poured his enthusiasm into the *Ain't It Cool News* website, launched in 1996. AICN talked about films far beyond what was seen on the screen and in minute detail, with an enthusiastic, excitable, wholly nonacademic, and nonprofessional attitude. With an open forum, Knowles built a network of talkbackers who had the latest dope on scripts, productions, actors, directors, and films. AICN gained renown inside the trade by generating positive word of mouth from talkbackers who attended early screenings, neutralizing professional criticism that a film was too long, or not worth its two hundred million dollar price tag (the talkers usually turned out to be right). Screenplays of hot films yet to be made and inside info no one in gossip-savvy Hollywood knew about started showing up on *Ain't It Cool News*. A handful of directors and writers clued into Knowles's fan zealotry, and realizing he was not an industry tool, embraced him and his website. The enthusiasm was real. He wasn't bought.

Four years after AICN began, its founder ranked number ninety-five on *Forbes* magazine's Hollywood Power List. He was famous for his website and famous for his birthday weekend Butt-Numb-A-Thons, a full twenty-four hours viewing Knowles's favorite movies, trailers, and shorts. Knowles also co-programmed Austin's annual Fantastic Fest in September, an eight-day meetup dedicated to sci-fi, horror, and fantasy.

After being run over by a cart containing twelve hundred pounds of movie and comics memorabilia, Knowles was confined to a wheelchair until 2012, when he regained his mobility. By then, Knowles had run up a $600,000 tax bill and *Ain't It Cool News* had lost some of its sizzle, reverting to its original intent as a hangout for movie geeks. But Knowles's celebrity, and the media and events he was attached to, were examples of another Austin outsider community whose impact and influence extended beyond the city and Texas. Austin bands were notorious for hardly ever being in it for the money, and fewer still actually made a living from their chosen profession. But they were all part of a community. The regulars who made all the special screenings at the Alamo, the discussion thread habitués who were on *Ain't It Cool News* every day, the Quentin's-in-Austin spotters—they weren't in it for the money, either. They were just film addicts who couldn't get enough. And Austin happened to be a great place for that.

The fourteenth annual Butt-Numb-A-Thon was peak Harry Knowles. On December 11, 2012, at the Alamo Drafthouse Cinema, Knowles screened some of his favorites along with world-first sneak previews of *The Hobbit* and *Mama*, followed by in-person Q&As with directors Peter Jackson and Andres Machietti, and *Mama* producer Guillermo del Toro, who also introduced a trailer for his forthcoming film *Pacific Rim*. Filmed birthday shout-outs to Harry from actors Simon Pegg, Nick Frost, and Brad Pitt, and directors Michael Bay and Paul Feig, popped up between features.

Harry Knowles was Jacob Knight's hero. Knight moved to Austin with his wife in 2013 to watch movies, pretty much the same reason why Rick Linklater moved to Austin thirty years earlier. Knight had gotten hooked attending Fantastic Fest. Shortly after making the move, Knight lucked into a hard-to-find ticket to Harry Knowles's Butt-Numb-A-Thon 15 and blogged about it.

> It's true. Four weeks ago, my wife and I packed up the car and drove three days, from Philadelphia to Austin (OK, well, we stopped in Kentucky to hang out with her dad and brother for a week and in Memphis to see Graceland and devour some BBQ spaghetti). The move was Fantastic

Fest's fault, as we had traveled down for vacation two years ago and completely fell in love with the city. Texas beer and barbeque are great, but nothing beat the constant cinematic inundation a relocation to the town promised.

I've wanted to attend Butt-Numb-A-Thon since I first read about it in high school. The annual birthday celebration for Harry Knowles, mastermind behind AICN, the mix of classic cinema and secret premieres sounded like a near perfect party. But the event was happening so far away from my tiny suburban town that it almost didn't feel real. Now that I was going to be in the area full-time, I figured it was foolhardy for me to not pursue my own personal chair at this shindig.

If it weren't for the wonderful Phil Nobile, Jr., I probably wouldn't have even attempted my first crash of the single-day film festival until next year—applying proper with everyone else. But a cold front ran through Texas, dumping snow and sending these warm weather lizards into a panic. Flights were cancelled and the roads were a mess, rendering travel for certain long distance attendees impossible. This led to Harry announcing on Twitter that there were going to be a minimum of nineteen seats available to those willing to brave the cold and hang standby.

I didn't see any of that. Phil emailed it to me late Thursday night (I'm bad at Twitter sometimes). But now that I knew there was even a remote chance of attending, there was no way I wasn't going to give it a go. So I suited up, down vest and all, ready to stand in the cold for a solid two hours with no guarantee of getting in. Fortunately, the Ritz was kind enough to let the line of hopefuls wait in the well between its two theaters, where it was far warmer than twenty-eight degrees.

The first film was scheduled to roll at noon. After most of the attendees arrived, pillows and blankets in hand and PJs covering many legs, raffle tickets were handed out at eleven. A half hour later, the standby denizens were all called down into the empty lobby, where the cinema sweepstakes was to be held.

Fourteen seats. That's how many were up for grabs. And there were twenty-seven of us total. By my calculations, that gave me over a fifty percent chance of getting in. But as the numbers were called, I felt my hopes sink, until all fourteen were granted entry and the tickets were seemingly gone completely. But Kristen Bell, the always-awesome event coordinator for the Drafthouse, told those of us who remained to stick around, as she might be able to squeeze a few more in. Minutes later, she was flipping through badges and motioned for us to come over—turned out we were all going to get a seat!

I couldn't believe it. All I could do was continuously thank Kristen as she walked us through obtaining our badges. And once I settled into my seat (which was front and center, three rows back), the reality of the situation finally dawned on me . . . I WAS AT BUTT-NUMB-A-THON!

When the waiter came, I could barely get my initial drink order out of my mouth. I was so ecstatic to even be in the room, as it felt like the only logical end of my journey to Austin. It wasn't until Harry Knowles' visage filled the big screen, welcoming us all to the fifteenth anniversary of the famed movie marathon that I was able to finally settle down.

Butt-Numb-A-Thon was real. And I was in attendance.

BNAT changed Jacob Knight's life, sort of. He would eventually snag a gig working the counter of Vulcan Video, which specialized in foreign, cult, and classic film rentals. In Austin, he got to watch all the films he wanted to watch.

The events, the theaters, the studios at the airport, the directors, the producers, the crews for location shoots—they were all businesses. Austin cinemania, like Austin music, was built on the premise of enjoyment and good times experienced on the receiving end—as a consumer, as a fan, as an all-out nut—which Austin seemed to articulate and accommodate better than most places.

The big difference between music and film in Austin was money. Making a film cost a whole lot more than making a record, and involved a lot more people. That translated into a very significant impact on the local economy. The Austin Film Society evolved into the go-to umbrella organization nurturing film in Austin, especially independent film. The society's membership included investors who fancied themselves producers, which made even more film possible.

Rick Linklater kept making films at a torrid pace, never sticking to a formula, always willing to overreach and take risks. His 2015 film *Boyhood* was filmed over twelve years in and around Austin, following the same characters as they grew up and aged before the camera lens. The film earned multiple Academy Awards and Golden Globe honors. The year before, Matthew McConaughey, who honed his acting chops in Linklater's *Dazed and Confused* and *The Newton Boys* in addition to his turn in the *Texas Chainsaw Massacre: The Next Generation*, won the 2014 Academy Award for Best Actor for his performance as Ron Woodroof, a character who'd lived with AIDS for seven years with only thirty days left to live, in the film *Dallas Buyers Club*.

Linklater broke the mold with two animated features *Waking Life* in 2001 and *A Scanner Darkly* in 2006, which used rotoscope technology to transform real actors into cartoon figures. (Conspiratorialist Alex Jones had cameos in both films.) *School of Rock* starring Jack Black became a major motion picture hit at the same time Linklater was collaborating with actor Ethan Hawke to write and make *Before Sunset*, the second of three low-key, dialog-heavy romantic dramas about Celine and Jessie, a couple played by the actors Juliet Delpy, a Jean-Luc Godard discovery, and the Austin-born Hawke. *Before Sunrise* premiered in 1995, nine years ahead of *Before Sunset*. *After Midnight* would follow nine years later, in 2013.

Then there was the very twisted, very hilarious art-influences-life tale of *Bernie*, Linklater's 2011 low-budget adaption of an East Texas true crime story by *Texas Monthly*'s Skip Hollandsworth. The lead character, Bernie Tiede, was a beloved funeral home director who murdered the elderly, somewhat insufferable woman who befriended him, and stuffed her in a freezer while giving away her money. The tragicomedy, starring Matthew McConaughey and Jack Black, brought attention to the real-life Bernie Tiede, who was serving a life sentence for his crime. An appeals attorney brought up Tiede's sexual abuse as a child and two judges agreed to release Tiede on bail to Rick Linklater's custody. He moved into a garage apartment behind Linklater's residence. But in 2016, Tiede was retried and sent back to prison.

That year, the Linkater-directed *Everybody Wants Some*, what he called the "spiritual sequel" to *Dazed and Confused*, hit the multiplexes, with an ensemble cast of jock college baseball players. *Last Man Standing*, released in 2017, was a coming-of-old-age saga about reunited army buddies. Linklater was also the subject of an authorized documentary film, *Dream Is Destiny*, directed by Karen Bernstein and produced by Louis Black, as well as a second documentary.

Linklater generated enough soundtrack work to launch Graham Reynolds's career as an alt-classical composer and performer, engaging in collaborations with DJ Spooky, the Austin Ballet, and the Austin Symphony, as well as Linklater.

In October 2003, three Austin films—Linklater's *School of Rock*, Robert Rodriguez's *Once Upon a Time in Mexico*, and Tim McCanlies' *Secondhand Lions*, a comedy filmed at Austin Studios about a shy kid sent to live with two wacky great-uncles in the country—landed in the box office top ten during the same week.

Thirteen years later, *Time* magazine's Best of Film list for 2016 included Linklater's *Everybody Wants Some*; Jeff Nichols's *Loving*, a historical drama about an interracial couple who marry in 1958 that Nichols wrote and directed; and *Tower*, the documentary by Keith Maitland about the Charles Whitman mass shootings from the University of Texas tower in August 1966 that killed four-teen people and injured thirty-one. Maitland utilized the same rotoscope ani-mation technique that Linklater did for *Waking Life* and *Scanner*.

"Look how different we all are—Robert, myself, Jeff Nichols, Mike Judge, Andrew Bujalski [whose mumblecore films, along with the Duplass broth-ers' work, followed in the footsteps of *Slacker*], all the documentaries being made," Linklater said. "There is no one [Austin] identity. We transcended that way back, that kind of regionalism. The three films cited by *Time* were very different from one another." The one common thread was the Austin Film Society. Keith Maitland and Jeff Nichols had received grants from the film society at times—grants that Rick Linklater helped dole out.

Linklater's go-to editor, Sandra Adair, made her directorial debut in 2017 with *The Secret Life of Lance Letscher* about the obsessive Austin collage artist.

"Here we are thirty-one years later, and it's different, but it's that same kind of feeling," Linklater said. "I realize the audience turns over. There's nobody from back then who's still around. The turnover's pretty quick. Austin turns itself over quite a bit. But I see a lot of young people who are very similar with the same kind of gleam in their eyes."

The Austin Film Society under the leadership of Rebecca Campbell grew up like the film directors and other movie people in Austin had grown up. The society purchased a flagging two-screen theater in a middle-aged strip center under renovation, and the Marchesa Hall and Theatre was born—a real hangout and home for the Austin Film Society. After extensive renova-tions, the venue was reborn in 2017 as the AFS Cinema and Hall twin-screen arthouse cinema and exhibit space. Film dominated the facility's schedule, but there was enough room and desire, programming-wise, to host pro wrestling matches, drag shows, burlesque performances, and art bazaars.

Future filmmakers were AFS priorities. The society was in schools and involved with education, grants, and an international exchange program. Summer camps, field trips, and an internship program were all part of the agenda. With a membership exceeding two thousand, and forty thousand people attending AFS events annually, the film society had become a very big deal. "There are so many things we've grown into," Rick Linklater said, his emphatic voice betraying the fact he still considered the society to be his baby.

"There's a lot of cross-pollination going on. There are cool funky film organizations for whom we are the behemoth. They're showing outdoor films; they're riding their bikes. We're the Man. That's what you get when you're a thirty-year-old organization. A rising tide lifts all boats: that's how we've approached it. Austin's too small. We're too small a community to be petty about anything. We're supportive of each other."

After all he'd accomplished, Rick Linklater still wanted to stay involved. "It's fun. It's the film society. It's the future. It's movies. It's our film culture."

He was just warming up. "I've always had an evangelical streak in showing movies publicly, hosting film series," he said. "The film society's like a kid who's grown up and out of the house. There have been some good long-term advisers—Chale Nafus, Charles Ramirez-Berg, Louis Black—the handful of people who were around then, who are still with us. Everybody in their own way went through growing pains. I remember Charles Ramirez-Berg saying, 'We used to sit around and talk about movies; now we're talking about money.' I'm like, 'I know, but we're only talking about money for this meeting because we have to.'"

Rick Linklater didn't have a choice. He *had* to.

"People have got to express themselves," he said. "People have got to tell stories. Film, it's a powerful medium. People are drawn to it. They're gonna make it work. That low-budget film has gotten even lower. *Slacker*, I was out of pocket like twenty-three thousand dollars. Now that number would be three thousand. You could make it digitally, edit it, have a watchable film for almost nothing."

He was right. Anyone has access to filmmaking in the digital world. An unprecedented number of would-be auteurs were taking advantage of it, meaning the field was more competitive than ever. "When I did *Slacker*, it was one of 210 submissions to Sundance," Linklater said. "*My gosh, 210 indie films submitted and only 20 are going to get in.* Now it's like six, eight thousand submissions. That little private film that you did, there's eight thousand of those. You know how good, or how special you have to be to be even noticed? It's a good time to be a filmmaker, but a hard time to break through or have any kind of cultural impact." But the spirit abided, and there was community to share that spirit with, created by a society driven by the simple desire to watch movies.

Toward the end of the summer 2015, Robert Rodriguez announced that in celebration of the twenty-fifth anniversary of the filming of *El Mariachi*, he would make another film for seven thousand dollars, while simultaneously filming a documentary of the project. "I'll have no crew; I'll just use friends—I've got some pretty cool friends I can put in front of the camera—but still no crew, no money," he said.

People wanted to paint Tom Sawyer's fence when the fence they were painting was interesting and fun. The alternative Austin business model remained valid—in the right situations.

8

Geeks

DELL, LORD BRITISH, RVB, CAPITAL FACTORY, AND THE TRANSLATOR

Enrolling at the University of Texas had been an easy decision. The precocious eighteen year old from Houston could have gone to Stanford, Harvard, MIT, or some engineering institution. The truth was, he could have just as well not gone to college at all, and kept doing what he had been doing in his spare time, tinkering with personal computers, the shiny new object consumers suddenly had to have. He was already making good money doing that. But enrolling at UT for the fall semester of 1983 kept his folks happy and let them hang on to their dream that he become a medical doctor. Home was a three-hour drive away.

The problem was the work Michael Dell had brought with him. In the back seat of the sporty white BMW he had purchased with earnings from selling subscriptions to the *Houston Post* were three computers. He was so good at upgrading clones of the IBM personal computers everyone was buying that computer users beat a path to his dorm at 2713 Dobie Towers once he was settled in. This kid knew what he was doing.

Michael didn't take much time to appreciate the birds-eye view from the next-to-the-top floor of the twenty-eight story high-rise dorm. The baby-faced kid didn't lurk downstairs at the Dobie Theater in the Dobie Mall like the film geeks did, or burn quarters at the video arcade, or hang in the record store. He didn't venture downtown to dance at Club Foot or hear bands on Sixth Street.

His world was right here at his desk, whenever he wasn't in class. "I was taking apart IBM PCs," he explained. "I was struck by the fact the components inside the IBM PC cost about four to five times less than they were selling the product for. That didn't seem fair to me. There had to be a better way to do that."

Dell gutted remaindered and outdated computers he'd purchased, adding memory and upping power to make them work faster and more efficiently, and then resold them. Clones had become popular because IBM, in response to the new Apple microcomputer, adopted open source code, allowing access to their computer architecture to encourage software and hardware innovation via new technologies from people like Mike Dell. Their input would lead to a better, lower-cost single user computer.

Studying wasn't easy when someone was calling or knocking at the door every hour, needing an upgrade or a new computer. But Michael Dell was hardly the typical college freshman. He was a gifted child, who at the age of eight responded to a magazine solicitation to "earn your high school diploma by taking one simple test." He showed a propensity for making money, earning two thousand dollars at age twelve by setting up a mail-order auction business aimed at stamp and baseball card collectors. He loved hanging around the local RadioShack electronics store and playing with the new computers being sold there.

At age fifteen, Mike Dell persuaded his mother and father to buy an Apple II computer, which he immediately began to disassemble. "My parents were furious," he recalled in his autobiography. "An Apple cost a lot of money in those days. They thought I had demolished it. I just wanted to see how it worked."

The summer before his high school senior year, he sold newspaper subscriptions for the *Houston Post*. Rather than cold call from a list of new telephone customers that the *Post* circulation provided, Dell observed that newlyweds and people who had just moved into an apartment or home were likely subscribers. He created a target mailing list on his computer, winnowed from marriage records publicly accessible at county courthouses and from mortgage company transactions. He saved his newspaper subscription earnings and paid cash for his BMW.

His dorm room computer business worked too well. Word of mouth spread. Attorneys and doctors started showing up. That led to him bidding on state contracts for computers, and winning several bids.

Concerned that Mike wasn't focusing on his classes, his parents staged an intervention, flying in and calling him from the Austin airport, which gave Dell just enough time to stash the computers he was working on in the shower stall of his roommate's bathroom.

His father confronted him. "You've got to stop with this computer stuff and concentrate on school. Get your priorities straight. What do you want to do with your life?"

"I want to compete with IBM!" Dell told his folks. He was stone serious.

His folks weren't buying it. They persisted until Mike agreed to give up his "computer stuff." He managed to keep his word for three weeks. But he couldn't stay away. He knew what he wanted to do: build computers that were better than IBM, and sell direct to the end user.

Dell returned to Austin early for the spring semester at UT so he could register his business, PC's Limited, with the State of Texas, and take out a classified ad in the *Austin American-Statesman*. He moved out of the Dobie into a two-bedroom condo without telling his parents.

Dell made it through the spring semester with a weak promise to his parents that if his computer business didn't work out over the summer, he'd focus on school. A week before freshman finals, the Dell Computer Corporation, doing business as PC's Limited, was incorporated with $1,000 in capitalization. In June, Dell racked up $180,000 in sales. Michael Dell did not return to UT as a sophomore that fall. By the end of the year, sales reached $6 million.

PC's Limited moved out of Dell's condo into a thousand-square-foot office in a North Austin business center, where three men built and upgraded machines while others took orders via telephone. A month later, the business moved into a new space more than twice that size. Five months after that, PC's Limited moved again into a 7,200-square-foot space for another six months before packing up and relocating to a 30,000-square-foot space in 1985.

While upgrading and rebuilding computers, Dell had figured out a more efficient and direct build-to-order business model. He would make and sell a computer to each customer's specification. Build-to-order and direct sales eliminated the need for inventory or a brick-and-mortar store. Dell's idea would become the industry standard. In 1985, Dell created the Turbo PC, the first computer of his own design, built in Austin by engineer Jay Bell. With an Intel 8088 processor running at 8 MHz, a 10 MB hard drive, and a 5.25-inch floppy drive, it was one of the first PC-compatible computers to compete directly against IBM.

Dell showed his serious business side when venture capitalist Lee Walker was appointed company president in 1986. Walker was instrumental in obtaining a line of credit for the company from Austin banks, and for recruiting George Kozmetsky, the dean of the UT School of Business, and Bob Inman, of defense contractor Westmark Systems, to Dell's board of directors. Walker helped articulate new goals for the company, specifically targeting large companies in addition to individual users, and setting their sights on expanding globally. Dell did sixty million dollars worth of business in 1986.

The year Micheal Dell was supposed to graduate, Dell Computers, as it was now called, recorded ninety million dollars in direct sales. Brick-and-mortar computer stores were rendered passé. The company expanded by 80 percent a year in its first eight years of existence, riding the tidal wave of the microprocessor. Dell Computers carved out a fat slice of the action as the first major computer company to sell their products direct to customers via the World Wide Web.

◉ ◉ ◉

High tech and Austin wasn't a love at first sight affair, like Austin and music supposedly were. It was a more formal relationship, built on common wants and needs—a relationship that was pretty much all business initially, but one that grew into something more. Austin was a small city of 159,000 in 1955, with a stable economy that revolved around the University of Texas and the State of Texas government. That's when five physicists and engineers founded a defense-contracting firm, Texas Research Associates, a spinoff of the University of Texas's Defense Research Laboratory. They aimed to do research and development of advanced electronics for military purposes. In 1962, another UT research spinoff, Textran, merged with Texas Research Associates to form Tracor, Austin's first tech startup, and the first publicly held company in Austin included on the Fortune 500 list of the largest public companies in the United States.

That was pretty much it, other than what was going on at the University of Texas' research facilities. In 1967, International Business Machines hired lawyers close to the chambers of commerce in Austin and in Dallas to secretly scout both cities as the site for an envisioned manufacturing plant. A search team showed up to look around, and after a series of talks, IBM announced Austin would be the site of a plant to make the IBM Selectric typewriter, the state-of-the-art word processing machine before there were home computers and word processors.

Motorola and Texas Instruments followed. Still, high tech research and development was largely tied to government, military, or university contracts and was largely being conducted out of the purview of most of the population into the early eighties.

A high-powered attorney changed that. In 1983, Pike Powers, a partner at Fulbright & Jaworski law firm who was serving as chief of staff for Governor Mark White, spearheaded a community push to recruit the Microelectronics and Computer Technology Consortium, founded the previous year as the largest research and development computer consortium in the United States.

Austin would be an ideal location, Powers told the public-private partnership. The University of Texas, eager to build upon its Balcones Research Center, offered to provide facilities for MCC's headquarters, and the deal was done.

The Semiconductor Manufacturing Technology, or SEMATECH, a not-for-profit consortium formed by the United States government and fourteen corporations to promote research and development of microchip manufacturing, and subsidized with Department of Defense contracts, landed in Austin four years later, again with Pike Powers leading the recruitment effort.

From those big ideas sprang the so-called Silicon Hills, referring to the northern, northwestern, and southwestern fringes of the city and adjacent suburbs, Austin's answer to Silicon Valley in Northern California. Pike Powers continued to play an instrumental recruiting role, helping persuade 3M, Applied Materials, and the biggest get of all, Samsung, to locate in the Austin area. Samsung invested more than sixteen billion dollars in plant construction and equipment in twenty years after it opened its first chip plant outside of Korea in suburban Round Rock in 1996. IBM, Samsung, 3M, Applied Materials, National Instruments, Motorola, Advanced Micro Devices, Bell Labs, Apple, Cisco, Cirrus Logic, Freescale Semiconductor, Trilogy software, Bazaarvoice, and Google all put down roots in the Silicon Hills.

MCC and Sematech were critical in building the kind of environment that encouraged a young homegrown company like Michael Dell's to thrive and prosper. Dell Computers went public in 1988, selling stock to amass capital. The June 22 initial public offering of 3.5 million shares at $8.50 per share increased Dell's market capitalization to $80 million. A ten thousand dollar investment at the first IPO grew to one million dollars in nine years, creating a class of Dellionaires in and around Austin, and infusing the local economy with more wealth than anything since the first real estate boom in the seventies.

No small part of Dell's success was due to smart hires. Management talent such as Lee Walker, Tom Meredith, and Kevin Rollins were as synonymous with the Dell brand as its namesake. In 1992, Michael Dell was recognized as the youngest CEO to ever appear on the Forbes 500 list of top American companies. Chips, processors, RAM, connectivity, and bandwidth may have been difficult concepts for a layperson to understand, but the money part was easy.

By the end of the nineties, technology had left all other industries in the dust. The Silicon Hills was central Texas's engine, powering unprecedented economic growth in Austin and surrounding communities for fifty miles in all directions. With a 48 percent increase in population in 10 short years, raising Austin's population to 672,000 residents, the city was no longer small, much less cheap or easy.

The same year Mike Dell enrolled at the University of Texas, another very bright future UT student from Houston named Richard Garriott formed a company with his brother Robert, his father Owen, and Richard's Clear Creek High School friend Chuck "Chuckles" Bueche. Origin Systems was created to distribute the Ultima game series that Richard had dreamed up. Existing distributors had not paid the hundreds of thousands of dollars owed for sales of the first two versions of Garriott's game. The new company's first release, Ultima III: Exodus, was a hit straight out of the box.

Richard Garriott wasn't just the creator of Ultima; he was the game's lead character, Lord British. A bright kid from a "dreadfully overeducated family," as he described them, he'd read Lord of the Rings and discovered the Dungeons & Dragons fantasy tabletop role-playing game about the same time the personal computer entered the marketplace. Garriott was hooked on D&D's interactive storytelling, which inspired the nineteen-year-old to try and write his own story The First Age of Darkness: The Story of Mondain the Wizard.

The self-taught gamer's career began with a high school job at a ComputerLand store in Houston, where he was exposed to Apple II computers. Between the Apples and D&D, Garriott wrote and produced his

Gaming guru and astronaut Richard Garriott, a.k.a. Lord British, at work, at play. (Photo by Will Van Overbeek.)

first computer game, *Akalabeth*, "a game of cunning, fantasy, and danger," whose name was copped from J. R. R. Tolkien. The floppy disk game came in a Ziploc bag. Richard's mother did the cover art. Twelve copies sold the first week at ComputerLand for twenty dollars each.

Akalabeth morphed into the *Ultima* series. From there, *Ultima Online* became the first massively multiplayer online role-playing game (MMORPG) that allowed computer users to play the game with other computer users. Garriott entered the University of Texas, where he joined the Society of Creative Anachronism, became an enthusiastic renaissance festival regular, and got into cave exploration and rock-climbing while he worked on Origin Systems and *Ultima*. But he wasn't getting much classroom enlightenment. "Most universities don't offer a curriculum beneficial for microcomputer applications," Garriott said. "They were still teaching mainframe business computers."

He dropped out of college his junior year ("my GPA sunk") and dove into game development full-time. Even though he was no longer at the university, Austin remained an ideal base of operations, since the city had the deepest pool of computer-literate creators and developers in the region. Talented creators who didn't know computers could always be taught.

True to Austin's contrarian nature, a parallel universe to the hardware companies had evolved in smaller, less obvious, but equally significant ways. The hardware companies made for Austin's fat tech wallet. Its tech soul, though, was rooted in small entrepreneurial startups, with games and social media leading the way.

Cool gaming in Austin predated the Internet. Steve Jackson Games, meaning Jackson and his friends, created imaginative card and role-playing board games, starting with the card game *Car Wars* in 1981. Software designers, code programmers, graphic designers, and musicians writing scores for games, such as George Alistair Sanger, the Fat Man of Team Fat, and even poster artists from the Armadillo World Headquarters, managed to carve out niches in this nascent alt tech universe.

Richard Garriott personally sought out the Armadillo poster artists and trained several as video game illustrators. For all the success of the early *Ultima* games, "there was no good art," he complained. Graphics were critical to a game's success. To Garriott, making the transition from creating music posters to creating scenes for *Ultima* or *Wing Commander* seemed natural. Armadillo poster artists Danny Garrett, Jim Franklin, Bill Narum, Micael Priest, Sam Yeates, and briefly Guy Juke might have thought otherwise at first, but they effectively infused funky old alternative Austin sensibilities into this slick high-tech platform.

Sam Yeates made a career out of game and concept art, following his stint at Origin with stretches at Digital Anvil, Ion Storm, Junction Point (which became Disney Interactive), and finally Rosetta Stone.

"In most any other city in the country at that time, if you tried to put a company together that included a couple of sport-coat-and-tie-wearing yuppies, some pocket-protector can't-give-you-a-good-handshake computer nerds, as well as some hippie-freak rock-and-roll poster artists, those three walks of life would not get along and respect one another," Garriott said. "When you come to Austin, those three walks of life are intermingled throughout the city." And at Origin Systems headquarters. "Austin was where I met the people who would become characters in my main stories," Garriott said.

Play mattered.

The one time Garriott crossed paths with Michael Dell was in 1988, five years after each had started their companies. Garriott had what Dell wanted. "PCs needed games to push their hardware sales," Garriott said. But the two did not do business together.

◎ ◎ ◎

The game's premise was simple: your party of four gathers in front of the gates of a medieval mansion guarded by gargoyles where you are graciously welcomed by Lord British, a tall blonde-bearded dude wearing a crown, speaking in what sounds like an English accent. You are told to wait. At the appointed time, five minutes later, Lord British returns with a couple of monks to inform you his house was once a monastery before it was taken over by evil spirits. Lord British guides the group from the gates to the ornate front door, which is flanked by griffins. As the door opens, a bolt of lightning flashes. One monk walking with the group falls limp, as if he's been struck dead. Lord British points the group to a campfire outside. There, another monk will lead everyone inside the house to search for the gargoyle talisman that will cleanse the house of evil spirits.

For the next forty-five minutes, the group explores the haunted mansion, discovering secret passageways to scurry through and spaces to crawl in while fending off demons, zombies, and assorted flying creatures. There is a boat in which to row across the flaming River Styx, an earthquake to survive, and trapdoors to avoid. Work your way through enough rooms and levels and you reach the dungeon, where a mad doctor holds the talisman. Grab that, and all evil spirits are banished. If you fail, the mansion—and the world—will continue to be haunted by evil spirits.

There are clues to follow, puzzles to solve, boxes to unlock, and doors to open. Choose wrong and you lose. Choose wisely and you could save the world.

The best part: this wasn't a video game at all.

This was a real-time immersive adventure staged in and around Richard Garriott's Britannia Manor, a fanciful, custom-designed six thousand square foot, three-story mansion perched on a bluff overlooking Lake Austin.

Richard Garriott, assisted by his overactive imagination, fifty thousand dollars, and a workforce of carpenters, technicians, and actors, all of them volunteers just wanting to do something cool, transformed his recently built residence into a life-size real-time interactive haunted house laid out like a video game. During the week leading up to Halloween in 1988, Britannia Manor opened to the public as a haunted house. The free admission was the hottest ticket in town. Several groups camped out for days at the gates of Garriott's home so they could be first in line.

The game was full-contact, especially for those thrown out of the dungeon, falling just short of the big prize talisman. Participants had to sign liability waivers before going in.

⦾ ⦾ ⦾

Four years after Lord British first opened Britannia Manor to the public for some for scary Halloween thrills, the Electronic Arts gaming company acquired Origin Systems for thirty-five million dollars.

Over its nine year run as an independent company, Origin nurtured an all-star lineup of developers. Chuckles Bueche went on to found Craniac Entertainment and develop popular games such as *Autoduel* and *2400 AD*. John Romero worked at Origin briefly before co-founding id Software, makers of *Doom* and *Wolfenstein 3D*, pioneering first-person-shooter games notorious for their graphic violence. Britt Daniel composed music for Origin games before starting the popular Austin band Spoon. Ralph Koster went on to design *Star Wars Galaxies* and other games for Sony Online Entertainment. Sheri Graner Ray founded Women in Games International. Writer Raymond Benson became "official continuation author" of James Bond novels. Warren Spector created *Deus Ex* for Ion Storm and then formed Junction Point Studios in Austin, which was bought by Disney Interactive, for whom Spector created *Epic Mickey*. Spector moved into academia to help articulate a game development academic track for the University of Texas, and then returned to gaming to work on *System Shock 3*.

Origin Systems and the *Ultima* series would inspire a French game developer named Raphael Colantonio to start Arkane Studios in 1999 in his hometown of Lyon, and then open a second Arkane Studio in Austin in 2006. *Dishonored*, an action-adventure video game, became Arkane's biggest hit when it was published in 2012, with several high-profile actors (including Carrie Fisher and Susan Sarandon) adding their voices to the big budget game. A sequel *Dishonored 2* was released in 2016, six months before Arkane's most ambitious title, *Prey*, a first-person shooter science fiction thriller set in a space station, made its debut on Xbox and several other platforms.

After Electronic Arts acquired Origin Systems, Richard Garriott left the company and resurfaced in 2000 with Destination Games, founded with his brother and Starr Long, the producer of *Ultima Online*. Destination Games eventually partnered with NCSoft, with Garriott heading their gaming division until his departure in 2008. That was the year he became the first second-generation American astronaut, following in the footsteps of his father, Owen, a NASA space pioneer. Rather than attempt to qualify for NASA's strenuous and lengthy astronaut training program, Garriott paid thirty million dollars (five million less than the amount Origin Systems sold for to Electronic Arts in 1992) to travel into outer space for twelve days as a tourist on the Russian TMA-13 and TMA-12 space capsules, to and from the International Space Station.

Outer space changed Garriott. He was no longer a gamer, but an adventurer and explorer. While in the space station he managed to make a short film, *Apogee of Fear*, collaborating with fantasy writer Tracy Hickman to make what Garriott proudly described as "the only science fiction movie filmed in space."

A film documentary *Man on a Mission: Richard Garriott's Road to the Stars* told the story of his space adventure. He went into further detail in the book, *Explore/Create*, published in 2017, in which Garriott explained his love of research and his appetite for knowledge. His friend Elon Musk blurbed the book as "a chronicle of wonder."

Garriott also co-authored *The Sword of Midras* with Tracy Hickman, which tied into the *Shroud of the Avatar* multiple-player game he designed for his new company, Portalarium, carrying on the spirit of *Ultima Online*.

On December 21, 2012, a day that marked the end of the Mayan calendar and the world, by association, or so some prognosticators believed, Richard Garriott hosted an end-of-the-world fundraiser on his sixty-five acre ranch west of Austin. The one thousand dollar ticket apocalypse bash benefitted the X Prize Foundation, on whose board Garriott sat. The foundation encouraged public competitions for technological advances that helped mankind. The end-of-the-world winging featured a thirty-five foot high pyramid and four end-of-the-world scenarios, including fire and brimstone, that the costumed revelers could party within. Stripper poles equipped with scantily clad dancers were strategically placed around the premises.

Play remained his guiding compass. Smitten with the desire to explore and armed with the financial wherewithal to go wherever he wished, Garriott dove in a deep sea submersible to the bottom of the Atlantic to view the wreck of the Titanic, canoed down the Amazon River, and participated in two expeditions to Antarctica in search of meteorites.

Garriott was able to do all that by anticipating the convergence of video and computer games and storytelling long before most of his peers and the public had a clue. Well-designed games were "the new movies," the preferred means of telling a story—only with games, the viewer could influence the plot line and determine the ending. Budgets for developing a major game escalated into the tens of millions of dollars—feature film territory—and the gap in gross receipts narrowed.

Garriott's best-known protégé, Chris Roberts, an Austinite relocated from Northern California who had grown up in Manchester, England, tried to have it both ways. Roberts rolled out *Wing Commander*, a space combat simulation game published by Origin Systems in 1990. A subsequent edition, *Wing Commander IV: The Price of Freedom*, released in 1997, ginned up loads of publicity for its then-astronomical $12 million budget. Nine years later, *Wing Commander* debuted as a major motion picture. The film, starring Freddie Prinze Jr., was made with a $30 million budget. No matter what gamers thought of the *Wing Commander* games, movie critics did not buy into the film. One reviewer roundly trashed the film as "excruciatingly earnest yet convictionless." The film bombed, grossing less than $12 million. Roberts left film and returned to gaming. He didn't need to mess with movies. In 2017 he developed a new game *Star Citizen*, with a movie-sized $141 million budget.

Not every tech idea turned into gold, even if tons of money were being bet on whatever the next big thing was. In 1994, the touts were focused on CD-ROMs. The compact disc with read-only memory promised storage capacity far beyond what a personal computer's hard drive and floppy disks could contain at the time. Human Code, the multimedia development startup founded by Chipp and Liz Walters and Gary Gattis, headquartered in a converted early twentieth century home at the corner of Fifteenth Street and West Avenues, introduced itself as the business that would make CD-ROMs part of everyone's life.

Human Code was about interactive learning, e-commerce, and games, all of which would be made accessible with the CD-ROM. Human Code's first product was a CD-ROM version of *The Cartoon History of the Universe*, commissioned by a book publisher. Unlike the book, the CD-ROM version had visuals and audio. Storytelling would never be the same—or so the theory went.

The Walters and Gattis attracted the interest of two heavyweights of the new tech world, venture capitalist David Boucher and Nicholas Negroponte of the MIT Media Lab, who were the principal investors in the startup.

Human Code's big bet on CD-ROMs would be its undoing. Computer processors were getting more and more powerful and the Internet more accessible. Why fuss with a disc when the same information could be gleaned online? Storage capacity, the bugaboo that made the brief age of the CD-ROM possible, would eventually be practically unlimited with the advent of cloud computing.

Before those developments took place, in 2000, the Sapient Corporation bought Human Code Inc. for $103.8 million in stock. Chipp Walters went on to design and deploy Google sites and apps and work on Elon Musk's HyperLoop mass transportation concept. The CD-ROM went the way of the floppy disk.

Richard Garriott and Chris Roberts might have been unsuccessful at translating a popular video game into film, but a handful of provocateurs among the next generation of gamers pulled it off. Rather than wait for the film industry to get hip to gaming, gamers in Austin exploited their native platform, the Internet, to do what film and television had previously controlled.

Booze played a critical role in this development, which made sense since Austin consistently ranked as one of the nation's drunkest cities. Drunkgamers.com started in 2001 with a purpose, albeit a pretty flimsy one. University of Texas Radio-Television-Film students Burnie Burns, Gus Sorola, and Geoff Ramsey got together, got drunk, and reviewed video games. Simple premise. In exchange for writing reviews, the guys behind Drunkgamers.com would receive advance copies of latest video games for free for the purpose of reviewing them. That was the plan, at least. The tepid response from game producers convinced the group to change their site's name from Drunk Gamers to Rooster Teeth and broaden their concept. And did they ever.

Burnie Burns also reviewed games for Xbox and posted gameplay videos of *Halo: Combat Evolved*, sometimes adding his own humorous voice-overs to the descriptions. That inspired the idea of an online serial. Joined by writer-director Matt Hullum and Joel Heyman, both of whom worked with Burns before Drunk Gamers went online, Rooster Teeth proceeded to develop a

Halo-inspired series called Red vs. Blue. The sci-fi comedy, which debuted in 2004, was built around the premise that "two groups of soldiers battle for control of the least desirable piece of real estate in the known universe—a box canyon in the middle of nowhere." RvB grew an audience in the millions through podcasts, a dedicated YouTube channel, and short films—all delivered with a wiseass attitude.

RvB was a form of machinima, the art of utilizing real-time images from existing video games and adding original or lifted dialog to create a cinematic production, meaning RvB might have looked like Halo, but was nothing like it.

By 2014, RvB claimed to be the longest running episodic web series and longest running American science fiction series of all time. Rooster Teeth, the company, grew to ninety employees before it was sold to a larger company offering larger budgets to create with—in the tradition of Electronic Arts buying Richard Garriott's Origin Systems, only with a happier working relationship. An office opened in Los Angeles. Matt Hullum directed Rooster Teeth's first feature film, the sci-fi comedy Lazer Team.

Rather than seek funding for the film through traditional sources, Rooster Teeth launched an online fundraiser through IndieGoGo in June 2014, cutting out the second-guessers and backseat drivers. The $650,000 target was reached in eleven hours, fueled by Rooster Teeth's passionate and substantial cult of followers. The fundraising campaign did not stop until just short of $2.5 million, the second-largest amount raised on the funding website. They'd make the film the way they wanted to, which was just the way their crowd funders wanted it. In September 2015, Lazer Team the movie premiered at Fantastic Fest in Austin.

Rooster Teeth's ability to tap into an audience of gamers who were steeped in Internet culture culminated with RTX, a three-day festival staged in Austin every summer, attracting more than sixty thousand registrants for a long weekend of seminars, screenings, games, discussions, and parties. Complementary festivals were staged in England and Australia.

◎ ◎ ◎

Chris Taylor arrived in Austin from Carnegie-Mellon University in Pittsburgh with all his possessions in his car. He didn't have an apartment. But he did have a job at Trilogy, the high-profile software and digital services company that was successfully recruiting the brightest engineering talent straight out of college. Within an hour of Taylor's first day at the office, he was on a plane to Las Vegas where he would pull an all-nighter . . . at the craps table.

"You couldn't have hand-chosen your friends any better," Taylor recalled.

Taylor was one of the Trilogy Mafia, alumni of the Trilogy corporation, along with folks like Heather Brunner, CEO of WP Engine; Vast CEO John Price; and Scott Francis, cofounder of B3, all beneficiaries of Trilogy's unorthodox recruiting methods, part of the company's strategy to create a culture, or cult, depending on one's point of view.

Other companies touted fringe benefits and community amenities such as professional sports teams and schools. Trilogy kept it simple, as John Price described it: "Money. Recruiters. Beer. Repeat."

Richard Florida, a professor of regional economic development at Carnegie Mellon University had taken note of this unconventional strategy in his May 2002 article in the *Washington Monthly*, "The Rise of the Creative Class." The article was an excerpted preview of the book of the same name, which examined the future of American cities in the twenty-first century. The article zeroed in on one particularly talented Carnegie-Mellon grad being chased by several corporations.

"I noticed one member of the group sitting slouched over on the grass, dressed in a tank top," Florida wrote. "This young man had spiked multi-colored hair, full-body tattoos, and multiple piercings in his ears. An obvious slacker, I thought, probably in a band. 'So what is your story?' I asked. 'Hey man, I just signed on with these guys [Trilogy Corporation in Austin].' In fact, as I would later learn, he was a gifted student who had inked the highest-paying deal of any graduating student in the history of his department, right at that table on the grass, with the recruiters who do not 'recruit.'"

This was a whole new way of doing business. When Florida graduated from college twenty years before, students dressed up for interviews to show they could fit in at the company they were interviewing with. Now the companies were wooing students like they were pro football prospects, doing whatever it took to get a desired "Yes." In the case of the Carnegie-Mellon grad, that meant taking him out drinking in Pittsburgh, and then flying him to Austin to drink and party some more. "We wanted him because he's a rock star," a Trilogy spokesperson explained to Florida.

◉ ◉ ◉

Florida wondered why the rock star did not consider staying in Pittsburgh:

I asked the young man with the spiked hair why he was going to a smaller city in the middle of Texas, a place with a small airport and no professional sports teams, without a major symphony, ballet, opera, or art museum comparable to Pittsburgh's. The company is excellent, he told me. There are also terrific people and the work is challenging. But the clincher, he said, is that, "It's in Austin!" There are lots of young people, he went on to explain, and a tremendous amount to do: a thriving music scene, ethnic and cultural diversity, fabulous outdoor recreation, and great nightlife. Though he had several good job offers from Pittsburgh high-tech firms and knew the city well, he said he felt the city lacked the lifestyle options, cultural diversity, and tolerant attitude that would make it attractive to him. As he summed it up: "How would I fit in here?"

This was "a profound new force in the economy and life of America," Florida wrote. The creative class wasn't a class but "a fast-growing, highly educated, and well-paid segment of the workforce" that practiced an ethos valuing "creativity, individuality, difference, and merit."

The subtitle of Florida's article got straight to the point: "Why cities without gays and rock bands are losing the economic development race. Density and universities are key."

The article appeared about the same time Austin Mayor Kirk Watson showed up in the studios of KGSR-FM in Austin to talk to morning show host Kevin Connor. After Watson did his on-air bit, promoting his Smart City initiative to bring residential living to downtown, the conversation continued off the air. "You know, I can't say this publicly, but I can say this to y'all," Watson told Connor and his crew in the studio while a song played over the air. "The key is tolerance. We tolerate and embrace people who are different. That's what diversity is all about. It's a great recruiting tool for Austin."

For all the talk of diversity, there was a perception that a lot was just that— lip service. Austin had been too small to harbor significant black and brown communities during the first half of the twentieth century, at least compared to San Antonio, Dallas, Houston, and Fort Worth, which were all much larger cities than Austin then. But even boomtown twenty-first century Austin was still too small for some folks. In 2010, Austin was the only major city in the United States with a declining African American population. City blacks had been pushed to the suburbs by gentrification. A rising star at IBM who'd grown up in Chicago and happened to be African American felt there was so little black community in Austin to plug into that he chose to attend church in Houston, commuting three hundred miles round trip every Sunday.

That did not deter Austin's third billionaire, after the homegrown Michael

Dell and John Paul DeJoria, the hair products titan from Los Angeles. Robert F. Smith, the head of Vista Equity Partners, a private equity firm, moved with the company he cofounded to Austin in 2000, following a productive run as a Goldman Sachs technology investment banker in Silicon Valley. Vista built a reputation as one of the ten best-performing private equity funds in the world. As the second wealthiest African American in the United States, Smith told the *New York Times* that he had a unique set of circumstances to deal with. "The biggest challenge I've faced is a degree of loneliness," Smith said. "Who is out there like me that I know?" His existential angst was not unrelated to where he chose to live.

By the early twenty-first century, the entrepreneur was the New Austin artist. You had to monetize to know success. For folks like that, with big ideas in need of investment capital, there was Capital Factory.

The prestigious top floor of the office half of the Austin Centre-Omni Hotel building at Seventh and Brazos Streets had been previously occupied by *Texas Monthly* magazine, the unofficial state magazine of Texas. The young white twentysomething male in the plain white T-shirt, black jeans, and surf sneakers riding up the glass elevator might have been a delivery boy or a maintenance repairman back when the magazine occupied the sixteenth floor. Instead, he was a partner in a startup company hoping to get

Inside Capital Factory, the startup incubator. (Photo by Joe Nick Patoski.)

into Capital Factory's accelerator program, the most difficult and the most rewarding track that Capital Factory had to offer. If he could effectively pitch the potential viability of the startup he was working on, they'd be one of the few chosen among the hundreds of applicants to get into the three-month program that paired ideas with capital.

The Texas Monthly offices had been all dark cherrywood paneling and carpet. Capital Factory cleared out the space and dressed it down: concrete floors with a minimum of industrial carpeting, drop ceilings removed to expose vents and pipes. This was a stripped-down workspace. There was no need and no one to impress with expensive fixtures.

The high-tech incubator held public tours of the premises three times a week. Desmond Thomas, a slim, dark-haired, olive-skinned, perfectly agreeable go-getter in his twenties, whose official title was Experience Coordinator for the Capital Factory, led the tours, walking around prospects, media folks, and VIPs while telling the story of Capital Factory's founder Joshua Baer, who was also a professor of entrepreneurship at the University of Texas. The president of the United States, Barack Obama, the cofounders of PayPal and Reddit, and one of Texas's two US senators had taken the tour. On this day, it was three men tied to startups looking for office space, a University of Texas marketing senior interested in getting involved with startups, a gamer with a California startup who needed space to connect with the home office on the West Coast, the accelerator program aspirant in the white T-shirt, and a German gentleman in a suit wanting to get into international business in Texas. Capital Factory had a program the German might be interested in, Desmond Thomas informed him upon introduction. Touchdown Austin provided a "soft landing pad for international companies seeking to enter the US market," he said. "We've already touched down three companies and one of them is doing rampantly well. Their target market is Texas." Touching down was a good thing in the startup world.

Prominently displayed in Capital Factory's main foyer was an infographic poster with the banner: "Austin Sucks: Please Don't Move Here, Here Are Some Reasons Why."

Factoids filled the poster:

158 People Move Here Every Day.
You Know That Fun, Flirty Feeling Of Being The New Girl In Town?
    Kiss It Goodbye After Day One.
Heat. I Hope You Like Humidity And Dripping Sweat With Temps Over

100 For Most Of The Summer. Your Smart Car Better Have An AC, Poser. This F***** Sucks!

I35 Traffic Blows. Trust Me On This One.

Public Transportation: What's That?

When It's Less Than 50 Degrees, Shit Shuts Down. You Don't Want To Know What Happens When It Rains.

People Talk About Kale All The Time.

Good Luck Finding A Boyfriend. This Is Adult Never-Never Land. Men Stay Children Til Their Late 30s, Then They Date One Of The I58 People Who Moved Here Today.

I Hope Your Dog Is Rescued . . . Because You Will Be Alone.

Dallas and Houston Are Amazing . . . You Should Move There.

Kammie Russell, an illustrator, visual artist, and author created the poster. She moved to Austin two years after earning her BFA from the University of Nebraska.

To the right of Capital Factory's main foyer, where *Texas Monthly*'s advertising and publishing departments used to be, was a room full of moveable tables seating four, most bunched together so eight people could sit at one table, underscoring Desmond Thomas's introductory statement that "number one, we're a community center." Numbers two, three, and four were the choices of spaces in which to work, including coworking, private desks, and offices, offering an ecosystem with access to mentors, along with discounted sponsored products and services, and the accelerator program with a venture fund.

Sixty young people stared intently into the screens of their laptop computers in this coworking space. Despite framed music posters hanging on the wall that announced "You're in the Live Music Capital of the World now," the room was eerily quiet. Most of those seated at the tables wore earbuds. At the back of the room were four telephone booths with window doors—minus telephones—so workers could have conversations on their smartphones if they needed privacy. A video screen nearby rotated images, including the official Capital Factory logo with the word "Funding" above the actual logo and "Coworking" below it.

This was the entry-level workspace. Membership bought access to the workspace, its Google fiber connectivity, printing, scanning, access to mentors and advisers, the coffee, tea, fruits, and vegetables in the well-stocked kitchen pantry, and the opportunity to work alongside other startup aspirants. Access for three days a week, Monday through Friday, between 9:00 a.m. and 5:00 p.m., cost two hundred dollars a month. Three hundred fifty dollars a month bought access 24/7. For $750 and a three-to-six-month contract, a starter-upper could get a desk with a Formica surface and an ergonomic chair in an open space with dividers. One man taking the tour suggested that with all the beanbag chairs scattered throughout the floor and kitchen privileges, you could live at Capital Factory while developing your idea. The Experience Coordinator's nonresponse intimated some members might be doing just that.

Several subcompanies operated within the Capital Factory premises, including Maker Square web developer and OwnLocal automated digital advertising agency for local electronic and print media. Classrooms offered local tech groups spaces to meet. Startup presentations could be produced at the in-house television studio.

Interfacing with the community outside the incubator was a high priority. In 2015, eight hundred events attended by more than forty thousand people were booked at Capital Factory. "We want to create this center of gravity for entrepreneurship," Desmond Thomas said. "A lot of the smaller meetups, such as Women Who Code, Austin Web Pipeline Users, stuff like that, are held in this classroom. If you're accepted into our accelerator program, we also have classes here every Friday called Capital Factory University, where we bring in high-level speakers to talk about particulars."

Capital Factory was one of the stops on the startup pub crawl that kicked off SXSW Interactive, the biggest week for technology in Austin. Thomas described the crawl as "basically a drunk show-and-tell with tech companies," with stops at Facebook, Visa, RideScout, and other prominent tech companies clustered downtown.

Seven hundred fifty members, thirteen conference rooms, and ten phone booths were spread over fifty-three thousand square feet of space occupying the sixteenth and fifth floors and half of the seventh floor. "We're going to take over the whole building," Desmond Thomas added casually.

The tour group perked up when the elevator door opened at the fifth floor, revealing another open area of wired tables and chairs in a temporary space. This was the Capital Factory accelerator program. More than one hundred candidates applied for the program every month. Five or so were accepted to interview with the board of directors. Applicants who passed muster received a package of products, services, credits, free stuff, and discounts worth more than a half-million dollars, and were matched with investing mentors. Convince two mentors to invest twenty-five thousand dollars in

WP Engine CEO Heather Brunner preaches diversity, transparency, and inclusion as core values. (Photo by Hans Ivery Odenrud, Finansavisen.)

your startup, and Capital Factory would match the investment, and work with other venture capitalists to match the investment too.

All you needed was a multimillion-dollar idea in search of a few million dollars.

◎ ◎ ◎

Heather Brunner started at WP Engine, one of the world's largest hosts for WordPress open source websites, when the startup was the first major tenant at the Capital Factory tech incubator. WP Engine was the first full-blown chief executive officer gig for the fifth-generation Texan. Brunner had earned leadership roles at tech companies ever since graduating from Trinity University in San Antonio in 1990 with a degree in international economics. She was known for her skills monetizing tech ideas, concepts, and innovations. She made it all real.

Like Capital Factory founder Josh Baer, Brunner, a self-described "hard charger," was once part of the storied Trilogy Mafia. She was also a sought after asset—a female in a male-dominated business.

The route to WP Engine was circuitous.

Brunner grew up in Houston enamored with her father's job traveling around the world for a Houston-based energy company. She accompanied him to the office to see how things worked and set her sights on a career in international economics. She learned to assert herself early on, working a temp job on the Houston Ship Channel to make ends meet while she finished college. Tiring of her male boss addressing her and her coworkers with terms of endearment, not their names, she confronted him one day in his office. "Could you please call me Heather, not honey, sugar, or babe?" she asked him, struggling to smile.

"He said, 'OK' and that was it!" she laughed. All she had to do was ask. By asking nicely, it was a whole lot easier for him to answer in the affirmative.

Brunner's postgraduate career started at Andersen Consulting in Houston. For eight years, her gig was back office automation, helping companies automate and convert their systems to digital on-site. During her five-year IT engagement with FedEx, she met the man who would become her husband in a Memphis dive bar.

As stimulating as her extended stays in Memphis and other cities had been, Brunner admitted to her boyfriend that she missed Texas. A master craftsman who designed and built furniture and loved to go out to hear music, he told Brunner he'd move with her to Austin or San Antonio maybe. "Houston and Dallas were not under consideration," she said.

Andersen Consulting, which would become Accenture, promoted Brunner to senior manager and parked her in Austin. She brought in the Memphis boyfriend in March 1995 for South by Southwest. "He was sold," she said. "In Memphis, we probably went out to hear live music five nights out of seven. He felt like he was home. I was back in Texas. We were enjoying the amenities of Town Lake and Zilker Park. There was a boom, and he was busy doing carpentry work, trim work. He was able to come in right away and establish himself, get work through word of mouth."

They married. Brunner moved on to open the Austin office for Oracle data management software systems. She became the first Oracle person in Austin, working with commercial clients starting in 1997. It was a step down but a more interesting challenge.

"I went from running this seventy-five million dollar project for the state of New York with hundreds of people involved, to me, a desk, a phone, and a green-and-white dot matrix printout that somebody from Houston shipped me in a box with a note: 'Here are all the people with Oracle licenses.' In eighteen months, we built an eighteen million dollar book." The next stop was Concero, part of the next generation of web-based strategies for corporate clients, and then Trilogy software.

Trilogy was on steroidal growth spurt providing technology services to large corporations in the electronics, automobile, and insurance sectors. The head of Trilogy John Price approached her at a party.

"I don't want to work at Trilogy," she coolly told to Price. "You guys are a bunch of assholes. The perspective in the marketplace is that you guys are an ivory tower, everyone's really arrogant. Why would I want to?"

Her remarks only made Price want Brunner even more. "We're trying to change that. You should talk to us."

"He knew that was the perception," explained Brunner. "While their strategy of Get the Top 1 Percent of Graduates to Come to Austin was really working in terms of incredible engineering talent and prowess, they needed to balance that with some common sense, some business practicum, so to speak."

Trilogy had a platinum rep among engineering talent. "Lots of overpaid young people buying expensive cars and speed boats, the entire company going on these massive trips," Brunner said, rolling her eyes. A month after the Fourth of July party, she went to work at Trilogy. One month later, 9/11 happened. "It went from Mardi Gras to sweeping up the beads overnight," she said. "What I saw through that 9/11 experience was how the company came together. There was this moment of How Can We Give Back?" Brunner saw that as an opportunity to better focus on customer service.

"Engineers needed a perspective around what they're building," she said. "It's not just something that's functional." Brunner was asked to be part of the Tiger Team that launched an employee incentive program to get every one of Trilogy's customers to agree their business benefited from their relationship with Trilogy.

"Very simple, very black or white."

Brunner represented Trilogy's next phase after recruiting its workforce and promoting solely from within—bringing in talent from the outside.

"I was the first leader at Trilogy to be a nonengineer leading an engineering team," she said. "Most of the people at Trilogy were hired off of campus and this was their first job. They did not have to work prior, whatever their circumstances. The perspective was skewed, coming to Austin, living high on the hog. At Andersen, I had to learn how to manage clients. I was used to earning the respect and trust of people who were different from me."

Brunner found a collaborator in Chris Hyams, the functional head of engineering at Trilogy who told her, "You teach me about the business side and I'll teach you about the engineering side."

Subsequent gigs at Coremetrics, which was all about customer experience analytics; B-Side, a platform attempting to be the Netflix of independent film ("It was too early, there wasn't the cloud"); a distressed tech bailout firm acquired by Trilogy founder Joe Liemandt; and Bazaarvoice, which offered user-generated content marketing solutions, led to WP Engine.

All along the way, Brunner preached transparency as the path to profitability. "Who really thought they'd want negative reviews on their website?" she said of her stint at Bazaarvoice. "Who thought that would be a positive thing that would be adopted? We had retailers like Williams-Sonoma and Macy's saying they would never do this. But they did. People saw how effective it was."

Brunner rode several waves where a sense of purpose beyond making money made a difference. "I was at the beginning of greenscreen, the beginning of ERP, web analytics, and now the beginning of social commerce," she said. "We walk the talk and urge our customers to share the good, the bad, the ugly. We do that internally too. It was really fun to be at the table to help to shape that as our mission."

Bill Wood and Morgan Flager at Silverton Partners, a spinoff of Austin Ventures, Austin's first venture capital investment firm, introduced Brunner to an entrepreneur named Jason Cohen and his company WP Engine. The Silverton partners thought Brunner would be a good addition to the company's board.

"I met with Jason at Maudie's," Brunner said. "We were supposed to meet for an hour. We went more than two and a half hours." Cohen was a graduate of LBJ High School in Austin who had studied computer science at UT. Like Brunner, he was a mentor at Capital Factory. WP Engine was the home of WordPress, an open source website building tool that users could build themselves. WordPress was growing like a weed. Twelve percent of all sites on the World Wide Web were built using WordPress's technology. The open source approach spoke to Heather Brunner's sense of higher purpose. "WordPress was an entry ramp to the web. The mission was to democratize publishing, and enable everyone, in every country, in every language, to have a voice." She joined the WP Engine board of directors.

During South by Southwest 2013, Brunner got a call from a very spirited Jason Cohen, who was out enjoying SXSW with a Silverton partner. "We think you need to be CEO of WP Engine," Cohen told her over the phone. Brunner was welcomed as the chief operating officer and president of WP Engine two months later. That summer she stepped into the role of chief executive officer. In the first 4 years with Brunner at the helm, the staff of 40 serving 8,000 customers grew into a workforce of 430 women and men in 5 offices, 3 in the United States, serving 60,000 customers in 130 countries. Capital Factory, having served its purpose as a startup incubator, was vacated for larger, snazzier headquarters occupying the tenth floor of Lavaca Plaza a few blocks west. Blowup photographs of Austin scenes including bands and nightlife greeted visitors in the atrium leading to the reception area, where the Core Values board was prominently displayed, adorned with signatures of WP Engine employees.

Higher purpose made the bottom line look even better, further improved by a $250 million infusion of capital from a private equity firm in 2018.

"The mission of democratizing publishing to bring their business, their voice to life, is happening," Brunner smiled confidently in her small office cubicle. "Twenty-seven percent of all websites in the world were built with WordPress," she said.

She name-dropped diversity, inclusion, and core values as much as she cited profit margins and growth rates. It was part of the company culture. "There's this vibe, this energy, and altruism," Brunner said. "Every year, we have all employees recommit to our core values, our ethos. This is what we stand for. Do the right thing. Customer inspired, we're here in service to our customers.

"People choose their tribe," Brunner said. She believed companies had supplanted schools and churches in the roles they once played defining culture and values. Diversity and inclusion weren't just buzzwords at WP Engine. The executive team was 65 percent female. A third of the employees did not have college degrees. A third were nonwhite. Five percent self-identified as LGBTQ.

"It isn't a quota. Women are given opportunities to thrive and grow. It makes no difference whether you're black or gay or Asian, or whether you're in Limerick or in Austin, or you're fifty years old or twenty years old. All those dimensions of diversity, we have to walk the talk. We have to honor and protect it. If people see that you're genuine, they're happy and they refer other people." Almost half of WP Engine's workforce had been hired through a referral from another employee.

Core values, an environment of diversity and inclusion, opening the doors wider, and helping people thrive were just as important as a credible financial performance to Brunner. Stressing community as much as raw profit was practically an Austin thing, with roots that could be traced back to the music community. In the world of tech, where recruiting talent was just as important as securing funding, the holistic approach gave companies like WP Engine a leg up on the competition.

"People do care about being in a place with a sense of purpose," Brunner said. For now, WP Engine fit the bill.

◉ ◉ ◉

Michael Dell, the college kid with a head for efficiency, grew into a titan of computing and finance. Dell outsold all other personal computers for a stretch until laptops became the preferred computing device, and then reigned as one of the top global sellers of laptops. Attempts at smart pads and smartphones were not as successful.

Dell had spearheaded the paradigm shift brought by affordable, accessible technology. But he wasn't ready to rest on his laurels and the considerable wealth he'd built as Austin's first billionaire. By 2013, the Age of the Personal Computer was in the rearview mirror. Smartphones were the platform of preference for consumer technology innovation. The big money was in the corporate sector.

Michael Dell partnered with the Silver Lake Management technology firm to take the company private, buying back stock in a $24.9 billion deal.

Going private gave Dell Technologies, as it would be called, more flexibility and nimbleness in decision-making and anticipating where technology was heading, as Michael Dell had been doing since he was a kid. As a private corporation, Dell management could take a longer view of the evolving digital age and data economy.

"We love being a privately controlled company, and I haven't found any downside to it," Dell said after the move. "We are focused on long-term success, not quarterly earnings-per-share and the short-term thinking that plagues many companies. We can think in a time horizon that is measured in decades."

Two years later, Dell Technologies bought the EMC Corporation, the world's biggest enterprise storage vendor, for $58 billion. It was the largest technology merger in history. The purchase cemented Dell's position as one of the world's largest server makers, allowing the company to better manage and store corporate data through cloud computing, which was where the action was.

"In essence, we acquired our own company, not other businesses," Dell wrote in the revised foreword to his book. In 2018, five years after Dell bought back stock and went private, the company once again became a publicly traded and owned entity.

Michael Dell was no longer an innovator and entrepreneur, but an industrialist who owned one of the largest tech companies in the world, overseeing a global workforce of more than 140,000.

The company's roots as the thousand dollar good idea—a thoroughly Austin trait—remained its guiding compass. "Dell bubbled up through a kind of Darwinian evolution, finding holes in the way the industry was working," Dell said. "We didn't become asset-high because it was a brilliant strategy. We didn't have any choice. Our lean beginnings created the strategic management principles that define our culture: Less is more. Information is better than inventory. Ingenuity is better than investment. Execution is everything. No excuses."

He had reached that graying-around-the-temples age and stature where Susan and Michael Dell were recognized as Austin's leading philanthropists, the Dell name affixed to everything from the University of Texas medical school to the Jewish center and the baseball park. His ideas made a lot of money for a lot of people and would continue doing so for years to come.

Technology rocked.

9

The Franklin Line

◉ ◉ ◉

Sunday morning, January 3, 2010, did not start well for Aaron Franklin. "It was gloomy, there was no one there," he said. "I was just sitting around." There happened to be the back of a parking lot on the north-bound frontage road of Interstate 35, just south of Thirty-Eighth Street. That's where Franklin had parked the funky Aristocrat Lo-Liner trailer that his girlfriend Stacy found on Craigslist for three hundred bucks. A second trailer held the smoker that Aaron had bought, which had belonged to his former employer John Mueller.

"This thing was just crappy enough for me to be able to work on," Franklin said of the Aristocrat. "It was busted. It is still really busted. Really polished a turd on that one. It was not a good trailer in any way. I stripped the whole thing down, sanded every square inch of that by hand, pulled down the walls, cut in the windows, relocated the door, gutted the whole thing, re-welded the bottom. My parents bought me a welder for Christmas to build barbecue pits because it was way cheaper than buying a barbecue pit."

Three men drove into the lot, parked, and approached the weathered Aristocrat. One had called in advance to ask Franklin if he was open on Sundays. He said he was driving in from Dallas to try out the barbecue Franklin was selling out of his trailer.

"Whatever meat I had, I served them," Franklin said. "Apparently they liked it." He gave the three customers banana pudding for dessert, on the house.

The men were BBQ bloggers, a new breed of enthusiast devoted to discovering and sharing places that smoked great barbecue, which in Texas starts with beef brisket.

The big guy from Dallas with the receding hairline was Daniel Vaughn, a recent arrival from Ohio whose day job was as an architect. His passion was the Full Custom Gospel BBQ blog he created, for which he traveled around Texas eating barbecue—neither grazing nor nibbling but finishing entire meals, including trimmings; several meals in a single day—and writing about it. He called himself the BBQ Snob. The two locals were Drew

Thornley, a UT law school professor, and Brad Istre, Thornley's partner on the Man Up! Texas Barbecue blog.

"I'd never heard of barbecue blogs," Aaron Franklin said. "I'd never heard of Twitter before, either."

Full Custom Gospel and Man Up! Texas BBQ both wrote glowing reviews on their blogs about their visit to Aaron Franklin's trailer.

Drew Thornley of Man Up! put Franklin in perspective:

The unique setup redefines urban BBQ (assuming it was ever defined): 1 man, 1 smoker, 2 trailers, and some picnic tables. And it totally works, as the brisket revealed. Now, I realize I didn't grow up in Texas, but I've eaten quite a bit of brisket since moving here in September 2007; and I can say with zero hesitation that the brisket was quite possibly the best I've ever had (and, lest you think I am prone to superlatives, I've never said this of any brisket). Smokey. Not too dry, not too moist. Perfect amount of outside char.

Vaughn waxed downright eloquent:

It was 10:45 when I stepped up to the locked chain link gate and Aaron, the owner, was arranging picnic tables in the front getting ready for his 11:00 opening bell. I sat there like a sad puppy dog until he unlocked the gate and happily invited me in for a few slices off the brisket he was just pulling from the pit.

We chatted for a bit as he unwrapped and sliced the meat, but I cut the conversation short knowing he had to get back to work, and I had to have some alone time with this beautiful beef in my front seat (too cold for picnic tables). I took a few bites, and the flavor was incredible. I had ordered the fatty cut on my previous visit, but lean cuts are more suited for brunch. The heavy black pepper rub helped create a crispy crust on the meat that also packed a wallop of smoke. Although this was lean brisket, the meat was incredibly moist and perfectly tender. After a few luxurious slices, I wrapped it back up and headed out onto I-35 back to Dallas.

As the radio played, I contemplated if this was the finest brisket that I've ever eaten as it called to me beneath the thin, greasy, and now transparent yellow paper. As I eyed the interstate with one eye, the other was watching as I carefully unwrapped the meat for another go. As the salty flesh passed my lips, I realized how an appropriate song can add so much to a special moment.

Man Up! Texas BBQ liked Franklin's so much, they returned with a team of twenty-one reviewers, all of whom gave their thumbs-up.

Franklin started hearing about it.

At the time, he was trying to do it all. "I used to make the sauce in little half-gallon batches, all three sauces, every morning. I was making the potato salad. I was cooking two briskets a day during the week and three on the weekend. At that point, I couldn't get rid of a rack of ribs, so I was cutting spares in half and tried to cook a half rack. I'd never cooked a rack of ribs until we opened up the trailer. They're too gosh darn expensive to waste.

"I was making potato salad one morning. There were five people standing outside the gate. I wondered what they were here for. People kept coming, stacking up. 'What's going on?'

"Eleven o'clock came around. 'I think they're here for food.' I was talking to myself, listening to music in the trailer. Super peaceful. Sleeves rolled up, having a good time. Opened up the gate at eleven, and the people kept coming in. The next day, there were a few more. That was Daniel's blog. Non-neighborhood people started showing up."

Lines formed well before the eleven a.m. opening as word spread. Just like at John Mueller's, where Franklin had previously worked, customers were offered complimentary thin slices of burnt ends, the crispy fatty end pieces of brisket, as they placed their order. The pork ribs and sausage were top shelf, but Franklin's beef brisket, the standard of Texas barbecue, was on a whole other level. "Slow smoked a minimum eighteen hours a day," he explained one midmorning while checking on one of his barrel pits as the line started snaking toward the street. That was a lot more smoking time than most pit masters required. The rub was salt and pepper. Nothing else. The wood was post oak.

He built a 500 gallon tank side cooker to accompany the old cooker from John Mueller's and a 250 gallon cooker in back behind the bamboo fence. "We were running a restaurant in a parking lot," he grinned. And it worked.

Franklin could measure the trailer's growing popularity in meat. "At first, I would go to Restaurant Depot and buy two briskets a day. Every day after lunch, I'd take the money out of the register and go buy meat, put it on, watch it until ten o'clock or so at night, try to make the perfect fire, try to do different things to make it sort of sustainable, improve the quality of fire. It was the biggest deal when I could buy one case of brisket, and I could cook that in a day. Then it was two cases. Wow. I'm buying two cases a day and I don't even have to store them. They come in, I rub them, put them on the cooker. This is great."

Aaron Franklin's BBQ was one of the most successful of a new breed of dining establishments that had popped up in Austin. Food trailers were the startup platform for aspiring restaurateurs in Austin, just as they had been in other cities such as Portland and Los Angeles. The size of trailers and their portability to move wherever and whenever necessary made them ideal test kitchens. If the idea worked, the trailer could go brick-and-mortar and become a real restaurant.

It was hardly a new concept. Carts vending hot dogs and ice creams were staples on the streets of New York and other cities in the northeastern United States, going back to the nineteenth century. Food carts started appearing on Guadalupe Street, one of the few pedestrian strips in Texas, and in other locations across from the University of Texas main campus in the early seventies. Salvation Sandwiches ("Live Good, What Is the Harm?"), a hippie sandwich vendor with carts scattered in locations near campus, offered cheap vegetarian fare in the form of an avocado-and-sprouts-on-whole-wheat-bread sandwich. Salvation, run by two displaced New York hippies, Roland DeNoie and his sidekick Michael Kleinman, filed a lawsuit against the University of Texas Board of Regents for the right to sell food on the university's sidewalks, a privilege heretofore limited to taco vendors. University officials banned Salvation from campus in September 1974, citing them as competition for vending machine sandwiches sold on campus, whose profits went to the Ex-Students' Association. DeNoie successfully sued UT and then successfully sued the Austin City Council for the right to sell on Austin's sidewalks.

Salvation's legal victories opened the doors for numerous campus-area food cart operations. The idea spread downtown to Sixth Street at night in the forms of hot dog, egg roll, and pizza carts. At the time, four-wheeled food trucks and trailers were pretty much limited to the taco trucks that worked construction sites.

The first star in the modern Austin food trailer movement was Torchy's Tacos, created by executive chef Mike Rypka. In 2006, Rypka took advantage of a newly reinterpreted city code that tolerated mobile kitchens to build a multiple trailer empire before making the trailer-to-brick-and-mortar transition. In seven short years, Rypka's idea grew from a single food trailer to Texas' biggest specialty taco chain with more than twenty locations.

There were trailers dedicated to bahn mi Vietnamese sandwiches, Yucatecan tacos, Cuban sandwiches, pork bellies, and Japanese street food (Love Balls). A local invention, the Mighty Cone, a concoction of sliced chicken wrapped in a tortilla cone topped with mango-jalapeno slaw and doused in ancho sauce, was created by Hudson's on the Bend chefs for the first Austin City Limits Festival's food court, so eaters could dine on the run with a minimum of spillage. Its popularity at ACL Fest led to a food trailer selling Mighty Cones year-round.

Bryce Gilmore, the son of Jack Gilmore, the chef behind Z'Tejas Grill, one of Austin's first Southwestern cuisine restaurants, and his own Jack Allen's Kitchen, was another trailer luminary. Bryce Gilmore trained on the job at the prestigious Boulevard restaurant in San Francisco before returning to Austin to open Odd Duck, a "farm-to-trailer" concept that combined two trends into one successful business. He soon opened a small table brick-and-mortar restaurant, Barley Swine, and then a permanent Odd Duck after being named one of Food & Wine magazine's best new chefs in 2011.

In response to all the exotic global cuisines being cooked up in trailers, old hidebound traditions such as southern comfort food and Tex-Mex were undergoing makeovers too. None came close to the transformation of Texas barbecue, which had been reborn as a trendy, hip thing. Texas Monthly established the position of Barbecue Editor and filled the position with Daniel Vaughn, who quit his architect job to write about barbecue, including a book, The Prophets of Smoked Meat: A Journey through Texas Barbecue (2013).

Barbecue was the centerpiece of Foodways Texas, a nonprofit headed by UT professor Marvin Bendele, founded in 2010 to preserve and promote the state's food cultures. Its annual Camp Brisket workshop held at Texas A&M was an instant hit, requiring participants to make reservations at least a year in advance. Academic Elizabeth S. D. Engelhardt did a deep dive into barbecue's folkways with Republic of Barbecue: Stories beyond the Brisket (2009), while longtime Texas food writer Robb Walsh mixed deep history with recipes in his Legends of Texas Barbecue Cookbook (2002).

Smoked meats were a Texas perennial, a tradition linked to meat markets owned by Germans, Czechs, and other central European immigrants in Texas in the late nineteenth century. Lacking refrigeration, the markets got rid of their unsold meat by slow smoking the week's leftovers into barbecue on Saturdays.

But barbecue around Austin had practically become frozen in time. Small funky joints such as House Park BBQ and Sam's seemed like they'd always been there, and turned out consistently good beef brisket, pork ribs, sausage, and even mutton. But it was pretty much same as it ever was. Until it wasn't.

In 1975, the first County Line barbecue opened west of Austin in a one-time speakeasy on a hilltop just off Bee Caves Road. The scenic setting, the family-style dining room layout, and the giant beef ribs, which were not part of the basic Texas BBQ menu, made the County Line a big hit. It was the nice kind of place where UT students could take visiting parents from out of town—that is, when a drive to the Salt Lick in Driftwood, the most Texas-looking BBQ destination establishment anywhere, was out of the question. County Line expanded to other scenic locations in Austin, San Antonio, Dallas, Houston, El Paso, Albuquerque, and Lubbock.

A tall black man with a booming voice and a gentle countenance who happened to be a storied pit master made his mark on Austin barbecue when he moved from Lubbock in 1982, following his musician friends Joe Ely, Butch Hancock, Jimmie Dale Gilmore, Jessie Taylor, Kimmie Rhodes, and Lloyd Maines.

C. B. Stubblefield was a gentle giant of a one-man barbecue enterprise, friendly to customers and visitors, protective when he had to be, and a pretty great cook. His menu carried the advisory: "There will be no loud talk or bad talk in this place." His original BBQ joint hosted Sunday night jams featuring the best musicians hanging around Lubbock in the seventies. But Stubb was becoming just as famous for the piquant, spicy sauce he concocted to accompany his smoked meats. Not for nothing did he declare, "Ladies and gentlemen, I am a cook." He could back it up.

Stubb first set up shop cooking at Antone's nightclub on Guadalupe Street, and then at his own standalone location in a faded motel restaurant at Forty-Fifth and Interstate 35. He struggled financially until his place was shut down by the Austin-Travis County Health Department for one too many code violations. Stubblefield defended kitchen conditions to a television reporter, saying, "The roaches and rats are God's creatures too."

C. B. Stubblefield and Joe Ely. (Photo copyright © 2017 by Bill Leissner.)

Two Lubbock expats who had relocated to Austin, Sharon Ely and Kimmie Rhodes, took notice Stubb was without a joint and encouraged him to bottle his barbecue sauce, drawing labels by hand and utilizing whisky bottles and jelly jars. Stubb sold whatever he and his friends could bottle. Sharon's husband, the musician Joe Ely, took samples to New York when he appeared on the *Late Night with David Letterman* television program, and word spread. With the help of backers, Stubb's Legendary Kitchen was incorporated in 1992, and his sauces started to appear on shelves of high-end groceries. Although Stubblefield passed away in 1995, the retail sauce business continued expanding, while a music club and barbecue joint bearing his name at Red River at Eighth Streets opened in what was once the One Knite Club.

The opening of the Austin Convention Center in 1992 exposed out-of-town conventioneers to Texas barbecue courtesy of its semiramshackle next-door neighbor, the Iron Works BBQ, housed in a red sheet metal building that once was really an ironworks. Ruby's, a joint just north of the University of Texas campus, introduced natural beef to Texas pits.

Barbecue was already going through something of a revival, with small-town joints within an hour's drive of Austin being discovered by tourists, many of them on semiorganized BBQ tours while attending South by Southwest. A lunch road trip to Lockhart, Luling, Taylor, or Llano became an annual ritual for hundreds of attendees.

Texas Monthly magazine seized upon the growing interest with the *Texas Monthly* BBQ Top 50 of the finest 'cue joints in Texas, as ranked by the popular magazine in 1997. A seven-person BBQ Swat Team traveled around the state, each judge racking up several thousand miles sampling and rating barbecue.

The first list in 1997, a second list in 2003, and subsequent lists applied modern restaurant criticism to earthy, timeless places that cooked and served smoked meats. Reactions were both heated (judges were accused of being "city boys") and startling ("You really prefer gas-fired smokers over wood-fired?"), and substantial enough to turn the Top 50 BBQ Joints list into a tradition.

In 1999, John Mueller of Louie Mueller's in Taylor, one of the Holy Trinity of Texas barbecue according to *Texas Monthly*, contacted the magazine to weigh in on what was happening in Lockhart, the self-proclaimed Barbecue Capital of Texas, and home of one of the other two Holy Trinity joints, Kreuz Market. A family feud between brother Rick Schmidt and sister Nina Sells had split Kreuz apart. Edgar "Smitty" Schmidt had bequeathed his business to his sons Rick and Don, and the building to his daughter Nina, when he died in 1990. Nine years later, sibling disagreement led to the family split.

In an elaborate ceremony involving hot coals carried in wheelbarrows,

Rick Schmidt moved Kreuz Market out of its historic location near the county courthouse to new quarters four-tenths of a mile away on the north edge of town that featured the biggest woodpile in the state of Texas. The high-ceilinged, smoke-tinted former location of Kreuz Market was taken over by Nina Sells, whose day job was county clerk for Caldwell County. Her husband and sons, all barbecue cookoff champions, manned the pits. The Sells renamed the place Smitty's, after Nina's (and Rick and Don's) dad.

People in Lockhart weren't complaining. Instead of one world-class joint, the town now had at least two. Black's and Chisholm Trail were also highly touted. John Mueller of Taylor couldn't help but weigh in.

"It's a pity what the family let come between them," Mueller said, issuing an invitation to inspect the new, historically accurate addition to the dining area of Louie Mueller's in Taylor, where John Mueller had spent the previous twenty years honing his smoking talent.

Two years later, in 2001, John Mueller opened his own joint in Austin, an establishment, as he noted in a handwritten note tacked to the door, that wasn't affiliated with Louie Mueller's of Taylor. Rumors and whispers had it that John Mueller had been banished from Louie Mueller's, something about him abandoning his family and running off with the hired help.

Regardless of the actual circumstances, Mueller's exile became the best thing to ever happen to Austin barbecue.

John Mueller BBQ opened on Manor Road on the near East Side in the same green building that once housed the grocery run by barrelhouse piano legend Robert Shaw. Located two blocks from the University of Texas Darrell K Royal Memorial Stadium, it was close enough to draw a steady university clientele. By bringing Taylor old school barbecue to Austin, Mueller raised the bar.

Mueller was a disruptive force, providing an alternative to the usual road trip required for real deal slow-smoked-with-wood barbecue. UT Football Coach Mack Brown made John Mueller's a regular lunch stop, and Brown's players, coaches, associates, and fans followed. Soon the concrete walls were adorned with jerseys and banners, and lines began forming outside the door before the 11:30 a.m. opening.

Demand grew fast enough to prompt Mueller to open a second location, which led to his downfall. He knew how to work a pit, not run multiple businesses. His marriage fell apart, his Manor Road lease suddenly expired, and five years after he appeared, Mueller's Austin experiment ended.

One of Mueller's employees was an affable kid with black frame glasses and prominent sideburns from Bryan, who learned a lot at John Mueller's, even though he was quick to point out "John never let me work the pit; only he did that."

Aaron Franklin was the quintessential alternative Austin immigrant.

"I grew up in a music store and a barbecue restaurant," he said of his growing up years in Bryan, ninety miles northeast of Austin. "My grandparents had a music store, a record store on the wrong side of town, then started selling guitars. My grandfather, Tommy Howard, was a pedal steel player who played with Bob Wills and all the old school country-western bands around Houston. For a few years, my parents had a barbecue restaurant in Bryan. It was a lunchtime spot, nothing special, but it certainly planted the seed for my future. I was into music, got into playing in bands. I wasn't interested in staying in Bryan-College Station." The home of Texas A&M University would not do.

"I was like 'I'm turning eighteen and I'm going to Austin.' I knew I wanted to go somewhere and do something different, but I didn't have a plan. Like most people, school's not my thing. I just like playing music, like hanging out. I like building stuff, that's pretty much at the top of my list.

"Austin was the little oasis of Texas where the free-spirited get to go and not be messed with," he said.

The commitment was sealed at a show at Liberty Lunch when a stranger offered him a beer despite the fact he was only eighteen. 'It was people on the back porch of Liberty Lunch, just hanging out, watching bands and stuff."

He moved two months later, on August 17, 1996.

"Anyone could move here," Franklin said. "You could be in a band. You could be an artist, wear a bikini, and ride your bike downtown. You could do whatever you wanted. I could afford to move here and just work random odd jobs and play rock and roll at night. That's what I did, and pretty much why I came here."

Franklin played in several bands as a drummer and as a picker of all kinds of stringed instruments. Some of the bands he played in toured outside of Austin. The most successful was Those Peabodys, the band he was drumming for when his life changed.

His girlfriend Stacy held down the steady job. Franklin made do with "a million things. I was a baker at Schlotzsky's for three months. I worked at an insurance place for about a year and a half, my *Office Space* experiment. They let me go on tour for weeks on end, come back for weeks, leave again, come back. I did that for a good while. Finally, they went, 'Your position has gone away.' I was 'Gawd, this is awful. I can't sleep at work anymore. I've been waiting for you guys to fire me forever.'

"I remodeled houses for a little while. I can tape-and-float like a crazy person. I was building houses, remodeling houses on my own. At the same time, I started doing backyard barbecues. I worked Little City [coffee and café] and John Mueller's place, just working the register."

His real education came at backyard barbecues. "Stacy and I had just gotten our first little place together up north on Guadalupe. I had a paycheck and went to Academy to buy us a grill. They had this New Braunfels cooker. Ninety-nine bucks. 'Oh, brisket. Never thought of that. Great.'" Never mind that he couldn't grill with a cooker.

"It sparked an interest," Franklin said. "On a Friday night, I'd go get a brisket at H-E-B for eighty-seven cents a pound, cheap, really crappy. I'm pretty sure it was select, frozen for decades, and addled with hormones. I didn't know, and I didn't care. I went and got a couple bundles of firewood, fired it up, sat down in the backyard, opened up a beer, and thought to myself, 'Wow, this is amazing. I wanna do this. Maybe that's what I'll do. Maybe I could open up a little barbecue joint like my parents had.'

"That brisket turned out pretty terrible. A month or two later, I did another one. That was the beginning of this whole barbecue thing. I did backyard barbecues, invited friends, then we'd play shows. We'd set up a date every summer to try to make it a big barbecue, a little bit bigger and better. I didn't really know what I was doing at all. But I was having a blast.

"There were a hundred fifty people showing up. I would do handbills like you passed out for shows. I'd be at Emo's and 'Oh, in two weeks, I'm having a barbecue.' I was handing them out, got a mailing list going. I'd make these really super rad flyers for the barbecue, invite only, suggested donation of five bucks to help cover food costs. I didn't really have a job. We would have one blowout barbecue every summer because it would take me a whole year to save up for that."

His girlfriend tolerated the growing obsession. Sort of. "It drove Stacy nuts," admitted Franklin. "*Gawd, will you shut up about barbecue? Stop talking about this stuff all the time!*"

Aaron Franklin couldn't help himself. "I'd never been so on fire, never been so excited about anything other than, like, playing drums and playing music."

But could he actually be a barbecue pit master? "I did want to make sure it was something I wanted to do," he said. "Can I take eighty hours of this? 'Cause it's going to be a lot of hard work. I wanted to test the waters. That's why I got a job at John Mueller's. I had two other jobs. That was my third job. I put in twenty-five, thirty hours a week on top of the other two jobs, made a whopping five-fifty an hour. Cut onions. Took it all in. 'Yup, this is pretty dang cool. I like this.'"

He started stockpiling in anticipation of someday opening his own place. "I wanted a small building, something built out of stone, and I wanted it funky and old. I wanted grease on the floor. Most people would think it's crappy. I call it character." Unfortunately, there was no money, so scavenging became the new stockpiling. He brought home leftover building materials from construction jobs. He found a warmer in San Antonio. He got his cooker from the guy who bought John Mueller's cooker after Mueller went out of business.

"I was being super junk-yard-y industrious, holding on to some extra materials with my sights set on building a barbecue trailer one day," he said. His friend Travis who had worked with him at Little City called one day: "Hey, I'm building this place. I've got a coffee roaster. You want to help me work on some windows?"

"Yeah, totally. I'm not doing anything. Sure."

Travis and Aaron met up, got a twelve-pack of beer, and hung some windows. "I ended up helping him build out that whole building, really just for fun," Franklin said. "I was so excited to build something." The building had been a Texaco service station that opened in 1951. "It was a kit building designed by the same guy who designed the Brownie camera," Franklin said. "I looked at the titles in back. I have a hardcore thing for Googie architecture. I got oddly excited working on this place: 'Yeah!' 'What do you need?' 'I want to do it!' 'I don't even care if I get paid. I just want to hang out and work on this building.'

"We were sitting drinking beer one night, painting some walls, and Travis said, 'Man, you should build that trailer and park it back here.'"

"Are you serious?"

"Sure, totally."

"That was the missing piece to the puzzle," Franklin said. "I didn't sleep for three days I was so excited. I went home and sat up all night at the kitchen table, thinking and drawing on paper, trying to figure everything out."

It would take another year and several more backyard barbecues. "But I had a goal at that point," he said. "It wasn't a pipe dream. It was very organically falling into place. A lot of good friends came together to help it happen. Having fun, hanging out, the true Austin spirit."

The Franklin BBQ trailer opened for business on December 2, 2009.

"It took eight years to build a three hundred dollar trailer," Aaron Franklin laughed. "It's like playing in a band. You practice. But you're never ready until you hit the road and start playing. You also can't rush these things. You can't rush out and try and get signed to a crappy label because you're going to fail. You're not ready. Same thing with opening a barbecue place. You need to have your ducks in a row. You need to be prepared. Don't half-ass anything. Just do it. But that means it might take forever. Eventually you've got to take the plunge. 'All right, this is as ready as we'll ever be. Let's go for it.'"

Opening day was nerve-wracking. "I don't remember any of it, hardly. I got to work at 3:00 a.m. I didn't have cooking time figured out. I didn't really know what I was doing. I had one pit; it came from John Mueller's place. That was a Godsend. The trailer, Travis offering the coffee roaster spot, and the pit all falling in my lap—the moons of Saturn were in alignment.

"It was rainy. It was cold. My friend Big Jeff was the first customer. It was the first outing for his newborn baby. He had that thing bundled up in forty blankets. We emailed twenty people, our homies from the backyard barbecues. Every single one of them showed up. Eleven oh one on the dot, twenty people lined up. They were all friends."

He cooked three briskets that first day.

"We had twenty-three cents in the bank. Stacy had a car wreck, and instead of fixing the car with the insurance money, we used the last couple thousand dollars to buy enough meat to open up the trailer.

"All that was unintentional. I just liked making barbecue."

Baptism by slow smoke was rough, Franklin admitted. "I'd never cooked every single day. I'd never cooked in the rain. I'd never cooked with green wood. Stacy worked on weekends. There was a chain link fence so I could cook at night and not be pestered by the hobos."

Franklin coveted a brick-and-mortar spot—a real eatery, the former location of Ben's Long Branch BBQ on East Eleventh, a block from the interstate and downtown Austin. For now, though, he would make do with a trailer parked in a dead lot, hauling in a few picnic tables for customers, and hoping the weather would cooperate. Most of the time it did.

Everything about Aaron Franklin, from his lean build to his easygoing manner and laid-back demeanor, busted Texas BBQ stereotypes. He proceeded to redefine the hidebound tradition and elevate it into something more. He cooked longer. He looked harder for better brisket to smoke. He experimented with wood. The day he overcooked his whole inventory of twelve large briskets, he gave it all away.

Almost a year to the day after Aaron Franklin opened his barbecue trailer, he signed a lease to occupy the old Ben's Long Branch location at 900 East

Eleventh Street. He needed the space. He was cooking up to twenty-four briskets and nine racks of ribs a day and had run out of room.

The permanent version of Franklin BBQ opened for business on March 12, 2011, the first day of South by Southwest. Like with his food trailer, the opening was an improvised affair, with Aaron Franklin leading the way on the construction. No contractors were involved. The business had zero debt.

"We were in mega crunch time," Aaron Franklin recalled. "That trailer could not support another South by Southwest. The seams would have ripped apart. It was too much. So the trailer closed for a couple days, we moved over here, pulled everything in. I was building fires while moving barbecue pits into place. I cut that door the day before we opened because we didn't have any way to get to the barbecue pits. I did it at ten o'clock at night, trying to saw in the dark with Stacy holding a flashlight."

The Flying-by-the-Seat-of-His-Pants method fit in with what he was selling. "It's all trial-and-error anyway," Franklin said. "People were lining up outside and I'm making the sneeze guard. Somebody else was cooking that night. I got here at three in the morning. There were people camping out on the wheelchair ramp. I'd gotten a text at 11:30 earlier that night: people are starting to show up."

The new restaurant was built to accommodate the same volume of business as the trailer, allowing that business might actually drop off a bit. Franklin thought he could keep the doors open until 7:00 p.m. daily. Instead, lines started to form at least two hours before the 11:00 a.m. opening. Closing time was around 1:00 p.m., when the meats sold out.

The Franklin Line turned into a ritual. Hip Austinites and, increasingly, out-of-town visitors interested in food queued up. A scene ensued. Offices pooled resources and rewarded their line-waiter with free lunch. Waiting meant making friends, taking pictures, reading smartphones, drinking beer, and eating breakfast tacos.

By slow-smoking dozens of briskets of Montana-raised beef for eighteen hours in one of his three barrel pits and slicing it all up and serving it until it was gone, Aaron Franklin had articulated a product (as pit masters blandly referred to their creation) that was so good, demand outstripped supply. Franklin responded by working with investors to develop a bottle version of his espresso coffee barbecue sauce, write a book, and launch a PBS television show. But he refused to expand his core business beyond what he could personally handle as pit master. He wanted to work the cookers, not manage a restaurant or oversee a chain. That was Dallas. He was Austin.

Aaron Franklin was recognized in 2015 with the prestigious James Beard

Award for best chef in the southwestern United States. The honor brought respect to what was once considered a street food, now considered as edgy and exciting as bone marrow or pork belly for young diners just beginning their own personal BBQ quests. Accordingly, wholesale prices for brisket shot up, rendering BBQ into a delicacy, no longer a workingman's lunch. Real old-style wood-smoked Texas barbecue with an Austin attitude turned into a trendy restaurant concept embraced in Brooklyn, Silver Lake, Amsterdam, and Paris.

Franklin's former boss John Mueller resurfaced. After two false starts, some out-of-town catering gigs, more than one battle with personal demons, and a 2011 revival in a trailer cut short by his sister who happened to be his main investor, Mueller settled into a spot behind one of the last remaining Mexican bars in East Austin, where he parked two pits, a trailer, and some picnic tables. Mueller had cultivated a reputation as the Bad Boy of Austin Barbecue for his food blog feuds and surly demeanor while smoking. His rural twang and his ruddy cheeks always left you wondering if he'd been drinking, working out in the sun too long, had rosacea, or just always looked like that because he was a hothead. It was all part of the show. Whatever his flaws, John Mueller had aged (for at least a little while) into the old school elder among a new breed of cookers, a third-generation pit pro who smoked outstanding brisket, ribs, and superior sausages for the natives and tourists, earning his own line winding out to the street. Presented with a bill from the State of Texas for ninety-two thousand dollars in unpaid taxes, Mueller shut down in 2016, and resurfaced in Georgetown the following year in a trailer he called the Black Box.

Three years before Aaron Franklin was recognized with the James Beard Award, another Austinite snagged the same honor. Paul Qui had taken Aaron Franklin's path in reverse. He ventured into food trucks under the East Side King banner after working his way up at Uchi, one of the most expensive restaurants in Austin, and at Uchiko. Uchi and Uchiko were creations of Tyson Cole, a curious Texan who started as a dishwasher at Kyoto in Austin before immersing himself in the art of sushi, learning Japanese language and culture as well as apprenticing with a master sushi chef. Armed with knowledge and practical experience, Cole opened Uchi, which generated a buzz and long waits when its doors opened in 2003, which earned Cole a James Beard Award in 2011.

Paul Qui knew nothing about Austin growing up, other than it being "the capital of Texas and the home of UT. That was about it." Qui's family had emigrated from the Philippines to Virginia in the nineties, where his first cooking gig was at an Orange Julius fast-food franchise. His mother kicked him out of the house and sent him to Houston, where his father lived. He soaked up that city's oversized Vietnamese scene, majored in art at college, slung dope on the side, but wanted to do something better with his life—like cook. That's when Austin landed on his radar. The shortest term and most affordable culinary school Qui could find was Le Cordon Bleu in Austin. In 2002, he moved, underwriting his relocation and tuition with five hundred Xanax pills a friend offered to front him.

Paul Qui's introduction to local cuisine was "migas, breakfast tacos, and barbecue," he said. "Austin was not a food town." It was simply a springboard to New York, LA, Chicago, Vegas, Houston—somewhere bigger with more restaurant action. Instead, he met Tyson Cole, who became Qui's mentor. His first month at Uchi, Qui worked for free—the alternative Austin business model in action.

"That model only works if the person working for free is learning something," Qui said. "I think it's the best way for someone with zero experience to get into the business. It's definitely less [expensive] than going to culinary school."

The second month, Qui's salary increased to seven fifty an hour. He stuck with it, persisted, and obsessed. "I spent all my money on cookbooks, knives, and *World of Warcraft*," Qui said. He was designated chef de cuisine before moving over to open Uchiko, another Tyson Cole concept that focused on Japanese farmhouse dining, as executive chef.

Once Uchiko was up and running, Qui started his own deal on the side, East Side King. Working with Moto Utsunomiya, who'd also worked at Uchi, they whipped up Asian-driven fusion dishes in trailers parked in the backyards of two East Side bars. Brick-and-mortar locations were later added at the Hole in the Wall bar, across Guadalupe Street from the University of Texas campus, and on South Lamar.

Another food truck co-owned by Qui and Utsunomiya, Thai-Kun, run by Thai Changthong, prepared O.G. Thai—the kind of Thai cuisine served to Thais, not the overly sweet variations that Americans preferred. Qui's name had become synonymous with new and exciting food, evidenced by Thai-Kun's inclusion on *Bon Appetit* magazine's Hot Ten for 2014—the only food truck to make the list—earning raves for the "incendiary" chow. (Chef Jesse Griffith's Dai Due in East Austin would make the Hot Ten list for 2015.)

Paul Qui's James Beard Award, ten years after he enrolled in culinary school, garnered respect from his peers. But he got considerably more mileage from winning the *Top Chef* award for season nine of that cooking competition television show on the Bravo network. TV made him a foodie superstar.

He finally opened the much-delayed Qui in East Austin in 2013, the year after his *Top Chef* turn, to considerable fanfare and sticker shock for the uninitiated. Emphasizing global fusion with a strong Filipino twist, Qui liked to cook with a blank slate, asking suppliers what was fresh, and riffing off that. Qui also launched another restaurant in a hip hotel in Miami.

But he wasn't leaving. What happened to that stepping-stone plan?

"I fell in love with Austin," he said, shrugging. What he found in 2002 still held thirteen years later. "It's about the energy and vibe as a whole. There's plenty to go around."

Qui opened Otoko, one of three restaurants that opened at the boutique South Congress Hotel, a very expensive, very small sushi bar.

He reemerged in the spotlight in 2016 as the very visible face of chefs in recovery after his girlfriend filed assault charges and he went public with his alcohol and drug addictions. His restaurant Qui would close, only to reopen in early 2017 as Kuneho, the Tagalog word for "rabbit," specializing in Japanese small plates with Texas and Filipino influences, such as trout roe migas and rabbit hand pies. Kuneho didn't last the year. But the chef Paul Qui was hardly finished.

Chefs were the new rock stars. Where you just ate mattered more than which hot band you just saw, even though playing in a band or knowing someone in a band remained a badge of pride in Austin. And it was no longer enough to be able to cook and serve. The modern state-of-the-art Austin restaurant required a designer, as well as a chef, along with investors, a marketing team, and a marketing strategy.

◎ ◎ ◎

Five years into his brick-and-mortar dream, Aaron Franklin admitted to having mixed feelings about pulling off the improbable. He was a certified Austin celebrity, a rock star chef. The new Eleven Austin apartments across Eleventh Street listed their proximity to Franklin BBQ as an amenity to prospective tenants.

Austin evolved into a barbecue scene unto itself, with numerous top shelf competitors in trailers and in joints. There was the comeback, subsequent demise, and revival of the John Mueller. La Barbecue, started by John Mueller's sister Lee Ann and headed by pit master John Lewis, who studied under Franklin and Mueller both, vied for top ranking by the BBQ bloggers until Lewis left to open a joint in Charleston, South Carolina. Stiles Switch, opened by Shane Stiles who took over at Louie Mueller's in Taylor when John Mueller left, ruled North Austin. Newcomers including Micklethwait, Kerlin's, LeRoy and Lewis, and Valentina's Tex-Mex served notice that the best BBQ in the world was in Austin, not some small town out in the boonies.

Aaron Franklin had become more settled about the Franklin Line. "The line is really tricky," he said. "On one hand we're so grateful and so blown away that so many people show up, and so many people care to stand in line, drink some beers, and hang out. That's South Austin [attitude] right there. It's the same thing as Liberty Lunch before I moved—'Hey, you need a beer?' 'Hey, we brought some extra tacos. Where you from?'"

"Hanging out, having fun, that's the Austin spirit," Franklin said.

Still, he admitted being troubled about so many people waiting for the doors to open. "It's so unintentional," he said. "Our goal is to make the best food that we possibly can, not live outside of our means. Do what we

BBQ king Aaron Franklin and his barrel smokers. (Photo by Wyatt McSpadden.)

do, and do it well. The Line brings in a whole other aspect. There's three hundred people standing out there and the food's not even ready yet. What if we mess up? People are so hypercritical of everything."

One enterprising kid sold his services as a Franklin Line stand-in, with Franklin's blessing. "We don't really like rules," he said. "If you're respectful to people in line, you're not being a jerk, you're not doing anything weird, you're not buying our food and holding it for many hours and then reselling it—who knows what safety standards you've adhered to. If you're not standing in line and letting twenty people join, and we don't notice that you're even there, you're doing a good job."

When adults joined the enterprising kid as line-placeholders, Franklin decreed no professional line-placeholders. The enterprising kid was grandfathered in.

"We don't want to tell people what they can and can't do," said an exasperated Franklin. "That's not what we do. We're going to have a good time. We're here to just be cool, man. Just be cool. It's just barbecue."

Three of Franklin's staff checked on the line throughout the morning, being especially vigilant during warm months.

"Hey your forehead is getting red—here, have some sunscreen."

"You're drinking too much—here, have some water."

"Your kiddo's hungry. We'll bring him snacks."

"We are really taking care of people," Franklin said. "This is grandma's house. They're here for a really long time. We've got chairs, we've got umbrellas whenever it rains that we'll lend to people. We're here to take care of everyone that's here."

The Franklin Line had produced three marriages, and at least one offspring. A wedding had been staged on the premises. "All while waiting in line for barbecue," Aaron Franklin marveled. "How cool is that?"

Franklin BBQ had maxed out, smoking and selling thirty-two to thirty-five thousand pounds of meat a month. "That's pretty ridiculous," Aaron Franklin said. Unlike most of the rest of Austin, he wasn't willing to scale up. "That's why we'll never get bigger. Because this is enough. We're cooking what we're cooking. We're cooking as much as we can cook and keep the quality up there. Obviously, if you do four briskets a day, they're going to be flawless. Doing a hundred is exponentially more difficult."

Seven cookers—five offsets, a six-foot by eight-foot rotisserie for ribs, and a sausage cold smoker—smoked meat twenty-four hours a day. Demand pulled Franklin off the pits. "I'm here every day, but I don't always cook," he said. "I cook for special events. All the business-y stuff has gotten to be so intense, twelve hours of my time is not available anymore. I can't cook a shift. I'm all over the place now."

So why didn't he just cash in and open multiple locations?

He shot a dirty look. "That's horrible. That goes against our soul. That goes against our true spirit. I don't want to sell out. We started this for a reason. We really cared about it. And goshdarnit, we still really care about it. I'm not willing to compromise that.

"People are always coming to me, saying, 'Why don't you franchise, or put it in every airport?' No. This is barbecue. That's not how this stuff works.

"I can cut a brisket and tell who rubbed it, who trimmed it, who cooked the first half, who finished it, and probably who went through it before serving it. I know the different styles of everybody. You try to spread that out or do that in multiple locations, it'd be horrible.

"Barbecue, you can't levitate like that. It's too crafty, and there's too much heart and soul involved to do that."

Thirty-seven years old, James Beard Award in his pocket, and Aaron Franklin wouldn't allow himself to bask in the glory of his achievements. He had to make sure it was all done his way. It was a business, and if he was going to turn out product worth raving about, he had to run it hands-on.

The thing that drew Aaron Franklin to Austin was not so easy to find anymore. "It's changing really quickly, and it's changing in a direction I'm not really a fan of," he said, admitting the same people griping about the change enabled the change. "It's getting so expensive that if I was eighteen all over again, I probably couldn't afford to live here. I couldn't afford to move here and just work random odd jobs and play rock and roll at night. That's what I did and pretty much why I came here."

He had an Old Austin soul with a New Austin realist's head. "I haven't been here forever but I've been here long enough to appreciate things that aren't around anymore," he said. "And I'm doing what I can to hang onto them. At the same time, we always have to evolve. You can't stay stagnant."

He was working harder than ever, and he was still smiling. "I'm giving it ten more years," Franklin said. "I'm still up at midnight, starting the next day's fires, but at nine in the morning, I've got a whole other job now, minding the business and all the other stuff."

Franklin understood too well the inevitability of change. He just didn't appreciate the warp speed it was occurring in Austin, and the values it was bringing. "I don't want to be a Debbie Downer, but it's sad. Love and labor—you used to be able to pull that off. Now, it's changed."

Aaron Franklin paused and pondered for a few seconds, but then brightened up. "But look at the alternatives. Anywhere else? Naaaahh. This is still the coolest place to be." He laughed, adding under his breath, "But it's not as cool as it used to be."

Outside the entrance of Franklin BBQ, a line had already formed, even though the door wouldn't open for another hour. One big fellow with a full gray beard sitting in a Texas Longhorns folding chair waited patiently, along with tatted-and-bunned hipsters more than half the man's age. Once upon a time, Billy Bob Sanders had been the imposing doorman at Soap Creek Saloon, the music club in the hills west of the city that felt like home to so many Austin folks of a certain age. Then Billy Bob became Archdeacon Niketas Sanders, a priest at St. Elias Orthodox Church, across the freeway and a few blocks west of Franklin's. He was a man of the cloth who knew his barbecue, and happy to spend this particular morning sipping from a can of Pearl Snap from Austin Beerworks, one of those cool kids local brews, waiting. If that was the price to get at the best brisket in Austin and therefore the world, passing a couple hours in the Franklin Line was worth it. What was the rush, anyhow? Changes were perpetual. Too often too many of those changes had been both overwhelming and soul-killing to the city that so many loved. Whatever was there for newcomers that Billy Bob Sanders greeted at Soap Creek Saloon all those years ago was there for newcomers in the Franklin Line. Same Austin, only different. Both Billy Bob and Niketas could tell you that.

10

Keeping Austin Weird

THE LOOKY-LOOS

◉ ◉ ◉

Agents of creative change in Austin were neither obvious nor conspicuous. They weren't attached to an institution, and their influence and impact could be dismissed as minimal. But those little things and those unsung people added up to cumulatively define and distinguish alternative Austin, which had become a tourist attraction unto itself.

Austin ranked second to only Las Vegas in the J. D. Power 2016 Destination Experience Satisfaction Study, praised for its "infrastructure and activities." Travelers spent a lot more money in cities they loved than disgruntled trav-

You haven't been to Austin if you haven't posed in front of the I Love You So Much graffiti on the side of Jo's Coffee Shop on South Congress. (Photo by H. H. Howze.)

elers did, the study concluded, and people who visited Austin—the Looky-Loos—were extremely satisfied.

They came to watch the bats emerge from underneath the Congress Avenue Bridge on warm summer evenings and take selfie photos with their smartphones at Stevie Ray Vaughan's statue on Auditorium Shores before going to get their pictures taken with James White at the Broken Spoke.

The tourists kept Austin weird once the creators became entrepreneurs, mainly because they spent money and bought stuff. Forget Dell, Matthew McConaughey, hit records, and best sellers. How about a night at Esther's Follies? A make-out session in your car at the Blue Starlite Drive-In south of the city? Hearing Jesse Sublett read from his book about the infamous Overton Gang at South Congress Books on the same avenue the hoodlums cruised during their hell-raising days?

Posing in front of the I Love You So Much graffiti on the side wall of Jo's Coffee Shop, waiting in the Franklin Line, shaking hands with Eddie Wilson at Threadgill's—these were highlights that made alternative Austin visits memorable.

Those in the know toured the funky memorial wall at the South Austin Museum of Popular Culture, honoring hipsters they'd mostly never heard of; crossed the Larry Monroe Bridge in Stacy Park, even if they were unfamiliar with the namesake's role in championing local music on the radio; checked out the Flatstock poster expo at the convention center during South by Southwest to spot Armadillo World Headquarters poster artists; nodded familiarly whenever the phrases "onward through the fog" or "709" were uttered; and viewed at least one film in costume during Fantastic Fest.

Whatever it was the tourists came to look at or do generally didn't exist wherever they came from. It was the unusual that didn't fit in anywhere else that made Austin Austin, which is why they were there to see it.

"You know that book by Dave Hickey, *Air Guitar?*" asked Liz Lambert, the hotelier who took South Congress Avenue upscale while defining hip hospitality with the Hotel San Jose, the Saint Cecilia, and the Magdalena. "He talks about the Looky-Loos—the people who come and look. It changes the nature of the thing. But I'm also a businessperson. There's no way you survive without the Looky-Loos. You can't keep the doors open. And if you can't keep the doors open . . ."

"Looky-Loos" was a term that the Fort Worth writer and art critic Dave Hickey learned from his father: "They were civilians, nonparticipants, people who did not live the life—people with no real passion for what was going on. They were just looking. They paid their dollar at the door, but they contributed nothing to the occasion—afforded no confirmation or denial that you could work with or around or against."

Spectators weren't creators, but they definitely kept the creators and the creative enterprises going.

As Austin cool and creativity evolved, Looky-Loos became a significant source of revenue, a necessary evil residents put up with because they spent money and then left town. Without them, those trendy restaurants with ceiling-high overheads would be trailers, if not fast-food franchises. Minus Looky-Loos, South Congress, East Seventh, East Eleventh, East Twelfth, Springdale, Burnet Road, and other cool street scenes would revert to their rough seventies-era ghost town ways.

Leslie, the bearded homeless drag queen with great legs and a penchant for showing them in a tight Speedo while pushing his grocery cart, was a Looky-Loo top score, usually easy to find around Dirty Sixth and Congress. After his death in 2012, a committee was formed to build a statue in his honor and two documentary films about him went into preproduction.

Looky-Loos watched the servers at Amy's Ice Cream who turned the process of scooping ice cream into an acrobatic art, and scrawled on the coloring books at Home Slice Pizza, whose owners were a doc film producer, an indie restaurant consultant, and a food writer and web mistress. They looked at film at the Alamo Drafthouse and looked at Armadillo World Headquarters history while dining at Threadgill's World Headquarters.

They toured Whole Foods Market's flagship store on Lamar Boulevard between Fifth and Sixth Streets and took home a whole Austin look by stopping in at Allen's Boots on South Congress for manly footwear. Visiting wannabe cowboys with more patience and money headed farther south to College Avenue and Texas Traditions boot shop. Head bootmaker Lee Miller apprenticed with the storied Austin bootmaker Charlie Dunn, celebrated as "the one to see" in a song Jerry Jeff Walker wrote back in the early seventies. Now it was the curly-haired Miller, a native of Vermont, who was the one to see to get feet measured for a handmade pair in exchange for a two thousand dollar good faith deposit and willingness to wait two years for delivery.

This new breed of tourist visited luthier Mark Erlewine to see models he built for ZZ Top and Johnny Winter, or booked a tour of Bill Collings's guitar factory west of the city, and then tried to figure how they could come up with seven grand for a custom Collings. They took the three-hour Austin Detours Live Music Crawl to meet Dianne Scott, the Oldest Female Bouncer in Show Business, who was the keeper of the back door at the Continental Club, and the club's historian. The petite Scott had made her way to Austin in 1987 from upstate New York and never looked back.

A few adventurous visitors even made pilgrimages to the Community First! Village for the homeless in deep east Austin, a twenty-seven acre master planned community of affordable, permanent tiny houses and RV homes for two hundred fifty chronically homeless residents. The village was imagined by Alan Graham, the founder of Mobile Loaves and Fishes, a volunteer nonprofit established in 1998 to provide food and clothing to the homeless, and promote a sense of dignity among the less fortunate. The sixteen million dollar project opened in 2015 with amenities including community gardens, Wi-Fi, walking trails, an outdoor movie theater, and health screenings. So much outside interest had been generated that a bed and breakfast was constructed to accommodate visitors and volunteers, which was exactly the idea.

"If we really want to profoundly change cultures and communities, we have to go live in these communities," Alan Graham said. "It's not enough just to give someone a sandwich. You have to move into a relationship with people. You have to be willing to share email addresses and telephone numbers and invite people over to your house for the holidays. It's just placing value on the human person and it goes both ways." Graham's organization included sixteen food trucks in five cities—eleven of them in Austin. Mobile Loaves and Fishes volunteers served four million meals to the homeless during its first eighteen years.

◎ ◎ ◎

As nice as it would be to say all these new visitors to Austin really cared about social issues, most came to Austin for the party. Austin was an honest town in which to get down—and not just during ACL Fest, South by Southwest, and Halloween.

On the heels of SXSW every spring came a tide of young black folks from across the South for the Texas Relays, a track meet that had evolved into Texas' African American spring break; roots music fans who liked to camp out and hear music played on wood instruments at the Old Settlers music festivals in Driftwood and Dale; the fifties retro kids, rockabillies, and gearheads turning up for the Lonestar Rod and Kustom Round-Up car show, described by *Jalopy Journal* as "the best damned car show in America"; hundreds of thousands of scooter buddies who joined forces to create the longest motorcycle parade known to mankind at the annual ROT (Republic of Texas) Biker Rally; the anything-goes local tradition of Eeyore's Birthday, celebrating the character from *Winnie the Pooh* and the libertine life; *Cinco de Mayo* and attendant *pachangas* celebrating Texas-Mexican Tejano heritage; and Juneteenth, the biggest holiday for African Americans in Texas, celebrating emancipation from slavery.

A freewheeling maypole at Eeyore's Birthday. (Photo by Marlon Taylor.)

Austin's indoor party of parties was Carnaval Brasileiro, jump-started in 1978 by a bored record store clerk who was inspired by the pre-Lenten holiday celebrated in Brazil and many other parts of the world. Mike Quinn was an ethnomusicology student of Americo Paredes and Gerard Béhague at the university, and a part-time world music expert at Discount Records on the Drag. A classmate in his Music of Brazil class invited Quinn to a Carnaval party organized by homesick Brazilians in 1976. He liked what he experienced so much, he would up helping put on the 1977 event, and then took over staging the whole thing in February 1978.

Quinn found a room that already had a dance floor and sound system, the Boondocks on East Fourth Street, a block east of Congress Avenue across the alley from the Greyhound bus station. He hired Armadillo poster artist Micael Priest to design a poster, which was affixed to light poles and bulletin boards throughout campus neighborhoods.

Quinn anticipated maybe four hundred people showing for Carnaval Brasileiro. One thousand paid the two dollar admission fee, about two hundred over legal capacity. A couple hundred more were turned away at the door. People dressed up. Jim "The Hawaiian Prince" Hughes, who worked at Oat Willie's, Austin's legacy head shop, came attired as a giant lobster. An improvised band of ethnomusicologists and members of Beto y Los Fairlanes provided the entertainment. Dancers in all forms of undress moved in unison to the pounding rhythm of drums and music. The club sold all the alcohol on hand, so the doors remained open past last call until four in the morning. The crowd danced so hard, the floor would have to be repainted.

The event grew exponentially larger and wilder by the year, attracting thousands of elaborately costumed revelers well into the twenty-first century. Mardi Gras was practically an afterthought.

◉ ◉ ◉

At twilight almost every evening from March through October, several hundred people gathered along the eastern railing of the Ann Richards Congress Avenue Bridge, and below, along the shoreline all the way to the *Austin American-Statesman*'s official Statesman Bat Observation Center on the southern shore. As the sun sank behind the hills west of the city, depending on the weather and the season, more than a million Mexican free-tailed bats emerged from underneath the bridge in a series of swirling columns to begin their nightly forage, consuming about fifty thousand pounds of moths, mosquitos, and other insects before returning home at dawn.

The bridge was summer residence of the largest urban bat colony in the United States. More than one hundred thousand people gathered at this spot every year to watch this spectacle of nature in the middle of a bustling city, a shining example of ecotourism. Bats, a much feared, much misunderstood flying mammal, were a very big attraction. At the south end of the bridge on the Barton Springs Road traffic island, *Night Wings*, Dale Whistler's eighteen foot high by twenty foot wide spinning aluminum sculpture, was installed

Crowds watch Mexican free-tailed bats emerge from beneath the Congress Avenue Bridge at dusk.
(Photo by Will Van Overbeek.)

in 1998. A bat festival was staged on the bridge every August, with vendors, bands, and spectators crowding the span to party in the name of the misunderstood winged mammal.

The crowds were there because of a curious biologist Merlin Tuttle, who jump-started the out-of-the-ordinary tradition of bat watching.

Mexican free-tailed bats had been considered a problem when they first appeared in large numbers in downtown Austin in 1981, shortly after the Congress Avenue Bridge reopened with a wider girth and new support. The bridge's reworked crevices made an ideal bat habitat. A colony of a hundred thousand or so moved right in, sparking controversy: the Congress Avenue Bridge had been taken over by bats! Something had to be done! Several civic organizations petitioned the city to eradicate the colony in the name of public safety, to eliminate chances of people contracting rabies from the little flying creatures.

A headline bannered in the September 23, 1984, edition of the *Austin American-Statesman* screamed "Bat colonies sink teeth into city." Those were fighting words to Merlin Tuttle, spoken out of ignorance and intolerance. Tuttle lived far away in Milwaukee, Wisconsin, where he was the curator of mammals at the Milwaukee Public Museum. He was also known as the guru of bats, world-renowned for his photography and passionate advocacy trying to correct the negative image many humans had formed toward the small winged mammals. In 1982, he founded Bat Conservation International in Milwaukee.

Mexican free-tailed bats and other relatives are seasonal residents of caves, nooks, and crannies around central Texas and the Hill Country. A colony of twenty-five million Mexican free-tailed bats spends summers in Bracken Cave, the world's largest bat cave, sixty-three miles south of downtown Austin.

Merlin Tuttle saw opportunity when he read past the *Statesman*'s frightinducing headline to learn a bat colony inhabited the reconstructed bridge downtown: Austin needed educating, and Bat Conservation International needed new headquarters.

"It's a laughing matter now, but it sure wasn't a laughing matter when you were trying to found an organization to convince people bats are OK and should be protected," Tuttle said. "I realized that any city with that many bats and that much news media with nothing better to talk about just might be the ideal place to center conservation efforts. I believed the people of Austin could be quickly educated that bats were valuable allies, not fearsome threats."

Tuttle and Bat Conservation International moved to Austin in 1986, and Tuttle started preaching. "It wasn't hard showing people that saving the bats under the Congress Avenue Bridge was in their best interests. Now, just as I'd hoped, it has become a world showcase how to live harmoniously, safely, and with great benefit, with large numbers of bats." Just in case, Tuttle wrote a book, *The Secret Lives of Bats: My Adventures with the World's Most Misunderstood Mammal* (2015), to have another platform from which he could correct the record.

⊙ ⊙ ⊙

The natural beauty of Austin was always a surprise to first-time visitors. The sight of the clear, pale blue waters of Barton Springs was startling. What was something so translucent and shimmering and pure-looking doing a mile from downtown? Imagine that. The fourth largest spring in the southwestern United States was right in the middle of the city, civilized with concrete embankments, a diving board, lifeguard stands, stairs, and ladders, shaded by a dense canopy of green.

Texas was a hellhole in the summer. With the exception of the mountainous Chihuahuan Desert of Far West Texas, temperatures never cooled below seventy degrees at night from June to September. A solid argument remained

A summer day at Barton Springs, where it's always sixty-eight degrees. (Photo by Martha Grenon.)

that if not for air conditioning, Texas would be a Third World country, and Houston would still be known as Murder City, USA. Texas heat could drive a person to kill another over not much. With AC, at least there was a better chance of coping and avoiding impulsive rash deeds.

Getting in Barton Springs guaranteed relief from that heat, once the body adjusted to the initial shock. The water was a constant sixty-eight degrees year-round. Dipping in a toe always brought a shudder.

The pool was a little more than one-eighth of a mile long. Four round trips equaled a mile. Nice view, too, although a swimmer could grow so complacent and in-the-zone to risk a head-on collision with another swimmer in a similar state of mind. There were no lines to follow at the bottom of the pool. With downtown skyscrapers rising above the verdant wall of trees beyond the deep end appearing close enough to reach out and touch, the contrast of the man-made world nudging up to this natural jewel pumping pure, cold spring water out of cracks in the rocks was one of those unique Austin experiences.

Barton Springs separated Austin from everywhere else. No other city had one of these. The abundant artesian spring water, a quality noted by Mirabeau Lamar in 1838, still made all the difference in the world.

Barton Springs was Austin's hardest-earned asset. In the early eighties, former governor John Connally and former lieutenant governor Ben Barnes, two of the most powerful politicians in Texas, partnered to build the Barton Creek Country Club, golf course, and conference center as the centerpiece of the exclusive 2,200 acre Estates of Barton Creek, a high-end development on Barton Creek, about eight miles upstream of Barton Springs pool.

The Connally-Barnes project cratered when the savings and loan scandal broke out across Texas, bankrupting developers, speculators, and bankers. Jim Bob Moffett and his New Orleans–based company, Freeport-McMoRan, which specialized in mineral extraction including the biggest gold mine in the world, bought the resort, golf course, and development for sixty million dollars in 1988. The next year, Moffett purchased another 863 acres east of the Estates of Barton Creek. The combined properties and other acquisitions became the Barton Creek Planned Unit Development, which had requested a waiver from the city's recently passed Comprehensive Watershed Ordinance. What was perceived as a done deal, executed behind closed doors, turned into a citizen revolt.

The chamber room had filled beyond capacity for the June 7, 1990, meeting of Austin City Council long before the weekly meeting had gotten underway. Outside, a growing knot of people jammed the sidewalks and spilled into the street, clogging Second Street and forcing police to reroute traffic.

The general public had an armchair view on the City of Austin's cable Channel 6 when the testimony began around 2:00 p.m. The majority of the early testifiers spoke in favor of Barton Creek Properties; its parent company, Freeport-McMoran; and its principal owner, Jim Bob Moffett, a former University of Texas football player who had parked his RV party ride outside council chambers and bragged about it. Even God, better known around Austin as retired University of Texas football coach Darrell K Royal, vouched for Moffett—a boisterous gentleman with rugged, dark features and the puffy semi-pompadour of a Southern preacher. Moffett himself proudly testified he made the best grades of anyone at UT . . . on the football team.

Outside in the streets, protestors carried signs that read "Developers: Go Build in Hell," "Hands Off Barton Creek," and "No Compromise." They made clear their displeasure wasn't just the threat of fouling Austin's natural crown jewel, Barton Springs; it was Freeport-McMoran's reputation as the single largest discharger of toxic pollutants into American waters, and the owner of the world's biggest gold mine in Indonesia, which emitted its own stew of toxic chemical runoff. Moffett's promise that he would never do anything to harm Barton Springs rang hollow.

As the evening progressed, the tide turned. Poets read poetry. People cried as they talked about their personal relationship with Barton Springs. Passions simmered. The council was beseeched, consistently and relentlessly: don't ruin Barton Springs.

One of the very last speakers was Coach Royal's son, who wanted to inform the gathering that not everyone in the family supported the development: "My name is Mack Royal," he said by way of introduction. "My father is a golfer. I am a swimmer. I love Barton Springs. I want hear a 'no' vote from each and every one of you. Thank you." His brief, concise message earned a standing ovation. "It was close to 4:00 a.m. It seemed to be the pivotal moment," Royal later said. "I actually thought that the deal was done and the council would give Jim Bob their vote in the end. I never expected every single one of them to vote no."

The city council voted unanimously to reject changes to the Comprehensive Watershed Ordinance to accommodate the Barton Creek planne development.

Thirty thousand signatures forced a referendum to protect Barton Springs by limiting and regulating development within the Barton Creek watershed. Austin musicians Jerry Jeff Walker, Bill Oliver, Joe Ely, Eric Johnson, Marcia Ball, and Kim Wilson performed at benefits. Don Henley, an East Texas musician and conservationist who worked in frat bands that played Austin in the sixties before forming the band the Eagles in the seventies, provided a generous donation.

Dire things would happen to Austin if the referendum passed, the old guard city leadership warned. The *Austin American-Statesman* editorialized against the Save Our Springs initiative. Jim Bob Moffett threatened to bankrupt Austin with lawsuits. George W. Bush political strategist Karl Rove was hired to sow doubt and fear. Economist Ray Perryman predicted passage of the initiative would cost Austin 140,000 jobs, a prognostication made in exchange for a $10,000 consultant fee.

The August 8, 1992, vote drew one of the highest turnouts for any Austin election. Sixty-four percent voted to limit development to a maximum of 15 to 25 percent of paved surfaces or impervious cover, and mandate pollutant levels in developed areas not exceed concentrations that existed before development occurred.

Looking back, the Save Our Springs initiative victory appeared pyrrhic. Jim Bob Moffett ultimately built out his Barton Creek Properties development, including a high-dollar resort and golf course. Moffett's real estate interests in Austin were spun off into a separate entity known as Stratus Properties, which went on to partner with Willie Nelson and his nephew Freddy Fletcher in building the W Hotel complex in downtown Austin, which included the new home of the Austin City Limits television series. That venture, Stratus CEO Beau Armstrong liked to point out, was not in the Barton Creek watershed.

The state legislature, at the behest of Austin developers and homebuilders, including Jim Bob Moffett and his minions, passed numerous bills to neutralize the SOS initiative and limit Austin's (and other cities') ability to control growth, regulate land use, and establish water quality standards. Austin bashing became blood sport at the increasingly Republican Texas legislature. Putting the screws to the left-leaning, Democratic-voting People's Republic of Austin was payback for out-of-town legislators having to work and live in Gomorrah for six months every two years.

Pollution and encroaching development subsequently did compromise the clarity and purity of the springs. But those negatives were offset by the fact Barton Springs pool continued to exist. Where else could you swim with endangered species within eyeshot of downtown?

The Barton Creek Uprising and passage of the SOS initiative altered Austin's political culture and ratified the city's reputation as the most environmental-friendly community in the state.

◉ ◉ ◉

On the first day of the new year, the air temperature at seventy-eight degrees with a slight southerly breeze and a few high clouds scudding across an otherwise deep blue sky, more than one thousand Austin residents stripped down to bathing suits to join the annual Polar Bear swim at Barton Springs—not that jumping in was particularly painful or challenging. The water temperature was a constant sixty-eight degrees year round. On a day like this, the water actually felt warm.

On the last day of the old year, the air temperature at seventy-nine degrees, no wind, and a brilliant blue sky overhead, a whole different crowd slowly poured out of fifty or so vehicles that had pulled into the first parking area of Milton Reimers Ranch Park, thirty miles from downtown Austin in the far western corner of Travis County.

People were out everywhere all over the back roads outside Austin, taking advantage of nice weather and the holiday break. The "At Capacity" sign at Enchanted Rock went up at 10:00 a.m. Cars were backed up waiting to get in to the Westcave Outdoor Discovery Center, a nearby cave grotto, and to the Hamilton Pool, another cave grotto at the opposite end of the same canyon.

Most of the people hitting the trail at Reimers Ranch were under forty. Many wore outdoor shorts; some carried backpacks. More than a few looked kind of scruffy; almost all were physically buff. Reimers, a one-time working cattle ranch, had trails for mountain biking, picnic areas, and summer swimming in the Pedernales River, whose pale green-blue waters curved around the base of a high limestone bluff, which was the ranch's distinctive landmark feature.

The trail descended into the tight, fern-choked Climbers Canyon. The unmarked pathway was slick, crisscrossing a babbling creek multiple times. Less than a quarter-mile in, a small cluster of people gathered underneath a jagged limestone overhang, all heads gazing up. Underneath the overhang, a slender woman with her hair pulled back in a ponytail hung upside down, spiderlike, clinging to the rock above her with the fingers of both hands splayed wide, while she tried to pull one leg up and plant it in a tight crevice in a single motion, in order to leverage her body up and over the lip of the overhang.

If she missed her plant, the rope tethered to a particularly large bearded man in a wool cap standing below would catch her.

The five men and two women watching from below craned their necks, eyes fixed on the climber pondering and planning her next move, quietly offering encouragement or an "ooo" or an "ouch" opinion over the potential solution to the problem she was trying to solve.

Climbing was big in Austin because there were plenty of places to climb along Bull Creek and Barton Creek, with destinations like Reimers and Enchanted Rock within a two-hour drive. This part of Texas would not be confused for major climbing destinations such as Boulder, Colorado, Yosemite in California, or even Hueco Tanks, east of El Paso. But for the place and time of year, Reimers, Enchanted Rock, and Barton Creek were little bits of all right. Similarly, a caving community thrived in Austin because Travis County was pocked with limestone caverns—not the biggest in the world, perhaps, but considering the location, they were some of the most conveniently accessible caves close to a major urban area anywhere.

Birding was a popular recreational activity because the city of Austin could claim more than 150 species around Lady Bird Lake, while Central Texas was regarded as having one of the most diverse bird populations in the Americas. The Golden-Cheeked Warbler and Black-Capped Vireo, two rare neotropical songbirds found in significant numbers only in the Hill Country, helped Victor Emanuel launch his global nature tour empire from Austin, initiating the first birding camps for young people and ultimately developing ecotourism economies in more than a hundred countries around the world.

Swimming was popular because of Barton Springs, Lake Austin, Lake Travis, Deep Eddy Pool, Barton Creek, Bull Creek, McKinney Falls, Krause Springs, and dozens of secret freshwater swimming holes.

Denver had a kayak run through downtown, and paddlers near San Francisco, Boise, Missoula, Charlotte, Atlanta, and Raleigh were surrounded by dependable whitewater. Austin kayakers had to wait for heavy rains to flood Barton Creek and the Class III and Class IV rapids that appeared overnight. Whenever flow levels were high enough, the creek got crowded quick.

Austin alternative rec was about taking advantage of what natural features existed, and about using the imagination when those features weren't enough. When climbing conditions weren't right outdoors, the world's largest bouldering gym beckoned on Springdale Road on the east side, hosting bouldering tournaments that attracted hundreds of lithe and rangy millennials from across the Southwest.

Surfers no longer had to check wave conditions on the Texas coast, two hundred miles away. Instead, they checked their wallets to see if they had the coin to surf the waves at NLand Surf Park. The first of its kind in North America, NLand looked like a ski resort built next to a rectangular seventeen-acre lagoon with a pier running down the middle. Every two minutes, a cable pulled a plow down the pier, leaving two fully shaped surfing waves of varying degrees of difficulty in its wake.

While Houston, Dallas, San Antonio, and Fort Worth all landed on the Top Ten Fattest Cities in America list at one time or another, Austin consistently landed on the fittest lists. The Texas Rowing Center claimed to be the nation's number one rental outlet for stand-up paddleboards, or SUPs, which had become as much a fixture on Lady Bird Lake as the flotillas of kayaks, sculling crews, and canoes.

The Hike-and-Bike Trail around Lady Bird Lake stretching for more than ten miles was one of the most congested running trails in the world, with one and a half million users, rivaled only by Central Park in New York and a park in Tokyo—at least that's what Lance Armstrong said. Once Austin's highest-profile athlete, Armstrong remained active and visible around the city following his confession of doping and cheating to win at cycling. He had amassed tens of millions of dollars, had a nice pad in Aspen, and enjoyed traveling the world. But he couldn't quite leave. He understood the Looky-Loos too well. "Somebody from out of state rolls up on a perfect day, and thinks, 'And I can walk from here to Chuy's and have a double margie and keep walkin'?' Dude. Still pretty great."

Sports were a different deal compared with other cities. No major league professional sports team called Austin home, although the San Antonio Spurs, the model franchise of the National Basketball Association, played seventy-eight miles south of downtown. If one spectated team sports in Austin, it mostly meant the University of Texas Longhorns, the richest athletic program of any university in the United States, which had an operating revenue of $215 million in 2017. The University of Texas Longhorns football team was more profitable than the National Football League's Denver Broncos, Pittsburgh Steelers, and Chicago Bears.

The Round Rock Express was an instant hit as a minor league baseball franchise under the direction of Hall of Fame pitcher Nolan Ryan and his sons, when the team started play in 2000, two suburbs north of downtown. The Express was one of the top-drawing teams in the minors, with attendance figures exceeding some major league baseball franchises. The northwestern suburb of Cedar Park hosted the minor league Texas Stars ice hockey team and the Austin Spurs of the National Basketball Association's developmental G League. In the midteens, the Austin Aztex began competing in professional minor league soccer before Major League Soccer's Columbus Crew relocated to Austin in 2019, and rugby fans cheered the Austin Huns, a startup team that beat the New York Athletic Club for the Division One national club championship in 2017.

But really, other than UT football, basketball, baseball, track, soccer, softball, and volleyball, spectator sports were pretty much beside the point.

That sentiment was expressed in a 1995 city bond election. Austin voters overwhelmingly rejected a ten million dollar bond issue to build a minor league baseball park in the Riverside-Pleasant Valley area, a couple miles east of downtown. A total of 49,111 voters opposed, and only 18,019 voters approved. The local electorate did not think much of corporate welfare for sports, no matter if bonds were paid off or not. Besides, who needed pros when the Horns were winning?

One significant exception to that perception was a retooled version of a fringe spectator sport born in the twenties during the era of dance marathons that became a popular sports programming staple on television in the fifties and sixties, usually paired with pro wrestling. Roller derby was an invented competition between teams of male and female skaters skating past and elbowing one's opponents on a banked track. With points and teams, roller derby was step up from pro wrestling, but just barely.

In the early aughts, roller derby was resuscitated and reinvented in Austin as a participatory sport for women of a certain nature and demeanor. The idea was hatched by an itinerant musician named Devil Dan Policarpo, who recruited four women to the Casino El Camino bar on Sixth Street to organize a roller derby skate infused with rockabilly and punk sensibilities, or as Policarpo cryptically envisioned it, a "crazy circus with these clowns unfortunately stabbing each other, these bears on fire on these unicycles."

It didn't take long for the women—Anya Jack, April Hermann Ritzenthaler, Heather Burdick, and Nancy Lynn Haggerty—to ditch Policarpo and launch Bad Girl, Good Woman Productions.

Ritzenthaler had fallen in love with Austin on visits as a high schooler from a small town north of Houston. "It felt real free," she said. "You could sneak into the bars. It was young, lots of cute boys. You could park anywhere. You felt safe." She moved in 1993 and worked as a paralegal, then as a massage therapist, and finally as a massage teacher. She was about to turn thirty on the afternoon she met the three women and Devil Dan at Casino El Camino. She helped spread the word for a second meeting. Fifty women showed up and a league was formed, she said, although "no one knew anything about skating."

Teams bought matching jackets. Ritzenthaler thought up two unique features for this version of Roller Derby: the penalty wheel, in which a penalized skater spun a wheel to determine her punishment, and Spank Alley, in which a skater charged with a blatant violation had to run a phalanx of spankers—fans who had winning raffle tickets sold at the games.

The first competition was staged at Skate World on June 23, 2002. Two hundred fifty fans showed up to watch the Rhinestone Cowgirls go up against the Hellcats, followed by the Putas Del Fuego versus the Holy Rollers. Two bands played between the skates.

A group of women skaters broke away from Bad Girl, Good Woman Productions, now known as TXRD, and the practice of skating on a banked track, like the classic version of roller derby. Texas Rollergirls, as they called themselves, skated on flat tracks, meaning a skate could be organized just about anywhere with very little set up. Both versions promoted a punk rock riot grrrls ethic, tongue firmly in cheek down to provocative skate wear (fishnet stockings were standard issue) and the stage names of skaters and teams (Helen Wheels, Freight Train, Polly Gone; Texecutioners, Hot Rod Honeys). The hits were real. The performance and show mattered more than the score.

Skates were held in the Austin Convention Center, the Palmer Special Events Center, and on the main soundstage of the Austin Studios at the old Mueller Airport, drawing crowds up to two thousand. Roller derby fever

Rolling and jamming on the banked track with the TXRD Rollergirls. (Photo by E. McGeehee.)

spread across Texas cities and to other cities with sizeable alternative populations, such as Portland, Minneapolis, and Brooklyn. National media including ABC's *Good Morning America*, *Spin* magazine, the *New York Times*, and National Public Radio's *All Things Considered* covered the phenomenon. More than seventy-five women's roller derby leagues formed in less than five years.

In 2005, the A&E cable television network filmed the reality series *Rollergirls* around the TXRD skaters, climaxing with the Calvello Cup, named for original roller derby bad girl, Ann Calvello, who watched the finals from her perch on a throne at one end of the arena, wearing a crown.

An eight million dollar marketing campaign for the A&E series plastered advertising on billboards, subway trains, buses, boardwalks, and telephone poles, with several skaters hyping the show with a six-city press tour. "Within six months after the first show, 250 new leagues had popped up," said April Ritzenthaler. "Canada went nuts because there were all these hockey rinks that were empty in the summer."

The creation of modern roller derby in Austin and the split between the TXRD and the Texas Rollergirls provided a focal point for the film documentary *Hell on Wheels* by Bob Ray and Werner Campbell. When the film premiered at South by Southwest Film in March 2007, skaters from the rival leagues had to be seated on opposite sides of the Paramount Theater. The dispute in Austin was also rehashed in the 2012 Australian film *This Is Roller Derby*.

Whip It!, a women's roller derby feature film based on the memoir of Austin rollergirl Shauna Cross that was shot partly in Austin, followed in 2009. Drew Barrymore directed the film with A-list actors Ellen Page, Juliette Lewis, and Kristen Wiig in lead roles.

By 2015, women's roller derby had grown to more than 450 leagues worldwide, prompting the Bob Bullock Texas State History Museum to roll out a women's roller derby exhibit to coincide with the X Games, an extreme sports olympics that was staged at the Circuit of the Americas racetrack east of Austin.

◉ ◉ ◉

The skanky, rink raunch look that defined the Austin version of Roller Derby was sort of a nostalgic throwback to a time when skank defined quarters of the city like South Congress Avenue.

"Whenever I'd play with Stevie Vaughan back in the seventies, I'd drive down from Fort Worth and usually stay at the Imperial 400," the saxophonist Johnny Reno said of his tenure in the Triple Threat Revue, the band that preceded Stevie Ray Vaughan's breakout combo Double Trouble. "Stevie was so broke that if he couldn't find a couch to crash on, he'd sleep in the dumpster out in front of the motel."

That South Congress was lowdown, blue-collar, and semirural. South Austin was once known as Bubbaland, and its main drag could be as rough as any thoroughfare north of the river back when Little Stevie Vaughan was getting his act together playing the Continental Club and the Aus-Tex Lounge up the block. South Congress was still fairly rough five years after SRV's first album shot up the charts in 1983, and remained that way at the time of the first South by Southwest in 1987.

Extending south from Town Lake to Oltorf Street and farther south to Ben White Boulevard, and beyond, the avenue retained a whiff of its sketchy past in the scattering of presixties motels and motor courts, remnants from when it was the main route to San Antonio. South Congress bars catered to customers with limited budgets. Its streetwalkers inevitably got a male legislator or state public official arrested every year or so.

Things started to change about the time the third and last version of Soap Creek Saloon shut down in 1985, after a five-year run at its South Congress and Academy location in the one-time lobby of the old Terrace Motor Inn. Around the corner, Willie Nelson and his investment group had transformed the old Austin Opry House and surrounding buildings into the Arlyn recording studio and the ARC rehearsal space, with other studios and spaces rented out to musicians. Lots of music people leased apartments on the grounds of the former resort hotel from Willie. But not for long. Nelson had moved most of his operations to the bankrupt Briarcliff Country Club he'd purchased west of Austin near the Pedernales River and Lake Travis. With the neighborhood around the original Willie World gussying up, and removing the skank, Nelson happily sold most of his South Austin properties at a handsome profit.

The transformation was plain to see from behind the windshield of a passing car: block after block of early and mid-twentieth century one-story and two-story storefronts reimagined with statuary and creative signage. The cartoon diorama above Jenna Radke's over-the-top costume and vintage shop Lucy in Disguise with Diamonds stopped traffic. The masks, jewelry, and wigs inside got people out of their cars and on the sidewalk. Lucy in Disguise, which planted its flag in 1984, was joined by the Magnolia Café South, Kent Cole and Diana Prechter's rehab of the Aus-Tex Lounge space in 1988, and Uncommon Objects, a stridently unconventional antiques and vintage shop that opened in 1991. Those pioneering shops endured hard times and the street's gradual bottom-up transition from rough to edgy to hip in order to be able to enjoy the spoils that came with the arrival of tourists in the early aughts. The shops, along with the existing infrastructure of wide sidewalks and head-in parking on both sides of the avenue, an abundance of shady oaks, visually appealing murals, and quirky people who gravitated to the action, made South Congress a desirable destination and Austin's biggest street scene.

Older businesses such as Allen's Boots and the Austin Motel complemented more recent arrivals like Yard Dog folk art gallery, Off the Wall antiques, and Vespaio Ristorante. The old Central Feed and Seed building turned into Güero's Taco Bar, where US President Bill Clinton stopped in shortly after the restaurant's relocation from its original East Oltorf address. After Clinton returned again, cleaning his plate a second time, owners Robb and Cathy Lippincott added the El Presidente—chicken al carbon taco, beef taco, tamale and guacamole, with rice and frijoles—to the restaurant's menu.

The linchpin of South Congress's rebirth and, really, the heart of the avenue was the Continental Club, a shotgun space shoehorned into a small half-block of fifties vintage storefronts with a script neon sign out front. Opened as a private supper club in 1955 that hosted the touring burlesque dancers Candy Barr and Bubbles Cash, the Continental had been reborn in the seventies as a rock and blues music club first under the direction of Roger Collins, Michael Summerdawg Carter, and Wayne Nagel, and then with Liberty Lunch's Mark Pratz and J-Net Ward. Steve Wertheimer quit his accounting job for the State of Texas to retrofit the club in 1987 into a roots rock and alt country showcase. Already famous as the best small music room in the city and maybe all of Texas, the Continental led to Wertheimer's second career as a hip developer.

After leasing and then buying the club, Wertheimer bought most of the block the club was on before purchasing other properties up and down South Congress. He expanded the hours of the Continental so that live music started in the afternoon and ran at least until 2:00 a.m. last call. He also utilized his club as a meeting place for custom hot-rodders like himself.

The birth of South Congress as a hip strip applied pressure on surrounding neighborhoods. Older residents on and near the avenue who appreciated the area's offbeat, under-the-radar character in the seventies and eighties started to complain about the noise and trash that came with the increased crowds. Cars parking blocks away from South Congress drew complaints from the surrounding Travis Heights and Bouldin Creek neighbors, forcing city ordinances limiting parking on many streets to residents. First

Thursdays, a street celebration when businesses stayed open late into the evening, grew so big and out of control that sponsoring merchants scaled back the monthly event to tamp down the crowds and the enthusiasm.

In 1998, voters approved a four million dollar bond issue to expand and improve sidewalks and other street infrastructure, including along South Congress Avenue. When city planners followed up the vote with a proposal to bring light rail to South Congress, the business owners and neighborhood blanched. Construction disruptions or outright street closings lasting six months to a year and a half would kill most of the small indie retailers. A completed, operating rail stop would raise leases for nearby businesses and chase the indies off the avenue altogether. Or so the reasoning went.

In order to continue thriving, South Congress merchants had to fight the light rail and its impact on the status quo.

City planners came away chastised. "It's a complicated area," George Adams, assistant director in the planning and development review department for the City of Austin told *Preservation* magazine. "Its development has been more organic, or market-driven, which complicates any attempt to do things. You start out with certain attitudes: 'What's wrong with these people? Don't they know we're trying to help them?' Over time, we've come to understand the benefit of doing things incrementally, how to make changes and accommodate the needs of the small businesses and of the residents. South Congress has taught us a lot."

Top-down, or government-subsidized, development was not the way South Congress wanted to go. The proprietors of the determinedly eclectic, independent, non-chain stores selling toys, haircuts, Halloween costumes, cowboy boots, and assorted knick-knacks spearheaded the redo, not some urban planner or master developer. South Congress succeeded because of its corporate-free businesses and pedestrian-friendly environment, not in spite of it.

Then it succeeded too well.

This new vibrant collection of cool, laid-back, independent enterprises included one that defined Austin style in and beyond Austin—the Hotel San Jose.

Liz Lambert, a square shouldered, pink-cheeked, blonde-haired West Texan had come to Austin as an undergraduate student at the University of Texas seeking a creative writing degree. She stayed through law school. "I'm from Odessa," she said. "Anybody who's a little bit different runs to Austin as fast as they can. You don't want to leave Texas, but there's nowhere else you want to live in Texas."

She left Texas, but she couldn't stay away. Working for the Manhattan district attorney's office in New York, Lambert kept remembering a visit back to Austin in March. "It was still snowing in New York, and I was driving in someone's borrowed pickup across the river without any shoes on and thinking 'How could I not be here?' A lot of people feel Austin was made for them: You're a Texan through and through, but there's not really many places in Texas you want to go."

Like thousands of others before and since, Liz Lambert moved back to Austin in 1994 without much forethought. "I didn't know what I wanted to do."

She found her calling after remodeling the Travis Heights house she shared with her girlfriend and spending too much time at the Continental Club. Owner Steve Wertheimer offered remodeling tips, since he had stripped much of the music room's interior to its original fifties-vintage décor.

The San Jose Motel across the street from the Continental, a thirties-vintage motor court that had devolved into a by-the-hour hotbed harboring all sorts of assorted street characters, became the object of Lambert's desires. Whenever she came to hang out with Wertheimer, she ended up gazing across the street. "The place was painted sea-foam green," Lambert said. "It had a red tile painted roof. It looked empty. I didn't know there were lots of people there. They didn't have cars, or luggage, or come out during the day."

Wouldn't it be fun to buy the motel? she kept thinking to herself. Fun, maybe. But as a business? Lambert knew it was risky. "South Congress was pretty empty, not real peopled. There weren't many things around. You couldn't get real coffee. Güero's wasn't next door." She closed on buying the motel

Liz Lambert of the Hotel San Jose and Steve Wertheimer of the Continental Club reimagined South Congress Avenue. (Photo courtesy of KCRW.)

in November 1995. "There were two liens I was able to qualify for. My mom co-signed the note, and I bought it for five hundred thousand."

Lambert intended a gradual room-by-room redo. Architect David Lake convinced her to go whole hog: kick out the tenants, close the motel, and remodel all at once. "David said to create interest, and for my financials to work out better, I needed more rooms." Lake designed two additional buildings with sixteen rooms across the veranda from the lobby.

David Lake and Ted Flato had already articulated a Texas vernacular for Hill Country homes, emphasizing airy, open spaces with wood and corrugated metal exteriors. Flato and Lake redesigned the San Jose into an understated, almost minimalist lodge of forty urban bungalows arranged around a Zen-like courtyard. Cacti lined the crushed granite walkways. The lobby encouraged visitors and guests to hang out and linger.

The Hotel San Jose was Austin's hip hotel from almost the moment it opened in March 2000—technically, it took a week for a seriously clogged sewage drain to be fixed first. Performer Hank Williams III described the layout as "half Mexican, half Japanese." Singer Raul Malo wrote and recorded a romantic song about the place. The adjacent outdoor dog-friendly coffee shop, Jo's, turned into the busiest corner on the emerging South Congress Avenue pedestrian strip. The repurposed hotel and coffee shop instantly blended in, testaments to how Lambert saw hospitality and place.

Rock N Reel nights were scheduled in the parking lot during warm months, with Austin bands performing between screenings of classic films. During South by Southwest, ten high-profile bands a day performed on a stage at South by San Jose in front of packed crowds in the parking lot for four days straight.

Tourists posed year-round on the side street of Jo's, where Lambert's girlfriend, Amy Cook, spray-painted "I Love You So Much" in cursive graffiti on the lime stucco exterior. The message was sufficiently iconic to warrant selling T-shirts.

South Congress Avenue was Austin's promenade. Everybody wanted to go to south to park their cars so they could walk South Congress's sidewalks and visit its eclectic shops. One of the new centers of South Congress street life was a small village of food trailers that sprang up on a city block at 1603 South Congress, the future site of a luxury hotel.

Mighty Cone, Jeff Blank's easy-to-handle staple, and Hey! Cupcake were the first of a swarm of trendy eateries to occupy the location. A Thai trailer, a Middle Eastern trailer, and a fried food trailer soon joined them. Before you knew it, people were calling the lot the Most Famous Food Trailer Park in

America. It wasn't just the opportunity to literally eat globally. It was the surrounding carnival of buskers, craftspeople, and bands that attracted gawkers, strollers, gourmets, and filmmakers shooting commercials and movies.

Liz Lambert had gone the extra mile making a film documentary of the pre-redo motel and the residents she was moving out before the makeover began. Guests of the new Hotel San Jose could watch the guests of the old San Jose Motel in *The Last Days of the San Jose*, available at the front desk.

Lambert followed the San Jose with Hotel St. Cecilia, a down-on-the-heels mansion built in 1880 on Academy Drive, a half block east of Congress, refashioned into an exclusive fourteen-room understated luxe lodge named for the patron saint of music and poetry. Rooms, some of which featured pages from old *Rolling Stone* magazines as wallpaper, fetched five hundred dollars a night.

The Lambert brand, formalized as the Bunkhouse Group, extended south to San Antonio, where she resuscitated the downbeat Mediterranean-styled Hotel Havana on that city's famed Riverwalk. She went eco-wild with El Cosmico in the small art town of Marfa in Far West Texas, where Lambert's family had roots. Lodging options on the twenty-one acre nomadic hotel and campground included vintage Airstreams and other trailers, teepees, tents, and a Mongolian yurt. Lambert's imaginative inventions and reinventions led to the Bunkhouse Group joining Standard Hotel Group of Los Angeles in 2015, providing capital for Lambert's Hotel San Cristobal project in Todos Santos, Baja California, Mexico, and more imaginations.

In 2016, Bunkhouse purchased the iconic Austin Motel, the one constant on South Congress since it opened in 1938. As South Austin gained cachet in the nineties, the Austin Motel became better known for its distinctive neon sign and message board sign ("So close, yet so far out") out front than for the rooms. The sign's tall, slender shape moved the actor Sandra Bullock, who lived in Austin for a stretch, to dub it the Penis Motel.

The Magdelena, "our third saint," named after the patron saint of fallen women, opened on South Congress a year later. "It's our homage to old Austin—to swimming holes, grottos, lake houses," Lambert said.

SoCo, as it was increasingly called, took on a trendy, upscale sheen.

Liz Lambert couldn't put her finger on the concept of a distinctive emerging Austin style, other than "it was nothing intentional. It's the Hill Country and having a bunch of hippies and cosmic cowboys move in. It's the water." Austin style was paying attention to what was around you. "By listening to the people of the place, looking at the architecture of the place, looking at the building materials you would use, the style of service you would have—all those things have to be part of the fabric," Lambert said. "We have friendly front desk people who happen to know who's playing at the Continental Club and what days Barton Springs is open."

Steve Wertheimer expanded his empire. The upstairs of the space next door to the Continental turned into the Continental Gallery, an even more intimate music room featuring jazz and blues heavyweights like Mike Flanigin, Dr. James Polk and his protégé Elias Haslanger, and neighborhood singer-songwriters Jon Dee Graham and James McMurtry. The downstairs was leased to South Austin Tattoo. Wertheimer's immediate neighbors to the south were the 10,000 Villages Fair Trade artisans sustainable goods shop, an Italian restaurant, a hat store, and the St. Vincent de Paul thrift store, whose parking lot accommodated a food trailer. The apparel store's previous tenant, Factory People, specialists in "clothes to listen to music in," and its owner Thomas Popov left the red and yellow Guns sign remnant from the previous occupant, Just Guns.

To keep his hot-rod buddies and himself happy, Steve Wertheimer bought the Avenue Barber Shop, the last place in town to get flattops with fender skirts and other vintage men's hairstyles, and restored the shop to its original 1933 look.

The old Trophy's/Big Mamou building two blocks south became C-Boy's Heart & Soul Bar in late December 2013, Wertheimer's other club for his personal favorite bands like Jimmie Vaughan's and Mike Flanigin's, occasional road acts, and private parties. Its name was a tribute to C-Boy Parks, the African American cook and manager of the Rome Inn just north of the UT campus who mentored Wertheimer in running an Austin club back in 1978.

In 2000, the year the Hotel San Jose opened and the official city population topped 650,000, a regular listener named Red Wassenich called in to the weekly broadcast of *The Lounge Show*, on the listener-supported, nonprofit KOOP 91.7. It was fundraising week, and Wassenich wanted to pledge money to the program devoted to mambos, cha-chas, exotica, and kitschy hi-fi sounds. The person working the phone at the station asked why Wassenich was donating.

"Because the show helps keep Austin weird."

The light bulb went off over his head as the words left his mouth. Wassenich, an Austin Community College librarian, immediately told his wife, Karen Pavelka, that he'd coined a phrase. "Let's do bumper stickers," she said. The Keep Austin Weird bumper sticker was born, as well as the Keep Austin Weird website.

Austin was weird, all right. Signs were everywhere: Daniel Johnston's weird "Hi, How Are You?" cartoon creature on a wall on Twenty-First Street at the corner of Guadalupe, Leslie the Drag Queen, Eeyore's Birthday, Spamarama.

Wassenich followed up with a book, *Keep Austin Weird: A Guide to the Odd Side of Town*, published in 2007. The phrase resonated. Smartasses in other cities responded with their own campaigns: "Keep San Antonio Lame," "Keep Dallas Pretentious."

◎ ◎ ◎

Shannon Sedwick came to Austin with a vision of a pool dancing in her head—only this was no spring-fed pool. A tall, stately blonde with wide eyes and a commanding presence that took over any room she walked into, Sedwick arrived from Fort Worth in the summer of 1968 to enroll in the drama department at the University of Texas, and write and act outside the classroom.

"I joined the staff of the *Texas Ranger* [the campus humor magazine] to learn how to write satirical comedy, and got involved with a show called *Now the Revolution* that was basically a Texas version of *Hair*. We got thrown off campus for nudity in the show, but not before it had caught the eye of Joe Papp, who invited the cast to come up to the New York Public Theater to perform the musical revue." Sedwick did not go.

"I felt it more important to stay in school," she said. "I was starting an independent film series on campus called 'The Museum of Light' with my partner, Michael Shelton. So I missed *Now the Revolution* changing to *Stomp* and touring Europe [a tour that future musician Joe Ely jumped on]. I chose the creative entrepreneur path in Austin instead."

Her friends in the touring company were starving artists. Sedwick was at least comfortable in her chosen path. She knew how to hustle. "Our film series was successful," she said. "We made a mint off the showings of *Naked Zodiac*."

Shelton and Sedwick eventually decided to find their own space and venture off-campus. "We started looking for a location to run a restaurant/performance space, and found an abandoned lumberyard built in the early nineteen hundreds at 405 West Second Street at the southwest corner of Guadalupe Street. The building that fronted the lumberyard had once been a restaurant run by the Texas School for the Blind. When we cleaned off the front of the building, we uncovered the name 'Liberty Lunch.'"

Reviving the building's old name, Sedwick and Shelton opened Liberty Lunch for lunch in 1976. Painter Doug Jaques created a surrealistic mural on the Guadalupe Street side of the building that featured a lion and lamb playing with a beach ball, a lizard with a cherry on its tongue, and a human hippie raising a baby up above a river formed from a waterfall spilling from a coconut. The old building's interior was remade into a large café/ small restaurant. "We had the first open kitchen in Austin [in the theatrical sense], with chef Emil Vogely making gumbo and New Orleans muffalettas," Sedwick said.

Sedwick and Shelton's theatrical backgrounds were put to use with their declared intent to establish "a minicultural center in the inner city area," a nice way of explaining the improvisational performances by the couple and their friends who were actors, dancers, singers, musicians, and poets. Collectively, they called themselves Esther's Hard Corps du Water Ballet. Events such as Mom's Apple Pie Bakeoff were imagined. A Gumbo Cookoff was held at dawn, with Chef Emil arriving in a Roman litter, holding a scepter with a wig hat adorned with boiled crawdads with smiley faces painted on them—his custom-designed Medusa of Gumbo Ya Ya headgear.

"Liberty Lunch was an overnight success with the *Texas Monthly* crowd," Sedwick said of the new slick statewide magazine whose offices were nearby, and whose young staff were some of her best customers. But the eatery would be subsumed in a couple years by the action around the backyard stage behind the lunch building. That's where the reggae band the Lotions and the pan-Latin band Beto y Los Fairlanes were attracting huge crowds that danced on the asphalt of the old lumberyard. Between music sets, Esther's

The cast of Esther's Follies kicks up a chorus line under the watchful gaze of Shannon Sedwick's likeness, at the original Sixth Street location. (Photo copyright © 2017 Bill Leissner.)

Hard Corps du Water Ballet, guided by Doug Dyer, performed short, offbeat theatrical skits, sometimes concluding with a dance around a lawn sprinkler in tribute to the performance troupe's inspiration, the campy, splashy films of the thirties and forties that starred Esther Williams.

Liberty Lunch, the restaurant, struggled to stay in the black after Chef Emil departed to work full-time at his other job as head chef at Jeffrey's, Austin's contemporary fine dining establishment that had opened in the old Clarksville neighborhood. Meanwhile, Liberty Lunch, the open-air club/concert hall out back, was drawing crowds of up to a thousand, functioning like the alternative Armadillo World Headquarters.

The founders had gotten distracted. With Liberty Lunch up and running, word spread around downtown about Sedwick and Shelton, the hippie couple who gussied up the old derelict lumberyard. The owner of a pool table supply company approached them. He knew about a small conjunto bar on Sixth Street that had just been shuttered due to too many shootings and police incidents. "He wanted us to run the bar and to use his tables," Sedwick said.

Esther's Pool opened for business on April Fool's Day 1977 at 515 East Sixth Street with a party. The following Friday a group of dancers, musicians, singers, poets, mimes, and comics showed up and improvised their way through the evening.

The patron saint and thematic inspiration for the bar was Esther Williams, the swimming champion turned movie star whose likeness in one-piece Speedo and bathing cap was the room's logo. Beside beer and wine, amusements were initially limited to pool tables and cigarette machines. But once Sedwick, Shelton, and company finished building a stage, which happened to be right in front of the windows facing Sixth Street, the show really started. Performers were guaranteed a rear-view audience of passersby, college students, transients, and patrons on their way to the adult bookstore down the block. Sedwick and Shelton made sure the stage was occupied by something different and entertaining. That idea evolved into the contemporary Austin-centric musical comedy troupe known as Esther's Follies.

Shannon Sedwick and Michael Shelton's comedy revue survived a fire at their 515 East Sixth Street location in 1983. They found temporary shelter at the old Ritz Theater on Sixth, and then permanently relocated to larger quarters at 525 East Sixth Street on the southwest corner of Sixth and Red River Streets, the former home of the JJJ Tavern.

Doug Jaques bathed the new exterior in another underwater mural in 1990, extending the theme that began at Liberty Lunch in 1976. The revue continued through the second decade of the twenty-first century, as Austin's longest-running stage production. For visitors, out-of-towners, newcomers, suburbanites, and natives, Esther's Follies was the most direct window to the city's alternative culture and its offbeat sensibilities.

The variety show was a communal effort, effortlessly parodying everything from Shakespeare to radio drama. Doug Dyer directed the musical productions. Skits were imagined by Terry Galloway. Recurring characters emerged, such as William Dente's comic opera singer Dame Della Diva, Margaret Wiley's Latin bombshell Chi Chi La Bamba, Shaun Branigan's almost loveable Rick Perry, and Kerry Awn's cheesy comic entertainer Ronnie Velveeta. When illusionist Ray Anderson joined the troupe, magic became an integral part of show. Linda Wetherby's female harmony singing groups Rotel and the Hot Tomatoes and the Blandscrew Sisters were both conceived at Esther's Follies. Sedwick had a reputation for channeling dead country singer Patsy Cline.

A typical Friday started with a live band, followed by the Follies for a couple hours, and then a band again. Proceeds were collected by passing the hat.

The unexpected was the norm. The gentleman entering the front door during the show totally naked except for an angel food cake strategically placed around his genitals? Part of the show, ladies and gentlemen. A Halloween show stopped by a troupe of giant ants, roaches, and other bugs swarming the stage, being chased out the door by an oversized Raid can? Show biz, baby.

Audiences embraced the topical satire, snappy blackouts, and anything goes attitude. Two to three hour marathons with more than thirty performers and pass the hat admission eventually slimmed down to an hour-long performance by a cast of twelve with set ticket prices. Sedwick described it as contemporary vaudeville inspired by old school troupes such as Sid Caesar's *Your Show of Shows*, and SCTV.

Esther's was its own little empire. "We grew into a comedy conglomerate, with a standup club, The Velveeta Room, and a catering company to handle corporate bookings and group sales," Sedwick said. "Our restaurant, Patsy's Café, named after Patsy Cline, my longtime favorite character in the show, caters all the big parties we host."

The show remained the thing, fresh topical fare the priority. Political commentary was delivered with a distinctive Texas kick. "We've been lucky to always have Texas sensibilities in our comedy, bigger than life, and too full of itself," Sedwick said, citing Texas politicos George W. Bush, Ross Perot, Ann Richards, Rick Perry, Ted Cruz, and Dan Patrick. She credited Esther's long-term success to the players growing up with their audience, "learning what makes people laugh, and making sure we provide what they need to have fun."

Sedwick admitted the concept probably wouldn't have worked in New York or Dallas. The Comedy Central television network filmed several shows hoping to capture Esther's quirky spirit for the small screen. But producers concluded it was Esther's was an Austin thing. And its creators were just fine with that.

Esther's was to Austin theater what Bob Schneider was to Austin music. They were hometown favorites who didn't necessarily translate beyond the city limits, characters who demanded you hear them on their own turf in order to understand and appreciate them to the fullest.

One of Esther's most beloved characters did not belong to the cast. Crazy Carl Hickerson worked the streets in front of Esther's showcase windows early on weekend evenings, spinning and balancing carnations and flashing his man-boobs, which earned spare change from the sidewalk audience. Crazy Carl had pretty much been doing the same act since the seventies, mostly on street corners. Those skills were tied to the deeper past of the self-proclaimed alter ego of Austin.

He was Crazy Carl, the Salvation Sandwiches vendor on the Drag in the seventies before he found his place as Crazy Carl selling flowers on street cor-

Crazy Carl Hickerson, street corner flower salesman, mayoral candidate, and inspiration for the bumper sticker "I'm Crazy Too, Carl." (Photo by Martha Grenon.)

ners, entertaining himself and passersby by performing tricks with his long-stemmed merchandise. His high visibility inspired runs for the city council and mayor seven different times. He may have been a hippie surviving on a limited income, but he articulated a prescient promarijuana, antigrowth, anti-nuke, progreen, pronude swimming platform, garnering 12,223 votes in 1979. Hickerson never won an election—he might have been too weird for that—but he paved a path for fellow street flower salesman Max Nofziger, who served nine years on the council and was its most ardent environmental advocate.

The flower gig was barely enough to get by. "I'm rather underemployed," Crazy Carl said. "Kind of like a lot of Austin." He was a star nonetheless, the inspiration of the bumper sticker "I'm Crazy Too, Carl," and the subject of the 2014 film documentary *Crazy Carl and His Man-Boobs: An Austin Love Story*.

It should be little surprise that a place known for welcoming and har-boring iconoclasts happened to foster a whole lot of music built on quirk and novelty. A thread of hard-headed individualism ran through Kenneth Threadgill's yodeling, John Clay's hollering, Turk Pipkin's miming (rolling the biggest joint in the world in front of a full house at the Armadillo), the Grey Ghost's barrelhouse piano trilling, Blind George McLain's improvised rants and vamps, Joe "King" Carrasco's table-jumpin', out-in-the-street walkin' brand of Tex-Mex, Randy (Biscuit) Turner's always startling drama queen stage improvisations, Glass Eye's edgy experimentalism, the organic extraterrestrial country sounds of Tommy Hancock and the Supernatural Family Band, carolyn wonderland's blues intensity, the comedic parodies dreamed up by Kinky Friedman, the Hickoids, the Austin Lounge Lizards, Pocket FishRmen, and Kerry Awn and the Uranium Savages, Gibby Haynes's subversive anarchy, Roky Erickson's blood-curdling yowls and yelps on top of horror movie lyrics, the out-where-the-buses-don't-run imagination of Shinyribs, and the one-man bands of Scott H. Biram, Homer Henderson, and (briefly) Shakey Graves.

They all played second fiddle to Daniel Johnston, a bipolar singer-song-writer-cartoonist-fabulist-naïve genius-hustler.

Daniel Johnston arrived in Austin in 1983, when the campus-area music scene was in the throes of the New Sincerity alt-rock explosion of bands at the Beach, the South Bank, the Continental Club, and other small, accommo-dating venues. He zoomed in on several people he determined were impor-tant enough to give them cassettes of the new albums he'd recorded, *Yip/Jump Music*, made in his brother Dick's garage in Houston with a toy chord organ and a Smurfs ukulele, and *Hi, How Are You?*, made in San Marcos where he moved in with his sister Margy shortly before he had a nervous break-

Daniel Johnston at Austin Music Awards with fellow songwriters Rich Minus and James McMurtry. (Photo by Martha Grenon.)

down. He moved to Austin after the breakdown, scored a gig at the campus-area McDonald's, and started handing out cassettes, informing passersby, "I'm Daniel Johnston and I'm going to be famous." He asked *Austin Chronicle* editor Louis Black to be his manager, and then went down the hall of the *Chronicle* building to ask the manager of the True Believers.

The tapes, with their hand-drawn covers featuring Jeremiah, the Innocent Frog, and the Happy Baby with the Giant Head, got circulated wide enough for Johnston to score a gig opening for avant-garde-ists Glass Eye. Glass Eye's audience was primed for what Johnston had to serve up: honest, sincere songs that were more than a little bit weird in content, performed in a sweet, sometimes falsetto by the songwriter himself, who projected the dual images of innocent and Out There.

Waterloo Records, Sound Exchange, and other indie record stores started selling the cassettes he'd been giving away, and Daniel Johnston's fan base expanded to include high-profile national music acts such as Yo La Tengo, Pearl Jam, the Flaming Lips, Beck, Tom Waits, Wilco, Death Cab for Cutie, and the Butthole Surfers—all of whom would make cover versions of Johnston's originals. To the eyes and ears of his growing cult, Daniel Johnston was like Jonathan Richman, the naïve singer-songwriter from Boston, but apparently minus the calculation.

Songs such as "Speeding Motorcycle" and "Sorry Entertainer," sung in a fragile voice that cracked without shame, attracted the attention of the crew that came to Austin to film MTV's *Cutting Edge* program for the music-focused cable television channel in 1985. Host Peter Zaremba, leader of the New York postpunk garage rock group the Fleshtones, palled around Austin with Joe "King" Carrasco and introduced the show with this incisive observation: "They say that ninety people a day move to Austin. The signs of growth are everywhere. Changes are not always welcome, however. Some of Austin's best clubs have disappeared. Liberty Lunch, one of tonight's featured clubs, won't be around much longer, either. Through it all, the bands survive; they play at parties, outdoors, and sometimes, yes, even in real garages. . . ."

The unlikely stars of the show were Timbuk 3 and Daniel Johnston. Timbuk 3 was a little-known, new-to-town husband-and-wife folk-rock duo from Wisconsin, Pat McDonald and Barbara Kooyman, accompanied by a beat box. Timbuk 3's appearance led to a record deal with the *Cutting Edge*'s sponsoring label, IRS Records, and a top ten pop hit, "The Future's So Bright (I Gotta Wear Shades)."

The enigmatic, curly-haired Johnston's innocent countenance provided plenty for the cameras to fixate on, especially when Johnston showed his cassette *Hi, How Are You?* and cheerily mentioned, "I was having a nervous breakdown when I recorded it."

The homemade, hand-drawn cassette and album covers, quirky songs ("Walking the Cow," "True Love Will Find You in the End"), fantasy story lines, and dreamed-up characters in the cartoon/music universe he created, and his determination that he was going to be famous, as he liked to tell any and all around him, made Daniel Johnston a superhero among DIY indie music enthusiasts.

That reputation turned mainstream when Kurt Cobain, leader of Nirvana, the biggest band in the world in the early nineties, sported a "Hi, How Are You?" T-shirt at the 1992 MTV Music Awards show. Cobain freely endorsed Johnston's music and his cartoons, the latter heavily influencing Cobain's own cartooning. In 1993, Cobain listed *Yip/Jump Music* as one of his favorite albums in the personal journal he kept.

Locally, Daniel Johnston became an institution unto himself, even though he was gone from Austin by 1990, largely due to too many fans' and friends' offers of illicit drugs, which did not mix well with the antidepressants he was supposed to be taking. The same year Johnston was cited by Nirvana's Cobain, Sound Exchange record shop owner Craig Koon commissioned Johnston to paint a mural of Jeremiah the Innocent Frog along with the

"Hi, How Are You?" phrase on the outside of the building, facing Twenty-First Street at the corner of Guadalupe Street, across from the University of Texas campus. In 2004, Sound Exchange closed and the mural was about to be painted over before community complaints convinced the building's new owner, John Oudt, to preserve the mural. In 2014, the building's even newer owners, David Roberts and Somyong Sukkij, restored the mural after Johnston's work was vandalized.

True to alternative Austin tradition, Johnston was the subject of a major documentary film, The Devil and Daniel Johnston (2005), that drilled deep into Johnston's bipolarity, his deepening manic-schizophrenia, and what life was like living with his parents on their small farm west of Houston. The film also captured Johnston freaking out at a Butthole Surfers show in 1986 after he dropped acid, and recalled the incident when Daniel's father was piloting him in his private plane to Austin and a delusional Daniel tried to crash the plane by removing the ignition key and throwing it out the window because he thought he was Casper the Friendly Ghost. The airplane affair led to one of several extended stays in mental hospitals. Another documentary, Hi, How Are You Daniel Johnston? (2015), focused on Johnston's live performances and artwork.

Where he had already enjoyed his first brush with fame as a performing musician on MTV's Cutting Edge, 2006 was the breakout year for Daniel Johnston as a visual artist. The prestigious Whitney Biennial in New York invited Johnston to exhibit more than a dozen of his pen-and-Magic Marker pieces, while a more extensive companion show was mounted at the Clementine Gallery in Chelsea. Drawings he once gave away were fetching more than one thousand dollars. A reporter from the New York Times profiling Johnston asked if Johnston would attend any of the New York events. "I'm not in any condition to go overseas," he responded. "It would wipe me out."

He was overweight, diabetic, and chain-smoked. He was bipolar. He was crazy. He was brilliant. He was his own worst enemy. But with his manic depression stabilized by new medications, Johnston got what he was chasing after. Over the years he managed to maintain and enjoy some semblance of celebrity as an Outsider Artist and Outsider Singer-Songwriter. Seven tribute albums had been recorded in his honor. A Houston theater company produced and staged a rock opera about him. He performed in Europe, Mexico, and South America. Exhibitions of his art were staged in Paris, London, Germany, Switzerland, New York, and Houston. In 2012, Johnston had his first comic book published, Space Ducks—An Infinite Comic

Daniel Johnston's iconic Hi, How Are You wall mural on Twenty-First Street near the corner of Guadalupe. (Photo by P. Kromer.)

Book of Musical Greatness, along with a companion album and smartphone app. Sales of Daniel Johnston merchandise, including original artwork, prints, and Hi, How Are You? tote bags, backpacks, and T-shirts, remained steady well into the twenty teens.

His name was Daniel Johnston, and he was famous.

But he was hardly the only offbeat Austin soul to gain international acclaim.

◉ ◉ ◉

Number Seventy-Two on TripAdvisor's list of things to see in Austin was the Cathedral of Junk at 4222 Lareina Street. This one-man monument of outsider art started honestly in 1988 as a small pile of hubcaps and a shopping cart in the South Austin backyard of Vince Hannemann. The pile grew into a work of art in a state of permanent progress with the addition of hundreds of shiny CDs, more than eight hundred bicycles, numerous typewriters, wheels, phones, toy horses, WWF action figures, and computer guts—all told, sixty tons of found objects wired together—much of it shaped into a thirty-three foot high tower that both adults and kids could climb into, an archway to walk across, and rooms to play hide-and-seek.

Word of mouth spread. Vanloads of tourists, gawkers, and curiosity seekers disembarked in front of Hannemann's home. Couples married at the cathedral. Visitors brought their own junk for possible consideration of adding to the pile. One constant was kids, always running around, always exploring.

Charging no admission and subsisting on donations, the Cathedral of Junk qualified as a genuine Austin tourist attraction and landmark, the perfect example of the Keep Austin Weird ethos the city and its boosters had embraced and promoted.

But in 2005, Hannemann got a visit from the city responding to a neighbor's complaint. The cathedral was out of compliance with city code. It must be closed. Defenders of the cathedral, including an architect and attorneys, pushed back. More than twenty volunteers removed forty tons of junk, including Christmas lights, cords, and other perceived hazards. The cathedral reopened.

It became an even bigger tourist attraction despite its diminished, safer scale, no matter how hamstrung rules enforcers tried to make it. Robert Rodriguez filmed a scene for his movie *Spy Kids 3D* at the cathedral. A ten-dollar donation per group was the new bottom line, even though the hours

Vince Hannemann admiring his backyard Cathedral of Junk in South Austin. (Photo by Joe Nick Patoski.)

were as sporadic as Vince Hannemann wished; otherwise the city would consider the Cathedral of Junk a business.

Vince Hannemann didn't look weird at first glance. His polo shirt, cotton dress shorts, white tube socks, running shoes, and short, semi-sculpted hair could have passed for the neighborhood look on this block and a half stretch of small midcentury semi-subdivision frame homes.

There were hints, though, such as the two-tone horn-rimmed glasses and the tattoos covering both arms. Then—ta da!—the letters inked on the outside of his fingers: one hand spelled "JUNK" and the other "KING".

Realizing a visitor wasn't a Looky-Loo, but a local who actually knew a little bit about the cathedral, Hannemann dropped his usual defensive posture and told his story. He grew up in Santa Fe, New Mexico, in a part of town not far from the city dump where rocks were plentiful. He built his first rock art sculpture / mission façade / fortress wall at age fourteen. He followed his mother to Austin as a young adult in 1989.

His first impressions of Texas played to stereotype. "Everybody seemed rich. You understand why the Mexicans go, 'Wow. It's crazy rich over here.'" His timing was good. "It was in the middle of a[n economic] bust, and that was kind of cool," he said. "Downtown was dead empty. Things were sort of affordable. People used to be able to afford to be slackers. Slacking went out the window with the economic upturn. The boom was real bad for slackers."

Hannemann didn't mind letting visitors know they'd arrived in Austin too late. "I've had people come and ask me, 'What's weird about Austin? Is that just a slogan?' I have to tell them, 'Now, yeah, it is. There's nothing weird about Austin anymore. Sorry. It's done. It's over.'"

Austin exceptionalism was like American exceptionalism, Hannemann contended. "Don't buy it. You're not exceptional if you say you are. Austinites aren't weird because they say they are. That's not weird."

Crab as he might, Vince Hannemann admitted he was kind of in awe that people came from around the world to see what he did. "They want to see something unusual. I've heard over and over again that this was the coolest thing they saw on their trip, bar none."

The reaction of kids was his greatest reward. "They see things differently," Hannemann said. "Once you get past a certain age, you're looking for meaning, or going down Memory Lane, and 'What are you trying to say?' The kids just run around, play hide-and-go-seek. They're having a good time. It's just a big fort to them. That's fun. A little girl saw all the CDs flashing around and said, 'Fairies!' A group of Girl Scouts gave me duct-taped roses that they had made and sang me a song. People write poetry about the cathedral. They'll draw pictures for me. I've got a few on the refrigerator. They'll send me Thank You cards. The kids make my day when they do that kind of stuff."

Just like Hannemann made so many kids' days. "I know it influences their brains in a positive way," he said. "It's going to stick in there and maybe help them in some way, to be brave, to do their own creative out-of-bounds thing that they want to. 'Well, that guy did that.' That's the one thing I really like here, that I give people permission. When I see that I've done that, I feel like this is a success."

Hannemann showed the buffer zone that had been cleared near the fence line, and a whole new tower rising beneath the oak trees. "This is the new staircase to the second floor," he said, tromping up winding stairs to a platform. "One of the things they made me do to get the city engineer to sign off on this was weight-test the platform. We put 400 gallons of water here to weight-test this. It's only 105 square feet. I defy anyone to build a 105 square foot platform 9 feet up in the air and load it up with 400 gallons of water."

Interactions with city officials and the endless stream of visitors made Hannemann realize the Cathedral of Junk was a public work of art. Dealing with the public, with city officials, with curiosity-seekers all was part of the art. "The authorities, my neighbors, everybody's impressions and mis-impressions, the Internet—all that stuff is part of it," he said. "That's my canvas. Where this is going to go, I don't know. I don't think the story has ended yet."

He couldn't take down the Cathedral of Junk if he wanted to. "No, no, no," he insisted. "Do you know what a huge uproar there would be? It belongs to the community, the way they use it. It means something to different people."

So what did it mean to the creator?

"It's an interesting journey, anyway," he said, growing quiet. "Just to go with the flow and see what happens." He understood the unintended consequences of what he started. "I could never anticipate that I would build a tourist attraction," Vince Hannemann said. "It's not something you plan. But I can imagine now what it had been like if you had been elected pope or been born into royalty. It's a lifetime job. It's not just you. There's a bigger thing to it. You're just occupying the office."

A slight smile broke across his crusty countenance.

"I still kind of fall between the cracks."

Free-spirited expressionism also manifested itself prominently at the graffiti park below Castle Hill a.k.a. Hope Outdoor Gallery at 1100 Baylor Street in old West Austin, the remains of a failed three-story eighties development whose foundations had been continuously painted over and over decades afterward, turning the site into a much-photographed destination in the spirit of the graphitized alleyways behind Mission Street in San Francisco—until the property was sold and redeveloped in 2018.

The Christmas lights of West Thirty-Seventh Street were another example of Austin's free-spirited expressionism. A group of residents in this long block of midcentury bungalows in Hyde Park, north of the university, conspired to haphazardly string lights between houses and even over the street, getting wilder and trippier every holiday season until the tight neighborhood started fragmenting after 2000.

11

Onward through the Fog

⊙ ⊙ ⊙

For a half-century, creative minds altered and reshaped a bucolic, semi-sleepy, laid-back state capital city in the middle of America into a dynamic city-state of global importance and appeal.

Accompanying Austin's ascendance was a significant spike in population, traffic, rents, and housing prices—the usual stuff that comes with economic growth. More and more newcomers didn't care where they happened to be. Austin's unique qualities, amenities, and attractions had nothing to do with them being where they were. They just wanted work. The city that had the lowest cost of living of the one hundred largest cities in the United States in 1970 happened to be the hottest jobs market in the United States during the aughts and teens.

Could a creative ethos continue driving the culture in a boomtown where money was held in higher regard than ideas? Wasn't Austin becoming just like everywhere else?

The 2016 departure of Alejandro Escovedo, a hometown music hero since his arrival in 1983, was neither unusual nor much noticed. Escovedo simply found a more welcoming housing situation in Dallas. Half a year in, he said North Oak Cliff, a historically blue-collar part of Dallas where he resided, seemed more interesting and diverse than Austin. The time had come to move on.

Austin had arrived at the maturation/saturation point of a Manhattan or a San Francisco. Limits had been reached. Austin, the city, had run out of space to expand. Previously derelict parts of the city were being retrofitted and rebuilt into hip neighborhoods, pushing a significant number of lower-income residents—artists, musicians, and entertainers among them—to older suburbs and nearby small towns. Lockhart, thirty miles southeast, with an architecturally significant county courthouse and several world-class barbecue joints, developed a reputation as an artist community, mainly because so many Austin musicians had moved there.

San Marcos, thirty miles south (a.k.a. Austin Jr.), with San Marcos Springs, the second largest complex of artesian springs in the southwest, and close to forty thousand students at Texas State University, always felt like Austin twenty or thirty years earlier. It continued to do so in spite of a population growth rate that in 2015 was even faster than Austin's. Many creatives simply hoofed it out of state, returning to old reliables California and New York as well as newer destinations such as Oregon, Washington state, and Colorado.

A few headed to Marfa in Far West Texas, a very small (population 2,424), very sophisticated art town, once the domain of minimalist sculptor Donald Judd. Following Judd's death in 1994, a wave of Houston attorneys and executives led by Tim Crowley, Dick DeGuerin, and Jeff Fort bought second homes and other properties, bringing in galleries, artists, and shop-keepers, mostly from Houston or from New York, California, and overseas.

When the South Congress hotelier Liz Lambert opened her funky, offbeat El Cosmico resort in Marfa in 2009, six years after former Austinite Virginia Lebermann and her business partner Fairfax Dorn opened the Ballroom Marfa arts complex, Austin cool kids began filtering west. Their numbers were substantial enough to move the Presidio County sheriff to affix a sticker to the rear bumper of his pickup truck: "Keep Austin in Austin."

By the start of the second decade of the twenty-first century, Austin back-lash was becoming as popular as Austin hype. John Nova Lomax, an Austin native, scion of the folklore Lomaxes, and a writer for the Houston Press weekly in 2011, declared Austin to be over in his article, "Finding Austin." Lomax reported the city was too crowded, too expensive, and let too many identi-fying icons fall to the wrecking ball to be the coolest city around anymore. Eddie Wilson, the Armadillo/Threadgill's trail boss, was quoted compar-ing the new Austin to "a good-lookin' chick who got knocked up and can't get into her britches anymore."

Lomax pointed out Austin didn't have much in the way of museums and institutional culture like Houston, Dallas, Fort Worth or San Antonio did. Traffic was soul crushing. Austin suffered from segregation, gentrification, and navel-gazing. Indie and funky were kaput. The sparkling shiny down-town skyline projected a corporate and ritzy vibe—perfect for Gilded Age vulgarians in search of a second or third home.

As Lomax saw it, Austin was a vapid Valley Girl of a wannabe city who liked to look at herself in the mirror just a little too much. Its citizens were smug and self-satisfied just being in Austin. Other Texas cities contained cool quarters too.

But Lomax missed the larger point: no one was moving to Dallas or Houston because they thought they were cool places. They moved for jobs, and then tried to ferret out whatever cool they could find. People were still moving to Austin because they thought it was cool, whether it was or wasn't.

Austin was what one made of it, more than ever. The canvas was no longer pristine and untouched. But it was constantly being painted over in imaginative ways.

Reinvention drove the creative continuum. So did age and perspective.

Stumbling upon the Broken Spoke on South Lamar Boulevard was more of a surprise in 2017 than in 1964, the year the rickety building on the southwestern edge of the city opened for business with a hitching post outside in case anyone rode in on their horse, a restaurant in front, and dancehall in back, surrounded by a sea of caliche for parking. Lacking lighting, the lot at night felt like being way out in the country.

Over the course of three years beginning in 2013, the Spoke shrunk, or least appeared to, as two symmetrical four-story condominiums rose up on both sides of the weathered honky-tonk. The Broken Spoke looked out of place and out of time, not unlike the last brownstone among the high-rise apartments on the upper west side of Manhattan.

The innards had been slightly improved and updated over the years, but not too much. Stepping inside was like walking into a genuine neon-lit Texas country dancehall because that's what the Spoke was. The narrow rectangular dance floor was slicked up like it was supposed to be, all the easier for sliding boots doing the Texas two-step. The ceiling was low enough to scrape the tops of cowboy hats, qualifying the venue as a honky-tonk. The ceiling was original, but a new roof had been constructed above it to conform to city code.

Anyone familiar with the Spoke over its fifty-year lifespan was pretty sure the new condos around it meant its time wasn't long. But any twenty year old who'd just arrived in Austin could have just as well thought, "How cool is this? An ancient kicker hangout where you can learn to 'dance country' right in the middle of a modern residential complex?" The iPhone photos of the exterior, and of James White welcoming visitors to his "tourist trap," were Instagram hits. To a younger generation, the changes were relative.

Stumbling upon the Broken Spoke scrunched between condominiums was not unlike stumbling upon a tree-shaded outdoor amphitheater in the middle of a mall in Bee Caves west of the city. A mall with its own music venue might have seemed kind of cool, but to anyone who'd attended a show at the Backyard between its opening in 1993 until it was landlocked

James White, proprietor of the honky-tonk and "tourist trap" Broken Spoke. (Photo by Will Van Overbeek.)

by Old Navy, Office Max, and Best Buy stores at the start of the 2007 season, the surrounding development was another kiss of death. The power center retailers ruined what had been a near idyllic open-air setting for hearing music. On the "shed" circuit of outdoor music venues in the United States, the Backyard had developed a reputation for having one of the most perfect natural environments to perform music in, with a gently sloping hillside surrounded by giant oaks. As the centerpiece of "the Shops at the Galleria," it was a very bad sign of progress. The venue would relocate nearby in 2010, but never regain its footing or reputation.

The steroidal growth that transformed other parts of the city arrived in East Austin around 2000. Over the next ten years, the number of African Americans declined by 27 percent to comprise less than 8 percent of the city's population; the number of Anglos in East Austin increased by 40 percent during that time. The number of Mexican Americans in East Austin dropped almost 10 percent.

Back in 1928, the City of Austin's Master Plan officially designated East Austin as the part of the segregated city where African Americans and Mexican Americans could live, and where industry should be located. Although segregation laws were eliminated in the fifties and sixties, an invisible line still ran through the city, roughly along Interstate 35 through adherence to a "gentlemen's agreement" that west was for whites and east was for minorities, similar to the unspoken city council rule that one council seat was for blacks, one was for browns, and the other five seats were split among white folks.

The "gentlemen's agreement" was finally ignored or conveniently forgotten when mostly white young people started moving east because that's where the affordable rents and housing prices were. Many older East Austin homeowners cashed out, with the majority of African Americans moving to Pflugerville, Round Rock, and other suburbs north of Austin, and Mexican Americans moving south to Kyle, Buda, and San Marcos.

East Austin turned into hipster central.

Several old East Austin Chicano bars such as the Scoot Inn and Hotel Vegas transitioned to cool kids clientele in the aughts and teens, along with the surrounding neighborhood. The most popular reinvented joint was the White Horse, at the corner of East Fifth and Comal Streets, which featured three to four bands on its small corner stage seven nights a week for no cover charge, with weekly dance lessons offered for young people who didn't know how.

On Sunday afternoons for several years, an elderly crowd of East Austin Mexican Americans turned out at the White Horse for the weekly *tardeada*, the late afternoon show hosted by Los Pinkys, the accordion-driven band well-versed in conjunto (the South Texas-Mexican sound popular in blue-collar cantinas). The gig was a real neighborhood gathering, with the elderly musicians outside during breaks, telling stories and passing around funny cigarettes and sipping beers, while younger Mexican American players discreetly lobbied for a sit-in spot during the next set. Inside, dancers surveyed the room for prospective partners when the music started up again. A tall scruffy-haired Anglo with a movie camera lingered around the edges. That was Lee Daniel, cofounder of the Austin Film Society, filming the scene.

The leader of Los Pinkys was another example of having to come to Austin to work his ideas out. Bradley Jaye Williams was a Saginaw, Michigan, kid who grew around two kinds of polka music—the Polish style he was raised on, and the Mexican style as performed by Latino immigrants who lived in Saginaw. Williams came up with the idea for Los Pinkys in San Francisco, where he landed after a brief career as a commercial fisherman.

Few people in San Francisco really understood what Williams was trying to do. Keith Ferguson, the hepcat bassist with the Fabulous Thunderbirds and the Tailgators who was passing through the Bay Area on tour, zoned right in on what Williams was about when he heard him playing on the street. "Either get yourself a monkey and a tin cup, or move to Texas," Ferguson advised him. "Because you're not gonna find anybody to play with [in San Francisco]." Williams took Ferguson's advice and moved in 1993.

Joining Williams in Los Pinkys at the White Horse was drummer Clemencia Zapata, a veteran in Austin's Mexican American music community and one of the few female drummers in conjunto, and Isidro Samilpa and Chencho Flores, two elderly accordionists, with more than one hundred years in music between them. Williams accompanied them on *bajo sexto* guitar.

The *tardeada* made palatable the transformation of East Austin. The corner of Twelfth and Chicon Streets near Sam's Bar-B-Q evolved from crack-dealers marketplace to hip bar strip. The East Eleventh Street corridor had been transformed so radically the transvestite hookers who once solicited from in front of Shorty's Fruit Stand had nowhere to relocate. They just went away. The Victory Grill, a remnant of the Southern blues chitlin' circuit, and Kenny Dorham's Backyard, an open space with food trailers named for the jazz trumpet player who came of age in Austin in the forties, were the only touchstones left testifying to Eleventh Street's heyday as a Little Harlem.

A piñata store on Cesar Chavez was evicted and the business destroyed, replaced with a café for cats.

Cecilia Balli felt like a fish out of water in this Austin. "As a Texas Mexican American who's lived in Brownsville, San Antonio, Houston, El Paso and Austin, this is the first city where I frequently would look around and find I was the only non-Anglo in the room, or maybe one of two or three," she said. Balli was one of Texas's leading Latina writers who moved to Austin in 2008 to teach at the University of Texas. "I'm talking about this happening in the restaurants and coffee shops in the heart of the city. But still, it was surprising to me to find that my ethnicity was something I noticed more while [in Austin]. I was dumbfounded when I found out 30 percent of the population was Hispanic. Even as the city fetishized tacos and other things Latin American [Day of the Dead was adopted as a local holiday and became another reason to party hearty], Latinos seemed invisible to me in mainstream Austin. I'd never felt so self-conscious, so not like myself, and so fetishized, almost, as a Latina."

Balli also observed that in Austin she always felt overdressed. Austin casual was not as easy as it looked.

Was this Austin postcultural, its image tied to youth or lifestyle, not ethnicity? The last place most aspiring blacks and Latinos in Texas wanted to move was the old 'hood or barrio. They wanted to live in the same places everyone else wanted to live. Cecilia Balli moved to Houston.

Every December, old Austin hippies and those who remembered them came out of the woodwork for the Armadillo Christmas Bazaar, a handmade fine arts and crafts market with bands, beer, and familiar faces to revisit the past with. The Armadillo World Headquarters may have died on New Year's Eve 1980, but the one concrete piece of the old hippie music hall's legacy, the Christmas bazaar, grew into one of Austin's longest-running arts and music festivals, drawing forty thousand shoppers over the fortnight before Christmas every year.

After the Armadillo was torn down, the bazaar moved to increasingly larger spaces at the Austin Music Hall, the Austin Convention Center, and the Palmer Auditorium, while staying true to its original concept of featuring merchandise created by the people selling them while local favorites serenaded the crowd. To make the concept viable, people paid a cover charge to shop. The crowds who showed up during the run up to Christmas didn't seem to mind. Many, it turned out, came just for the music and conversation.

Austin's alternative history was officially enshrined at the South Austin Museum of Popular Culture, a small space adjacent to the Planet K head shop at 1516-B South Lamar Boulevard, which opened as a museum in 2004. Michael Kleinman, the owner of Planet K and the property, offered the space for the museum to a group of poster artists from the Armadillo. Former Armadillo World Headquarters staffer Leea Mechling took charge and oversaw exhibits and events at the museum, initially focusing on Armadillo poster artists Jim Franklin, Micael Priest, Bill Narum, Danny Garrett, Sam Yeates, and Ken Featherston, and then broadening to other alternative subjects such as underground cartoonist (and poster artist) Gilbert Shelton, who

Memorial Wall at the South Austin Museum of Popular Culture, honoring artists, writers, performers, philanthropists, and other contributors to Austin's alternative culture. (Photo courtesy of the South Austin Museum of Popular Culture.)

Close-up of the Memorial Wall at South Austin Museum of Popular Culture. (Photo courtesy of the South Austin Museum of Popular Culture.)

returned to Austin from his home near Paris, France, underground comic pioneer and graphic novelist Jack Jackson, and oddball sculptor and imagineer Bob "Daddy-O" Wade.

Mechling's husband, Henry Gonzalez, a charter member of the Armadillo poster art squad, created and maintained the memorial wall outside the museum, painting Mexican-style *retablas* honoring more than 150 deceased Austin hepcats. Some of the subjects such as Doug Sahm, Stevie Ray Vaughan, and Townes Van Zandt were well-known. Others like Danny Roy Young, D. K. Little, Keith Ferguson, Mambo John Treanor, raul salinas, and Ed Vizard were legends to insider Austin outsiders. In 2016, Henry Gonzalez joined his departed friends on the wall.

◉ ◉ ◉

No matter how old one was, or how long one had been in Austin, you could still wander into a strip mall on Brodie Lane and step back in time to catch an old Austin vibe at the Evangeline Café, Curtis Clarke's homey Cajun operation that featured some of the city's finest roots musicians crammed into a small corner during and after the dinner hour. You could sit at the counter of the Frisco Shop on Burnet Road, order a Frisco burger or Top Chop't sirloin from a waitress you feel like you've known forever, and be teleported back to 1960 to the main Night Hawk on South Congress, or the campus Night Hawk on Guadalupe, even though the Frisco Shop itself had changed locations on North Burnet Road in recent years.

If old Austin weird was worth memorializing, institutions lingered to

Austintatious mural on the Twenty-Third Street wall of the University Co-op, created in 1974 by the Austintatious art collective (Kerry Awn, Rick Turner, and Tom Bauman) and restored in 2014. (Courtesy of the Austintatious Artists.)

address that need. Oat Willie's, the premier head shop in Austin in the late sixties, maintained three locations in the city. Onetime Oat Willie's employee Michael Kleinman went a few steps farther than his old employer, opening eighteen Planet K shops located around Austin and San Antonio.

The Shoal Creek Saloon at Ninth and Lamar and the ABGB beer garden/pizza joint/music room on Oltorf just off South Lamar felt like they had been around forever, instead of just a few years. The Sahara Lounge and the Skylark Lounge on the east side and Sam's Town Point on the deep south side were the kind of neighborhood hangs that felt like extensions of someone's living room.

Maria's Taco X-press on South Lamar stayed true to the old Austin spirit, starting with the giant likeness of owner Maria Corbalan lording over the premises from the roof to free-form wall art and murals, salvaged furniture, cheap breakfast and street tacos, good music, and hippie church on Sundays featuring live gospel, migas, and mimosas.

A few blocks farther south, above the produce section of the second H-E-B Central Market, shoppers could behold "The History of Austin, Texas," a triptych mural drawn and painted by poster artist and muralist Kerry Awn, which provided a bird's eye view of Awn's version of alternative Austin.

Looking back extended to media. Thorne Dreyer reimagined The Rag, the underground newspaper he founded and edited in the late sixties and early seventies, into a multiplatform information delivery system that included an online blog, a weekly radio program that aired on KOOP community radio, a book, and a three-part documentary film.

Similarly, the Austin Sun biweekly from the seventies was revived online with former writers and artists contributing new and archival material. The Ghetto online community kept alive the spirit of Austin's first real hippie hangout in the early sixties—the campus area apartments known as the Ghetto where Janis Joplin lived.

Austin Community Television evolved into ChannelAustin, three separate city-owned programming channels managed by the Austin Film Society. Channel 10 was the longest-running public access television channel in the nation.

Eeyore's Birthday Party in Pease Park, the hippie free-for-all lovefest / skin show / Ultimate Drum Circle somehow survived, mainly because it happened only once a year.

Chicken Shit Bingo apparently existed once a week to remind folks that what once was, still was, if you knew where to look. Crowds packed Ginny's Little Longhorn Saloon, a humble, honest honky-tonk at 5434 Burnet Road

Sunday afternoons to play the game. While a live band performed, participants lined up to buy a numbered ticket for two dollars until all the tickets were gone. A well-fed house chicken was brought out to traipse around
atop a plastic bingo board until the bird took a shit. Whoever held the ticket
with the number where the shit landed won the pooled cash.

The two Threadgill's provided perhaps the easiest looks back. The southern comfort food heavy on vegetables was as much a throwback as the locations themselves. The south location on Riverside Drive at Barton Springs
Road served as the Armadillo World Headquarters'—and Austin's—de-facto
music museum. The North Lamar location, the site of the weekly hootenannies hosted by Kenneth Threadgill in the sixties, was filled with Janis Joplin
memorabilia.

The Armadillo was easily the most iconic institution of old cool lost
Austin. So when the Burley Auction Barn, fifty-five miles south of Austin,
opened its doors on the east side of New Braunfels on a sunny, chilly Saturday
morning in mid-January of 2015 to hold an Armadillo auction, fans were
ready. A standing-room-only crowd several hundred strong filled the barn,
which was already jam-packed with 520 artifacts and baubles from the past.
A line of more bidders and lookers stacked up outside the entrance and
snaked around the metal warehouse.

Eddie Wilson was clearly enjoying being the trail boss of the Armadillo
again, reflexively scanning the crowd, fetching poster artist Micael Priest
from out of the line and escorting him to a seat on the front row, shaking hands with well-wishers, and recognizing faces from the past. The
scrunched remains of a plastic water bottle in his left hand provided the
only hint of his nervousness.

Eddie Wilson felt like it was time. He was seventy-two years old. Surgery
that removed part of a cancerous lung two years earlier had left him complaining about feeling fuzzy-brained. Heavy rains the previous spring
had flooded the warehouse filled with collectibles behind the original
Threadgill's restaurant on North Lamar. The insurance company was going
to pay for moving and storing the items, but Wilson thought better of it and
decided to put most of the stash up for bid.

Wilson, the beer lobbyist turned hippie, promoter, entrepreneur,
restaurateur, sometimes could no longer recognize, much less afford, the
city he was attached to, despite his complicity in defining it. He might as
well let go.

Young people flocking to new restaurants all over Austin, dropping big
bucks for exotic, zoomy cuisine, seemed to have taken Threadgill's for
granted. The two restaurants were touchstones of an Austin they never knew.

Threadgill's was their parents' and grandparents' restaurant, the last refuge of Austin hippies.

The bags under Wilson's eyes hinted that he knew full well he was about to jettison one of his defining assets, his deep collection of Austin and Texas cultural ephemera. "I slept well," he said, clutching the plastic water bottle that had now been twisted into a bent ribbon.

For five decades or so, Wilson hung out in similar auction barns, bidding, buying, and accumulating. Now he was on the other side. The throng of elder hippies, California poster collectors, restaurant and bar owners, good ol' boys, and crafty horse traders was ready to relieve him of the possessions and pay a handsome price for the privilege.

Shortly before the 10:00 a.m. start, head auctioneer Robb Burley took the stage. He fit the silver-tongued Texas auctioneer stereotype to a T. His lean frame was adorned in pure cowboy—western hat, starched snap-button western shirt, pressed Wranglers cinched at the waist by a wide leather belt fronted by a shiny buckle the size of a VW hubcap, spit-shined boots.

The first thing Burley did was announce Burley Auction's website had crashed. Too many bidders had converged online. The start would be delayed. Once again, demand outstripped infrastructure, an old story to anyone who'd been around Austin as long as Eddie Wilson.

"We did a Roy Rogers sale and it didn't hold a candle to this," Burley announced to the gathering as he introduced Wilson. "This is the first one where I've gained weight. Eddie's mamma raised him right, because he sure fed us."

Burley's bidding cadence was rapid-fire but articulate, his arms gesticulating with each phrase. Burley's two assistants working the bidders were similarly attired and wired. The Armadillo, where the hippies and rednecks found common ground in music, beer, and marijuana, had come full circle. The cowboys and longhairs were rubbing shoulders again.

Wilson admitted feeling somewhat floored. "I've spent my entire life trying to put butts into seats," he said, scanning the crowd. "This is the most successful I've ever been." He heaped praise on the Armadillo staff, particularly the poster artists, citing Jim Franklin and Micael Priest, both of whom were in attendance.

Priest, using a cane and perfecting an Ol' Grampa delivery, stepped up to the podium to tell how he was commissioned to paint the mural for the cover of a Jerry Jeff Walker album, with Walker to be photographed in front of the mural. But Walker got drunk and didn't show, and Priest was never paid for the commissioned work.

Wilson informed the gathering that all proceeds from bidding on the mural, which had hung from the ceiling of Threadgill's World Headquarters, would go to the artist, who was residing in subsidized housing. "Priest is finally going to get paid," Wilson told the gathering.

After the mural was auctioned for eight thousand dollars, Priest leaned toward Wilson and whispered, "That covers my costs, and I made a thousand and a half. Thank you."

Trays, mugs, clocks, signs, and other collectibles advertising beer, some dating to the dawn of the twentieth century, went fast. A tricked-out neon sign for the defunct Grand Prize Beer brand fetched twenty grand. A sign that once hung in the historic Buckhorn Saloon in San Antonio, home of Lone Star Beer, with rattles from rattlesnakes spelling out "Minors and Students Must Not Enter Here" commanded nine thousand, plus commission.

The Armadillo piano went for $22,500. The Goode Co. restaurant family from Houston, whose empire included a music venue called the Armadillo Palace, made the winning bid.

Most Armadillo World Headquarters items, although nowhere near as old as most of the beer memorabilia, fetched considerably higher prices than anticipated. Posters that had been estimated to sell from one hundred to four hundred dollars each sold for more than a thousand dollars a piece, including the first Armadillo WHQ poster from 1970, and Willie Nelson's first Fourth of July Picnic in 1973, both drawn by Jim Franklin.

No poster came close in the bidding to the giant mural of bluesman Freddie King hitting the note of his guitar with an armadillo emerging from his heart that Jim Franklin had painted. The mural, commissioned by rock and roll icon Leon Russell, had hung inside the Armadillo World Headquarters. Now it would hang wherever Steve Wertheimer wished. The Austin club owner and South Congress Avenue empresario paid twenty-nine thousand dollars for the mural.

An original Armadillo hand-tooled leather shoulder bag, made by Craig Weller, a cofounder of Whole Foods Market, went for twenty-four hundred dollars. A pair of size twelve quad A handmade cowboy boots with marijuana leaves adorning the boot tops created by master bootmaker Charlie Dunn for Don Hyde of the Vulcan Gas Company was purchased by the Cavender's Boot City retail chain for seven thousand dollars.

The auction generated more than a half-million dollars in revenue. A few months later, Wilson staged a second auction of Armadillo posters at Threadgill's World Headquarters with all proceeds going directly to the artists who created the posters.

Following several months of anguish, Eddie Wilson bit the bullet in late

2014, agreeing to a new lease for Threadgill's World Headquarters at twenty-one thousand dollars per month, a steep increase from the previous lease at seven thousand a month. The threefold rise was the price of admission to continue being a player in Austin's booming restaurant trade. Thirty-five years after the Armadillo World Headquarters closed, real estate developers were still the enemy.

Three years later, Wilson negotiated another lease for the south location at an even higher price. He said it was his civic duty to keep the place going. The remaining photos and ephemera in the restaurants told a story that needed telling. The clusters of bright neon in the south location's bar and backroom that identified defunct Austin establishments, such as Jake's on West Fifth Street, the M&M Courts on far South Congress where Hattie Valdes operated a well-known house of prostitution, and the Night Hawk restaurant were historical markers. Eddie Wilson wasn't interested in selling anything more. "And I'm not going anywhere either," he said defiantly.

◎ ◎ ◎

Austin hubris wasn't going anywhere either.

Hometown hero Lance Armstrong, superstar cyclist, high-profile cancer survivor, and one-name Austin celebrity turned out to be a liar and a cheat. But before he was exposed, and even afterward, Armstrong played an instrumental role in redefining Austin.

His seven Tour de France victories popularized cycling in a city where all sports, professional and amateur, once upon a time revolved around the University of Texas, in a state where cars and pickups were kings of the road. The Livestrong Foundation had raised hundreds of millions of dollars for cancer awareness and created a global fashion trend with yellow rubber Livestrong wristbands. Thirty million sold the first year at a dollar each.

Armstrong was happy to bask in the limelight and party in the clubs with his buds when he wasn't competing. His cycling victories attracted the first non–University of Texas megacrowds in the streets of downtown Austin, gatherings that exceeded 100,000 people. His wins provided the underwriting, and his victory parties provided the practical experience for the future C3 Presents production team and the Austin City Limits Music Festival.

Ever since his first Tour de France win in 1999, Armstrong had been hounded by accusations of cheating to gain the winning edge by using banned performance enhancing substances such as growth hormones, steroids, and blood transfusions. Even if the accusations were true, insiders insisted it really wasn't such a big deal since doping was common in cycling, a sport where a single tenth of a second made all the difference in the world.

But that was before Armstrong had ruined the lives and careers of others, lashing out while defending himself. The grains of evidence piled up, and continued to after he stopped racing. When Armstrong refused to testify in front of the US Anti-Doping Agency in 2012, he effectively admitted doing pretty much what he had been accused of. He was stripped of his seven Tour de France titles.

Lance came clean over the course of two nights on national television, beginning on January 17, 2013, when he confessed to doping and lying about it to TV personality Oprah Winfrey. The two personalities conducted the interview seated in a hotel suite at the Four Seasons in downtown Austin. Winfrey's OWN cable channel secured first rights to air the interview.

Some 28 million viewers in the United States and 190 other countries watched the once-mythic American hero, who overcame the impossible odds of beating cancer to become the champion of champions, tell America's most beloved television talk personality that it was all "one big lie." He injected drugs for an extra edge in all seven Tour de France races he won, he said. And he'd do it again to win.

He was a bicycle racer doing what everyone else had been doing, he reasoned. And now he wanted to come clean.

Maybe it was how he came off when Winfrey pointed out he'd destroyed lives and careers with his previous denials. Honest expressions of sorrow or contrition were not in his repertoire. It made the sting of deception a little harder for Lance true believers to take.

Austin's hero was not as advertised. Cancer survivors and the tens of millions with their Livestrong bracelets felt hoodwinked. Lance Armstrong was chastised. He was no longer the arrogant, smooth-talking prick who also happened to be an exceptionally talented racer.

That planned trail along the north bank of Lady Bird Lake, was that still the Lance Armstrong Bikeway? Mellow Johnny's, his downtown bicycle shop with all the Tour de France jerseys hanging on the walls above the tricked-out racing and off-road bikes, was that still a must-see for tourists? Where had all those images of Armstrong that had decorated the walls of several 24 Hour Fitness gyms around Austin gone?

Two weeks after Lance Armstrong's televised confession, Willie Nelson was interviewed on his bus, Honeysuckle Rose, parked outside of a dancehall called Nutty Jerry's near Winnie, on the edge of the East Texas rice prairie; he declared he was in Armstrong's corner.

"If it [doping] is a bad thing to do—and in some instances and with some age groups, it would be a bad thing—but I don't know any sport that's drug-free, from professional football to wrestling," Willie said. "Do you?" He took a long drag from a fat joint of premium marijuana bud, and slowly exhaled. "I know some of those old wrestlers who took better pain pills than you ever saw, because they went through a lot of pain. There's a lot of sports out there that depend on drugs to get them [participants] to the next big town."

If marijuana was considered a performance-enhancing drug, Willie Nelson was as much an abuser as Lance had been with whatever he was taking. Willie never took the stage straight and sober. "We oughta look at it like, 'Let's don't judge 'til you've walked in that man's shoes. Let's not tell him how to live or what to do,'" Willie said. "That's what we were all taught early in life. 'Judge not, lest you be judged.' I don't think any of us can afford to be judged too close or harshly. Who knows what brought everything on and why everything was like it was? I think BC, Billy Cooper [Willie's onetime driver], said it pretty good: 'It's my mouth and I'll haul coal in it if I want to.'

"I know one thing that comes to mind when all that happened," Nelson said. "I had an arm that I couldn't use. I hurt it really bad when I was playing golf. George Clooney told me about a doctor in Germany. I went to see him. He took blood out and recharged it with a lot of healing qualities, put it back in, and my arm got OK. It's about one hundred percent now. You just can't throw everything in one big bag and say, 'That's bad.'"

Willie and Lance were friends. "I've passed a couple emails back and forth, but he got real busy," Nelson said. "I didn't want to bother him."

Any advice offered?

He nodded and exhaled again.

"Fuck 'em."

Willie and Lance were giants, and both knew it. But Willie had one clear advantage, Lance Armstrong contended: time. "Our [life] curves are similar," he said. "But he's thirty, forty years faster. And it's probably why he can appreciate that [career] arc, look back and go, 'All right.' He's genuine." Armstrong wished he could speed up his sentence for lying and betrayal and be as old as Willie was, be able to look back on it all.

"There's no doubt over time people will soften to this thing [admitting to cheating and lying]. Some already have. This was such a bad time. Maybe we shouldn't even call it a bad time. It was just a time. The set of circumstances were so . . . it was the perfect storm."

The rise and fall of Lance Armstrong demonstrated how easy it was to buy into the hero myth, no matter how uncool and unheroic the reality might have really been.

Austin's harsh reaction came with the territory. It had been mad love when he was the hometown champion. "On the flip side of that, that's why the city is pissed," he said. "Maybe partly pissed, partly disappointed, partly upset, partly confused—a lot of things. I was their guy."

Lance remained a man about town, when he was in town. He appeared in the 2016 film mockumentary *Tour De Pharmacy*, playing himself, and making a joke of confessing to doping.

He reemerged in the public eye hosting "The Forward Podcast with Lance Armstrong," interviewing friends and familiars like University of Texas football coach Mack Brown, the singer Seal, politicians Wendy Davis and Rahm Emanuel, tennis star Chris Evert, football players Ricky Williams and Bo Jackson, and author Malcolm Gladwell, conducting some interviews in his wine cellar.

Other than strategizing during a race, Armstrong never had to be creative to be who he was until now. A podcast worked like radio: fill up a fixed amount of airtime. Heavy friends were cool, but if engaging conversation wasn't part of the hang, the audience tuned out, no matter who you once were. Armstrong got especially engaged whenever talking about life after careers with retired athletes. Going low-tech with a podcast with no hype or backup was part of the redemption process.

Armstrong made clear he could have just as easily ducked out, gone somewhere else, but he stayed—at least part of the year. Aspen is extremely pleasant in the summer. "Austin is my city," he said. "I had a family here. I lived here full-time. I loved coming back here. I talked about Austin all the time, brought the team here. This was home."

Austin felt so much like home, that when asked about changes in the city, he hesitated before offering, "It's slipping." The usual suspects were cited. Cost of living. Traffic. Undersized infrastructure. Not enough bicycle transportation.

"Austin's slipping," he said softly.

⊙ ⊙ ⊙

Armstrong was hardly the only hip local to fall from grace. The Austin film community was rocked in 2017 by charges of sexual predation and intimidation leveled at Devin Faraci, who wrote content for the Alamo Drafthouse, and at Harry Knowles, who was dismissed from Fantastic Fest after being accused of making crude sexual remarks to women. Criticism was directed at Alamo founder Tim League, who decided to give Faraci a second chance without informing Alamo staff. Some younger staffers told League he was keeping deadbeats and miscreants on the payroll out of loyalty; he needed to clear out the deadwood.

Laid-back, small big city Austin had added an energetic, sometimes overly aggressive overlay when it grew large. Former slackers settled into straight gigs with six-figure incomes and weren't apologizing. Any lingering hint of casual was helped along by a torrid, humid climate that intimidated out-of-town suits unaccustomed to the way "bidness" gets done locally. And yet business somehow got done.

Exponential growth stretched existing infrastructure to the point of bursting at the seams, at least by American standards. Construction no longer kept pace with development. Sprawl pushed farther out from the city center. The seven miles of Interstate 35 that ran through Austin was the most congested highway in Texas, costing drivers close to one million hours of delay annually at a price pegged at $201 million.

Richard Florida, the urban theorist who focused on Austin in his first writings about the creative class and creative cities, sounded a warning. Between 2000 and 2014, the size of Austin's creative class remained static at 34 percent of the population. In 2000, that was good enough for Austin to rank number four behind San Jose, Washington, DC, and Boston in metro areas with the largest percentage of creative class workers. By 2014, so many cities had embraced the idea of having a creative class that Austin dropped to number ten.

Florida questioned his own original thesis with the book *The New Urban Crisis: How Our Cities Are Increasing Inequality, Deepening Segregation, and Failing the Middle Class—and What We Can Do about It* (2017). Creatives brought their own baggage.

And yet cool kids, older retirees, second-home buyers, speculators, and rapidly growing Asian and Indian immigrant communities continued moving in. In 2012, Asians composed 6.3 percent of the city's population, the highest percentage of Asians in Texas, and the tenth-highest percentage of Asian Americans nationally. Asian Americans would soon surpass African Americans in numbers in Austin, which was already a minority-majority city. Anglos lost their majority status in 2005 and were not expected to regain that majority in the coming decades. Austin was turning into a singles and couples city. From 1970 to 2000, the percentage of families with children living in the city dropped from 32 percent to less than 14 percent.

Surrounding suburbs with cheaper homes and theoretically better schools were the new family hubs. Austin's metropolitan area population doubled in twenty years, surpassing two million in 2015.

Music begat film begat food begat high tech, and whatever Austin was was directly tied to the big/small city circa 1970, when people began arriving in significant numbers for all the wrong/right reasons. They had a band. They were artists, dancers, and filmmakers needing a low-hassle, warm weather respite that wasn't like anywhere else in Texas, or anywhere in the United States, really, so they could work out their ideas. Money wasn't supposed to be the object. That was the realm of realtors, car dealers, bankers, lawyers, and politicians. Something new and different was the aim.

But without much oversight or grand vision, as cool built upon cool built upon cool, it eventually grew into a commodity unto itself, and money did become the object. Austin was a great place to live, to go to school, to retire, to be an entrepreneur—if you could afford it. The old and new versions clashed.

The Austin City Limits Festival expanded to a two-weekend affair in 2012, extending to a full month C3's takeover of Zilker Park to prepare and teardown, including the reseeding of the "great lawn" as it was now called. Residents living near the park complained of festival fatigue and demanded the city return the space to its original intended use as a public park.

Residents of the nearby Bouldin Creek neighborhood behind Terry Black's Barbecue, a business on Barton Springs Road across the street from the Palmer Center, complained of being choked by smoke coming from Black's barbecue pits. Sacrilege! When BBQ is outlawed, only outlaws will have BBQ.

The Westin, a high-end high rise chain hotel at Fifth and San Jacinto Streets that advertised its proximity to the night life of Sixth Street, sued an open-air club on nearby Sixth Street for playing electronica music late into night. The beats bugged the guests.

The artist in twenty-first century Austin had to be some kind of entrepreneur, or have a hustle. Unless oil and gas royalties, a trust fund, or outside money were part of the portfolio, being an Austin artist in the second decade of the twenty-first century just cost too damn much. Slackers had been priced out of the city.

A day didn't pass that something didn't happen to make even the most romantic local wonder if Austin had choked on its own success. Anyone sitting in the darkened Marchesa Theater in 2015, watching *Outlaw Blues*, the Peter Fonda directed B movie filmed in Austin in 1977, could feel it. The plot was corny and predictable, but the scenery was awe-inspiring. The

Warehouse District between Sixth Street and the river really looked like a warehouse district with real warehouses. Downtown was wide-open, airy, and full of light. The hills west of town had yet to be fully occupied. Austin looked stunningly pristine and inviting. Looking back made contemporary Austin seem like a theme park for the rich.

The Rainey Street neighborhood, a historic blue-collar residential district one block west of Interstate 35 near the banks of Lady Bird Lake downtown, flipped all at once in the late nineties, after residents voted to sell out to developers en masse. Chain Drive, a gay leather bar, made the first incursion into the neighborhood of simple two-bedroom frame houses. Soon almost every structure on the street was a bar or restaurant, most catering to a young, hard-drinking crowd. High-rise apartments and condos rose to the south by the lake. At the north end of Rainey was the 16-story, 360-room Van Zandt Hotel, promoted as "a refined riff on Austin's world-famous music scene," complete with its own music and social media director. It was the kind of high-toned place that its alleged namesake inspiration, the late singer-songwriter Townes Van Zandt, would've never stayed in, unless somebody else was picking up the tab.

The Hotel Van Zandt was across the street from a block-long compound on Red River Street south of Cesar Chavez Boulevard, at the top of the Rainey Street neighborhood, home of the G'Raj Mahal Indian food trailer when the bar scene got hopping. For at least forty years, the compound had been alternately known as Red River Motors or Washington Motors, the used car lot/car repair businesses of Doug Breeding and Artie Osborn, which amounted to a collection of cars and buses in various states of repair and disrepair in the backyard and alleyway in the back of three frame houses. Breeding and Osborn liked to sell cheap rides found at auctions to folks on a limited budget. That meant musicians—including the real Townes Van Zandt—along with mechanics, lost young people, and the crusty ne'er do wells who frequented Red River. (Van Zandt had to be eighty-sixed from the premises for reasons Osborn would not go into.)

Singer Lou Ann Barton, bassist Speedy Sparks, and teen rockers Will and Charlie Sexton had lived at Red River. The place achieved some kind of fame being featured in the 1980 film *Roadie*. Lead character Travis Redfish's modified Cadillac wrecker truck from the film became part of the evolving yard art. Red River also got a cameo on MTV's *Cutting Edge* program, featuring new music talent back in the mideighties. While showing host Peter Zaremba around the premises, musician Joe "King" Carrasco prophetically declared of the compound, "This is the last bastion of Austin soul, the final holdout of what Austin's all about. If this place ever goes, then Austin's gone."

The hippies were gone from Red River by the time the Hotel Van Zandt went up.

Like many of younger hipsters who'd just arrived in Austin, some of the wayward musicians, mechanics, and wanderers of Red River moved a few miles east, to a new compound owned by Artie Osborn on Hergotz Street in the largely Mexican American neighborhood of Montopolis.

"Is Austin still weird?" Red Wassenich rhetorically asked himself. "Yes. Arguably less so, but in doing the new edition of my book, I had to go out looking and it's still there." Many of the weird sites cited in the first edition of Wassenich's book *Keep Austin Weird: A Guide to the Odd Side of Town* had bit the dust. Spamarama, the beloved party/festival dedicated to the potted meat product, which enjoyed a run from 1978 to 2007, was one victim; Gerry Van King, the bass-thumping King of Sixth Street, retired; Leslie Cochran, the cross-dressing street celeb, passed away.

Wassenich's catchphrase had been codified into an annual music festival and 5K run. "Money changes everything," he said. "And Austin's getting too wealthy for eccentrics to slack successfully like they used to, but it's still there, especially in people's attitude." Age determined reactions. "In doing my [revised] book I came to the conclusion that old-timers think Austin's no longer weird; newcomers do, and love it."

Joe Bryson, whose Inner Sanctum Record Store west of the University of Texas campus had been Austin's iconic indie record shop in the seventies into the eighties, transitioned seamlessly from Inner Sanctum Joe to Condo Joe, realtor. Selling condominiums was like selling records, he said, only with a whole lot more zeros attached to the number at the end of each transaction.

Bryson took the leap in 1985, two years after his record merchant career ended. He couldn't open another record shop. John Kunz and Waterloo Records had filled that void and were doing quite well. "Life is too expensive now to do what I did back then," Bryson said. "The rent at Inner Sanctum started at eight hundred dollars a month and never went above twelve hundred a month in the thirteen plus years I owned and ran the store. No way that happens now. You could eat lunch at the Stallion or Scholz Garten or the Chuck Wagon on campus for a buck. I'm not sure how beer was paid for, but it always seemed like there was plenty to go around. It was no big deal to go to people's homes and share dinners.

"These days it takes money to live and eat. You have to make a decent living to afford to live here. For creatives, we are killing the goose that laid the proverbial golden egg. This is a creative town, but you have to be a successful creative to live here. Since most creatives are not successful starting off, that makes it difficult for them to stay while they are developing their audience. It's a real barrier. The concept of a 'starving artist' is real, but there has to be some other source of support through family, friends, or a job, to just keep the artist going."

Austin at its core still had the friendly vibe and relaxed style that drew him there, Condo Joe Bryson said. "Yeah, we have a lot of outside people making it different, but I think this city affects them more than they affect us. There's still an openness and appreciation of the good life that ties us all here."

⊚ ⊚ ⊚

If money was the measure, the Austin brand fetched a very good price.

Whole Foods Market, the elder of cool Austin food brands, fetched $13.7 billion when Amazon, the largest online retailer in the United States, bought the grocer in 2017. The purchase was Amazon's biggest to date, and effectively disrupted the entire retail grocery sector.

Hotelier Andre Balazs, known in hospitality circles as the king of the "antihotel," scooped up 51 percent of hotelier Liz Lambert's Bunkhouse Group for an undisclosed sum, estimated in the tens of millions.

In 2017, Tito Beveridge landed on the Forbes 400 list of the richest people in America. His handmade vodka distillery had made him worth an estimated $2.5 billion.

Deep Eddy Vodka, one of several craft liquor startups in the Austin area following in the footsteps of Tito's Vodka, was bought by Heaven Hill distillers of Kentucky. The five-year-old brand had doubled in volume annually since it was launched, making it an attractive prospect. Analysts estimated the purchase price between $165 and $300 million.

No local buyout was quite as sweet as McCormick & Company spice purveyors' purchase of Stubb's BBQ sauce for $100 million cash. What began as C. B. Stubblefield's one-man barbecue operation in Lubbock had grown into a grocery shelf staple and restaurant condiment. Oddly the depiction of Stubblefield on the labels of his barbecue sauces evolved over the years since his death in 1995 into kind of a genteel Uncle Ben character who bore vague resemblance to the real person.

For all the big money pouring in, the musicians who poured the foundation of Austin's creative sector scrambled to make ends meet.

A 233-page city-commissioned survey of 1,900 musicians issued in June

2015 concluded the Live Music Capital of the World was close to a permanent fade. Clubs featuring music had a tough time with escalating leases and a declining customer base. Half the musicians living in Austin earned less than $25,000 annually, barely above the poverty line. Most subsidized their music habit with outside jobs and income.

Fortunately, music and musicians were considered important enough to justify support infrastructure. Musicians had been helping each other get clean and sober ever since Stevie Ray Vaughan rehabbed and encouraged others to do the same in the mideighties. In the aughts and teens, powers in charge attempted to address personal and professional challenges musicians faced through organizations, panels, committees, surveys, studies, roundtables, and initiatives.

Sims Ellison of the band Pariah, who took his life in 1995 after Geffen Records dropped the band's recording contract, inspired the SIMS Foundation, established to provide mental health and addiction recovery services to musicians. Robin Shivers, a philanthropist and manager of singer-songwriter Troy Campbell, spearheaded the push to establish HAAM—the Health Alliance for Austin Musicians—in 2005 to make health care accessible for low-income uninsured working musicians. Tech executives in Austin established the nonprofit Black Fret Foundation. A pool of more than a thousand art patrons contributed $1,500 each, and awarded multiple $10,000 grants to music artists to play locally and to tour.

The music division of the City of Austin's economic development department worked with the private sector and nonprofits to create opportunities for musicians and to referee conflicts between the music community and the general population. The number of full-time residents living downtown had swelled from four thousand in 2000 to more than ten thousand in 2015, a direct result of Mayor Kirk Watson's Smart City initiative to increase density in the central city to stem sprawl, a policy that succeeding mayor Will Wynn embraced. As the downtown population grew, so did noise complaints about loud music. The city responded by creating the Music Venue Assistance Program to help clubs deal with sound issues experienced by their new neighbors.

Eventually the studies, panels, surveys, and expert opinions reached the same conclusion: rapid growth and an unprecedented influx of outside money had rendered Austin unaffordable for the creative types that had given the city its identity. Half of Austin's musicians were eligible for publicly subsidized housing, if only such housing existed.

"You can't pay your bills with cool," said Josh Logan, front man for local rock band the Blind Pets. After rent for his duplex was jacked up from $1,050 a month to $2,000, he decided he'd tour for the following year and live in his van.

Ironically, the starving writer didn't necessarily have to dream of New York anymore. The Michener Center, the Texas Book Festival, and *Texas Monthly* magazine opened Austin to the literary world. "It created this two-way street," Steve Harrigan said. "People would come down here and we'd go up there, up there meaning New York. It helped put Austin on the map, and didn't take away from us writing about Texas. The phrase Texas writer is so . . . you want to be more than that, even if Texas is what you write about. We had to make sense of where we were and how we could succeed without being at the center of the universe.

"It's still a struggle. It's still hard to break through that barrier. On the other hand, I don't want to have to move. I never did. It's a struggle to make a living by writing. Very few people can do it. For me, it's the only thing I can do. I can't play an instrument. Making a living is one thing. Being part of a thriving community is another."

Austin was the right place at the right time for Steve Harrigan. "Austin was alive," he recalled about experiencing the city for the first time. "Had I gone somewhere else, New York, LA, Paris, I probably would have felt that thrill of being in a place that seemed to be happening, having a pulse. But there was a modesty about Austin that conformed to my own ambitions. Even though my ambitions were Titanic in some ways, they were also scaled to a city of this size and energy.

"Not to say I'm a slacker," he said. "But I'm not competitive. I guess that's the thing. People who live here are not trying to outdo each other, or outflank each other."

Harrigan said he had to keep reminding himself about community, especially since he was in the business of teaching at the Michener Center. "It's possible to be envious at the breaks some of the younger people have and the avenues they have that weren't open to you, but it's also very satisfying, the success they're having, that's a continuum, that they really are part of this community. It feels like the new crop coming up."

Michener fellows such as Dominic Smith, Fiona McFarland, Smith Henderson, Philipp Meyer, and Jake Silverstein didn't just learn about writing. They learned about writing from this particular place. "We've helped pass on that sense of community," Harrigan said. "You have to filter out the elements of self-congratulation and the self-justification, but Austin is fairly special that way. It's changed in that what used to be accessible to everybody is now institutions with gatekeepers, like *Texas Monthly*, for instance. You can't walk in and say, 'I'd like to write this story for you.'"

Harrigan complained about the traffic like everyone else, but the complaint was tempered. "It still feels like, if there's someone you really want to get it know, that's still doable," he said. "You can meet people. You can hang out with people. There's still a berserk creative energy. It's a little more codified. It's a little more stratified."

Still, some aspects of modern Austin left him flummoxed. "There are all these conferences with all these people walking around with badges," he said. "And these fancy restaurants—it's mysterious to me. Where is all this money is coming from? Who are these people? Where are they getting their money? Why are they wasting it here?"

He more or less liked what he saw. "It was a good writing town then. It's better now. It's more connected to the rest of the world. It feels less insular, less cut off. But it still has the same sense of common purpose, friendliness, and accessibility that it did then."

Too much money and too many people weren't the only elements threatening to smother the creative spark. Not enough water was becoming a constant. There simply wasn't enough of it. The regional water supply came mostly from a string of six dammed-up stretches of the Colorado River upstream of the city. The dams and the lakes they created were part of a rural electrification and flood control project pushed by area congressman Lyndon B. Johnson in the thirties and forties.

For seventy-five years the dams worked as intended, passing water through during flood events and conserving water in reservoirs during dry spells, otherwise creating recreation opportunities around what was called the Highland Lakes. An extended drought that peaked in 2011 pulled nearby lake levels down to 30 percent capacity, some of the lowest levels since the dams were constructed. Two more years of drought would have spelled disaster. Without water, Austin couldn't grow, or even subsist, for that matter.

Climatologists forecast much drier conditions in the Austin area through the end of the twenty-first century. The Chihuahuan Desert is creeping toward Austin's doorstep. Declining availability put limits on watering landscapes and greenery, and threatened the water-dependent, chip-making sector of the city's high tech community. Rich folks residing in Old West Austin, including the governor of Texas, Greg Abbott, got around water restrictions imposed by the city of Austin by drilling their own water wells so they could water their lawns all they wanted, even though such drilling compounded the water shortage.

The end of the Anything Goes era was nigh. Viability of place was at risk. Then, just when the future appeared darkest, the rains came. And somehow, some way, the old outsider alternative Austin attitude managed to poke through the glitz and glam frequently enough to suggest the vibe remained.

Gaming guru Richard Garriott proposed a self-financed elevated rapid transit system in and around the University of Texas campus to help alleviate Austin traffic gridlock. SXSW managing director Roland Swenson rejiggered the Bowie Street sign outside his office to read "David Bowie Street" to honor the iconoclastic rock star upon his death.

April Ritzenthaler of Texas Rollergirls insisted the alternative Austin that had been critical in getting women's roller derby going was still there, even though it wasn't as easy to find. "The spontaneity is gone," she said in 2015. "There is just so much shit going on all the time, and traffic is terrible. You have to negotiate your day. It used to be, someone would call you up and say 'Hey, let's go meet over here!' 'Yeah, sure!' You can't do that anymore. And you have to factor in not being twentysomething. The older you get, the less tolerant you are. You can't be as relaxed as you used to. You can't be half-assed anymore."

South Austin matured as the neighborhood of choice for young and cool-focused newcomers. Everybody still wanted to go south to park their cars so they could promenade South Congress's spacious sidewalks and visit its eclectic shops and socialize in its bars, restaurants, and clubs.

In 2015, the South Congress Hotel opened on the site previously occupied by the Most Famous Food Trailer Park in America. Rooms started at $350 a night. Three restaurants operated on premises. One was a very small sushi bar created by Paul Qui that carried the reputation as the most expensive restaurant in the city.

Steve Wertheimer admitted turnover and upscaling along South Congress Avenue made him miss the Just Guns store down the block. "We don't own it like we used to."

He told the daily newspaper in 2017: "I hear a sucking sound every day with the soul being slowly drained out of this area. The local folks, who made this street so attractive by breathing new life back in the area, are having a difficult time remaining here."

Had success spoiled South Congress? "It kind of has," Liz Lambert said with a slight wince. "There are still little refuges, like the San Jose, like Jo's, the Continental Club, places like Bird's (barber shop) that are so Austin-driven, even if they've only been here for a few years, like the Magnolia and

Güero's. I live in the neighborhood. I don't like traffic. I don't like driving through. But I still think it's a special place."

She sounded like a local with some added perspective.

"Outsiders and freaks are really important to the DNA of Austin," she said. "I don't know what you do, but you can't price those people out. The trick is, can the creative class afford to live in Austin? That's why people go to places like Marfa, which is even getting expensive. I'm curious what's going to happen in Detroit. Suddenly it's affordable."

What Liz Lambert had pulled off twenty years before couldn't be done now, she acknowledged. "I couldn't afford to buy this property on South Congress. This was everything coming together in a perfect storm. Who knew?"

In 2017, Uncommon Objects, one of the cornerstones of the South Congress revival since it opened in 1991, relocated farther south to Fortview Road to cluster with other businesses forced to move away from South Congress by higher rents—Vulcan Video, End of an Ear, and Hill Country Weavers. Uncommon Objects manager Van Harrison didn't bother fighting the inevitable. "It's a natural evolution of the neighborhood. These things happen."

"I can't believe the change in such a short time," Liz Lambert said. "I remember picking up the phone and calling Steve Wertheimer and saying, 'Steve, there are cars on South Congress! People are parked on South Congress!' I was so excited." Lambert paused and exhaled slowly. "It wasn't that long ago."

The alternative mainstreamed. Outsiders turned into insiders. The creative class became part of the larger community. "On the one hand, there is something in the water," filmmaker and animator Mike Judge said. "People in this line of work come to Austin. On the other, I didn't want to be away from my kids. If I lived in Albuquerque or some remote place, it might be a little weird to make movies, because I might be the only one doing it. It's nice to know other people in Austin who are doing it too, so if you tell your kid's schoolteacher what you do, she's not shocked, or she doesn't think you're lying."

Community remained a defining difference, Rick Linklater insisted. "It's why BookPeople is still around and Waterloo Records is still around: because Austin has a population that gives a shit, that's literate, searching, cool, and cares about community. They would rather go to a screening and be around people, making an outing, have conversations with people in the lobby, see an old friend—that all means something.

"Austin was ready for this. It just hadn't been available, what the film society did. Subsequently, what South By has done with their film festival, the Austin Film Festival, all these other festivals—Austin was ready to be a film town, too. It just didn't have the mechanism. But it was sitting there waiting. Just like it was ready to be a high tech town. It's always been a music town. It was ready. It just needed someone to make that available."

The Austin Film Society, the Alamo Drafthouse, Fantastic Fest, and Rick Linklater were of a kind. "We're all in it together," Linklater said.

He mocked the moaners who inevitably showed up to complain how much better Austin used to be. "*Oh, the eighties in Austin! Rents were so cheap. I was on the guest list at every show. I never paid cover,*" he said, feigning dreamy remembrance. That part of old Austin Linklater liked. It was the other reality of that place and time he had no nostalgia for. "If you were ambitious or wanted something to happen, it wasn't gonna happen," he said. "It was so tough just getting something going. There wasn't much. It was kind of volatile too. It felt like it could go away at any second. I think that's how music people felt: 'Hey, we're a band, but if we don't get that deal, we're gonna go poof!'"

Rick Linklater, the indie filmmakers' indie filmmaker, and the Austin Film Society were the establishment now. "There are cool funky film organizations that look at us as the behemoth," he said. "They're showing outdoor films, they're riding their bikes. We're The Man. That's what you get when you're a thirty year organization. A rising tide lifts all boats: that's how we've approached it. Austin's too small. We're too small a community to be petty about anything. We're supportive of each other.

"Cut back to 1990. You couldn't be a filmmaker in town [without me knowing you]. Now, there's a ton of young filmmakers I've never met. There's so much going on that I don't pretend to know. I don't have my finger on the pulse." He had his finger on a camera, and he wasn't letting go.

◉ ◉ ◉

Leave it to a kid to straighten it all out.

Nineteen-year old Joanna Wu bounced into Mozart's coffee house with a spring in her step, practically crackling with energy. It was her only week off between the end of summer school and the start of fall classes at the University of Texas, and she was determined to make the most of it.

Wu might have been born and raised in Austin, but she didn't really know Austin. "I grew up in Northwest Austin, the suburb area near Round Rock," she explained. "I didn't really experience Austin the way people know it as. All the essentials and all my friends were nearby. There wasn't much need to go downtown." If the family went out to eat, it wasn't to some farm-to-table bistro in East Austin. Dining out was Olive Garden or maybe a favor-

Joanna Wu taking a break while pondering med school and/or film school.
(Photo by Joe Nick Patoski.)

ite Chinese restaurant that reminded her father, a computer programmer for IBM, and her mother, a microbiology research assistant at the University of Texas, of their hometowns in southeastern China. A good chunk of her leisure time was spent watching television or going to the movies. She was a big fan of the sitcom *Friends* and *West Wing*.

The March after she turned sixteen, Joanna Wu's Austin view expanded considerably. She'd reached the minimum age to be eligible to volunteer for South by Southwest. Three thousand young people would be accepted for positions where they'd work for free, once again affirming the appeal of the alternative Austin business model. In exchange, the volunteers had a close up view of SXSW craziness.

"It was an extreme way of seeing it," Wu said. "That week I was downtown, hanging out, walking around, experiencing the buzz that Austin has.

It was awesome. I loved it. It was exciting. I know South By is the big event, but no matter when you are here, there's local bands everywhere. People are walking down Sixth Street. Austin is a very open, kind city. You can have a conversation with someone waiting in line or just walking down the street.

"I grew up in a conservative family. Downtown Austin is not very conservative by any means. So it's a new experience for me, like that. There are a lot more people out, chilling, than where I grew up."

For SXSW 2013, Wu was an audio-visual tech for interactive and film conference panels. "I'd hear people talk about their projects, learned about films, saw a couple of them. I wanted to learn more." She got the bug.

The SXSW volunteer gig led to an unpaid summer internship in 2014 at Arts + Labor, the film production company for the music documentary *Sir Doug and the Genuine Texas Cosmic Groove* (2015). Three years of volunteering at SXSW and her Arts + Labor stint led Wu to add film school to her long-term educational goals, which already included med school. "I like being able to help people in their greatest moment of need," she said of the medical path. "You can do something about it."

Film's appeal was its complexity. "I loved watching behind the scenes clips of *Friends* on YouTube—they go through everything, all the aspects, props, editing, Foley artists, every little detail. I thought it was fascinating how they made everything fit together. That whole mesh of crap—somehow it all fits. The logic part of my mind wants to give that a shot, see how it works. And being able to tell a story."

So, medical doctor or film director? "I could go either way." She had the chops to do both.

Wu loved telling out of town friends about Austin. "Food's great. Music's great. Everything's great. Except the traffic and public transit are terrible. That's my two points. That's it."

SXSW opened up new worlds to her, but surprisingly music was not one of them. "I'm not the biggest music fan," she said, almost as a confession. Wait a minute. Didn't everyone love music in Austin? "Honestly, I don't go out of my way to hear it, but I'll hear it," she said. How could she *not* hear it? "It's everywhere." But she had her limits. "During the music part of SXSW, I go home. There are too many people. I'm tired. It's the end of the week."

OK, so Joanna Wu wasn't a party person. Academics came first and that wasn't going to change. But still, Austin was the only place for her to be.

"Aren't we trying to make people go away because there's too many people?" she laughed. "You know the saying, 'Come and visit Austin, but I hear

Dallas and Houston are great.' Austin is very different from the rest of Texas. Austin's got everything. There is always something going on. Music to hear, food to eat, an abundance of really smart people. Everyone's here."

Chasing pre-med and film degrees at the same time was challenging. Doing that while using her free time to hang out with friends, party, go to Barton Springs, and even go and listen to music now and then—that was her Austin. This was her place now, just as it had been for others before her, people who were outsiders, who thought outside the box.

The outsiders continued pouring in, even as an increasing number of old-timers decided to relocate.

Austin's cool, all right. But you should've been here ten years ago.

12
On the Road Again

⊙ ⊙ ⊙

It had been close to two years since I had heard Willie Nelson and Family in concert, and this show on April 22, 2017, a week before Willie's eighty-fourth birthday, was close to where I lived. "Better see him now," I told myself. It's easy to take Willie for granted when you've become pretty well convinced he will go on forever.

He had been a constant in my life since I'd hit Austin in 1973, as well as a childhood memory from the early sixties, vaguely recalled as an impressionable Saturday evening talking head on KFJZ-TV, Lively Eleven, pitching the acts who would be playing the Cowtown Jamboree at Panther Hall later that night.

So I trekked to the Whitewater Amphitheater on the Guadalupe River about fifty-five miles from downtown Austin.

A late April cold front brought chilly winds and lowered evening temperatures into the fifties. The setting was fairly bucolic, with giant shade trees and the river running behind the giant stage. The amphitheater and its balconies and elevated seating areas were filled to capacity with contemporary variations of rednecks, mostly, and hippies. Beer flowed prodigiously. The scent of high-quality weed could be detected now and then, but no cloud hovered above the stage like it did whenever the band played the Fillmore in San Francisco. Several dozen Comal County sheriff's deputies, firemen, and EMS personnel on hand for the concert might have had something to do with it.

Like Austin, so much had changed about Willie since I'd first seen the family band play on a flatbed trailer to showcase the new 1974 models at McMorris Ford, a site now occupied by GSD&M, the biggest ad agency in the Southwest.

The bubble had grown tighter around him. Gates Moore drove Honeysuckle Rose next to the stage while the opening act, Kasey Musgraves, finished her set. Willie's spirited take-charge wife Annie functioned as manager and gatekeeper, letting in a radio disc jockey to record a promotional bit with Willie about his latest album God's Problem Child, but forgoing the usual meet-and-greet.

Sister Bobbie was on board. So were daughters Paula and Amy, and youngest son Micah. Larry Gorham, the Hell's Angel who was Willie's longtime bodyguard, now white-haired and reserved, stood near the bus waiting to escort his boss to the stage. Tuning Tom, keeper of Willie's battered Martin guitar Trigger, prowled the backline, making sure everything was in place and in tune while Budrock the Illuminator, longtime lighting director Buddy Prewitt, visited with his daughters.

Paul English, Willie's drummer and lifelong sidekick and partner in crime, dressed in black, circulated among the small crowd clustered outside the bus. Paul had been dealing with memory issues, and his once-menacing presence seemed benign, almost gentle. Paul's younger brother Billy handled most of the drumming responsibilities, while Paul worked shakers and rhythm instruments, assisted by Micah Nelson.

Kevin Smith, the new boy who'd joined the band three years earlier following the death of longtime bassist Bee Spears, sat in a hospitality trailer with his wife, Justine, his daughter, and a friend, showing photographs of a recent show at the Houston Rodeo, a sellout performance in the seventy thousand capacity NRG Stadium.

Mickey Raphael, a Willie Family member since those McMorris Ford days, materialized three minutes before taking the stage, dressed in black like Paul.

Gates Moore pulled the bus even closer to the side of the stage to deposit Willie into the green room behind the stage.

With the band in place and hitting their notes, Willie materialized from the back of the stage to the roar of the crowd. A large cowboy hat covered his gray pigtailed head. The cuffs of his mom jeans were stuffed inside his black boots. Whether it was the outsized hat, the outsized stage he stood on, distance, perspective, or time, he looked diminutive, smaller than life, not larger, like Wee Willie Nelson, his old radio disc jockey handle.

He did not engage in his usual ritual of making eye contact with as many members of the audience as he could. Instead, it was one strum, two strums, three strums, four strums on his guitar Trigger, marking the beginning of "Whiskey River," the song that opened every show. With Mickey's wailing harmonica joining the guitar, Willie started singing, "Whiskey River take my mind." Only, he was talking his way through the lyrics as much as he was singing them.

He shook his right strumming hand, as if it was cramping up, or maybe something was wrong with the guitar. Was Trigger out of tune? Willie shifted into the opening guitar line of "Still Is Still Moving," his nineties-era anthem to roadwork and life its ownself.

It went no further. Willie put down his guitar before singing a word of the song, left the stage, and went to the bus. His son Micah left the stage, following behind him. Kevin Smith keyed on Bobbie Nelson, leading the rest of the band through an instrumental interlude. And another. And a third instrumental. No one from the band said anything, but rather soldiered on, as if they'd gone through this drill before.

Jody Denberg, the radio disc jockey who had interviewed Willie on the bus about his new album before the show, stood by the side of the stage, visibly nervous. "What's going on?" he asked no one in particular. Everyone was wondering the same thing.

Had Willie played his last song? Were we the ones to bear witness?

Heart attack? Carpal tunnel redux? Too cold and windy? Guitar out of tune because of the chill? A cranky eighty-three-year-old man in no mood to play?

My stomach felt queasy. I felt scared, sad. I thought I was there just to have a good time and see Willie.

During the third instrumental, ten minutes in, as other heads in the gaggle on the side of the stage glanced back toward the bus, wondering what was up, Willie reappeared onstage.

He plowed right into "Good Hearted Woman," talking his way through the song, and segued into "Mamas (Don't Let Your Babies Grow Up To Be Cowboys)." He was back in the pocket, shouting the word "Mamas" forcefully enough, and then flailing his right arm, with his hand sort of to his ear, to urge the crowd to fill in the rest of the words—which they dutifully did. The wave was short and to the point. He knew the reaction that was coming. It worked.

The rendition of Hank Williams' "Rolling in My Sweet Baby's Arms" was perfunctory.

Then came "Nuages," the Django Reinhart instrumental. From the first lines, picked out on individual strings, followed by full-body strums, Willie flashed command and chops with certitude. The strums were accompanied by more hand shaking, as if he was having trouble making chords and holding the guitar pick. But he was Willie again, badass on fire.

Nothing dramatic or newsworthy happened that night. It turned out to be another Willie Nelson show, the same as ever since before he got to Austin. He played "Whiskey River" a second time because he was Willie and he could do that, and none of the five thousand in attendance much cared he was repeating himself.

He and the Family finished the set joined by daughters Paula and Amy onstage, closing with his paean to cannabis, "Roll Me Up and Smoke Me When I Die." The crowd roared their appreciation and gave him a standing ovation. Willie walked along the front of the stage making eye contact like he usually did at the start of a show, and shook hands with fans. The band did not play an encore. Instead, Willie threw out a few bandanas, signed autographs for a couple on the front row, waved good-bye, and that was that. Honeysuckle Rose pulled out of the venue before most of the audience had made it to the parking lot. There was a show to play in Lubbock the next evening.

Source Notes

Articles

1. Seat of Future Empire, Home of the Armadillo

"Tower of Light: When Electricity Was New, People Used It to Mimic the Moon" by
   Megan Garber, *The Atlantic*, March 6, 2013.
"Austin's Moon Towers, Beyond 'Dazed and Confused'" by Mark Oppenheimer, *New
   York Times*, February 13, 2014.

2. City of the Violet Crown, the Gay Place

"Billy Lee" by Al Reinert, *Texas Monthly*, February 1979.
"Return to the Gay Place" by Jan Reid, *Texas Monthly*, March 2001.
"Notes on Mad Dogs: On Being Young, Talented, and Slightly Insane in Old Austin"
   by Clay Smith, *Austin Chronicle*, January 26, 2001.
"Who Needs Breasts, Anyway?" by Molly Ivins, *Time*, February 10, 2002.
"Salon of the West Dobie, Bedichek, and Webb: A Friendship to Stand the Test of
   Time" by Steve Moore, *Austin Chronicle*, July 4, 2003.
"Molly Ivins, Columnist, Dies at 62" by Katharine Q. Seelye, *New York Times*, February
   1, 2007.
"I Was an A-List Writer of B-List Productions: Reflections on a Career Writing Made-
   for-TV Movies" by Stephen Harrigan, *Slate*, July 11, 2012.
"Why Indie Bookstores Are On the Rise Again: Borders and B&N Tried to Compete
   with Amazon, and Failed. Independent Stores Can't Even Try—Nor Do They Have
   To" by Zachary Karabell, *Slate*, September 9, 2014.
"Reading American Cities: Books about Austin" by Michael Barrett, *The Guardian*, September 4, 2015.

3. Willie Nelson in Groover's Paradise

"Uncle Zeke's Rock Emporium" by Chet Flippo, *Rolling Stone*, October 12, 1972.
"Viva Tex Mex . . . Viva MD 20/20 . . . Viva Freddy Fender!" by Joe Nick Patoski, *Zoo
   World*, June 1974.
"Willie Nelson: The Emperor of Austin" by Joe Nick Patoski, *Zoo World*, July 1974.
"Tornado Warnings from Texas" by Joe Nick Patoski, *Zoo World*, September 1974.
"Armadillo World Headquarters: Uptown at the 'Dillo'" by Joe Nick Patoski, *Zoo World*,
   September 1974.
"Blaze Foley" by Michael Allison, *Austin Songwriter*, undated.

"Feeding the Fish: An Oral History of the Butthole Surfers" by John Morthland and Joe Nick Patoski, *Spin*, November 1996.

"A Walking Contradiction: The Legend of Blaze Foley" by Lee Nichols, *Austin Chronicle*, December 24, 1999.

"Ruling the Roost: The Live Music Capital's Notorious Captain of Industry" by Andy Langer, *Austin Chronicle*, June 1, 2001.

"The Rise and Fall of Blaze Foley" by Joe Nick Patoski, *No Depression*, August 31, 2006.

"G-L-O-R-I-A" by Michael Hall, *Texas Monthly*, August 2009.

"Austin Found" by Julie Vadnal, *Elle*, July 26, 2011.

"Shakey Graves: The Truth about Austin's Music" by Hilary Hughes, Esquire.com, March 14, 2014.

"Spoon, the Molecular Gastronomists of Rock" by Dan Koisaug, *New York Times Sunday Magazine*, August 1, 2014.

"Gary Clark Jr. on His New Album" by Tom Mann, *Faster, Louder*, September 11, 2015.

4. Austin City Limits

"Lone Star Hoo-Haw" by Joe Nick Patoski, *Texas Sun*, December 5, 1974.

"Stratus Quo? Even as Tom Hicks Moves in, Beau Armstrong Can't Shake the Ghost of Jim Bob Moffett" by Amy Smith, *Austin Chronicle*, December 1, 2000.

"Lance Armstrong Has Something to Get Off His Chest" by Michael Hall, *Texas Monthly*, July 2001.

"A2K Meets 'ACL': The Point Man behind 'Austin City Limits' Music Festival, Promoter Charlie Jones" by Andy Langer, *Austin Chronicle*, September 20, 2002.

"Austin Welcomes Lance Home" by Ted Arnold, *Pez Cycling News*, August 16, 2004.

"Armstrong's Business Brand, Bound Tight With His Charity" by Stephanie Sauljan, *New York Times*, January 13, 2013.

5. Whole Foods Market

"The 'Yuppie Chow' Market: Austin's Grocery Stores Duke It Out" by Amy Smith, *Austin Chronicle*, July 28, 1995.

"Whole Foods Is All Teams" by Charles Fishman, *Fast Company*, April 30, 1996.

"Fajita History" by Virginia Wood, *Austin Chronicle*, March 4, 2005.

"A Whole New Ball Game in Grocery Shopping" by Bruce Horovitz, *USA Today*, March 8, 2005.

"John Mackey, Whole Foods Market" by Sonia Reyes, *Adweek*, October 10, 2005.

"Food Fighter: Does Whole Foods' C.E.O. Know What's Best for You?" by Nick Paumgarten, *New Yorker*, January 4, 2010.

"Whole Foods' Organic Capitalism" by Elizabeth Flock, *Forbes*, October 20, 2010.

"Whole Foods CEO John Mackey Calling Obamacare Fascist Is Tip of the Iceberg" by Emma G Keller, *The Guardian*, January 18, 2013.

"Whole Foods Takes Over America" by Beth Kowitt, *Fortune*, April 10, 2014.

"When We Were Small: Whole Foods" by J. D. Harrison, *Washington Post*, July 30, 2014.

Whole Foods advertisement, *Austin American-Statesman*, May 28, 2015.

"17 Tweets about Whole Foods That'll Actually Make You Laugh" by Jarry Lee,
    BuzzFeed, February 4, 2016.
"Why Amazon Bought Whole Foods," by Derek Thompson, The Atlantic, June 16, 2017.

6. South by Southwest

"Huey P. Meaux Was the Crazy Cajun" by Ivan Koop Kuper, The Rag (blog), September
    22, 2011.
"The History of SXSW Interactive" by Chase Hoffberger, The Daily Dot, March 12, 2012.
"Brad and Jennifer: Is It Puppy Love or Just Pitt Bull?" by George Rush, Joanna Molloy,
    Marcus Baram, K. C. Baker, New York Daily News, May 22, 1998.
"20 Years of SXSW Film and Interactive," SXSW World, February 2013.
"What Happened at SXSW" by Nisid Hijari, Entertainment Weekly, April 8, 1994.
"Tweets Will Power Doritos' 62-Foot SXSW Vending Machine Concert Stage" by Brian
    Anthony Hernandez, Mashable.com, March 6, 2013.
"SXSWi Uncensored: The Complete Oral History as Told by the Entrepreneurs, Geeks,
    and Dreamers Who Remade the Web" by David Peisner, Fast Company, February 26,
    2014.
"South by Southwest's Unpaid Labor Problem: Why It's Risking a Class Action Law-
    suit" by Charles Davis, Salon.com, February 26, 2014.
"Edward Snowden: 'The NSA Set Fire to the Internet. You Are the Firefighters'" by
    Cory Doctorow, The Guardian, March 10, 2014.
"Edward Snowden Urges SXSW Crowd to Thwart NSA with Technology" by Kim
    Zetter, Wired, March 10, 2014.
"Jimmy Kimmel Live from Austin During SXSW 2014" by Sean L. McCarthy, The Com-
    ic's Comic, March 11, 2014.
"SXSW Q. and A. | Tilda Swinton" by Ted Scheinman, New York Times, March 11, 2014.
"Shakey Graves: The Truth about Austin's Music" by Hilary Hughes, Esquire.com,
    March 14, 2014.
"SXSW Film Head Janet Pierson Puts Her Stamp on the Austin Festival" by Kim
    Voynar, IndieWire, March 26, 2015.
"IFP Screen Forward: 5 Questions for SXSW Film Director Janet Pierson" by Scott
    Macaulay, Filmmaker Magazine, September 23, 2015.

7. Austin Film Society

"The Slack Track" by Joe Nick Patoski, Texas Monthly, April 1991.
"The Power Couple: Elizabeth Avellan and Robert Rodriguez" by Joe Nick Patoski,
    Texas Monthly, May 1998.
"The Eyes of CinemaTexas: A Brief Reminiscence" by Louis Black, Austin Chronicle,
    October 17, 2003.
"Mike Judge: The 41-Year-Old Writer, Director, and Animator on Hank Hill's Texan-
    ness, the Inspiration for Beavis and Butt-Head, and the Case for Burning Down
    Harvard" by Evan Smith, Texas Monthly, October 2004.
The Austin Film Society Tenth Anniversary Retrospective, official program, 1995.
Austin Film Society: 20 Years 1985–2005, official program, 2005.

"King for a Day" by Steve McVicker, *Texas Observer*, May 2, 2008.

"Slack to the Future: Austin Gets Older; 'Slacker' Stays Forever Young" by Marc Sav-
lov, *Austin Chronicle*, January 21, 2011.

"Profiles of Innovation: Celebrating Screenwriters: Barbara Morgan's Austin Film
Festival" by Kevin Benz, *Austin Culturemap*, October 2, 2012.

"Austin's Year in Film" by Matthew Odam, *Austin American-Statesman*, January 4, 2013.

"Journal Profile: Rebecca Campbell" by Patricia Rogers, *Austin Business Journal*, March
22, 2013.

"The Austin Film Festival at 20" by Matthew Odam, *Austin American-Statesman*, October 20, 2013.

"Butt-Numb-A-Thon 15" by Jacob Knight, *Cinapse*, December 20, 2013.

"Mike Judge Interviewed by Dave Davies" *Fresh Air*, National Public Radio, April 17,
2014.

"Surviving 'Jaws' while Floating on the Water in New Braunfels" by Patrick Beach, *Austin American-Statesman*, July 20, 2015.

"Rodriguez Wants to Make a Film for $7,000" by Joe Gross, *Austin American-Statesman*,
August 30, 2015.

"Leatherface Tops List of Iconic Texas Horror Villains" by Matt Levin, *Houston Chronicle*, November 9, 2015.

8. Geeks: Dell, Lord British, RvB, Capital Factory, and the Translator

"Serious Fun" by Joe Nick Patoski, *Texas Monthly*, January 1991.

"Inman's Business Record Includes Bankruptcy of Defense Contractor" by Stephen
Labaton, *New York Times*, December 20, 1993.

"It's All History: The Rise and Fall of Cedar Street" by Michael Bertin, *Austin Chronicle*,
January 30, 1998.

"Interview with Richard Garriott, Executive Producer, NCSoft Austin" by Kyle Acker-
man, *Frictionless Insight*, March 17, 2002.

"The Rise of the Creative Class" by Richard Florida, *Washington Monthly*, May 2002.

"Census Data Depict Sweeping Change in East Austin" by Juan Castillo, *Austin
American-Statesman*, April 23, 2011.

"Richard Florida's Creative Class, 10 Years Later" by Jon Talton, *Seattle Times*, July 14,
2012.

"Dancing the Apocalypse Away, Extravagantly" by Sonia Smith, *New York Times*,
December 30, 2012.

"How Millionaires Celebrate End-of-Days" by Sonia Smith, *Texas Monthly*, January
2013.

"Beginnings: A Panel about Entrepreneurism with Michael Dell," *SXSW Interactive*,
March 2014.

"A Private Equity Titan with a Narrow Focus and Broad Aims" by David Gelles, *New
York Times*, April 10, 2014.

"Going Private Is Paying Off for Dell" by Michael Dell, *Wall Street Journal*, November
24, 2014.

"SXSW Interactive: 'Money. Recruiters. Beer. Repeat.' Building the Trilogy Network"
by Andrew Hickey, WPEngine.com (blog), March 16, 2015.

"Victim, Gunman Identified in Downtown Austin Omni Shooting" by Calily Bien and Eric Janzen, KXAN Television, July 6, 2015.

"Bigger, Better, Bolder: How Austin Brings Texas Flair to Startup Culture" by Gabe Duverge, *Concordia University Online*, July 22, 2015.

"Dell Acquires EMC for $67 Billion: The Price Tag Includes Shares in a VMware Tracking Stock" by Stephen Lawson and James Niccolai, IDG News Service, *Network World*, October 12, 2015.

"Legacy of Freescale to Endure in Austin" by Kirk Ladendorf, *Austin American-Statesman*, December 7, 2015.

"High-Tech Visionary Is Texan of Year" by Kirk Ladendorf, *Austin American-Statesman*, December 6, 2016.

"Year Saw Big Tech Deals, Booms In Houston, Jobs" staff report, *Austin American-Statesman*, December 25, 2016.

"Austin's Arkane Studios Grows to a Full Studio, Spreads Its Wings with 'Prey'" by Omar Gallaga, *Austin American-Statesman*, May 4, 2017.

9. The Franklin Line

"Pit Split" by Joe Nick Patoski, *Texas Monthly*, February 1999.

"Top 50 BBQ Joints in Texas," *Texas Monthly*, May 1997, May 2003.

"The Hot 10 2014: Thai-Kun, Austin, TX (No. 8)" by Andrew Knowlton, *Bon Appetit*, August 19, 2014.

"How I Went from Being a Terrible Drug Dealer to Top Chef," by Paul Qui, *Vice*, April 10, 2015.

"Barbecue Trailer John Mueller Meat Company Seized by State" by Nadia Chaudhury, *Eater Austin*, August 29, 2016.

10. Keeping Austin Weird: The Looky-Loos

"Serious Fun" by Joe Nick Patoski, *Texas Monthly*, January 1991.

"So Long, Liberty Lunch: Club's Fans Offer a Tearful Toast to a Local Landmark" by Chris Riemenschneider, *Austin American-Statesman*, August 2, 1999.

"When Every Town Big Enough to Have a Bank Also Had a Professional Baseball Team: The Game Returns to Austin after World War II" by Alan C. Atchison, *Southwestern Historical Quarterly*, October 1999.

"Wide Open Heart: Accordion Man Bradley Jaye Williams" by Christopher Gray, *Austin Chronicle*, February 18, 2000.

"Lance Armstrong Has Something to Get Off His Chest" by Michael Hall, *Texas Monthly*, July 2001.

"Man-Child in the Promised Land" by Randy Kennedy, *New York Times*, February 19, 2006.

"The Dude of Roller Derby and His Vision" by Michael Brick, *New York Times*, December 17, 2008.

"A Junk Pile Grows in Texas, but Is It Art? Austin Project Bugs Neighbors, Attracts Hoards of Tourists" by Ana Campoy, *Wall Street Journal*, April 24, 2010.

"21 Year Old 'Cathedral of Junk' Dismantled After Neighbours Complain" by Lloyd Alter, Treehugger.com, June 16, 2010.

"It's Just Different Here" by Joe Nick Patoski, *Preservation*, July/August 2010.

"Census Data Depict Sweeping Change in East Austin" by Juan Castillo, *Austin American-Statesman*, April 23, 2011.

"Can Austin Keep Itself Weird?" by Richard Parker, *Austin American-Statesman*, October 25, 2012.

"The Twenty Colleges That Make the Most Money on Sports" by Cork Gaines, *Business Insider*, September 11, 2014.

"Austin's Original Weirdo Crazy Carl Hickerson Gets His Own Documentary" by Erica Lies, *Austin Culturemap*, October 23, 2014.

"Twenty-Five Years On, a Look Back at a Barton Springs Showdown" by Asher Price, *Austin American-Statesman*, June 21, 2015.

"After 25 Years, Recalling the Barton Springs Showdown" by Asher Price, *Austin American-Statesman*, June 22, 2015.

"Behind the Design: Liz Lambert, Bunkhouse Hotels" by Natalie Marchbanks, *Block Print Social*, June 25, 2015.

"Hotelier Standard Strikes a Rare Deal" by Craig Karmin, *Wall Street Journal*, July 14, 2015.

"Finding Home: At Community First Village, Homeless People Can Find Shelter, Regain Dignity, Reconnect with Family" by James Barragan, *Austin American-Statesman*, December 8, 2016.

"Report: Austin No. 1 Tourist Destination in Southwest, No. 2 in U.S. Business" by Gary Dinges, *Austin American-Statesman*, November 4, 2016.

11. Onward through the Fog

"Armstrong's Hometown Celebrates Again," Associated Press, ESPN.com, July 23, 2000.

"Stratus Quo? Even as Tom Hicks Moves in, Beau Armstrong Can't Shake the Ghost of Jim Bob Moffett" by Amy Smith, *Austin Chronicle*, December 1, 2000.

"Creative Capital? In the City of Ideas, the People with Ideas Are the Ones with Day Jobs" by Michael Erard, *Austin Chronicle*, February 28, 2003.

"Austin Welcomes Lance Home" by Ted Arnold, *Pez Cycling News*, August 16, 2004.

"Richard Florida's Creative Class, 10 Years Later" by Jon Talton, *Seattle Times*, July 14, 2012.

"Asian-American Demographics," AustinAsianChamber.org, January 1, 2013.

"Armstrong's Business Brand, Bound Tight with His Charity" by Stephanie Sauljan, *New York Times*, January 13, 2013.

"What Nobody Says about Austin—Is Austin the State's Most Segregated City?" by Texas Monthly staff and Cecilia Balli, *Texas Monthly*, February 2013.

"The Man Who Fell to Earth" by Michael Hall, *Texas Monthly*, March 2013.

"Willie Turns 80" by Joe Nick Patoski, *Texas Music*, Spring 2013, Issue 54.

"The Fight Over Keeping Austin Weird: Is the Hippest City in Texas Selling Out Its Oddball Charm?" by Hilary Hylton, *Time*, July 5, 2013.

"The Long Road to Redemption" by Selena Roberts, SportsOnEarth.com, September 24, 2013.

"F1 Race Boosts Austin's 'Brand'" by John Maher, *Austin American-Statesman*, November 10, 2013.

"South by Southwest's Unpaid Labor Problem: Why It's Risking a Class Action Lawsuit" by Charles Davis, Salon.com, February 26, 2014.

"Career Ambitions, Higher Cost of Living Erode Austin's 'Slacker' Vibe" by Marty Toohey, *Austin American-Statesman*, June 6, 2014.

"Meet the Man Who Studies Indie Music Economies (Yes, He's in a Band Too)" by Danielle Paquette, *Washington Post*, September 8, 2014.

"Austin Declares Two-Year Ban on New Street Events in 'City's Core,'" by Ben Wear, *Austin American-Statesman*, November 27, 2014.

"Austin's Economy No. 1 (Again)," *Austin Business Journal*, December 6–12, 2014.

"Austin Is Working on Its Love-Hate Relationship with Live Music" by Theresa Everline, *Next City*, January 8, 2015.

"Armadillo World HQ Auction Draws Big Bids" by Omar L. Gallaga, *Austin American-Statesman*, January 18, 2015.

"Report: Austin's Advanced-Industry Growth Fastest in U.S. Since 1980" by Dan Zehr, *Austin American-Statesman*, February 3, 2015.

"Here's What's Really Ruining Austin (and It's Not SXSW)" by Kriston Capps, *CityLab*, March 13, 2015.

"Survey: Austin's Music Culture in Danger of a Permanent Fade" by Lilly Rockwell, Deborah Sengupta Stith, and Peter Blackstock, *Austin American-Statesman*, June 2, 2015.

"Popular Stubb's Sauces Sold in $100 Million Deal" by Gary Dinges and Lori Hawkins, *Austin American-Statesman*, June 25, 2015.

"Music Census Sparks Talks of Bolstering Opportunity" by Marty Toohey, *Austin American-Statesman*, July 20, 2015.

"How a Space-Faring Entrepreneur Intends to Fix Austin's Traffic Woes" by Michael Theis, *Austin Business Journal*, August 13, 2015.

"Heaven Hill Brands Buys Deep Eddy Vodka" by Tripp Mickle, *Wall Street Journal*, August 20, 2015.

"Boom Times Test Austin's Music Scene" by Ana Campoy, *Wall Street Journal*, August 25, 2015.

"Austin Tops Big-City U.S. Economic Growth since Recession, Study Shows," *Austin Business Journal*, September 29, 2015.

"Top Ten Demographic Trends," Ryan Robinson, City of Austin Demographer, Planning and Zoning Department, City of Austin, Austin, Texas, October 1, 2015.

"West Loop Isn't Worst Freeway in Texas" by Dug Begley, *Houston Chronicle*, October 30, 2015.

"The Winners and Losers of the U.S. Creative Class" by Richard Florida, *CityLab*, December 7, 2015.

"On a Roll: Austin Metro Area's Population Surpasses 2 Million" by John Egan, LawnStarter.com, December 9, 2015.

"Record-Setting Austin Home Prices Could 'Normalize' in 2017" by Chris Betts, KVUE-TV, December 8, 2016.

"Saxon Pub: Same Spot, New Landlord for Austin Music Venue" by Shonda Novak, *Austin American-Statesman*, November 9, 2016.

"Gary Keller's All ATX Steps Up Its Game as an Advocate for Local Music" by Peter Blackstock, *Austin American-Statesman*, December 6, 2016.

"New Development in Store for South Congress Avenue" by Shonda Novak and Lori Hawkins, *Austin American-Statesman*, January 31, 2017.

"Uncommon Objects Leaving South Congress," *Austin American-Statesman*, September 27, 2017.

12. On the Road Again

"I Saw Willie Nelson Perform Saturday Night and It Was Beautiful and It Was Sad" by Brendan Meyer, Guide Live, *Dallas Morning News*, April 23, 2017.

Interviews

Don Hyde, Eddie Wilson, Bob Simmons, Jim Franklin, Houston White, George Majewski, Joe Bryson, Joe Gracey, John Kunz, Leea Mechling, Carlyne Majer, Hank Alrich, Doug Sahm, Marcia Ball, Bobby Earl Smith, Mark Pratz, Shannon Sedwick, Terry Lickona, Lance Armstrong, Bruce Scaife, Patty Lang Fair, John Mackey, Louis Black, Roland Swenson, Hugh Forrest, Eve McArthur, Janet Pierson, Nancy Schaefer, Huey P. Meaux, Rick Linklater, Robert Rodriguez, Elizabeth Avellan, Richard Garriott, Chris Roberts, Hugh Forrest, Heather Brunner, Aaron Franklin, Paul Qui, John Mueller, Vince Hannemann, Brigid Shea, Liz Lambert, Steve Wertheimer, Merlin Tuttle, Ray Benson, April Ritzenthaler, Mack Royal, Joanna Wu

Books

The Gay Place by William Brammer, Houghton Mifflin Harcourt, New York, 1962.

The Improbable Rise of Redneck Rock by Jan Reid, Heidelberg Press, Austin, 1974.

An Illustrated History of Austin by David C. Humphrey and William W. Crawford Jr., American Historical Press, Sun Valley, California, 1991.

Stevie Ray Vaughan: Caught In the Crossfire by Joe Nick Patoski and Bill Crawford, Little, Brown and Company, New York, 1993.

Air Guitar: Essays on Art and Democracy by Dave Hickey, Foundation for Advanced Critical Studies, Los Angeles, 1997.

Austin Music Scene: Through the Lens of Burton Wilson by Burton Wilson with Jack Ortman, Wild Horse Press, Austin, 2001.

The Rise of the Creative Class: And How It's Transforming Work, Leisure, Community, and Everyday Life by Richard Florida, Basic Books, New York, 2002.

Direct from Dell by Michael Dell with Catherine Friedman, Collins Business Essentials, New York, 2006.

Who's Your City?: How the Creative Economy Is Making Where to Live the Most Important Decision of Your Life by Richard Florida, Basic Books, New York, 2007.

Land of the Permanent Wave: An Edwin "Bud" Shrake Reader by Edwin "Bud" Shrake, Steven L. Davis, University of Texas Press, Austin, 2008.

Willie Nelson: An Epic Life by Joe Nick Patoski, Little Brown, New York, 2008.

Austin Chronicle Music Anthology by Austin Powell, Doug Freeman, University of Press, Austin, 2009.

Chainsaws, Slackers, and Spy Kids: Thirty Years of Filmmaking in Austin, Texas by Alison Macor, University of Texas Press, Austin, 2010.

Cosmic Cowboys and New Hicks: The Countercultural Sounds of Austin's Progressive Country Music Scene by Travis Stimeling, Oxford University Press, New York, 2011.

SXSW Scrapbook: People and Things That Went Before, Peter Blackstock, Jason Cohen, and Andy Smith, editors, Essex Press, Austin, 2011.

Distant Publics: Development Rhetoric and the Subject of Crisis by Jenny Rice, University of Pittsburgh Press, 2012.

The Handbook of Texas Music, Texas State Historical Association, Austin, 2012.

Lost Austin (Images of America) by John Slate, Arcadia Press, Mount Pleasant, South Carolina, 2012.

The Rise of the Creative Class Revisited: 10th Anniversary Edition by Richard Florida, Basic Books, New York, 2012.

Austin, Wildsam Field Guides, Wildsam Press, New York, 2013.

Austin's Waller Creek: Promise for Tomorrow, Philip H. Fry and Carolyn H. Wright, editors, Loflin and Associates, Austin, 2013.

The Handbook of Texas, Texas State Historical Association, Austin, 2013.

Republic of Outsiders: The Power of Amateurs, Dreamers, and Rebels by Alissa Quart, The New Press, New York, 2013.

Seat of Empire: The Embattled Birth of Austin, Texas by Jeffrey Stuart Kerr, Texas Tech University Press, Lubbock 2013.

Austin Film Society tenth anniversary monograph, 2004.

Austin Film Society twentieth anniversary monograph, 2014.

Outlaw: Waylon, Willie, Kris, and the Renegades of Nashville by Michael Streissguth, It Books, New York, 2014.

Homegrown: Austin Music Posters 1967–1982, Alan Schaefer, editor, University of Texas Press, Austin, 2015.

Armadillo World Headquarters by Eddie Wilson and Jessie Sublett, TSSI Publishing, Austin, 2017.

Explore, Create: My Life in Pursuit of New Frontiers, Hidden Worlds, and the Creative Spark by Richard Garriott with David Fisher, William Morrow, New York, 2017.

The New Urban Crisis: How Our Cities Are Increasing Inequality, Deepening Segregation, and Failing the Middle Class—and What We Can Do about It by Richard Florida, Basic Books, New York, 2017.

Passages from *The Gay Place* by William Brammer and Edwin Bud Shrake's description of Austin in the book *Willie: An Autobiography* used by permission of both authors' estates.

Index